RACE AND MIGRATION IN THE TRANSPACIFIC

Looking at a range of cases from around the Transpacific, the contributors to this book explore the complex formulations of race and racism emerging from transoceanic migrations and encounters in the region.

Asia has a history of ceaseless, active, and multidirectional migration, which continues to bear multilayered and complex genetic diversity. The traditional system of rank order between groups of people in Asia consisted of multiple "invisible" differences in variegated entanglements, including descent, birthplace, occupation, and lifestyle. Transpacific migration brought about the formation of multilayered and complex racial relationships, as the physically indistinguishable yet multifacetedly racialized groups encountered the hegemonic racial order deriving from the transatlantic experience of racialization based on "visible" differences. Each chapter in this book examines a different case study, identifying their complexities and particularities while contributing to a broad view of the possibilities for solidarity and human connection in a context of domination and discrimination. These cases include the dispossession of the Ainu people, the experiences of Burakumin emigrants in America, the policing of colonial Singapore, and data governance in India.

A fascinating read for sociologists, anthropologists, and historians, especially those with a particular focus on the Asian and Pacific regions.

Yasuko Takezawa is Professor at the Institute for Research in the Humanities, Kyoto University. Cultural Anthropology, Race and Ethnic Studies, American Studies.

Akio Tanabe is former Professor at the Department of Cultural Anthropology, Graduate School of Arts and Sciences, the University of Tokyo. Anthropology, History, South Asian Studies.

Routledge Advances in Asia-Pacific Studies

RACE AND MIGRATION IN THE TRANSPACIFIC

Edited by Yasuko Takezawa and Akio Tanabe

Routledge
Taylor & Francis Group

LONDON AND NEW YORK

Cover image: Yasuko Takezawa and Akio Tanabe

First published 2023
by Routledge
4 Park Square, Milton Park, Abingdon, Oxon OX14 4RN

and by Routledge
605 Third Avenue, New York, NY 10158

Routledge is an imprint of the Taylor & Francis Group, an Informa business

British Library Cataloguing-in-Publication Data
A catalogue record for this book is available from the British Library

ISBN: 978-1-032-21019-3 (hbk)
ISBN: 978-1-032-21020-9 (pbk)
ISBN: 978-1-003-26639-6 (ebk)

DOI: 10.4324/9781003266396

Typeset in Bembo
by KnowledgeWorks Global Ltd.

CONTENTS

FIGURES

TABLES

CONTRIBUTORS

Katsuya Hirano: Associate Professor at the University of California, Los Angeles. History, Early Modern and Modern Japanese History.

- *The Politics of Dialogic Imagination: Power and Popular Culture in Early Modern Japan.* Chicago: University of Chicago Press, 2013.
- "Thanatopolitics in the Making of Japan's Hokkaido: Settler Colonialism and Primitive Accumulation." *Critical Historical Studies* 2, no. 2 (2015):191–218.
- "Regulating Excess: Cultural Politics of Consumption in Tokugawa Japan." Giorgio Riello and Ulinka Rublack eds., *The Right to Dress: Sumptuary Laws in a Comparative and Global Perspective.* 435–460. Cambridge: Cambridge University Press, 2019.

Ryuichi Narita: Professor Emeritus at the Department of Integrated Arts and Social Sciences, Japan Women's University. Japanese History, Cultural History.

- *How "History" Can Be Narrated: A Critique of the "Nation's Story" of the 1930s* (in Japanese). Tokyo: NHK Books, 2001.
- *Taisho Democracy*, Volume 4 of the Series: Modern Japanese History (in Japanese). Tokyo: Iwanami, 2015.
- *The Asia-Pacific War in Memories and Epistemology: Iwanami Series of the Asia-Pacific War* (in Japanese). Co-edited with Yutaka Yoshida. Tokyo: Iwanami, 2015.

Takeshi Onimaru: Professor at the Faculty of Social and Cultural Studies, Kyushu University.

- "Itinerary, Revolution, and Port Cities: Comparative Study on Maritime Port Cities as Arenas for Asian Revolutionary Movements." In *Changing Dynamics and Mechanisms of Maritime Asia in Comparative Perspectives*, edited by Akita, S., Liu Hong, Momoki, S., 213–223. Singapore: Palgrave Macmillan, 2021.

- "Financing Colonial State Building: A Comparative Study of the 19th Century Singapore and Hong Kong." In *Emerging States and Economies: Their Origins, Drivers, and Challenges Ahead*, edited by Shiraishi, T. and Sonobe, T., 101–118. Singapore: Springer, 2018.
- "Shanghai Connection: The Construction and Collapse of the Comintern Network in East and Southeast Asia." *Southeast Asian Studies* 5, no. 1 (April 2016):115–133.

Hiroshi Sekiguchi: Associate Professor at the Institute for the Study of Humanities and Social Sciences, Doshisha University. Buraku History, Japanese History.

- "'Racialization' and the Global Development of Governance Techniques: Problematizing the Buraku in Modern Japan," *Politika*. Paris: EHESS, 2021.
- "Toyohiko Kagawa's Social Welfare Activities and Scientific Racism." In *Dismantling the Race Myth Series, Vol. 2 Science and Knowledge*, edited by Toru Sakano and Yasuko Takezawa (in Japanese), 105–137. Tokyo: University of Tokyo Press, 2016.
- "Academia and the Awareness of Buraku Issues in the Early 20th Century" (in Japanese). *Social Sciences* 91 (2011):125–147.

Yasuko Takezawa: Professor at the Institute for Research in the Humanities, Kyoto University. Cultural Anthropology, Race and Ethnic Studies, American Studies.

- *Breaking the Silence: Redress and Japanese American Ethnicity*. Ithaca: Cornell University Press, 1995.
- *Racial Representations in Asia*. Edited by Yasuko Takezawa. Kyoto/Melbourne: Kyoto University Press/Trans Pacific Press, 2011.
- *Trans-Pacific Japanese American Studies: Conversations on Race and Racializations*. Edited by Yasuko Takezawa and Gary Y. Okihiro. Honolulu: University of Hawai'i Press, 2016.

Akio Tanabe: former Professor at the Department of Cultural Anthropology, Graduate School of Arts and Sciences, the University of Tokyo. Anthropology, History, South Asian Studies.

- *Caste and Equality in India: A Historical Anthropology of Diverse Society and Vernacular Democracy*. London: Routledge, 2021.
- *Human and International Security in India* (co-edited with Crispin Bates and Minoru Mio). London: Routledge, 2015.
- *Democratic Transformation and the Vernacular Public Arena in India* (co-edited with Taberez A. Neyazi and Shinya Ishizaka). London: Routledge, 2014.

Yu Tokunaga: Associate Professor of History at the Graduate School of Global Environmental Studies with a joint appointment at the Graduate School of

Human and Environmental Studies, Kyoto University. Immigration History, American Studies.

- *Transborder Los Angeles: An Unknown Transpacific History of Japanese-Mexican Relations.* Oakland: University of California Press, 2022.
- "Japanese Farmers, Mexican Workers, and the Making of Transpacific Borderlands." *Pacific Historical Review* 89, no. 2 (Spring 2020):165–197.
- "Japanese Internment as an Agricultural Labor Crisis: Wartime Debates over Food Security versus Military Necessity." *Southern California Quarterly* 101, no. 1 (Spring 2019):79–113.

Kazuyo Tsuchiya: Associate Professor at the Department of Area Studies, Graduate School of Arts and Sciences, the University of Tokyo. Twentieth Century US History, Race and Ethnicity, and Gender History.

- "'Jobs or Income Now!': Work, Welfare, and Citizenship in Johnnie Tillmon's Struggles for Welfare Rights." *Japanese Journal of American Studies* 22 (2011): 151–170.
- *Reinventing Citizenship: Black Los Angeles, Korean Kawasaki, and Community Participation.* Minneapolis: University of Minnesota Press, 2014.
- "Rethinking the Demise of the National Welfare Rights Organization: Systemic Racism, Gender, and the Anti-welfare Ideology" (in Japanese). *The American Review* 55 (2021):75–95.

Crystal Uchino: Assistant Professor at the Department of Global Communications, Doshisha University. Social History, Cultural Studies, Ethnic Studies.

- "The Case of Leslie Satoru Nakashima and His Breaking News Dispatch." *Hawaiian Journal of History* 53 (2019):1–29.
- "Born Under the Shadow of the A-Bomb: Atomic Bomb Memory and the Japanese/Asian American Radical Imagination, 1968–1982." *Social Systems* 22 (2019):103–120.

PREFACE AND ACKNOWLEDGMENTS

This book elucidates the history and structure of race and racialization that has emerged from migration and encounters in the transpacific. The focus on the transpacific—a space where the racial experiences of Asia and those of the transatlantic are intertwined—offers insightful perspectives for a global understanding of race and its multifaceted characteristics beyond Euro-American-centric views of race and racism. We aim to intervene in dominant discourses about race that are based predominantly on the transatlantic paradigm of Western racism by shifting attention to experiences in the transpacific toward broadening perspectives and understandings of racialization experiences.

The collaborative research project that generated this book began in 2016. In the several years that followed, the contributors met regularly at Zinbunken, the Institute for Research in the Humanities of Kyoto University, to discuss our work. The highlights of earlier versions of our chapters were presented at one closed and two public seminars in 2020. We are deeply grateful to the commentators, Tomohito Baji, Mariko Iijima, Yoshiyuki Kido, Katsuro Nawa, and Koji Tsuda, for their insightful and constructive comments.

Two anonymous reviewers also helped us clarify and enrich our discussions, and we owe them a debt of great gratitude. We wish to thank Simon Bates, our editor, for his sincere and continued support. We would also like to express our deep appreciation to Lyle De Souza and Crystal Uchino for their valuable comments and copy-editing. Takamichi Serizawa, Minako Saigo, and Fumiko Nakamura provided indispensable assistance and support to carry out this project. Much appreciation also goes to the translators for their great work. Special thanks go to Tetsuya Suzuki and Hirokazu Ohashi at Kyoto University Press for their useful comments and kind advice. Tomohiro Yoshimura's perceptive feedback made an invaluable contribution to the project.

Generous funding from the Grant-in-Aid for Scientific Research (S), "Integrated Research into the Processes and Mechanisms of Racialization" (No. 16H06320), was provided by the Japan Society for the Promotion of Science. A grant to support the publication of this anthology was received from Zinbunken of Kyoto University. We also appreciate their support of the project through seminars, workshops, translations, and other related activities.

We would be delighted to have a broad readership of both students and scholars in the fields of ethnic and racial studies, migration studies, Asian/Asian American studies, anthropology, sociology, history, literature, transpacific studies, and other related fields. We hope this book stimulates further discussion on race and contributes to a greater pluralization of knowledge across these fields and beyond.

1

INTRODUCTION

Yasuko Takezawa and Akio Tanabe

This volume examines processes of racialization emanating from and underpinning transpacific migrations along with the various encounters engendered therein, as well as instances of empathy and solidarity within and across multitudinous forms of racialization. It focuses on unraveling the ways multilayered experiences of racialization, both Asian and transatlantic, are interwoven in the transpacific while unpacking affective alliances that obliquely transverse these categories. We contend that transpacific experiences epitomize the complex racialization processes and raise potentialities for abating racism in today's world.

Transpacific, in this volume, refers to movements, relations, and systems across the Pacific Ocean. It entails dynamic social, political, and economic interactions engendered in this transoceanic space. In this regard, this book echoes Viet Thanh Nguyen and Janet Alison Hoskin's approach to the transpacific, using the term as "one of those 'spaces of interaction,' which is not itself a 'region'... but which does define flows of culture and capital across the ocean" (Nguyen and Hoskins 2014: 7). Transpacific Studies has attracted a great deal of attention over the past decade, especially in area studies, Asian American studies in North America, American studies in Asia, and diasporic/transnationalism studies. Scholars have approached various dimensions of the transpacific: Asian American history (e.g., Kurashige 2017), gender studies (Choy and Wu 2017), U.S. Occupation of Japan (e.g. Koshiro 1999), and other interdisciplinary studies (e.g., Armitage and Bashford 2014; Plüss and Chan 2012; Takezawa and Okihiro 2016).

The growing political and economic importance of the Pacific Rim has significantly increased global recognition of the word "transpacific," from the TPP (Trans-Pacific Partnership Agreement) to East Asian security issues, the expansion of Chinese power, and a rise of tensions between US and its allies versus Russia, China, and North Korea, in addition to an increase in Asian immigration to North America. The latter, in particular, is directly relevant to the field of transpacific

DOI: 10.4324/9781003266396-1

studies. Referring to *World Migration Report 2020,* international migrants compose 3.5 percent of the world population (International Organization for Migration 2019: 2). More than 40 percent of international migrants were born in Asia, with the US being the primary destination country since 1970 (International Organization for Migration 2019: 25–26). In fact, Asian Americans/Asians are not only the fastest-growing group in the US but, according to Pew Research Center, are projected to become the largest immigrant group (36%) by 2055, surpassing Hispanics/Latinx (34%) (Budiman and Ruiz 2021).

Arguably, since the last decades of the twentieth century, the global center of mobility, flow, and exchange has gradually shifted from the transatlantic to the transpacific (Sugihara 2001, 2014). The increasing connection between Euro-America and Asia, however, has also brought intensified friction and conflicts. Violence and hate crimes directed at citizens and immigrants of Asian descent have increased dramatically amid the turmoil of the COVID-19 pandemic, particularly in Europe and North America. To consider the recent movements of Asian immigrants and exclusionary reactions to them, in conjunction with the socio-economic and ideological changes such movements bring about, it is necessary to draw attention to the nexus of experiences of racialization in the transpacific that offer a broadened engaged perspective with which to articulate our approach to race.

In pursuit of approaches to overcome the current wave of racism in this globalized environment, this book endeavors to understand the ways in which encounters with others engender various forms and structures of domination, discrimination, and exclusion in different aspects and phases of the transpacific. In doing so, it also explores possibilities for human solidarity and alliances on cultural and affective levels outside the constraints imposed by those structures. This book aims to study the past experiences, ongoing struggles, and collaborations between immigrants and various communities in the transpacific in pursuance of a means to resist new attempts at racialization.

1.1 Transatlantic and Transpacific Experiences of Racialization

It is nearly an established academic discourse that race is a modern Western construction.[1] Race studies have predominantly been premised on transatlantic experiences between white settlers and enslaved Black people or subjugated Indigenous peoples, as represented by studies on slavery, settler colonialism, scientific racism, and their legacies in modern Europe and the Americas, where the binary between Self and Other was marked mostly by skin color and other visible phenotypical differences. Without doubt, the experience of racialization in the transatlantic exerted an immeasurable influence on the history of humanity and continues to reproduce racial discrimination and inequality to this day. Nevertheless, as Yasuko Takezawa, an editor of this volume, has argued, race relations of the transatlantic are far from universal (Takezawa 2005, 2011, 2020). Transatlantic slavery marked a fundamental turning point in human history, especially in the transatlantic world, but the experience of mass migration across a vast ocean is an exception rather than the predominant rule in terms of the history of human migration.

Asia has a long history of ceaseless and active internal migration. Human genome research reveals that the continuous and multidirectional migration of people in and across Asia throughout history has resulted in complex genetic diversity with various but continuous gradients of phenotypical differences (The Hugo Pan-Asian SNP Consortium 2009). Consequently, many of the historically marginalized and discriminated groups in Asia, particularly East Asia, are phenotypically indistinguishable. That is, their physical differences are "invisible" and their physical appearance is no different or continuous from that of the majority and other groups in the societies they live in. As a result, the traditional system of rank order among groups of people in Asia often consisted of a multitude of "invisible" differences in complex entanglement, including descent, birthplace, occupation, and lifeway. It should be noted, conversely, that although phenotypical or skin color differences between the majority and the minority were "invisible," the differences deemed innate were often expressed in terms of "visible" differences that conflated cultural and bodily characteristics. So, the features of *Burakumin* and Dalits who were phenotypically indistinguishable from the majority were often talked about in terms of "visible" traits such as (imagined) facial features, hairstyle, clothing, or bodily gestures, in addition to other "invisible" traits such as smell, touch, speech, and innate character.

Although phenotypical differences are invisible, the belief persisted and prevailed for many centuries that subordinate groups exhibit "innate and unchangeable/unchanging" temperamental traits or capabilities characteristics which were inherited by successive generations. Burakumin in Japan, Dalits in South Asia, and *Paekjŏng* in Korea all have a long history of suffering racialization and institutional discrimination in legal, economic, and social domains since premodern times, with the stigmatized discourses of "impurity" and "innate differences" determined by their group ancestry.

It should be noted that this kind of racialization and institutional discrimination against peoples whose differences were phenotypically "invisible" was, in fact, widespread beyond Asia, covering the whole Eurasian continent in the premodern world. Yasuko Takezawa points out strikingly similar patterns of racialization in the Middle Ages regarding Jews in Spain, those called "Gypsies" in Romania, and *Kawaramono* in Japan (the majority of whom later became Burakumin), especially in the discourses on their characterizations and relationships with kings or rulers (Takezawa 2020). Jews and "Gypsies" were initially newcomers to Spain and Romania, respectively, but they had not migrated far across an ocean, and the Kawaramono were non-settlers originating from the same region as the settlers. These people were not physically different from the majority but were nevertheless distinguished by clothing and other visual markers and segregated in designated residential districts. The rigid institutionalization of their social status followed their marginalization and racialization in social practice in the Middle Ages.

The ultra-long-distance movements of people across the Atlantic Ocean beginning from the end of the fifteenth century and the encounters of geographically and genetically distant peoples brought about the prerequisite conditions for new forms of racialization based on the color-line, or "visible" differences. With the gradual establishment of dominance and hegemony in the transatlantic world by the West, experiences of racialization came to be primarily colored by the colonialist legacies of slavery and conquest of Indigenous people. While only a very few states in seventeenth-century colonial America classified the population by skin color, most states shifted to a skin color-based system of classification after the beginning of the eighteenth century, driven by the expansion of slavery and an increasing desire to control the Indigenous populations. While physically indistinguishable minorities of European origin, including Jewish, Irish, and Polish immigrants, suffered relentless exclusionary violence, and while the very boundaries of whiteness itself shifted in light of socio-political and economic circumstances, the white/colored racial binary based on visible difference was forever front and center.

Beginning in the nineteenth century, waves of another kind of long-distance transoceanic migration occurred, this time across the Pacific Ocean, which resulted in new encounters of people of widely different origins. As Asian immigrants started to arrive on the West Coast of the US, they were not only confronted with the white/colored binary structure of racism but also experienced racialization along forced nation-state identifications and categorizations such as "Chinese," "Japanese," "Korean," and "Hindu (Asian Indian)." Further, Burakumin, Paekjŏng, and Dalit within these groups experienced double racialization and discrimination inside their respective immigrant communities as well as outside.

In this way, the transpacific became a space for the formation of multilayered and complex racial relationships, as these physically indistinguishable yet multifacetedly racialized groups encountered the hegemonic racial order deriving from the transatlantic experience of racialization based on visible differences. This book aims to intervene in race studies by endeavoring to elucidate such complexities in the history of transpacific experiences of racialization and resistance to it.

1.2 Redefining "Race"

Before proceeding further with our discussion, we would like to clarify our definition of race and the ways it contributes to our analysis of the racializations and race relations in the transpacific. If we expand our perspective beyond modern transatlantic experiences, we may characterize race as entailing the following characteristics:

1. Bodily characteristics (visible or invisible features, including temperaments and abilities) are believed to be transmitted from generation to generation and thus determined by descent.[2] Hence they cannot be (readily) changed by environment or external factors.

2. A strong tendency of exclusion and aversion is associated with racial systems of classification, and a clear hierarchical order is assumed between different groups.

3. This exclusionary and hierarchical order manifests itself in association with the political and economic structure of power that institutionally controls resources. Race thus cannot be reduced to prejudice or ethnocentrism but instead results from an organized process of social differentiation and boundary-making, often linked with conflicts of interest.

Takezawa has argued that the concept of race has three dimensions: "'race in the lowercase' (race), 'Race in the upper case' (Race), and 'Race as resistance' (RR)" (Takezawa 2005, 2011). The term "race" in the lowercase refers to cases when the concept has emerged without any modern Western influence. In this paradigm, assumed differences between socially delineated groups are believed to be inherited and unalterable by the environment, these groups are conceived as hierarchically ordered in social systems and institutions, and group boundaries are delineated with legal, political, and economic inequality.

"Race" in the upper case signifies race as defined and characterized by "scientific" and "biologized" concepts, i.e., the belief that it is possible, through scientific and biological methods, to classify and map humans in terms of their racial ancestry. Examples of "Race" include, but are not limited to, "Caucasian," "Mongolian," and "Ethiopian/African" races constructed in Europe and reframed in North American social contexts during slavery, colonialism, and the exclusion of "undesirable" immigrants. "Race" also applies to some categories used in genetic studies and ancestry DNA testing today.

RR is race created and reinforced by minorities themselves as agents who mobilize racial identities within a repertoire of several other possible identities to fight against racism. This aspect of race thus results from a proactive resistance against hegemony and social domination. Furthermore, RR indicates the use of race as a discursive strategy to expose existing racial discrimination and provide a common focus for identity politics.

These three dimensions are not inextricable from one another but reinforce the concept of race through their mutual connections. For example, some of the "races" which existed in the Middle Ages were turned into "Races" in the modern period by applying "race science" and embedding the quantified "differences" in a racial hierarchy, thereby legitimizing the idea of biological superiority and inferiority. Genetic studies of people from historically marginalized "races" like the Ainu and Taiwanese Indigenous peoples have tended to essentialize their origins and genetic "differences" as "Races" through their representation and analysis. The recent backlash against the Black Lives Matter movement, the 1619 Project, and "critical race theory" rejects RR, which was born of historical discrimination against "races" and "Races." In turn, it reconstructs and remobilizes whiteness as a sociopolitical category, giving white supremacy a new guise.

When migrations transplant race relations from one society to another, relationships that had previously existed in their specific contexts overlap, producing a new relationality. The following sections will consider what happens when people who had been "races" in Asia cross the Pacific to the Americas, where they find themselves caught up in race relations built around R in the upper case "Races;" what kind of racialization is created when American policies based on R in the upper case "Races" are introduced to Asia; what kinds of empathy RR can arouse in other minorities; and what are the alternative alliances and solidarity that can transverse these racial categories.

1.3 The "Transpacific" as a Multicentered and Multilayered Arena of Racialization

According to Nguyen and Hoskin (2014), the "transpacific" has two contrastive dimensions. The first dimension involves the Pacific as a space of exploitation and expansion advanced by European, American, and Asian (imperial) powers. The other dimension refers to the Pacific as a contact zone where collaborations, alliances, and friendships are created in opposition to the first dimension through alternative narratives of translocalism, oppositional localism, and oppositional regionalism among minoritized and marginalized people.

The notion of the Pacific as a "contact zone" shares a conceptual basis with Lionnet and Shih's (2005) "minor transnationalism," which underscores the limitations of prevailing conceptions of transnationalism based on binary models of above and below, the utopic and the dystopic, and the global and the local.[3] Instead of only looking at the vertical oppression from above and the resistance from below, "minor transnationalism" examines the lateral minor-to-minor transnational networks that have the potentiality of connecting those on the margins without having to go through the center.[4] Such horizontal relationships developed by minority and diasporic peoples draw our attention to "the creative interventions that networks of minoritized cultures produce within and across national boundaries" (Lionnet and Shih 2005: 6–7).

Our volume has been much inspired by the notion of "minor transnationalism" (Lionnet and Shih 2005), and we have consciously paid attention to complex relationships involving multiple racial or intra-racial/ethnic groups instead of familiar dichotomies such as whites versus Asians. We also concur with Nguyen and Hoskin (2014) regarding the importance of being sensitive to aspects of exploitation and expansion by major powers as well as collaborations, alliances, and friendships among minors in our discussion of the transpacific.

Drawing inspiration from these works, the chapters in this volume elucidate the entangled and complex character of race and racialization in the transpacific that defy the vertical and horizontal binary. We note that while relationships among different margins are indeed important and worth paying attention to, it is also notable that minor-to-minor relationships are more often than not influenced, though never defined, by vertical relationships. Lateral relationships between margins can also influence vertical relationships. Thus, there are complex relationships between the vertical and the horizontal spaces beyond the binary opposition. There exists not only vertical space of exploitation by majors and horizontal space of minor-oppositional alliances but also complex interracial/interethnic relationships that obliquely cut across both spaces, involving both major and minor.[5]

The relevance of this point is elucidated when considering the complex nature of the transpacific space. It contains not only plural imperial centers, including the US, UK, Japan, and China, that compete and collaborate in the transimperial/transcolonial racial orders, but also multilayered levels of marginalization based on the encounters and combinations of various forms of hierarchized differentiation, including the white/colored binary; racialization based on nationality; and discriminations within nationalities. Here, plural forms of racialization meet and create new dynamics. In particular, the racial order of Western origin premised on "visible" phenotypical differences and that of Asian origin founded on other often "invisible" differences collided and formed complex racial orders that continue to reorganize themselves or be deconstructed in their respective social contexts. It is this dynamic, multicentered, and multilayered complexity that characterizes race and racism in the transpacific.

We must consider not only vertical and horizontal relations but also oblique relations between multiple major and minor actors who struggle to consolidate or redefine their positions vis-à-vis others at different levels of centrality and marginality, employing various forms of differentiation and alliances. The sum is the complex, entangled, and interwoven arena of interaction that transverses various categories and positionalities, involving dominance, competition, and resistance together with collaboration and alliances among various majors and minors. By paying attention to complex processes in shared transpacific experiences, our volume seeks to contribute to and intervene in the field of race studies and transpacific studies.

1.4 Racial Domination, Flows, and Assimilation

Transpacific dynamics took a turn in the mid-nineteenth century when direct interactions began between American and Asian peoples. During this time, the US strengthened its domination and began to show more imperialistic inclinations, occupying the Philippines and Guam due to the Spanish–American War of 1898 and annexing Hawai'i in the same year. These islands became significant American military strongholds in the Pacific. The British expanded and consolidated its formal and informal empire in the late nineteenth century across India, Southeast Asia, and parts of China (Gallagher and Robinson 1953). In response to the Western impact, Japan and other Asian countries gathered momentum toward the formation of nation-states, where each of them explored a new national/racial order based, in part, on the racial order it had learned from the West. Imperial Japan went on to racialize peoples and groups in its neighboring countries, dominating and oppressing them in its colonies, even though a majority of them had no "visible" physical differences.[6] Within its own country, Japan treated domestic/colonized minority groups such as the Ainu, the Ryukyuan (Okinawan) people, and Burakumin as different "races" based on biometric measurements and skull forms by adapting Western scientific racism and used it to justify land grabbing and exploitation of resources and labor.

By the late nineteenth century, the Indo-Pacific sphere had become a shared and contested arena among various imperial powers such as the US, Japan, and Britain.[7] Here, a key to imperial rule was setting up a colonial racial order of multiple subjects with the imperial self at the center.

Notably, the racialization process took place in such a transimperial/transcolonial space where modern knowledge and technology of governance based on "Race" moved across oceans and met regional and local orders of "race." This transoceanic process gave birth to new hybrid racial orders, where the pre-existing forms of racialization were incorporated into "scientific" knowledge on Race, resulting in chimerical forms of racialization. For example, the Japanese, who were striving to modernize under threat from Western powers, borrowed from North American settler colonial policies toward Indigenous people, and this import of knowledge played a decisive role in the occupation of Ainu Mosir and the racialization of the Ainu as a "useless race doomed to extinction" (Hirano, Ch. 2). In Singapore, the British colonial government created the category of "Chinese" in contrast to residents of Malaysian and Indian descent and racialized them as the target of control, suppression, and discrimination since they were seen to be "at the root of the problem" and a threat to the imperial order (Onimaru, Ch. 5). The British also attempted to understand and rule Indian society through a racial order where imported knowledge on Race was applied to groups differentiated by caste and religion, thus substantializing and perpetuating the pre-existing "race" categories in India (Tanabe, Ch. 6).

The transimperial formation of power in the Pacific is also related to the establishment of a new economic order, which prompted the transpacific movement of labor. One of the focuses of this volume is the flows of migrants stimulated by the development of capitalism in the transpacific and the labor issues and racial tensions that arose out of it.

The expansion of the Japanese empire was concomitant with the flows of colonial settlers to Hokkaido, Taiwan, and Korea, engendering racial encounters, tensions, and alliances (Narita, Ch. 7; Hirano, Ch. 2). There was also an increase in Chinese and Indian migrants across and within Southeast Asia (Onimaru, Ch. 5) and South Asia (Tanabe, Ch. 6). The migration of Chinese and later Japanese and other peoples in Asia to the Americas from the mid-nineteenth century marked the beginning of a new history in the transpacific.

The US was the chosen destination for a disproportionately large number of Asian emigrants. Many of them came to a new land in pursuit of better economic opportunities (Sekiguchi, Ch. 3; Tokunaga, Ch. 4; Tsuchiya, Ch. 9). For example, the Japanese laborers who emigrated to the US before World War II largely came intending to work for a short period to send money home to support their families in Japan. These immigrant laborers, however, were in a precarious and vulnerable position, having no social standing or economic security, and rather than protest their outrageous treatment at the hands of their employers, they did their best under the difficult circumstances to ensure their survival. Such efforts might have appeared to strengthen the assimilationist tendency in Asian immigrants to the US and provided the historical backdrop for the creation of the racial stereotype of Asians as a "model minority." When Frantz Fanon talked about how a colonized person tends to "try, in her body and in her mind, to bleach (the world)," he was referring to the assimilationist impulse on the part of the colonized living under an overwhelmingly asymmetrical power structure, but the socio-economic conditions in which these immigrants found themselves stimulated that same impulse (Fanon 1967: 45).

The power structures that encourage or compel such assimilation are also germane to the experience of the Ainu, who were stripped of their land and endured systemic racism. Needless to say, the power structures of immigrant society are different from those that sustain the settler colonial regime of Indigenous dispossession. However, as discrimination is a matter of life and death for most immigrants who often stake everything on surviving within a society governed by a dominant racial group, the same is true for the experience of Indigenous peoples like the Ainu, whose means of subsistence is ripped from them. As Hirano (Ch. 2) argues, the power structures that connect immigrants and Indigenous peoples are a racist form of governance: what Giorgio Agamben (1998) called "inclusive exclusion." To put it another way, when a group of people is included in society as a "minority," the dynamics of racist exclusion are necessarily at work. Being brought into society as "other" places racial boundaries between them and the majority, and discrimination and exploitation are normalized as the form of governance. Minoritized people then come to crave assimilation as a way of transcending those boundaries and freeing themselves from the shackles of discrimination.

1.5 Continuities and Discontinuities through Migration in the Transpacific

Within the dynamic of assimilation and differentiation, inclusion and exclusion, centering on the hegemonic structures, there were also transnational, multifaceted forms of categorization and racialization. This is because race and racism in the transpacific were influenced not only by the structure of imperial dominance by major powers but also by the encounters between various categories and differentiations that people from different origins carry with them.

Immigrants often bring prejudice and discriminatory practices from their homelands to their new destinations. In this sense, there is both temporal and spatial *continuity*. After emigrating to the West Coast of the US, Burakumin continued to experience discrimination and oppression at the hands of mainstream or a larger society of Japanese immigrants who, themselves, were excluded by white society (Sekiguchi, Ch. 3). There were unspoken but persistent practices of discrimination such as the refusal to serve tea to Burakumin visitors and the disapproval of marriage to Burakumin. The second-generation Japanese American *hibakusha*, who were born in the US but returned to Japan and experienced the atomic bombings in Hiroshima or Nagasaki, faced silencing and marginalization as a double minority within a larger Japanese American community that sought acceptance by white society (Uchino, Ch. 8). Korean and other Asian immigrants might have already been prejudiced against African Americans in their home countries and carried this prejudice with them when migrating to North America (Tsuchiya, Ch. 9). Similarly, Japanese immigrants purportedly looked down upon Chinese immigrants as "half-civilized" and inferior. The prejudice acquired in Meiji Japan through the introduction of race theories from the West was further intensified after Japan's victory in the First Sino-Japanese War of 1894–1895. This modern perception of the Chinese is in sharp contrast to the great respect and adoration of China in Japan that existed from ancient times to the early modern period (Iriye 1980; Wang 2004).

On the other hand, migration often generates *discontinuity* between the immigrants' countries of origin and new destinations. For example, referring to Sekiguchi (Ch. 3), none of the Buraku immigrants from Fukui, Japan, were engaged in leather production or shoemaking, occupations traditionally associated with Burakumin. Transpacific migration provided them with the opportunity to erase obvious markers of being Burakumin, if not the complete freedom from prejudice and discrimination.

Transplanting scientific racism in Asia also engendered discontinuity. As Hirano (Ch. 2) suggests, the Japanese had harbored a prejudicial view of the Ainu based on visual differences and heavily exploited them for economic profits since the seventeenth century. This "racial" attitude toward the Indigenous people gained a new dimension under the influence of scientific racism (Race in the upper case "R"), rearticulating the difference as genetically predetermined.

Moreover, by transplanting physically "invisible" races from Asia into a system of racial classification based on "visible" charateristics, transpacific spatial movements brought about changes in the internal relations of these groups. Because the physical differences in question were invisible to the larger society, these groups most frequently employed the following two strategies: The first was to suppress and silence minorities within the group – so-called double minorities – to keep their differences and thus their very existence from becoming visible and noticeable, even as this reproduced discrimination against them. The second was to emphasize the difference from other groups of Asian origin precisely because it was not visible. People from Asia, including the Japanese and Chinese, mobilized their national identities and emphasized their differences in order to be accepted. Through a close reading of Japanese-language literature, Narita (Ch. 7) explores how the Japanese who emigrated to Manchuria emphasized racial differences to distinguish themselves from other Asians, giving birth to a form of immigrant

nationalism. Whichever strategy they use, immigrants are often either unconscious of or indifferent to their own status as perpetrators of discrimination even
as they are caught up in their own victimhood of white racism.

1.6 Affective Alliances: Oblique Transversality

The new racism in the age of globalization manifests as a move to turn groups
that pose risks to nations into "others" (Onimaru, Ch. 5; Tanabe, Ch. 6). The
increasing mobility and hybridity under globalization have made those in the
majority feel that their status is being threatened and worry or fear that they
will become the target of exclusion. Thus, fear and anxiety amid globalization
lead to violence against and exclusion of minorities (Appadurai 2006). These
minorities are often labeled with "race" terminology based on their ethnicity,
native country, or religion. This is the racialization of "dangerous others." In this
political-cultural formation of the majority and the minorities, people belonging
to minorities also often take part in marginalization and discrimination of other
minorities, as in the case of multiple racial/ethnic relationships in the US or the
majority Japanese immigrants against Burakumin and hibakusha.

The racialization of minorities continues relentlessly because it ties in with
the populist politics of majority formation within and across a nation under the
never-ending act of differentiating between self and other. Amid anxiety over
the increased fluidity of social order caused by globalization, people try to side
with those who discriminate rather than those discriminated against on the
preconscious affective level.

Today, differentiation and discrimination based on various distinctions in the
name of maintaining order are occurring widely and producing new versions of
racialization by linking with the "politics of affect" (Massumi 2015) to blame
others for one's own anxiety. Here, the racialization of others and minorities
through more affective and fluid differentiation under populist majoritarianism is
intensifying in combination with the "politics of control" (Deleuze 1992; Rose
2000). As globalization continues to bring heterogeneous peoples into intense
interaction and conflict, this volume's attention to the politics of racial othering
in encounters between different social and historical groups and the ways in
which different racial regimes intersect and interact in forming a new kind of
hegemonic order will offer a critical insight into the current mode of racism.

To understand the complex modalities of racialization and racism in the transpacific and to fight against racism, it is not enough to point out the fallacy of
biological racism and the social construction of race. In the academic world,
biological race theory has been rejected, and the view that race and ethnicity
are social constructs is widely accepted. In society, an awareness of equality and
human rights pervades, and racial discrimination as an idea has been widely
rejected. Some people still try to exclude immigrants and minorities, but many
claim that they are only concerned about risks to their society and that they are
not racist. In this situation, when almost everybody knows and claims, at least at

the verbal level, that race and racism are not tenable, why are certain groups of people still demarcated as inherently different, dangerous, or inferior and why do disparities in health, income, education, employment, and various other domains still persist along racial lines?

There is no doubt that social systems play a fundamental role to produce and reproduce racism and racialization. Whereas it is indeed necessary to critique and reform social systems, it is also mandatory, in the face of persistent racial discrimination, to expand and deepen our critical gaze to the unverbalized, affective level of racism and racialization. For, in our understanding, racial discrimination persists because the *"othering" process is embedded in the deeper affective domain,* which operates at the preconscious level. Affect is experiential intensities at the virtual level that are prior to and/or outside the conscious and subjective experience of phenomena at the actualized level (Massumi 1995; Shouse 2005). The perspective on affect invites us to look at the potentialities of life as an entanglement of heterogeneous and shared intensities that lie beneath the surface of what is consciously seen and cognized (Nishii and Yanai 2020: 3–4). Even when the conscious cognition changes and admits that racism is an unfounded social construction, the working of the "racialized affect" (Berg and Ramos-Zayas 2015), that is, the preconscious process of the body-mind that does the "othering" at the virtual level, often remains persistent. "Differential intensities of affect" often survive conscious critique (Connolly 2002: 10). It is important to focus on the workings of such presubjective, heterogeneous, and virtual intensities of affect in understanding race and racism precisely because it is this affective level beneath what is consciously cognized and conceptualized that forms the foundation of the racializing process. The shared and preconscious affect caters to the persistent construction of "others" with imagined "innate difference" (Tanabe, Ch. 6).

Yet, it is important to note that affect does more than the reproduction of discrimination. Humans have "powers to affect and be affected" (Massumi 2002: 15, after Spinoza's *Ethics* [Part III Def. 3] in Spinoza 1985 and Deleuze 1988: 123–124). We have the potential of transforming the self in its susceptibility and capacity of being affected by others. That is why affective interactions can generate empathy, that is, shared senses and emotion, between people. The human capacity to be affected is not a weakness but a strength for creating bonds and alliances (Hardt 2015). An affect can break down barriers between groups for the very reason that there is a preconscious cross-over of corporeal intensities which transverse racial categorizations and differentiations. The power of affect generated by literature (Narita, Ch. 7), exhibition (Uchino, Ch. 8), theater (Tsuchiya, Ch. 9), art (Takezawa, Ch. 10), food, music, and dance, as well as simply working, chatting, and being together (Tokunaga, Ch. 4) are prime examples. These experiences and the reflections on them can sometimes support building empathy, cooperation, and solidarity between minorities as well as across minor-major boundaries. The role affect plays is key in considering both discriminations deriving from non-biological registers of difference, and sympathy, cooperation, and solidarity as protest against small-r "races" and capital-R "Races" and also toward alternative anti-racist alliance beyond RR.

In this context, this volume views the transpacific as a field of potential affective alliances where dynamic interracial/interethnic relationships emerge through the encounters and negotiations of multiple minoritized groups (Lionnet and Shih 2005). The transpacific and the West Coast of the US, in particular, have offered unique opportunities for minor-to-minor interactions where Black and Indigenous peoples with a long history of phenotype-based or color-line-based racialization and colonization, Central and South American immigrants, and Asian immigrants who flooded in over a relatively short period of time encountered one another in a white-dominated society. Moreover, Japanese immigrants of Burakumin, Okinawan or Korean backgrounds were subjected to double discrimination stemming from Japanese racial order and white supremacism and marginalized further not only in the US but also in other Japanese diasporas. The minors and the majors participate in the shared transnational space, structured by uneven power relations yet rife with potentialities for transversing racial categories.

By paying attention to such transversal moments and spaces, this volume examines the kinds of empathies that develop amid the struggle against exploitation and discrimination engendered by white society between Japanese and Mexican immigrants (Tokunaga, Ch. 4); Korean immigrants and Black Americans (Tsuchiya, Ch. 9); second-generation Japanese American hibakusha and third-generation community activists on the one hand and other Asian Americans on the other (Uchino, Ch. 8); and Asian American artists and other transborder migrants and minorities (Takezawa, Ch. 10) to illuminate the types of interracial engagement that have led to the formation of new alliances rather than to hatred. Through these case studies, we highlight the power of affect, which expands potentialities for empathy, cooperation, and solidarity between minorities, migrants; diagonally crossing borders of marginalization and discrimination, and bringing about affective bonds while respecting differences. Such oblique transversality that crosses multiple borders and categorizations across minors and majors has the power of affecting and transforming the entire structure of racism.

Globalization gives rise to not only exclusion and conflict but also new encounters and interactions. A new power of imagination is generated therein. Imagining a new and productive socio-culture in the age of globalization from people's activities in art, theater, literature, and hopefully scholarship – this is where we find a glimmer of hope. It would reverberate through the politico-economy and slowly change its direction. The study of transpacific migration and race in this volume offers a useful perspective to understand the relationships between the hegemonic racial order based on the politico-economic domination by the state and capital, on the one hand, and the discriminatory customs and sense and affect formed at the social and cultural levels on the other, and to consider how to overcome such entangled racism.

We believe that multicentered and multilayered perspectives on the nature of racialization, such as those offered in this volume, are essential for deepening our understanding of racism in the globalized world. At the same time, this volume proposes that we pay attention to the oblique transversality that may abate the present racism. The current challenge is to dismantle and unravel the entangled racial order and reconnect affective ties and alliances through and beyond differences. Our only starting point may be to reencounter and communicate with racialized others to disentangle ourselves from preset categories and prejudices and then begin to dialogically search for transversal ways to achieve alliance and solidarity. It is our differences that offer opportunities for self-transformation through dialogue and alliances. Alternative globalization beyond racism may be reached by encountering the singularity within each person beyond superficial labels and categories; communicating with others to reach an understanding of differences rather than commonalities, and pursuing the potentiality for empathy and solidarity that cut across majors and minors by making human diversity into a source to richer imagination instead of using it to exclude or exploit.

1.7 Chapter Contents

1.7.1 Part I: Encounters, Entanglement and Solidarity

Chapter 2, "Settler Colonialism as Encounter," by Katsuya Hirano examines the Ainu experience of modernity in the context of the development of Hokkaido, Japan. The "encounter" between Ainu and modernity was a violent experience that led to settler colonial dispossession and domination of the Ainu under the Meiji government. Hirano explores how the settler colonization of Ainu land, oriented toward creating and accumulating capital, racialized the Ainu and their traditional mode of labor. The Matsumae domain, a vassal state of Japan's premodern Tokugawa government, had treated the Ainu as an exploitable labor force in premodern times. On the other hand, Meiji Japan reconfigured them as a useless population, as opposed to Japanese settlers, for its drive to develop industrial capitalism. Therein lay the "politics of racialization," or the politics of "race" based on evolutionism, that regarded the Ainu as a "vanishing race" or a "dying ethnicity," as in the cases of Indigenous peoples in the US and Australia.

Chapter 3, "Burakumin Emigrants to America," by Hiroshi Sekiguchi marks a ground-breaking first study in Japanese American studies, Japanese migration studies, as well as Burakumin studies both in the US and in Japan. No previous study of Burakumin immigrants in the US has succeeded in proving even their existence with accurate and reliable historiographic evidence. In California, Burakumin faced double logics of "racialization" – namely, transatlantic and transpacific – which intersected with each other. Japanese immigrants collectively suffered discrimination between whites and Blacks in the transatlantic racial order, and the Burakumin among them were subjected to further discrimination within the Japanese expatriate community who brought with them the racism which was grounded not on phenotypical differences but the discourses of persistent centuries-old non-visual "racial differences," a form of racism ubiquitous in Asia.

In Chapter 4, "From Anti-Japanese to Anti-Mexican," Yu Tokunaga considers the inter-group relationship between Japanese and Mexican immigrants in California during the 1920s by examining the chain of racialization experiences in a white-dominant society. Arguments for and against immigrants from these two countries were closely linked as anti-Japanese campaigns, which had resulted in Japanese exclusion in 1924, influenced pro-Mexican labor advocacy as well as anti-Mexican nativism in the late 1920s. Although there was a growing class divide between Japanese and Mexicans, they shared common ground as nonwhite residents fighting racism. Tokunaga also casts a spotlight on sympathy and empathy for Mexican immigrants some Japanese immigrants showed concerning the anti-Mexican movement.

1.7.2 Part II: Empire and Effects of Categorization

Chapter 5, "Colonial Rule and 'Category'," by Takeshi Onimaru, examines how the British colonial administration in Singapore dealt with the organization of "secret societies" and communists by Chinese immigrants. It discusses the ethnic categories used for law-and-order enforcement in colonial Singapore. On the practical level, the authorities attempted to address the problems associated with secret societies and communist activities based on thorough investigations of the actual conditions. The prevailing discourse, however, was that Chinese immigrants and residents were the root of all the problems. This stemmed from the "racialization" of threat groups by categorizing invisible subjects and making them visible.

Chapter 6, "The Virtualization of Race," by Akio Tanabe, discusses race in modern and contemporary India. The imperial-colonial racial orders based on religion, caste, and race used to form the backbone of governance in India. Over time, however, the country has moved from a population-based approach to governance to an individual-based strategy involving the world's largest biometric ID system called Aadhaar. Today, threat groups have become implicitly linked to the categories of "race" through latent racial affect, that is, a collective sense of racial differences at the preconscious level. As the racial order based on caste and religion created under the colonial regime becomes less tangible and more latent, it becomes more difficult to criticize and change, even though it remains persistent. One of the ways to uncover and tackle latent racism is to directly appeal to the affective level.

In Chapter 7, "Racism in Imperial and Post-Imperial Japanese Language Literature," Ryuichi Narita discusses the persistent nature of the concept of "race" focusing on cultural elements of race. A concatenation of concepts of "Japan," "Japanese language," "Japanese national," and "Japanese literature" had previously constructed the Japanese race as self-evident. This chain has been broken and segmented to form the concept of "Japanese-language literature," which has come into use recently. Narita analyzes Japanese-language literature produced by Japanese and non-ethnic Japanese authors from the imperialist to post-imperialist eras. The experiences of writers of "Colonia" literature in Brazil and non-ethnic Japanese writers in Japan led to a search for new perspectives and identities that criticized racism by challenging dominant cultural essentialism.

1.7.3 Part III: Minor Alliance, Memory, and Affect

Chapter 8, "A Japanese American Critique of the Atomic Bomb and Its Up Againstness" by Crystal Uchino, examines attempts by Japanese Americans in 1995 to remember the atomic bombing of Hiroshima and Nagasaki amidst controversies over American and Japanese national narratives of World War II. While the Smithsonian Museum was forced to make a significant change to the contents of its planned exhibit of the Enola Gay due to conservative interests, a coalition of Japanese Americans produced an alternative exhibit to reveal the background of the bombings and the experiences of survivors, including Japanese American hibakusha. Uchino draws attention to how a critical remembering of the atomic bomb was constructed by crossing borders in the Pacific as Japanese American remembering interfaced with dominant U.S. narratives and growing demands for the redress of Japanese colonial violence in Asia. Examining discourses about war responsibility, she also points out challenges to coexistence between Japanese Americans and their Asian-American neighbors and between Japan and its Asian neighbors.

Chapter 9, "The 1992 LA Uprising and the Politics of Representation" by Kazuyo Tsuchiya, carries out a critical re-examination of the historical understanding of the LA Uprising and discusses how the plural and multilayered memory of the incident can be represented. The LA Uprising has often been positioned as the first "multiracial riot" between Black Americans, Koreans, and Latinx in US history. Tsuchiya argues that such a focus obscures disparities, poverty, and systemic racism faced by these groups: Koreans, as transpacific migrants from the east; Black Americans, coming earlier from the American South and struggling at the bottom of the transatlantic racial order; and Latinx, as trans-border migrants from the south; all suffer systemic racism, resulting in their marginalized economic niches and distinctive communities. She then examines the play *Twilight: Los Angeles*, 1992, actor and playwright Anna Deavere Smith's ground-breaking attempt to create an unvarnished, multilayered, and three-dimensional depiction of the uprising history by listening to the voices of various actual participants' and putting their words together.

In the final chapter, "Unravelling and Connecting in the Transpacific," by employing both concepts of "major-transnationalism" and "minor transnationalism" within the context of contact zones in the transpacific, Yasuko Takezawa analyzes the works and narratives of two artists, Yoko Inoue and Jean Shin, who immigrated from East Asia, one from Japan, the other from the Republic of Korea to the US, both of whom are currently based in New York. Both artists use objects that have crossed the Pacific into the US as motifs: Inoue uses them to re-examine multilayered US-Japan power relations after World War II and their economic complicity in the Korean War, while Shin uses broken pieces of celadon donated by a pottery town in Korea to make an ethnically symbolic mosaic art in a Koreatown in New York. In her analysis, Takezawa highlights the empathy that arises between the artists and other transmigrants and minorities, which in turn generates new connections and communities.

Acknowledgment

We would like to express our deep gratitude to Katsuya Hirano for taking his time to engage in a discussion with us and give valuable comments for this introduction.

Notes

1 This is a very persistent academic discourse. For example, in a recent article, Amitav Acharya says, "there is little question that the emergence of racism as a *scientific, profitable, offensive, geopolitical* and *normative* basis for organizing world order came only with the rise of European global dominance, which began in the sixteenth century CE and morphed into the era of American primacy after the Second World War" (Acharya 2022: 24, emphasis in original). There have indeed been such mutually reinforcing racial and world order-building by Europe and America, and this point is well taken. We should remember, however, that this consists of only one aspect, though a very important one of the complex phenomena of race and racism. Furthermore, it should be noted that the discourse that connects the construction of racism with the West, even when aiming to critique the West-centered formation of the racist world order, in fact, may end up privileging the Western agency in history. In this connection, Tomohito Baji's argument on the interlinkage between the development of Japanese international theories (International Relations) and the creation of a Japanese-centric racial order in imperial Japan is significant. Baji correctly points out, "While the critique of white international theories has uncovered anti-non-white racism entailed in them, it has usually missed how racial hierarchies within the non-whites were constructed and how they were embedded in non-western knowledge" (2022: 168). His endeavor to fill in the "lacuna behind the bifurcated categories of the colour line" echoes with the aim of this volume and is indeed commendable for establishing a global history of racism sensitive to its multicentered and interconnected character (ibid.).
2 Although some previous research also addresses descent in its definition (e.g., Miles 1989; Rex 1986), these theories are primarily constructed around the paradigmatic examples of racial relationships between "whites" and "Blacks" defined by the "one-drop rule," or between Jews and majority white Europeans in Europe, and did not include racialized groups in Asia in their focus.
3 Lionnet and Shih, citing Sarah J. Mahler, refer to "transnationalism from above" in the sense of elite-controlled macrostructural processes. "Utopic views of globalization," according to them, celebrates the overcoming of national and other boundaries for the constitution of a liberal global market, in contrast to "dystopic visions of globalization," which problematize their consequences such as environmental and health hazards. They also correctly point out that the transnational can occur across national, local, or global spaces beyond the local/global binary model (Lionnet and Shih 2005: 6–7).
4 The concept of "minor transnationalism" resonates with Gilles Deleuze and Félix Guattari's idea on "lateral and nonhierarchical network structures," that is, "a rhizome" (Lionnet and Shih 2005: 2). However, Lionnet and Shih also point out that even Deleuze and Guattari "end up falling back into a recentered model of 'minor literature'" where "the minor's literary and political significance rests on its critical function

within and against the major in a binary and vertical relationship" (ibid.). A minor literature is not expected to be written in a minor language but defined by Deleuze and Guattari as "that which a minority constructs within a major language" (ibid.).
5 In this sense, Lionnet and Shih are certainly correct when they say, "the minor and the major participate in one shared transnational moment and space structured by uneven power relations" (2005: 7).
6 Japan remodeled the Western racial hierarchy into a Japanese-centric order (which used the self-designation "Yamato people") and applied it in its imperial expansion and colonial rule in Asia (Baji 2022; Takezawa 2021).
7 The Japanese contested the Western hegemony over the hierarchical racial order in the first half of the twentieth century, which in turn led to complex relationships of both collaboration and exploitation with the racial minorities in the West (Onishi 2013).

References

Acharya, Amitav. 2022. "Race and Racism in the Founding of the Modern World Order." *International Affairs* 98(1):23–43.
Agamben, Giorgio. 1998. *Homo Sacer: Sovereign Power and Bare Life*. Translated by Daniel Heller-Roazen. Stanford: Stanford University Press.
Appadurai, Arjun. 2006. *Fear of Small Numbers: An Essay of the Geography of Anger*. Durham and London: Duke University Press.
Armitage, David and Alison Bashford, eds. 2014. *Pacific Histories: Ocean, Land, People*. Basingstoke and New York: Palgrave Macmillan.
Baji, Tomohito. 2022. "Colonial Policy Studies in Japan: Racial Visions of Nan'yo, or the Early Creation of a Global South." *International Affairs* 98 (1):165–182.
Berg, Ulla D. and Ana Y. Ramos-Zayas. 2015. "Racializing Affect: A Theoretical Proposition." *Current Anthropology* 56 (5):654–677.
Budiman, Abbey and Neil G. Ruiz. 2021, April 29. "Key Facts about Asian Americans, A Diverse and Growing Population." Pew Research Center. https://www.pewresearch.org/fact-tank/2021/04/29/key-facts-about-asian-americans/. Last accessed on January 19, 2022.
Choy, Catherine Ceniza and Judy Tzu-Chun Wu, eds. 2017. *Gendering the Trans-Pacific World: Diaspora, Empire and Race*. Leiden: Brill.
Connolly, William E. 2002. *Neuropolitics: Thinking, Culture, Speed*. Minneapolis: University of Minnesota Press.
Deleuze, Gilles. 1988. *Spinoza: Practical Philosophy*. Translated by Robert Hurley. San Francisco: City Lights Books.
Deleuze, Gilles. 1992. "Postscript on the Societies of Control." *October* 59:3–7.
Franz Fanon. 1967. *Black Skin, White Masks*. New York: Grove Press.
Gallagher, John and Ronald Robinson. 1953. "The Imperialism of Free Trade." *The Economic History Review*, New Series, 6 (1):1–15.
Hardt, Michael. 2015. "The Power to be Affected." *International Journal of Politics, Culture, and Society* 28 (3):215–222.
International Organization for Migration. 2019. *World Migration Report 2020*. Geneva: International Organization for Migration.
Iriye, Akira, ed. 1980. *The Chinese and the Japanese: Essays in Political and Cultural Interactions*. Princeton: Princeton University Press.
Koshiro, Yukiko. 1999. *Trans-Pacific Racisms and the U.S. Occupation of Japan*. New York: Columbia University Press.
Kurashige, Lon, ed. 2017. *Pacific America: Histories of Transoceanic Crossings*. Honolulu: University of Hawai'i.

Leys, Ruth. 2011. "The Turn to Affect: A Critique." *Critical Inquiry* 37 (3):434–472.

Lionnet, Françoise, and Shu-mei Shih. 2005. *Minor Transnationalism*. Durham: Duke University Press.

Massumi, Brian. 1995. "The Autonomy of Affect." *Cultural Critique* 31:83–109.

Massumi, Brian. 2002. *Parables for the Virtual: Movement, Affect, Sensation*. Durham: Duke University Press.

Massumi, Brian. 2015. *Politics of Affect*. Cambridge: Polity Press.

Miles, Robert. 1989. *Racism*. London: Routledge.

Nguyen, Viet Thanh, and Janet Hoskins. 2014. "Introduction: Transpacific Studies: Critical Perspectives on an Emerging Field." In *Transpacific Studies: Framing an Emerging Field*, edited by Viet Thanh Nguyen and Janet Hoskins, 1–38. Honolulu: University of Hawai'i Press.

Nishii, Ryoko and Tadashi Yanai 2020. *Afekutusu: Sei no Sotogawa ni Fureru [Affectus: Touching outside Life]*. Kyoto: Kyoto University Press.

Omi, Michael and Howard Winant. 2014. *Racial Formation in the United States*. 3rd Edition, New York: Routledge.

Onishi, Yuichiro. 2013. *Transpacific Antiracism: Afro-Asian Solidarity in Twentieth-century Black America, Japan, and Okinawa*. New York: New York University Press.

Plüss, Caroline and Chan Kwok-bun, eds. 2012. *Living Intersections: Transnational Migrant Identifications in Asia*. Dordrecht: Springer.

Rex, John. 1986. *Race and Ethnicity*. Milton Keynes: Open University Press.

Rose, Nikolas. 2000. "Government and Control." *British Journal of Criminology* 40:321–339.

Shouse, Eric. 2005. "Feeling, Emotion, Affect." *M/C Journal 8* (6). https://doi.org/10.5204/mcj.2443.

Spinoza, Benedictus de. 1985. *The Collected Works of Spinoza*, Vol. 1. Edited and translated by Edwin Curley. Princeton: Princeton University Press.

Sugihara, Kaoru. 2001. "Oceanic Trade and Global Development, 1500–1995." In *Making Sense of Global History: The 19th International Congress of the Historical Sciences Oslo 2000 Commemorative Volume*, edited by Solvi Songer, 55–69. Oslo: University of Oslo.

Sugihara, Kaoru. 2014. "The Economy since 1800." In *Pacific Histories: Ocean, Land, People*, edited by David Armitage and Alison Bashford, 166–190, 347–348. Basingstoke and New York: Palgrave Macmillan.

Takezawa, Yasuko. 2005. "Transcending the Western Paradigm of the Idea of Race." *The Japanese Journal of American Studies* 16:5–30.

Takezawa, Yasuko, ed. 2011. *Racial Representations in Asia*. Kyoto and Melbourne: Kyoto University Press/Transpacific Press.

Takezawa, Yasuko. 2020. "Racialization and Discourses of 'Privileges' in the Middle Ages: Jews, 'Gypsies,' and Kawaramono." *Ethnic and Racial Studies* 43 (16):193–210.

Takezawa, Yasuko. 2021. "Japan's Modernization and Self Construction Between White and Yellow." In *The Routledge Critical Whiteness Studies Handbook*, edited by Shona Hunter and Christi van der Westhuizen, 160–170. London: Routledge.

Takezawa, Yasuko and Gary Y. Okihiro, eds. 2016. *Trans-Pacific Japanese American Studies: Conversations on Race and Racializations*. Honolulu: University of Hawai'i Press.

The Hugo Pan-Asian SNP Consortium. 2009. "Mapping Human Genetic Diversity in Asia." *Science* 326 (5959):1541–1545.

Wang, Ping. 2004. "Nihonjin no Chūgokukan no rekishiteki hensen ni tsuite" [On the Historical Changes of the Japanese "China Perception"]. *Hiroshima Daigaku Management Kenkyū* 4: 261–269.

PART I

Encounters, Entanglement, and Solidarity

2

SETTLER COLONIALISM AS ENCOUNTER

On the Question of Racialization and Labor Power in the Dispossession of Ainu Lands

Katsuya Hirano

2.1 Introduction

When we examine Hokkaidō's "opening" as a history of encounter brought about by settler colonialism, in what way should we reconsider the modern experience of the Ainu, the Indigenous people of the land? Encounter, in the strictest sense of the word, refers to an unexpected meeting or a situation in which an opportunity for unanticipated interaction with the other arises. Settler colonial encounter is neither an inevitable consequence of historical progress nor a manifestation of the Cunning of Reason, contrary to the persistent belief of some Hegelian historians. It is, rather, a particular historical condition created by a state-led capitalist program designed to plunder and rob another society. Therefore, settler colonial encounters are diametrically opposed to the principle of free and equal exchange of ideas and goods or non-hierarchic mixing of different cultures and are instead founded on the systemic use of violence for dispossession and destruction. One figure that speaks eloquently of this matter is Aimé Césaire, a poet and leader of the Negritude movement who was born in Martinique, an island forcibly incorporated after a brutal invasion by the French military during the seventeenth century. Probing colonialism's violent subjection of Indigenous communities, Césaire asks: "of all the ways of establishing contact [between cultures], was [colonization] the best?" (Césaire 2001, 33). Colonial encounter is never "an excellent thing that blends different worlds." Rather, it serves only to "decivilize the colonizer, to brutalize him in the true sense of the word, to degrade him, to awaken him to buried instincts, to covetousness, violence, race hatred, and moral relativism" while completely dehumanizing the colonized (Césaire 2001, 35). Indeed, "there could not come a single human value" in colonial encounters, as Césaire affirms (Césaire 2001, 34).

This chapter examines the settler colonization of Ainu Mosir ("the peaceful land of humans" as the Ainu people called Hokkaidō) as an encounter in the following

DOI: 10.4324/9781003266396-3

two senses of the term. The first is the encounter between the Indigenous Ainu and the Wajin (Japanese) settlers; the second is the encounter between the Meiji government's emigration policy and the American settler colonial expansion called the Westward movement. This structure of encounter was primarily formed by the politics of racialization—meaning the ranking and categorization of human beings into different types based on perceived innate abilities derived from particular physical traits such as skin color and bodily measurements—which gave birth to the modern world order. In the racial hierarchy of Hokkaidō's opening, white American and English experts hired to advise settler-colonial development were at the apex, followed by the Wajin settlers, while Ainu and Korean workers were relegated to the lowest strata. There were, moreover, further subdivisions. Within Wajin settler society, capitalists, pioneers, and prisoners occupied different rungs on the ladder, while there existed further partitions within Ainu communities between the Hokkaidō Ainu and the Karafuto Ainu.

As is commonly known, Wajin immigration to Ainu Mosir did not begin during the Meiji period (Enomori 1997). Until the later part of the seventeenth century, the early modern Tokugawa government (*bakufu*) had authorized the Matsumae clan to claim the southern part of Ainu Mosir as its domain and to establish a monopoly system of trade posts by outlawing the extensive Ainu trade networks covering Karafuto, the Amur River, Tsugaru, and various northeastern domains. The Matsumae clan forcibly restricted Ainu trade while simultaneously imposing iniquitous exchange conditions on the Ainu. For most Ainu, these unfair trading conditions led to their becoming destitute; moreover, those who did not subordinate themselves to Matsumae control could neither buy goods nor trade and were threatened with the selling of their children for labor or sexual exploitation. As the Ainu became increasingly resentful of the injustices suffered under the Matsumae clan, an armed coalition began to resist Wajin domination in 1669 in what is now known as Shakushain's Revolt or Shakushain's War (Hirayama 2016; Walker 2006, 48–72). In 1688, following the suppression of this rebellion, the Tokugawa *bakufu* forbade both Ainu use of hunting weapons and Wajin migration to Ainu Mosir in order to prevent further uprisings and conflicts.

In the eighteenth century, as the areas of "Ezo" (蝦夷, or "barbarians" as the Wajin called the Ainu) covered by Matsumae trade underwent financial and technical complications, Wajin merchants started managing this system on behalf of the Matsumae lord. The Ōmi (present-day Shiga) merchants, who had ties to the lord, were given exclusive trade rights with the Ainu and built up a vast enterprise centered on marine goods such as herring, chum salmon, cherry salmon, and sea cucumbers. Ainu would fish these using their small towlines rather than in large-scale operations. They maintained a limited measure of freedom through their ability to transport their catch and barter at different trade posts but still faced exploitation as they could only sell their goods on severely disadvantageous terms (Hokkaidō—Tōhokushi kenkyūkai 1998, 105–106). In addition, many young Ainu men were pressed into corvée labor, leaving the women by themselves in *kotan* (Ainu village) vulnerable to sexual assault and forced concubinage by

Wajin (Iewallen 2019, 10–17; Matsu'ura 2002, 107–109). In 1856, Ainu Mosir was incorporated as Japanese territory by the Tokugawa *bakufu*, who, in the name of asserting its settler-colonial claims against an expanding Tsarist Russia, launched a policy of assimilation. The Ainu were forced to adopt Wajin names, clothing, hairstyles, as well as be forbidden to wear earrings, have facial tattoos, or worship Bear spirits. At the same time, colonists were encouraged to immigrate to Ezo to open wet paddy fields and promote the development of agriculture.

At first glance, the pre-Meiji Ainu encounter with the Wajin seems highly analogous to what came after. For example, both the Tokugawa *bakufu* and its Meiji successor implemented a policy of Wajin migration and agriculturation as well as Ainu assimilation. The early modern form of Ainu exploitation was predicated on visible markers of difference such as custom, habits, external appearance, and even language. The Wajin essentially viewed the Ainu as visibly different foreign "barbarians" (夷), as expressed in the word "Ezo" (蝦夷). In this regard, the idea presented in this volume's introduction about the distinction between pre-modern mode of racism based on "invisible differences" and racism of the "phenotypically visible differences" of Euro-American scientific racism in modern times is not directly applicable to the historical relations between the Ainu and the Wajin. Both early modern and modern forms of racialization in their relations were predicated on the notion of notable cultural and physical differences. It can be argued, therefore, that the early modern form of racial hierarchies supplied a crucial condition for the germination of the modern form in Meiji Japan's settler colonial policies in Hokkaidō.

We cannot, however, draw simple parallels or a linear continuity between the early modern and modern forms of racism. Modern racism was born, as the introduction also suggests, out of a biological conception of difference, as well as the shift toward the classification of human life according to distinct genetic types. This speciation of human beings ranks them based on the principle of "survival of the fittest" derived from the Social Darwinian view of the world. Which race is the most fit for survival? And which one is to prosper, advance, or dominate? The Darwinian principle of evolution constitutes the core epistemology of new notions of civilizational progress. Within this framework, civilization is seen as a unilinear and hierarchical development of humanity as a progressive force of history necessarily divides the human beings into superior and inferior, vigorous and feeble races. Modern civilization thus is synonymous with the new hierarchical configuration of humanity: it determines who is to survive and who is to vanish, connecting life and death to observable markers of genetic difference. This biological articulation of hierarchies among human species as a corollary of evolution signifies a radical break between early modern and modern epistemologies, and it is this fundamentally new articulation of difference that gave rise to the virulent notion that the Ainu lacked suitability for existence in the world of modern civilization. In this regard, Takezawa's distinction between r and R, as seen in Introduction, to underscore the crucial difference between pre-modern and modern forms of racism is absolutely helpful. Both early modern and modern forms of Japanese racism toward the Ainu were predicated on "visible difference," but the epistemological assumptions about the "difference" differed radically from each other.

The understanding of the Ainu as a "vanishing race" emerged precisely at the moment the notion of survival of the fittest rose to the surface as a new hegemonic ideology in modernizing Japan. We see that this discourse of fitness offered a deadly rationale for settler-colonial policies designed to use emigrant labor to build up social and economic foundations for the opening of Hokkaidō. Policymakers pursued settler-colonial policies with the following questions in mind: whose and what sort of labor power was to contribute to frontier development and the modernization of Japan? Who was to "cultivate the land" and "increase the volume of agricultural exports" to earn more foreign capital? (Bessho 1882). The Meiji government saw the forms of Ainu labor used to sustain a hunter-gatherer lifestyle as obstructing the acclamation of the land and thus the development of large-scale agriculture for the accumulation of capital, while also regarding it as a manifestation of the Ainu's racially inferior character. Thus, Meiji Japan's settler-colonial policies in Hokkaidō were aimed primarily at eradicating the Indigenous form of life. Put differently, the question of labor power was at the heart of Meiji leaders' understanding of the survival of the fittest, and the Ainu's form of labor signified the ultimate expression of racial inferiority, thus of humans to be eliminated.

As described earlier, under Tokugawa-era Matsumae trade post and contract labor systems, Ainu were hired and allowed to trade goods, although they were frequently defrauded and overexploited by Wajin merchants. Then, during the Meiji period, the policy of frontier opening by way of the theory of natural selection both replaced the trade posts and contract labor systems and disparaged the Ainu solely as "ignorant and foolish" types who offered nothing but futile labor and pursued a useless existence. In short, modern settler colonial encounters shifted the labor power of the Ainu from useful to dispensable according to the theory of natural selection. It was said that only the Wajin had the requisite labor power and intelligence required for the labor to engage in the frontier development considered necessary to build up Hokkaidō's modern agricultural industries. As Japanese colonizers occupied Ainu Mosir from 1869 on, the Ainu's immiseration and impoverishment worsened, and a debate emerged in Japanese society between those who believed that the Ainu people should be left to themselves to face extinction and those who advocated for assimilation policies as part of a larger governmental relief effort. Simultaneously, these policy debates went hand in hand with the process that forced the Ainu to live as "the survival of the ancient past," "the exotic object for display" and "the object of racial sciences" that aroused the curiosity of Wajin and European scientists (Chikappu 2001, 240–247; Roellinghoff 2020, 295–310; Sasaki 1934, 1). In "vanishing," "protection," "spectacle," and "specimen," whichever term one may use, we see the ways in which the Ainu were subsumed by the modern racial order.

The plunder of Ainu Mosir and the development of the US Western frontier, which resulted in the dispossession of Indigenous peoples, occurred side by side. Those who partook in the latter experience played a pivotal role in the opening of Hokkaidō. This fact is of great importance for our understanding of Hokkaidō's settler colonialism as a matter of encounter. From the late nineteenth century on, Japan closely studied the example of American westward expansion when designing methods for the plunder of the lands of the Indigenous people, along with their rivers, forests, and other support systems, for the development of capitalistic industries. This history of dispossession was also part of a larger global moment in which Indigenous peoples in Australia, Canada, Russia, and the Pacific Rim were seeing systems of plunder erected upon their lands. This global moment of indigenous dispossession coincided with the spread of capitalism across the entire globe and was deeply tied to the process of violent expropriation (i.e., enclosure or colonial rule), which Rosa Luxemburg, following Karl Marx, referred to as the "accumulation of capital" via the "struggle against natural economy" (Luxemburg, 2003, 348–365).

In his book *The Sublime Perversion of Capital*, building on Luxemburg's discussion of the use of violence as integral to the system of capitalist accumulation, Gavin Walker theorizes that the originary moment of capitalist formation, or so-called "primitive accumulation," involves all manner of extra-economic forces that serve to subsume and mobilize labor power. Referring to labor power as the outside of capital, Walker defines its place in the capitalist system: "We are always inside [the capitalist system], but this inside contains the substance of the exterior, the material forces [like political, social, and ideological forces] of the outside's originary enclosure, which can never be fully erased" no matter how much capitalism develops (Walker 2016, 139). In other words, the human creative power called labor power is always the necessary element in the production and reproduction of capital, but it constitutes the outside of capital because it can never be created and mobilized by capital itself. Labor power serves capital only when it is captured by a variety of extra-economic forces such as law, politics, ideology (common sense, readily accepted social values, etc.), as well as education and media, along with other elements emerging from civil society. It can be said that racism, one of the most virulent ideologies in modern times, is such an extra-economic force that directs how labor power is subsumed under capital.

Racism, as Etienne Balibar and Immanuel Wallerstein have pointed out, allows for the differentiated subsumption of labor power, which in turn creates and justifies conditions under which the labor power of racially minoritized people can be exploited in an extreme manner (Balibar & Wallerstein 1991, 34–35). Put another way, racism plays a decisive role in normalizing the creation of a distinct type of labor force subject to heightened exploitation. But in examining the history of frontier development in Hokkaidō, one crucial lesson we should derive is that capitalism's subsumption of labor power often designates a particular form of labor as disposable, even useless. In order to mobilize the labor power needed for the creation of capital in Hokkaidō, the process of labor division evolved through racial differences that, without exception, were founded on a distinction between "useful" labor (that of the Wajin settlers) and its "futile" counterpart (that of Indigenous people). This differentiation of usefulness/futility is part of capitalism's general tendency to separate "worthy" from "unworthy" life, which is a prerequisite for the continued existence of what we call biopolitics. The biopolitical management of labor power under racialized capitalism reveals itself most vividly in encounters between racialized labor groups. Chapter 4 of this volume by Yū Tokunaga, who analyzes the racial partitioning between immigrant Mexican and Japanese labor in California, illuminates one such case. Chapter 5, by Takeshi Onimaru, also attests to such encounters in his examination of how the ethnic, rather than racial, categories utilized often arbitrarily to manage diverse immigrant populations in Singapore separated the Chinese population from Malay immigrant labor. In this chapter, by centering my discussion around the term "encounter," I examine the ways in which the settler colonization of Hokkaidō, oriented toward creating and accumulating capital, racialized Ainu labor power (along with their long-established connection to the land) in relation to that of Japanese immigrants, as well as the way racialization also transformed Ainu lives.

2.2 *Terra Nullius*—The Logic of Plunder and Occupation

"Vanishing race" was a term imposed upon the Ainu, as well as many of the globe's Indigenous peoples, as the modern era began (Brantlinger 2003; Dippie 1982). It naturalized the settler-colonial process of subjecting these peoples to regimes of dispossession, poverty, and death as a "law of progress." It was, furthermore, closely associated with another deadly concept, that of *terra nullius*. Beginning in the seventeenth century, the concept of *terra nullius* laid the foundation for the capitalist concept of private property: only those who cultivated and reclaimed the land could be in possession of it. Grounding land ownership in the labor of cultivation, *terra nullius* negated Indigenous people's relationship with nature and their lands since their ways of life were based mostly on the commons, that is, hunting and gathering. *Terra nullius* offered a legitimating logic to settlers' plunder and occupation of lands belonging to Indigenous peoples.

Terra nullius—mushuchi/無主地 in Japanese—connotes land unclaimed or not owned by anyone (Fitzmaurice 2007, 1–15). In international law, *terra nullius* generally refers to land whose inhabitants have not established political structures such as a state or a region/territory which has not undergone sufficient development or cultivation. Originally, this concept was refined by the father of international law, Hugo Grotius (1583–1645), who claimed that a land "inhabited by no one" can be "discovered," occupied, or subjugated even by means of violence in a fully legal fashion. According to Yogi Hendlin, Grotius understood the triumph of civilization as entailing the "converting [of] things through use and seizure into owned property" (Hale Hendline 2014, 146). Thus, for anyone to be considered a member of the civilized world, one must transform land into property through labor and organized activities. The political theorist John Locke (1632–1704) further elaborated on this idea by offering a theory of private property in the context of Colonial America. For Locke, anyone who uses his labor to cultivate, improve, or reclaim land can use its products exclusively, as well as claim ownership of it by enclosing it from the commons (Locke 1989, 290–291). In the Lockean conception of property, God commands humankind to subdue the land or to appropriate it for the sake of individual wellbeing (Locke 1989, 292). Thus, the possession of the land becomes the expression of God's ordinance insofar as "whatsoever he tilled and reaped, laid up and made use of, before it spoiled, that was his peculiar Right; whatsoever he enclosed, and could feed, and make use of, the Cattle and Product was also his" (Locke 1989, 295). The ability to conquer nature, improve it, and derive value from it by labor is God's endowment unique to humans and functions as a clear indicator for what legitimates private property. Therefore, to leave the world untapped as commons can be said to oppose God's will, given that the world should be used diligently and rationally by humans for their own happiness (Locke 1989, 291). Furthermore, one can increase the value of land through the application of labor, which allows for the production of crops such as wheat, barley, and sugar. For Locke, "(L)and which is left wholly to Nature [commons], that has no improvement of Pasturage, Tillage, or Planting, is called, as indeed it is, waste: we shall find the benefit of it to amount to little more than nothing" (Locke 1989, 297).

This Lockean understanding of *terra nullius* was applied by British colonizers not only to the land of Indigenous Americans but also to that of Aboriginal Australians, whom the colonizers defined as "savages" incapable of practicing agriculture and, by extension, using the reason or mental faculty required for civilizational progress. For the colonizers, this signified the Aborigines' being as anomaly, half-human even, because they did not follow God's commands. It was claimed that because the land they inhabited was still a commons, which the inhabitants subsisted off of through a hunter-gatherer lifestyle, their lands were considered a wilderness in need of a new master who obeyed God's will. Based on this belief, in the name of God and Reason, the conquest and genocide of Aboriginal Australians were carried out (Jalata 2013, 1–12). In other words, the theory of *terra nullius* not only excused the plunder of Indigenous lands but also supported the logic of ethnic cleansing (removal, expulsion, genocide). Such logic of colonial looting and massacre was crucial to the birth of the private property system and its patterns of land use, ultimately shaping the theoretical foundations of the modern imperial world.

The Japanese approach to colonization in Hokkaidō is no exception to the rule. Frontier expansion in Hokkaidō was very much influenced by Lockean political philosophy as applied in the United States, in which context the concept of "empty domicile" was particularly important in its ideology of so-called Manifest Destiny (Madley 2004, 167–192). According to the Manifest Destiny framework, human civilization was transmitted through the ancient Roman

empire, the British Empire, and finally, American westward expansion, the ultimate purpose of which was, as John L. Sullivan put it in 1845, "to overspread
and to possess the whole of the continent which Providence has given us for the
development of the great experiment of liberty and federated self-government
entrusted to us" (McCrisken 2001, 68). As the white settlers' expansionism fused
with the conception of God-given mission of "civilizational progress," Indigenous
peoples were forcibly relocated to and decimated in conquered territories like
Texas and California (Cumings 2009; Lahti 2018). The encounter with Indigenous
peoples on the frontier was eventually extended to include encounters with various "others," as Bruce Cumings explains:

> [T]he encounter with non-white peoples to the west (was) increasingly seen
> as numerous, an obstacle to expansion, and alien to a new nationalist concep-
> tion of what it meant to be an American. The alien was the Other, his cul-
> ture was the antithesis of the Anglo-Saxon creed, assimilation was out of the
> question given the stain of race, and so this garden-cum-empire was fueled
> from one end to the other by virulent racism. Blacks in the South, Indians on
> the frontier, Mexicans in California, eventually Filipinos, Chinese, Japanese
> and Koreans—all suffered outrageous abuses and indignities.
>
> *Cumings 2009, 90*

Echoing Cumings, Ueda Makoto argues that we ought to reconsider and reex-
amine Commodore Matthew Perry's "opening" of Japan as part of the larger
process of Manifest Destiny (Ueda 2018, 109–110). From Oregon to California,
and then crossing over into the Pacific, American expansionism led to incursion
into Japan—fulfilling Christopher Columbus' dreams of reaching distant lands
filled with gold in the East.

One individual whose conception of civilization, like that of his contemporaries,
was shaped by the ideology of American westward expansion was Horace Capron
(1804–1885). In 1872, after moving to Japan to advise the Hokkaidō Kaitakushi,
the Development Commission tasked with settler-colonizing Ainu Mosir, Capron
wrote to Colonel Warren, an army colleague who lived in San Francisco:

> The great tidal wave of civilization which then was sweeping across the
> American continent, seems only to have paused upon its western coast to
> gather for its passage over the broad Pacific in its westward progress around
> the world. It has reached the Asiatic continent, and your dreams of the great
> future benefits to your city and state in this connection are at last to be realized.
>
> *Capron 1872*

Capron's view, as expressed in his letter, was shared by many Americans who
viewed Japan's recent "opening" as a monumental opportunity to expand
their businesses to sell their products not only to Japan but also to other East
Asian nations. In this regard, the Capron mission signified the continuation of

American westward expansion in a way that promised an unprecedented opportunity for American economic expansion beyond its Western limits.

Capron was one of the "hired foreigners" in Hokkaidō who lent their expertise to lay the blueprint for the colonization of Ainu Mosir. When he met with Kuroda Kiyotaka (1840–1900), Undersecretary of the Kaitakushi, in 1871, he was serving as the Commissioner of the United States Department of Agriculture under the presidency of Ulysses S. Grant due to his well-known success with crops and livestock. Capron had also been involved in Indian removal from 1851 to 1853 under President Millard Fillmore's commission, which forcibly relocated the Cherokee, Comanches, Creeks, Delaware, Kickapoos, and Shawnee tribes in Texas to new territories. The US government carried out these relocations in accordance with the view that "Indians hindered western expansion, and as such could only be thought of as a 'barbaric' obstruction" (Saruya 1982, 187). Capron's expertise in agriculture and experience in resettling Indigenous peoples made him a compelling pick to oversee the economic development of Hokkaidō.

Between 1869 and 1879, Meiji Japan hired 75 foreign experts for the Hokkaidō settler-colonial project. Of them, 45 were Americans. As the head of the first American advisory commission to Hokkaidō, Capron brought with him in 1871 civil engineer A.G. Warfield and chemist and geologist Thomas Anticell to investigate the soil quality and geography of the island. Benjamin Smith Lyman succeeded Anticell in 1874 and joined the team as a geologist and mining engineer. Lyman carried out extensive geological surveys with his 13 Japanese assistants to explore coals, oilfields, iron, sulfur, and gold. He made the first geological map of Hokkaidō that detailed all minerals "discovered" on the island (Figure 2.1). Lyman was also active in advocating dairy farming and recommended the extermination of bears, wolves, and wild dogs by "offering bounties, as is done in other countries" because their presence "in the mountains will perhaps be some hindrance to the introduction of sheep and even larger cattle" (Yamada 2011, 117). The Hokkaidō Development Office put this advice into law in 1877 (Yamada 2011, 123–124). Lyman was not alone in recommending the mass killing of native wildlife species for the sweeping ecological domination of Ainu Mosir. Seeking to build livestock industries in the new colony, the Hokkaidō Development Office put together a team of American specialists who had gained expertise in the methods of settler-colonial reconstitution of the American West. Among them was Edwin Dun, who was a rancher from Ohio and lived in Hokkaidō as an advisor for the development of farms from 1876 to 1883. Soon after his arrival in this new Japanese colony, Dun started horse breeding programs to raise high-quality ranch horses and proposed the purchase of strychnine to poison wolves, bears, and wild dogs at new ranches such as the 35,000-acre Niikappu Ranch, one of the imperial estates (Walker 2004, 263). Meiji Japan followed Dun's advice, and native wolves were wiped out as a result. Hokkaido literally became the first experimental ground for the US to apply its project of Manifest Destiny in Asia.[1]

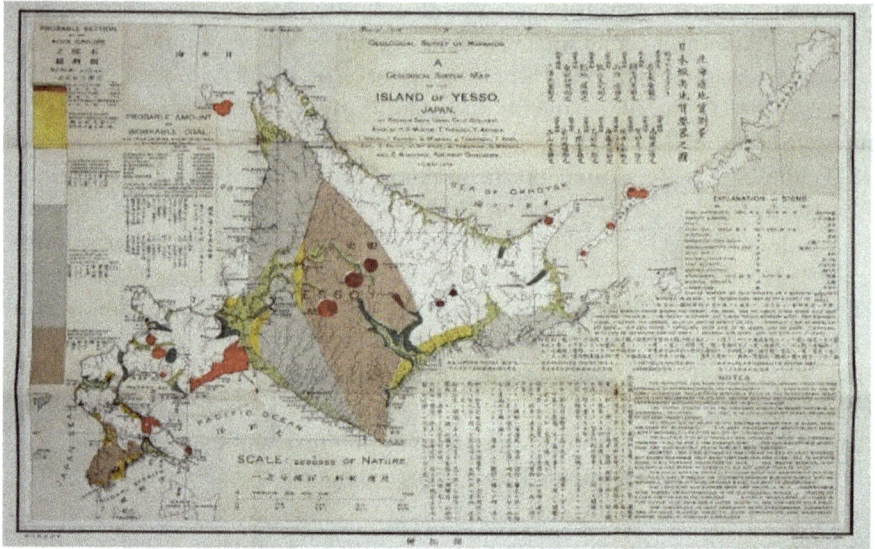

FIGURE 2.1 Lyman Made and Published the First Geological Map of Hokkaidō in 1876
Source: Hokkaidō University Library

It is important to point out that Meiji Japan, suffering from its "inferior" status vis-à-vis the Western imperial nations within the global structure of civilizational hierarchies, did not agree with the White supremacist presumption of Manifest Destiny, but it did deploy the notion of historical progress and the Lockean conception of *terra nullius* whereby it came to view the Ainu as "primitive" and unfit to claim any right to their ancestral lands. The Meiji government also regarded the system of private property and desire for it as the driving force behind civilizational progress, thereby deeply internalizing capitalistic notions of land ownership. We could say that Japan, for all of its vigilance against Western imperialism, created its own experiment of "manifest destiny" in the name of bringing "civilization" to the "Land of Barbarians."[2]

Surely, Japan's policy of settler-colonization in Hokkaidō did not use the brute force of extermination as often seen in the likes of European and American's handling of Indigenous peoples. Probably, the longstanding trade relations between the Ainu and the Wajin from the early modern period onwards—which involved overexploitation and slave-like relations—prevented the blatant use of force, at least in part. Also, thanks to years of overexploitation and sexual colonization, the Ainu population had been decimated by the start of the Meiji period (lewallen 2019, 16), and the impossibility of armed resistance after the failed revolts of the seventeenth century was likely a contributing factor as well. Still, the absence of military conquest and warfare integral to European and American expansion does not exclude the Ainu from the global history of Indigenous dispossession. Rather, Japan's dispossession of the Ainu should be understood in terms of the long process of settler-colonization of Ainu Mosir, which spanned two different political regimes (the Tokugawa feudal system and the Meiji capitalist system) from the seventeenth century on. It reached the peak in the late nineteenth century where Meiji Japan's modern settler-colonial policies systemically negated Ainu forms of social, economic, and cultural life and labeled them as a "vanishing race" destined to be extinguished.

2.3 Living to Die—Prison Labor and Primitive Accumulation

In order to grasp the logic that dispossessed the Ainu by incorporating them into the Japanese empire, we must now turn our attention to the mobilization of prison labor in Hokkaidō. An examination of prison labor enables us to understand the ways in which the Ainu were rendered as "vanishing" and became dispossessed of their land.

The Meiji government's frontier expansionism gave birth to the image of the Ainu as "backward and feeble," meaning that they were perceived not as an exploitable and disposable labor power but rather as a race on the "verge of extinction." It was believed that the Ainu became subject to the iron law of "survival of the fittest" as a result of their abject encounter with the more valiant and progressive Wajin. This encounter was considered inevitable as nothing could halt or alter the progression of history, a history in which the feeble and backward Ainu would vanish sooner or later. This assumption about the Ainu's fate was the underlying logic of the Wajin's aggressive settler-colonial emigration to Hokkaidō since the government considered Wajin to be far better suited than the Ainu to achieve their two urgent goals of building up a prosperous colony and defending Japan's borders against Russia.[3] From the early 1870s to the mid-1880s, the Meiji government encouraged ex-samurai and poor farmers to immigrate to the new land. But the harshness of winter, insect damage to crops, insufficient capital, as well as lack of complete modern infrastructures such as roads, schools, hospitals, and railways, led to delays in the implementation of emigration policies (Asada 2004, 38–39). In 1885, while inspecting the difficult living conditions of Hokkaidō "pioneers," Kaneko Kentarou (1853–1942) remarked that "already so many years have passed since immigration, and [the settlers] still live in thatched huts with dirt floors and lead a harsh life. They can no longer bear such hardship, and in the end, have dispersed. They have borne witness to countless other scenes of misery" (Takakura 1947, 128). With the aim of pushing forward their lagging frontier, the Meiji government launched a new policy. From 1886 through the Russo-Japanese war of 1904–1905, the government built up infrastructure such as roads, railways, ports, and bridges by mobilizing prison labor, as well as developing coal mining. At the time, Iwamura Michitoshi (1840–1915), who headed the new Hokkaidō Office established in 1886, proclaimed to Wajin village heads across the whole territory that "henceforth we will no longer promote the emigration of the poor, but bring in rich immigrants," just as nobles, merchants, landlords and other agents of *naichi* capital began devoting themselves to frontier development (Kuwahara 1982, 165). This marked the beginnings of massive capitalistic investment in Hokkaidō. In June of 1886, the Regulations Concerning the Sale/Disposal of Hokkaidō Land Act was promulgated to encourage investment in Hokkaidō by increasing the acreage of nationally owned "undeveloped properties" that could be sold, thereby creating a loophole for large-scale capitalist investors. An additional Law Regarding the Disposal of Nationally Owned Undeveloped Lands was then passed in 1897, which greatly facilitated the acquisition of land in Hokkaidō, thereby accelerating the immigration of poor farmers from *naichi* (Tanaka & Kuwahara 1996, 14). It goes without saying that these land policies designed to accelerate immigration and capital investment were modeled after the US's Homestead Act of 1862.

Prison labor was composed of so-called felons, a group that included vagabonds and struggling peasants who had lost their lands and turned to a life of crime as a result of the Land Tax Reform of 1873–1881 and Lord Finance Minister Matsukata Masayoshi's deflationary policy, as well as participants in the Satsuma Rebellion of 1877 which challenged the legitimacy of the newly established Meiji government. In order to build up the infrastructure needed to advance the capitalistic development of Hokkaidō, the Meiji state turned to exploitable "semi-slave" prison labor. This semi-slave labor force labored up to 10 hours a day under extremely cruel conditions for paltry wages and often worked to the point of death by way of malnutrition, overwork, or disease. They were under constant surveillance and bound by iron balls and chains while working outside the prison. If they attempted to escape, they were beheaded on-site and their bodies left to rot.

About 95% of the prisoners were between 20 and 50 years old, with those in their 30s representing more than half of all prisoners (Chōsenjin Kyōsei Renkō Chōsadan 1974, 105 & 147). Between 1886 and 1889, the total number of prisoners increased from 4,209 to 7,000 (Chōsenjin Kyōsei Renkō Chōsadan 1974, 105). 30 to 50% worked in mining and construction, while 20 to 30% were engaged in farming and reclamation (Tanaka 1986, 108–109). Their annual mortality rate ranged from 2.5% to 13%, depending on the type and conditions of labor. Men within the same age range in the general population had a mortality rate of about 1%, making this rate extremely high and close to the rate in contemporary prisons (Chōsenjin Kyōsei Renkō Chōsadan 1974, 108). In 1887, Sorachi Prison reported 265 deaths out of 1,966 prisoners, a 13.5% mortality rate, while Kushiro Prison had 83 deaths out of 790 prisoners, marking a 10.5% mortality rate (Tanaka 1986, 126). Abashiri Prison—established in 1890 for the purpose of building a central highway—reported over 200 deaths out of 1,397 prisoners in 1891, an extraordinary mortality rate of 15.7% (Tanaka 1986, 126). The main causes of death were infectious diseases, skin conditions, pulmonary diseases, and digestive and nutritional diseases, pointing to extremely harsh working conditions, an unhygienic environment, and an inadequate diet that were common in mining and construction sites (Tanaka 1986, 122–123). Okada

Asataro, a law professor who conducted a survey about the prisoners' working conditions in mines, observed in 1893 that the prisoners worked 12-hour shifts, their drinking water was filthy, and they ate and excreted in the same place, all of which contributed to chronic digestive and pulmonary diseases as well as high mortality rate (Shigematsu 2004, 54).

What these extremely exploitative conditions signified was that frontier labor was foisted upon those whom the Meiji authorities took as essentially worthy of death, that is, those who were considered to be absolutely disposable objects. This semi-slave labor was different from that of poor farmers, who were "free labor" created by enclosure movements: they were forced off the land, completely severed from their means of production, and made to move and float along with the flow of capital with only their labor to sell. Prison laborers were neither free to sell their labor nor free to move in conjunction with capital. In other words, they were forced to work at a fixed place until their death as unfree labor. Until the Russo-Japanese War, frontier development in Hokkaidō was supported by this prison labor. From the Russo-Japanese War on, a wage labor system emerged in rural villages in both *naichi* and Hokkaidō and the resulting labor market came to replace the prison labor system. This meant that in Hokkaidō a labor market was formed on the basis of the consolidation and relocation of large and heavy industries and the small to medium food industries that had been transplanted during the early Meiji period by local capital. Prisoners forced into unfree labor preceded the formation of this market and allowed the Meiji government to deal with the knotty problem of labor shortages for its management of Hokkaidō as the first modern colony. It should be noted that the mobilization of prison labor for frontier development occurred across different sites like Australia, the eastern United States, French Guiana, Algeria, and New Caledonia, as well as Russian Siberia and Sakhalin. The Meiji government's policy of frontier expansion should be seen as part of this broader historical context of the development of prison labor used since the late eighteenth century (De Vito and Lichtenstein, 2013).

Tsukigata Kiyoshi (1846–1894), the Chief Prison Administrator of Hokkaido, presented the idea of mobilizing prisoners for frontier development in 1885 and explained the benefits of this particular type of labor to Kaneko Kentaro, then in the middle of an inspection tour in Hokkaidō: "Our government should relocate prisoners and convicts who have been punished and exiled elsewhere to Hokkaidō to reclaim this land unused for millennia and bring about generations of prosperity and wealth to our nation" (Tanaka 1986, 104). He then added, "when it comes to frontier colonization, the most urgent matter is the convenience of roads and transport infrastructure," wherein one could "force prisoners" to work so as to "build roads where there are no roads, lay bridges where there are none, and clear out all the thorny shrub," as well as "cultivate wastelands" (Tanaka 1986, 104).

Kaneko, who was ordered to go on the inspection tour by Itō Hirobumi (1841–1909), put out his report on "An Inspection of the Three Hokkaidō

Prefectures," in which he explained the advantages of mobilizing prison labor for road construction in the following way:

> Transferring prisoners to Hokkaidō achieves two objectives: first, it helps to open and cultivate unlimited resources that were left unused over thousands of years for the benefits of our nation; second, it provides the prisoners with employment. Among the most urgent tasks is the construction of roads and bridges as well as the development of coal mining .... Furthermore, the true benefit of using prisoners is that their wage can be much lower than ordinary laborers' (ranging from one-third to one-fifth of the average wage) and even if they die of hard and unbearable working conditions, their death is different from the tragic cases where the laborers leave their corpses in fields and mountains for their wives and children to collect. To begin with, prisoners are roughnecks .... Their death in fact contributes to reduction in the number of prisoners, lifting much strain from the expenditure of prison systems. We can achieve our objective of reducing the prison expenditure by more than half. This is precisely what we call killing two birds with one stone.
>
> *Kaneko 1885*

We can sum up Kaneko's ideas regarding prison labor as follows: (1) since prisoners are individuals who have committed crimes, it presents no problem that they should be left to die on the fields due to hard labor; (2) in addition to the fact that the death of prisoners is far from being a tragic situation since no one laments it, it helps reduce the number of prisoners and prison's expenditure; and (3) the wages of prisoners are less than half of that of regular workers, and therefore use of such labor helps reduce the cost of frontier development. The logic outlined in these three points communicates the absolute subordination of human life to economic efficiency.[4] Because of the crimes they committed, these prisoners were deemed unworthy of living and simply keeping them in prisons was a financial drain. As a result, they could be worked to their last breath, giving rise to the notion that prison management and frontier development costs could be effectively and simultaneously reduced. This is what Kaneko calls "killing two birds with one stone."

Kaneko likely learned this logic of pure economic efficiency from his time at Harvard Law School, where he studied Social Darwinism and the conservatism of Edmund Burke. After returning to Japan in 1878, he served as the first president of Nihon Hōritsu Gakko (present-day Nihon University). Kaneko continued to be an influential conservative figure in academic and political circles for his defense of elitism within Japan and promotion of imperialism outside. The most salient example of his conservatism can be found in his unwavering identification with Edmund Burke's antagonism toward the French Revolution. In order to counter and quell the significant influence of Jean-Jacques Rousseau's *The Social*

Contract, introduced as *Minyakuron* in Japanese among the activists of the Popular Rights Movement of the 1880s, Kaneko devoted himself to the translation of excerpts from Burke's *Reflections on the Revolution in France and Appeal from the New to the Old Whigs*. Published under the title *A General Theory of Politics* (政治論略, *Seijiron ryaku*), the book was less an abridged translation than a skillful rendition that offered a conservative response to the contemporary politics of political radicalism (Matsumura 2014, 46). *Seijiron ryaku* was widely read among imperial families, oligarchs, and intellectuals, propelling Kaneko to the status of leading conservative theoretician. Kaneko believed in an elite-led polity structured around the axis of national essence (国体, *kokutai*) and imperial authority and was adamantly opposed to popular participation in politics (Matsumura 2014, 48). To him, democracy was a dangerous idea that threatened the integrity of the Japanese nation. Indeed, Kaneko convinced the Meiji government to send radical members of the Popular Rights Movement to prisons in Hokkaidō to condemn them to prison labor. Methodically following the logic of survival of the fittest and national interests, Kaneko argued that those who demonstrated mental and intellectual weaknesses would harm the nation and, therefore must obey the directives of their superiors (Matsumura 2014, 52). The sacrifice of the lesser was acceptable if the well-being of the nation called for it. For Kaneko, the death of a certain population was even necessary for the nurturing of life among more desirable members of the national community. Prisoners embodied such a population to be sacrificed to build a stronger and wealthier nation.

Kaneko's thought emblematizes precisely what Achille Mbembe calls the necropolitics of slavery.[5] According to Mbembe, necropolitics is where life exists only as an expendable object. What determines life's expendability is not an ordinary sense of death but a death whose existential meaning is completely obliterated. In other words, death is not understood or chosen in relation to the fulfillment of life. In necropolitics, death holds absolute power over life in a way that completely renders it senseless. Human existence is reduced to mere physical being to be objectified and exploited until its expiration. In Hokkaidō, a prisoner's life was recognized only with regard to its utility and expendability as labor power. A 1902 government report on prisoners building the Kitami highway between Asahikawa and Abashiri described the conditions as follows: "Runaways are immediately captured and beheaded, and the bodies of those who died of illness and exhaustion are abandoned in the fields and the mountains and exposed to rain and wind" (Shigematsu 2004, 48) (Figure 2.2). Within the first several months of construction, 186 of 1,115 laborers died and 914 fell ill. The report also noted that due to unbearably harsh conditions not only in this highway construction but also in all other mining and construction works, 639 prisoners ran away between 1881 and 1891, 57% of which were captured and 18% were beheaded (Shigematsu 2004, 58). As Kaneko had proposed, these prisoners were exploited to a maximum degree, were subjected to capital punishment, and left to rot after their death.

FIGURE 2.2 Kabato Prison in 1882. The Kabato prisoners were mobilized for the construction of the highway

Source: Hokkaidō University Library

Prisoners' circumstances differed qualitatively from those of immigrant workers who constituted the proletarian class in the new colony. Immigrant workers became what Marx called the "industrial reserve army." For Marx, the population of the industrial reserve army constantly drifts between employment and unemployment and thus constitutes the pool of labor power most effectively exploited to maximize surplus value. Therefore, penal laborers and the reserve army of labor differ decisively in their forms of labor, as well as how the logics of life and death are brought to bear on them. The proletariat that survives only by selling labor power gradually loses its utility value as a means of producing surplus value as capitalists accumulate variable capital and expand constant capital. While those who are employed lose their jobs and sink to the status of the reserve army of labor, the relative surplus population of the reserve army increases and puts more pressure on those who are employed. As a result, the employed become increasingly subject to capital's logic of exploitation, being forced to meet demands for overwork, while the reserve army is thrown more into job insecurity and chronic poverty. This is how the proletariat's historical character as an expendable object is deepened.

This downward spiral of impoverishment, which takes place in inverse proportion to the expansion of capital, manifests itself most vividly in what Marx calls "pauperism" or "the hospital of the active labor-army and the dead weight of the industrial reserve army" (Marx 1977, 797). Marx divided this group into three categories: those who are capable of working but remain unemployed, vagabond orphans, and those who are incapable of working because of sickness, injuries, age, or physical disabilities. They all form an integral condition of capitalist production and accumulation, but as visible victims of the capitalist system, they are also the beneficiaries of charitable works and social reform movements designed to compensate for capitalism's severity. In short, this "hospital" is the capitalist form of pauperism. Yet, precisely because they are paupers, their status as the dead weight of the reserve army does not sentence them to death but rather to a state of being kept alive so that they remain a cheap commodity for capitalists to purchase and exploit. In short, they constitute the lowest stratum of what Michel Foucault calls a biopolitical regime.

On the contrary, a Hokkaidō prison laborer's life was predicated on their eventual ultimate disposability—death. Prisoners lived in a necropolitical world where they served as an absolutely expendable labor force. For the sake of cost-benefit performance, Hokkaidō prison laborers were expected to die after having been maximally exploited. If we are to compare them to regular waged workers who maintain their ability to freely sell their labor to the capitalist (though it should be kept in mind that their freedom is to be made and fully utilized for exploitation), Hokkaidō's "semi-slave" prison laborers did not have this freedom. Unable to move and sell their labor power, prisoners could not receive decent wages or proper working conditions. This necropolitics of prison labor points to, to borrow Achilles Mbembe's words, "death-in-life," a form of existence in which one is neither alive nor dead, a phantom state between life and death. "This life is a superfluous one," as Mbembe puts it, whose value "is so meager that it has no equivalence, whether market or—even less—human" (Mbembe 2019, 38). Prisoners' lives were a "living hell," an Abashiri prisoner noted (Kuwahara 1982, 182).

2.4 The Inclusive Exclusion of the Ainu

What is the relationship between the Ainu and the politics of death surrounding prisoner labor? The politics of death among Hokkaidō prison laborers was predicated on the politics of death among the Ainu, that is, their expulsion from the land or expropriation of their means of sustenance. The Ainu's population fell from 17,362 to 16,700 between 1873 and 1897 as they were driven to the fringes of the island, while the number of Japanese settlers reached over one million by 1903. In 1931, 15,960 Ainu were counted, overwhelmed by 2.7 million Japanese settlers. By this time, the Ainu represented only 0.6% of Hokkaidō's population (Okuyama 1950, 194). The Ainu, in Okuyama Ryō's words, "became worthless in terms of the quality and quantity of labor power as the settlers dramatically increased in number" and continued to occupy most arable lands and commercial centers (Okuyama 1950, 195). This process of Ainu's decimation recalls the late historian Patrick Wolfe's thesis on the "logic of elimination," which he developed through analysis of the "genocidal dispossession" of Indigenous peoples around the world (Wolfe 2006, 387–409). In order to probe this eliminatory politics as distinguished from the necropolitics of prison labor in the settler-colonial history of Hokkaidō, I use Foucault's "thanatopolitics" in the original sense of the word. Thanatopolitical forms of violence point to the sovereign's exclusive power over determining worthy and unworthy life, who should live and who is to die. Within the context of modern biopolitics, power over life and death entails a logic of elimination rooted in non-military and non-violent biological sciences, which we usually refer to as racism. As Foucault put it, "race or racism is the precondition that makes killing acceptable .... Once the State functions in the biopower mode, racism alone can justify the murderous function of the State" (Foucault 2003, 256). For Meiji policymakers to view prison labor as indispensable for Hokkaidō's settler-colonial development, they had to assume the Ainu to be a vanishing race. The Ainu were then viewed as having neither right nor ability to live freely in their native places because they had left the vast, resource-rich land unexplored and uncultivated for centuries. Given their "inherent" inability to diligently cultivate the land, the Ainu could serve no function in the primitive accumulation of capital needed to bring about frontier development. Thus, their presence and their ways of life were nothing but an obstacle to Japan's drive for modernization. In a 1923 report on the "former Hokkaidō natives," Kōno Tsunekichi described the Ainu as (1) possessing only primitive knowledge and therefore incapable of managing complex and structured tasks; (2) economically unskilled and lacking the ability to increase capital and develop industries; (3) having the patience to do the work that they like, but easily growing tired of regular occupations; (4) lacking a sense of responsibility with regard to their duties and thus incapable of jointly operating businesses, for which employers have difficulties trusting them when hiring them (Kōno 1980, 58). According to Kōno, because of these inherent deficiencies, the Ainu could find no rightful place in the modern world. Such racialized notions of the Ainu provided the rationale that naturalized their dispossession as a matter of historical inevitability.

The label of "vanishing race" resulted from the installation of the capitalist mode of production in Hokkaidō, through which the Ainu were rendered as a useless population and subsequently replaced by prison laborers. If prisoners were to be called on to bear the burden of opening the "wilderness" and building up infrastructures for modern industries, then the Ainu had to be relocated to barren lands as a necessary condition of frontier development. With regard to the methods of exercising power over the Ainu and prison laborers, the key difference is that the former is founded on racism. As mentioned earlier, for Foucault, racism draws a sharp line of demarcation between who should live and who is to die. In racializing the Ainu and their ways of life, Meiji policymakers rationalized a doctrine of elimination by dispossession in terms of a biological logic of survival of the fittest. In its 1926 "Outline of the Former Hokkaidō Natives," the Hokkaidō government presented the view that the Ainu "fall far short of (average) human intelligence such that they have been the losers in the struggle for survival, and their livelihoods have fallen rapidly into distress" (Kōno 1980, 34). The Ainu's inclusion into Imperial Japan meant simultaneously elimination by dispossession that drove them to destitution and death, and racism rationalized this mode of inclusive exclusion of Ainu's life as their unavoidable fate, as the theory of social evolutionism insisted in Japan and elsewhere.

One could say, based on what has been discussed thus far, that the modern Ainu experience cannot be analyzed using a traditional, class-based approach. This is why traditional Marxist analysis, which takes the contradiction between labor and capital as the primary locus of historical inquiry, has always overlooked the ways in which the destruction of Ainu communities constituted an essential element of the birth of Japanese capitalism or the process of primitive accumulation. Class and race were predicated on distinct, albeit interconnected, logics in the formation of modern society. Markers of class difference such as gender, education, and property ownership served as necessary preconditions for the production of surplus value, but it is essential to recognize that the racial differentiation imposed upon the Ainu was a crucial first step needed for that type of necessary condition to come into being. Those who were discriminated against based on racialization were exposed first and foremost to the possibility of forms of violence including dispossession, exclusion, and elimination before they could be imagined as potential wage laborers. This seems to be precisely the point that Marx called "the most merciless barbarism" exercised by the State in the process of primitive accumulation.[6]

Let us summarize the argument thus far. We can put forth at least three aspects of the structure of encounter known as Hokkaidō settler colonialism that relate to the politics of life and death. First, biopolitics was a system of labor designed to absorb the population of landless peasants created by earlier land reforms and deflation and of former samurai following the abolition of the Tokugawa status system. This settler-colonial policy was initiated as part of the centralization of the Japanese nation-state's sovereignty over its declared territory and the inception of capital accumulation. Neither saw much success until the turn of the twentieth century, with the influx of zaibatsu capital. Second, necropolitics relied on unfree penal laborers to resolve the stalemate in the reclamation of Hokkaidō by settlers described above. Prison labor was tasked not only with the reclamation of the "wilderness" but also with the construction of social and economic infrastructures necessary to bring in more settlers and industries. Their expendable labor was deemed essential for Hokkaidō's transformation into a land of capitalist production and accumulation. Third, thanatopolitics expropriated Ainu Mosir, displaced the Ainu people, and rendered them as a vanishing race. I would like to emphasize that death worked as the principal logic for both the necropolitics of prisoners and the thanatopolitics of the Ainu people but assumed different roles: prisoners faced death through overexploitation, whereas the Ainu were targeted for elimination. In the former case, death was an integral element of so-called primitive accumulation, whereas in the latter case, death was a precondition of primitive accumulation.

What needs to be stated here is that the relationship between settler colonialism and primitive accumulation in the case of Hokkaido ought not to be understood in terms of historical progression, nor should it be understood as following development in stages. While Marx understood primitive accumulation as capital's "prehistory" and a sort of transition into full-fledged capitalism, Ainu peoples' experience of the thanatopolitics of elimination did not necessarily precede prison laborers' necropolitics of expendability. Necropolitics, furthermore, did not precede the process of proletarianization in which workers, upon losing their lands and means of production, were forced to relocate continually to sell their labor. Rather, we should think of these three elements that shaped the relationship between settler colonialism and primitive accumulation as a synchronic, multi-layered, and mutually interdependent set of relations. Japan's imperial capitalist project depended on a political form in which these three elements were inextricably linked. The expropriation of Ainu Mosir, along with the racism that supported it, was in no way a transient phase of capitalist development. Rather it was a constitutive and continuous element of the structure of imperial Japan's national capitalist formation. Even after a large number of "free" laboring Japanese began settling in Hokkaidō due to massive displacement following the Matsukata deflation and the Russo-Japanese War, the Ainu still continued to live in a state of dispossession as their lands remained occupied and their access to means of sustenance was denied. This structure of continuous occupation and dispossession was predicated on a hierarchy of forms of labor (settlers = free labor, prisoners = unfree labor, Ainu = useless labor) around which the politics of life and death was organized. In the next section, I would like to explore a form of life under thanatopolitical conditions.

2.5 Social Death—Living as the Dead

Itō Sanka, the chief editor of *Hokumon News*, wrote in 1898 that "the rapid degeneration of the Ainu race is caused not by the law of so-called natural selection, but by the naked cruelty and sheer evil of the law of jungle, of a conscious act of elimination by the Japanese. It is not natural but rather human selection that is responsible for their near-extinction" (Itō 1998, 460). Here, Itō points out the fact that the racist concept of natural selection provided the Meiji government with a pernicious rationale for positing the Ainu as an object of elimination rather than exploitation. According to the government, the Ainu suffered not as a result of settler-colonial dispossession but as a result of their innate incapability: Ainu faced the imminent danger of extinction not because of decimation but because of the Law of Nature.

This tenet of racism, which naturalizes the acts of violence that took place during the formative years of Imperial Japan, manifested itself most vividly—and perhaps most perversely—in the academic discourse and government policies that made the Ainu people into an exotic spectacle for tourists and a rare specimen to be studied for the classification of human species. By the time of the Russo-Japanese War of 1904–1905, the image of the Ainu as an ancient, vanishing ethnicity was firmly established. Needless to say, the Ainu people and their ways of life never died out: some successfully became farmers by taking advantage of the

Former Native Protection Law (FNPL) of 1899, while others lived on curtailed hunting and gathering while working as manual laborers in the timber industry. But even after FNPL was implemented, many Ainu faced poverty and sickness. As article one in the law stipulated, only those who were willing to farm could be the beneficiaries of the State's protection (Ogawa & Yamada 1998, 409). Article two, however, imposed strict regulations on even the terms of acquisition and ownership of land that the Ainu people managed to obtain from the government by cultivating it. The rights of pledge, mortgage, easement, retention, and priority were all denied, and no right of lien or statutory lien was granted. Only the right of inheritance was recognized (Ogawa & Yamada 1998, 409; Sekiguchi, Tabata, Kuwahara, & Takizawa 2015, 189–190). This amounted to a virtual denial of *jus disponendi* and therefore violated modern terms of private ownership that guaranteed owners the rights to use, profit, and disposal.

The "land ownership" granted to the Ainu people exemplified a state of exception in which standard terms of modern ownership were suspended. This ownership was neither legal nor illegal, but a-legal as it constituted a zone in which the State could exercise extralegal power to determine arbitrarily the terms of legality. Initially, the State deprived the Ainu of their lands by denying them access to the right of ownership in the name of *terra nullius*. FNPL then allowed the indigenous people to "own" their lands—but only for cultivation and inheritance. FNPL's inclusive exclusion of the Ainu in the modern system of private ownership was predicated on and justified by the notion that "former natives must live under the supervision of the Japanese settlers because they didn't possess the ability to govern and produce" (Ogawa & Yamada 1998, 409). The racist view of the Ainu's innate incompetence in self-governance, production, and self-management came to form the very basis of their relation to the land. In his 1911 research report titled "Former Natives in Hokkaidō," Kōno Tsunekichi explained, "The Ainu are naturally incapable of accumulating assets because they seriously lack the concept of thrift" (Kōno 1980, 26). His report utterly ignored the fact that the government's imposition of private ownership and its heavily restricted use was directly responsible for the Ainu's hardships. Racist reasoning substituted and covered over the settler-colonial history of expropriation and dispossession (As Kazuyo Tsuchiya's analysis of the "inter-racial conflicts" discourse during the 1992 LA riots demonstrates in Chapter 9, racism performs this kind of substitution that erases, or deflects our attention from, dominant and complex structural relations of socio-economic inequalities).

Compiled twelve years after the implementation of FNPL, Kōno's report indicated that the Ainu temporarily became farmers as a result of "protection" provided by the law, but also stated that quite a few "gave up and returned to fishery as migrant workers, leaving agricultural work in the hands of their wives and children" (Kōno 1980, 29). A report compiled in 1916 showed that conversion to farming was progressing steadily, with an estimated 2,354 of 4,007 Ainu households (57.4%) engaged in farming; however, each household's income was only one-quarter of the average income for a Japanese farming family (Sekiguchi, Tabata, Kuwahara & Takizawa 2015, 199–200). The total land area allotted to all of the Ainu from 1899 to 1910 was about 17,000 acres, but most of it was barren and unfit for farming (Kōno 1980, 55). Thus, the report recognized, "The arable land that led to profit or became the source of sustenance is very limited" (Kōno 1980, 27). Crucially, as stipulated in FNLP, land left uncultivated for fifteen years had to be returned to the government.

The report also touched on the Ainu's participation in fishery. It described their traditional way of fishing as "unsuitable for a larger scale of fishery" developed and monopolized by the Japanese settlers and Zaibatsu conglomerates such as Mitsui (Kōno 1980, 29). Some Ainu tried to develop their own fisheries but failed. In fact, the Meiji government had banned the Ainu's traditional fishing practices under the pretext of protecting salmon from their "primitive" and "abusive" practices in 1876 despite the fact that salmon was their staple food. By the time Kōno conducted his survey, Ainu had already been deprived of their main means of sustenance. Therefore, as the report summed up, "most former natives continue to live on small catches or seek employment by the Japanese as workers" (Kōno 1980, 29).

Very few Ainu were able to find employment through the labor market in mining or construction. Even when they did, they found themselves at the bottom of labor hierarchies, together with prisoners and other racialized workers such as Koreans. Some voluntarily became soldiers to prove their worth as loyal imperial subjects, but many accepted their lives as museumized objects. From the late nineteenth century to the end of WWII, Ainu people were "displayed" at various museums, world fairs, and expositions as the living remnants of the ancient past. The social evolutionary framework of anthropology, shaped largely by Charles Darwin and Herbert Spencer (1820–1903), guided the designs of these displays and presented the Ainu as the antithesis of Japan's civilizational might and advancement (Danika 2010, 591–614). For example, six Ainu people were exhibited at the Louisiana Purchase Exposition of 1904, along with the Apache of the American Southwest and the Igorots of the Philippines, all described as "primitive" or representing "pre-civilized native life" (Trennert 1987, 211–212). As much as the US turned Native Americans and Native Filipinos into objects of "spectacle, commodity, and spoil of American conquest," Japan used the Ainu to make an imperialist spectacle of the conquered (Swensen 2019, 439).

The museumization of life, a form of social death, disavows or displaces the historical encounter between colonizers and the colonized.[7] Museumization in Hokkaidō was predicated on framing the Ainu as ancient beings disconnected from the present conditions of history, frozen in the Stone Age, and imprisoned in permanent stagnation. This conception of the Ainu as an accidental leftover from the prehistoric past, worthy of only preservation and display, worked as the epistemological condition for the call for their protection. Accordingly, since such a race of people could never serve as useful labor power for the capitalist development of the land, this race found its rightful place in modern society only as a remnant of the past to be observed and studied. This condition of absolute exteriority—to be folded into capitalist time and space not as labor power but as a living fossil—is what defined the status of the Ainu in imperial Japan. In other words, they were subsumed neither by the biopolitics of able workers nor by the necropolitics of expendable labor but by the thanatopolitics of a useless population.

This logic of absolute exteriorization of the Ainu people is one of the most elementary logics of capitalism. The museumization of the Ainu signifies the most distinct marker of the Other of the interior: an eternally abject subject deemed utterly incapable of surviving independently in the world of capital. While figured as redundant to both the necropolitics of disposable labor and the biopolitics of population management, the Ainu were to be kept "alive" only in the form of a dead object, a vanishing and vanished species, for anthropological, historical, and biological investigations. These disciplines served to recode Indigenous people as the reflection of capitalist society's own prehistory, the past that it claimed to have overcome and progressed from a long time ago. In short, museumization served as a mirroring device through which the capitalist world could articulate the historical inevitability of its own emergence and domination.

This image of the fossilized Ainu drove a significant number of Ainu young men to attempt to transform their abject lives by enlisting as imperial soldiers. In 1896, only one Ainu man was enlisted. By 1910, the number of active Ainu soldiers rose to 136, with 382 more in the reserves. In his 1911 report, Kōno noted that 63 Ainu soldiers fought in the Russo-Japanese War. Three died in battle and five of illness, and two were seriously injured. Kōno praised these Ainu for performing the duty of loyal imperial subjects. As historian Enomori Susumu argues, "The Russo-Japanese War as an imperialist conflict played a decisive role in cultivating Ainu men's sense of citizenship and loyalty towards the State" (Enomori 2008, 457). In fact, the Meiji government honored Kitakaze Isokichi (1880?–1969), an Ainu soldier who volunteered to fight for imperial Japan during the war, as a war hero for his "extraordinary contributions" to the empire by promoting him to the officer rank of lance corporal and awarding him one of the most prestigious decorations (Enomori 2008, 456).[8] A number of biographical accounts of Kitakaze were published in newspapers, magazines, and even children's books (Hokkai Taimusu 1905; Kimura 1937, 258–280). Teachers promoted patriotism among the children they taught by reading aloud about Kitakaze's extraordinarily brave actions at Ainu and other schools in Hokkaidō (Muramai 1942, 62).[9] The stories emphasized his courage, education, perseverance, sincerity, and diligence. Kitakaze's humble background as an Ainu person and a laborer was always linked to his physical and mental strengths (Hokkai Taimusu 1905; Kimura 1937). After Kitakaze returned to his hometown of Nayoro, Hokkaidō, he donated large sums of money to a shrine and a local primary school and gave the students pencils and notebooks. His fellow Ainu called him the "most decent person among human beings" (Fujimura 1982, 311;

Sato 2001, 5). One Ainu individual recalled him fondly as the pride of the Ainu, a hero who helped them win respect and prove themselves worthy of status equal to the Japanese. Kitakaze himself found gratification in the fact that he was "the only Ainu person who received a decoration from the Emperor" (Nayoro Shinbun October 6, 2006).

Kitakaze's story reflects the paradoxical structure of desire that both propels and is propelled by assimilation. This desire drives those whose lives are rendered abject by racism to overcome racism's barriers by willingly participating in the imperialistic nationalism that undergirds the racism. Paradoxically, the colonized seek to conquer the negativity of their lives by identifying themselves with the values that support that negativity. They desire to overcome their social death by positively responding to a State's call for actual death—both murdering others and putting themselves in the line of fire. These paradoxical desires opt for "honorable" death over abject death caused by sickness and poverty resulting from dispossession or social death engendered by the museumization of life. On August 24, 1934, an Ainu reader using the pseudonym "Angry Student" contributed a short essay to Otaru News:

> We Ainu never fall behind others in recognizing the exceptional state in which we all live. Our sincerity in understanding our imperial soldiers' hardships [in battle] and extending our sympathies to them is no less than ordinary Japanese persons can offer. However, we are very indignant at the assumption that we Ainu can demonstrate our support for the soldiers only through inhumane spectacles. There are so many other ways such as becoming soldiers to contribute to our country.
>
> *Ogawa & Yamada 1998, 399*[10]

Patriotic devotion to the country became one of the means by which Ainu men sought to overcome discrimination and attain equality, and this devotion was measured by willingness to kill and die for the nation. For a "vanishing race," only death could supersede death. This perverse supersession was the ruse of assimilation—the paradox of double negation through which the colonized sought to "redeem" their subjectivity in perpetual subjection.

If Ainu men sought their redemption by enlisting in Japan's imperial wars, many Ainu women attempted to free themselves from the curses of racism by marrying Japanese men. A 1926 report compiled by the Hokkaidō government attributed the rapid decline in Ainu population in the town of Monbetsu to the fact that "former native women are keen on marrying Japanese men while adamantly refusing marriage with the same race" (Kōno 1980, 32). Ainu women's desire to "Japanize Ainu blood" and thus rid themselves of any Ainu "traces" through interracial marriage precipitated their general tendency to assimilate into Wajin society (Kōno 1980, 33). As Franz Fanon posited in *Black Skin, White Masks*, within a colonial society in which white patriarchal power structures determined modes of social interaction, colonized men's masculine subjectivity was negated while male colonizers became the object of longing and desire for colonized women. White men in power embodied wealth, power, social status, beauty, virtue, and advanced civilization, and intermarrying with them served, as was commonly believed, as the only way by which colonized women could rid themselves of their racial inferiorities and overcome the social discrimination and economic hardships accompanying those perceived inferiorities. A woman of color would "try, in her body and in her mind, to bleach (the world)" (Fanon 1967, 45). All she wants is "a kind of lactification. For, in a word, the race must be whitened" (Fanon 1967, 47).

It comes as no surprise that, within the context of settler colonial encounter in Hokkaidō, many Ainu parents, especially mothers, encouraged their daughters to marry Japanese men to remove the stigma of Ainu identity and to overcome its attendant socio-economic hardships. Ishihara Mai, an anthropologist at the University of Hokkaidō, explains that Ainu women's attempt to seek "mixed blood" with Wajin men was very common because they considered it the only means by which to "attain equal status with the majority by ridding themselves of Ainu physical traits and assimilating into Japanese society" (Ishihara 2018, 86). Just like Ainu men had to seek liberation through fundamental self-negation, Ainu women's strategy of survival was defined by the aporia in which their liberation was imaginable only by way of self-effacement. Looking back on Ainu's past in 2001, the late Chikappu Emiko, an Ainu weaver and activist, remarked that Ainu people's "hope to live with dignity and live their lives to the fullest" had been robbed and shattered since Meiji Japan colonized Ainu Mosir (Chikappu 2001, 248).

2.6 In Closing

To conclude this chapter, I would like to make the following point: racist epistemology operates on *tautology*. "The Ainu are incapable of survival because they are Ainu" is the essence of racist discourse. It precludes historical understanding of the process by which the Japanese government expropriated the Ainu's lands and drove them into poverty in the name of progress and protection by reducing the cause of their suffering to racial attributes. It leads to the view that all the Ainu's misfortunes were a result of their being a feeble race. Kindaichi Kyōsuke (1882–1971), one of the founders of Ainu linguistic studies at Tokyo Imperial University, always expressed his sympathy toward the Ainu people by referring to them as "a pitiful people left behind the progress of civilization," demonstrating precisely the tautological logic that naturalized the Ainu's near "extinction."

It is necessary to understand the museumization of life in relation to the commodification of labor power. These two phenomena of modern reification could emerge only where a capitalist system and a modern nation-state form a foundational structure of social relations. Marx's concept of so-called primitive accumulation helps explicate the historical processes that make labor power into a commodity because it reveals "the process which takes away from the laborer the possession of the means of production; a process that transforms, on the one hand, the social means of subsistence and of production into capital, on the other, the immediate producers into wage laborers" (Marx 1977, 874). But this general theory of primitive accumulation is not directly applicable to the experiences of many Indigenous peoples around the world.

Indigenous peoples did not become wage laborers but were made into members of "vanishing races" as a result of being dispossessed of their means of sustenance. This difference is crucial, and it compels us to reflect on the received discourse of primitive accumulation—how the Marxian discourse on colonialism in the context of primitive accumulation has precluded a serious reflection on the dispossession of the Indigenous peoples as an integral and generative process of capitalist formation. The problem originates from the fact that there is a disregard within the concept of primitive accumulation for how racialization—its tautological structure of reference—factors into the process of dispossession. As I stated earlier, racist logic posits that Indigenous people suffer because they are indigenous. Franz Fanon called this logic "the originality of colonial context" (Fanon 1968, 40). In describing the colony as a place where "economic reality, inequality, and immense difference of ways of life never come to mask the human realities," Fanon concludes:

> When you examine at close quarters the colonial context, it is evident that what parcels out the world is to begin with the fact of belonging to or not belonging to a given race, a given species. In the colonies the economic substructure is also a superstructure. The cause is the consequence; you are rich because you are white, you are white because you are rich. This is why Marxist analysis should always be slightly stretched every time we have to do with the colonial problem.
>
> *Fanon 1968, 40*

Fanon's insight elucidates the missing perspective on race that demands a complication and alteration of Marx's formulation. Although Marx recognizes settler colonialism as one of the constitutive components of primitive accumulation, his primary concern rests on the origin of labor power that enables the accumulation of capital. In his discussion of the theory of colonization advanced by British economist E. G. Wakefield (1796–1862), Marx is primarily concerned with how Wakefield explicates the relationship between labor and capital, that is, how to prevent European settlers from becoming landowners so as to turn them into wage laborers and make them dependent on capitalists. Marx's exclusive emphasis on this particular question came from his conviction that Wakefield's theory of colonial policies revealed a secret central to the birth of capitalist society: how its emergence depended on extra-economic means, that is, the state's deliberate efforts to produce wage laborers. But precisely because of this perspective on the formation of wage laborers among settler communities, Marx failed to ask how settlers too utilized extra-economic means to expropriate or plunder the lands from the Indigenous people, to rationalize and institutionalize the dispossession, and to turn such dispossession into the precondition for land ownership and the commodification of social relations. And most decisively: what was the role of racialization in all of these processes?

Marx, therefore, fell short of developing an analytical perspective on the process of settler colonization because his primary aim was offering a systematic and teleological account of the birth of labor power that produced capital. This omission is possible only by accepting the notion that Indigenous people's encounters with capitalist regimes are episodic, even insignificant to capitalist modernity on the premise that they do not constitute a substantive and structural component of capitalist labor power. In this respect, Marx's formulation of primitive accumulation inadvertently follows the thanatopolitical logic of elimination by erasing the truism that settler-colonial domination is a *continuous affair of Indigenous dispossession* that works as an elementary structure of settlers' permanent occupation of lands and resources. What erases this truism is the work of racism. To paraphrase Fanon, our examination of settler-colonial encounters must start with a reckoning with the fact that class existed as race and race existed as class in settler-colonial society in such a way that constitutes the enduring structure of the plunder and dispossession of Indigenous communities.

If, as Marx put it, "capital comes [into the world] dripping from head to toe, from every pore, with blood and dirt," the proletarianization of peasants as a result of expropriation of the means of production constitutes only one aspect of the birth of capital (Marx 1977, 926). What needs to be taken into consideration here is how primitive accumulation has been linked to the dispossession of Indigenous people's means of sustenance and how this relation of dispossession in settler-colonial society has been sustained as an integral part of the mechanism of capitalist accumulation. The thanatopolitics of racist dispossession is key to these questions. It condemns Indigenous people to extreme destitution and sickness by permanently occupying their ancestral lands while also depriving them of their history and thus subjecting them to the most grotesque form of reification, namely museumization. The museumization of Indigenous lives, in turn, erases or legitimizes the historical process of dispossession and its reproduction by representing them as survivors of the ancient. It encloses Indigenous lives within the logic of death, rendering them living fossils. It is the most grotesque form of reification in that it drives Indigenous people to social death and implants in them the compulsive desire to seek redemption in a way that is never redemptive but only self-destructive. This aporia is the ruse of assimilation as expressed so eloquently by an Ainu activist in the late 1990s:

> It (assimilation) is a violent yet powerful ruse that makes you feel as if your being Ainu is a shame, an utter unhappiness. You come to see yourself as belonging to an inferior and uncivilized race that is about to die out, that

should have never existed in the first place. You suffer from your own misfortunes, primitiveness, and cultural backwardness as a cursed being. You are made to feel worthless to the point that you want to wipe out your bloodline.

Narita and Hanasaki 1998, 147

Whether assimilation or honorable death for Imperial Japan, Ainu's settler colonial encounter with modernizing Wajin left them trapped in a violent cycle of self-negation.

Needless to say, not every Ainu resigned to the seemingly unending state of self-deprecation and self-hatred. But the struggle to free oneself from such a state was often accompanied by much agony. Let me close this chapter by recalling the words of anguish written by Iboshi Hokuto, an Ainu poet who passed away in 1929 at the young age of 27. Just before his death, Iboshi wrote this poem, expressing the agony of struggling against the violence of racial discriminations, as well as uncontrollable hatred and premonition of violence brought about by unendurable contempt and insults.

My solitary thoughts:

As an Ainu, from the time we were children, we endured much unendurable contempt from others.

We were weak, and we received insults we couldn't bear. Had we been stronger, who could bear such insults in silence?

We hated them with the depths of our hearts, to the point where we would have bullied them … As we reminisce on past events, how many times have we spontaneously clenched our fists?

However, we were honest.

Truly, we were sincere.

Even if we couldn't bear to receive their insults today, the next day we truly believed them, sincerely looking for their love.

Comrades (*Utari*)! Why are we weak?

What an insult they gave us yesterday! Think of it, think of their insults. I'm sure you can't forget. Then why do you believe them? Why don't you take revenge on them?

My heart cried out.

And then, and then, we got fired up planning our revenge. To this day, we still dream of taking revenge on them, even though we are frightened by the horrors of our sins.

Weakness leads to suffering—Heresy leads to sorrow.

How many times will we curse them and our society?

But we were honest.

Whenever we let our heart grow wild, we feel deep sorrow. And unbearable regret turns into warm tears, endlessly overflowing.

Iboshi 1984, 103–104

Acknowledgments

I would like to thank Tomohito Baji, Katherine Capuder, Jessica Cattelino, Takashi Fujitani, Akhil Gupta, Mariko Iijima, John Leisure, Katsuro Nawa, Toulouse Roy, Yasuko Takezawa, Akio Tanabe, Lorenzo Veracini, Gavin Walker, Jack Wilson, and Lisa Yoneyama for their helpful comments on drafts of this chapter.

Notes

1　For more details on the US's impacts on the formation of Hokkaidō as a Japan's settler colony, see Hirano (2015), 191–218; (2022), 135–153.
2　Discussing Japan's adaptation of American settler colonialism, Eiichiro Azuma also makes the same observation and calls it "a Japanese Style manifest destiny" (2019, 16).
3　Sanetomi Sanjo presented these ideas to Emperor Meiji as a national policy in 1869. *Meiji Ninen Hōrei Zensho* no. 843 (1887).
4　These three points resonate with the discourse on prison laborers in the US. See Hartnett.
5　In my view, Mbembe's theorization of necropolitics covers too many forms and instances of death caused by sovereign power and governmentality; moreover, the structural connection he makes between biopower and necropower is unclear. I find his discussion of slavery, especially his point that "slave life, in many ways, is a form of death-in-life," to be the most cogent and useful aspect of the article. It is in this specific sense that I am using the concept of necropolitics. Achille Mbembe (2003, 11–40).
6　Marx uses this phrase to refer to the means by which the expropriation of the direct producers was accomplished in the pre-history of capital. Marx (1977, 928).
7　Here, I am expanding Orland Patterson's concept of social death to include museumization. Other scholars have applied the concept to the holocaust, apartheid, slavery, and institutional segregation. See Orland Patterson (1982).
8　Kitakaze lived from 1800 to 1969. He was born into an Ainu family. He was also known as a skilled sculptor of bear figures.
9　In 1910, 92.2% of Ainu children were enrolled in primary schools. Out of 2,072 students, 688 went to Ainu schools established as a part of FNPL. See Masato Ogawa (1997, 163).
10　It is known that a number of Ainu men fought WW2 as "imperial Ainu soldiers," but the exact number is unknown.

References

Asada, Hideki. 2004. *Hokkaido Kaihatsu Seisaku no Rekishi* vol. 1 Meiji-hen. Sapporo: Ishikarisamitto.

Azuma, Eiichiro. 2019. *In Search of Our Empire*. Berkeley: University of California Press.

Balibar, Etienne and Wallerstein, Immanuel. 1991. *Race, Nation, Class: Ambiguous Identities*. London: Verso.

Bessho, Hirotake. 1882. *Takuchi Shokumin no gi nitsuki Kenngi*. Sapporo: Hokkaido Daigaku Hoppo Shiryōshitsu.

Brantlinger, Patrick. 2003. *Dark Vanishings: Discourse on the Extinction of Primitive Races, 1800–1930*. Ithaca: Cornell University Press.

Capron, Horace to Warren, February 25, 1872, Horace Capron Papers, Box 1, Folder 4, Manuscripts & Archives, Yale University Library.

Césaire, Aimé. 2001. *Discourse on Colonialism*. New York: Monthly Review Press.

Chikappu, Emiko. 2001. *Ainu Mosir no Kaze*. Tokyo: NHK Shuppan.

Chōsenjin Kyōsei Renkō Chōsadan. 1974. *Chōsenjin Kyōsei Renkō, Kyōsei Rōdō no Kiroku*. Tokyo: Gendaishi Shuppankai.

Cumings, Bruce. 2009. *Dominion from Sea to Sea: Pacific Ascendancy and American Power*. New Haven: Yale University Press.

Danika, Medak-Saltzman. 2010. "'Transnational Indigenous Exchange: Rethinking Global Interactions of Indigenous Peoples at the 1904 St. Louis Exposition' Alternative Contact: Indigeneity, Globalism, and American Studies," *American Quarterly*, 62 (3), 591–615.

De Vito, Christian and Lichtenstein, Alex. 2013. "Writing a Global History of Convict Labor," *International Review of Social History 58* (2), 285–325. Cambridge: Cambridge University Press.

Dippie, Brian. 1982. *The Vanishing American: White Attitudes and U.S. Indian Policy*. Kansas: University Press of Kansas.

Enomori, Susumu. 1997. *Hokkaidō Kinseishi no Kenkyu*. Sapporo: Hokkaidō Shuppan Kikaku Center.

Enomori, Susumu. 2008. *Ainu Minzoku no Rekishi*. Sapporo: Sofukan.

Fanon, Franz. 1967. *Black Skin, White Masks*. New York: Grove Press.

Fanon, Franz. 1968. *The Wretched of the Earth*. New York: Grove Press.

Fitzmaurice, Andrew. 2007. "The Genealogy of Terra Nullius," *Australian Historical Studies*, vol. 38. London: Taylor and Francis.

Foucault, Michel. 2003. *Society Must Be Defended*. New York: Picador.

Fujimura, Hisakazu. 1982. "Kokoro no Bunka," in *Chūo Kōron*, vol. 12. Tokyo: Chuo Koronsha.

Hale Hendline, Yogi. 2014. "From Terra Nullius to Terra Communis in Advance," *Environmental Philosophy*, 11 (2), 141–174.

Hirano, Katsuya. 2015. "Thanatopolitics in the Making of Japan's Hokkaido: Settler Colonialism and Primitive Accumulation," *Critical Historical Studies*, 2 (2) 191–218. Chicago: University of Chicago Press.

Hirano, Katsuya. 2022 Forthcoming. "Settler-Colonialism, Ecology, and Expropriation of Ainu Mosir: A Transnational Perspective," in Edward Melillo and Ryan Jones, eds., *Migrant Ecologies: Environmental Histories of the Pacific World*, 135–153. Honolulu: University of Hawai'i Press.

Hirayama, Hiroto. 2016. *Shakushain no Tatakai*. Sapporo: Jurōsha.

Hokkaidō-Tōhokushi, kenkyūkai, ed. 1998. *Basho Ukeoisei to Ainu*. Sapporo: Hokkaidō Shuppan Kikaku Center.

Hokkai Taimusu. 1905. "Yukan naru Kyudojin" *Hokkai Taimusu* August 4, 4–5. Sapporo: Hokkai Shinbun.

Iboshi, Hokuto. 1984. *Iboshi Hokuto Ikō Kotan*. Sapporo: Sōfūsha.

Ishihara, Mai. 2018. *Chinmoku no Auto-ethnography*, PhD thesis submitted to the University of Hokkaidō.

Itō, Kazan. 1998. "Hokkaidō Kyūdojin Hogoron," in Ogawa Masato and Yamada Shinichi, eds., *Ainu Minzoku: Kindai no Kiroku*. Tokyo: Sōfūkan.

Jalata, Asafa. July 1, 2013. "The Impacts of English Colonial Terrorism and Genocide on Indigenous Black Australians," *Sage Open, Vol. 3*.

Kaneko, Kentaro. 1885. *Hokkaidō San'ken Junshi Fukumeisho*. Sapporo: Hokkaidō Daigaku Hoppō Shiryō Shitsu.

Kimura, Tsuyoshi. 1937. "Ainu Tamashii no Kaiyūshi," in *Kōdankurabu*, vol. 9. 258–280. Tokyo: Kodansha.

Kōno, Tsunekichi. 1980. "Hokkaidō Kyū dojin," in Motomichi Kōno, ed., *Ainushi shiryōshū*. Sapporo: Hokkaidō shuppan kikaku sentā.

Kuwahara, Makoto. 1982. *Kindai Hokkaidōshi Kenkyu Josetsu.* Sapporo: Hokkaido Daigaku Shuppan.

Lahti, Janne. 2018. *The American West and the World.* London: Routledge.

lewallen, ann-annalise. 2019. "Gendered Technologies of Resistance: Centering Ainu women's Responses to the Sexual Colonization of Ainu Mosir" in Hokkaidō 150: Settler Colonialism and Indigeneity in modern Japan and Beyond, *Critical Asian Studies* 51 (1), 1–40 London: Taylor and Francis.

Locke, John. 1989. *Two Treatises of Government.* Cambridge: University of Cambridge Press.

Luxemburg, Rosa. 2003. *The Accumulation of Capital.* London: Routledge.

Madley, Benjamin. 2004. "Patterns of Frontier Genocide 1803–1910: The Aboriginal Tasmanians, the Yuki of California, the Herero of Namibia," *The Journal of Genocide Research,* 6 (2), 167–192. London: Taylor and Francis.

Marx, Karl. 1977. *Capital,* vol. 1. New York: Vintage Books.

Matsumura, Masayoshi. 2014. *Kaneko Kentaro.* Tokyo: Mineruba.

Matsu'ura, Takeshirō. 2002. *Ainu Jinbutsushi.* Tokyo: Heibonsha.

Mbembe, Achille. 2003. "Necropolitics" *Public Culture* 15 (1),11–40. Durham: Duke University Press.

Mbembe, Achille. 2019. *Necropolitics.* Durham: Duke University Press.

McCrisken, Trevor B. 2001. "Exceptionalism: Manifest Destiny," in *Encyclopedia of American Foreign Policy,* vol. 2, 2nd edition. New York: Charles Scribner's Sons.

Naikaku Kanpō Kyoku. 1887. *Meiji Ninen Hōrei Zensho,* no. 843. Tokyo: Naikaku Kanpō Kyoku.

Muramai, Hisakichi. 1942. *Ainu Jinbutsu Den.* Tokyo: Heibonsha.

Narita, Tokuhei and Hanasaki, Kōhei. 1998. *Kindaika no nakano Ainu sabetsu no Kōzō.* Tokyo: Akashi Shoten.

Ogawa, Masato. 1997. *Kindai Ainu Kyōiku Seido Kenkyu.* Sapporo: Hokkaidō Daigaku Shuppan.

Ogawa, Masato and Yamada, Shinichi, eds.1998. *Ainu Minzoku Kindai no Kiroku.* Tokyo: Sōfūkan.

Okuyama, Ryō. 1950. *Shinkō Hokkaidōshi.* Sapporo: Hoppō Shoin.

Patterson, Orland. 1982. *Slavery and Social Death: A Comparative Study.* Cambridge, MA: Harvard University Press.

Roellinghoff, Michael. 2020. "Osteo-Hermeneutics: Ainu Racialization, De-Indigenization, and Bone Theft in Japanese Hokkaido," *Settler Colonial Studies,* 10 (3), 295–310. London: Taylor and Francis.

Saruya, Kaname. 1982. *Seibu Kaitakushi.* Tokyo: Iwanami.

Sasaki, Katsutaro. 1934. "Introduction," in *Ainu Doka no Senjū.* Sapporo: Hokkaido Shogun Kōseidan.

Sato, Yukio. 2001. "Kitakaze Isokichi wo Shinobu," in *Kikan Ainu Bunka,* vol. 16. Sapporo: Ainu Bunka Tomo no Kai.

Sekiguchi, Akira, Tabata, Hiroshi, Kuwahara, Masato and Takizawa, Tadashi, eds. 2015. *Ainu Minzoku no Rekishi.* Tokyo: Yamakawa.

Shigematsu, Kazuyoshi. 2004. *Shiryō Hokkaidō Kangoku no Rekishi.* Tokyo: Shinzan Sha.

Swensen, James R. 2019. "Bound for the Fair: Chief Joseph, Quanah Parker, and Geronimo and the 1904 St. Louis World's Fair," *American Indian Quarterly,* 43 (4), 439–470. University of Nebraska Press.

Tanaka, Osamu. 1986. *Nihon Shihonshugi to Hokkaidō.* Sapporo: Hokkaidō Daigaku Shuppan.

Tanaka, Akira and Kuwahara, Masato. 1996. *Hokkaido Kaitaku to Imin.* Tokyo: Yoshikawa Kōbunkan.

Takakura, Shinichirō. 1947. *Hokkaidō Takushoku Shi*. Tokyo: Kashiwaba Shoin.

Trennert, Jr., Robert. 1987. "Selling Indian Education at World's Fairs and Expositions, 1893–1904,". *American Indian Quarterly*, 11 (Summer), 203–220.

Ueda, Shin. 2018. "Kaiko to Kaikoku," *Gendai Shiso: Meiji Ishin no Hikari to Kage*. Tokyo: Seidosha.

Walker, Brett L. 2004. "Meiji Modernization, Scientific Agriculture, and the Destruction of Japan's Hokkaidō Wolf," *Environmental History*, 9 (2), 248–272. Oxford: Oxford University Press.

Walker, Brett L. 2006. *Conquest of the Ainu Lands*. Berkeley: University of California Press.

Walker, Gavin. 2016. *The Sublime Perversion of Capital: Marxist Theory and Politics of History in Modern Japan*. Durham: Duke University Press.

Wolfe, Patrick. 2006. "Settler Colonialism and the Elimination of the Native," *Journal of Genocide Research 8* (4), 387–409. London: Taylor and Francis Group.

Yamada, Shin'ichi. 2011. *Kindai Hokkaidō to Ainu Minzoku*. Sapporo: Hokkaido Daigaku Shuppankai.

3

BURAKUMIN EMIGRANTS TO AMERICA

Historical Experience of "Racialization" and Solidarity across the Pacific

Hiroshi Sekiguchi

3.1 Introduction

This chapter analyzes the politics of the racialization of Burakumin as a double minority within the Japanese immigrant community in the US, as well as the solidarity in their struggle against discrimination that developed across the Pacific between Japanese immigrants on the West Coast and Burakumin in Japan.

Burakumin, a minoritized group in Japan, has long faced discrimination in Japanese society, despite the fact that they are no different from other Japanese people in terms of their skin color and other physical characteristics, language, and religion. Historians have a consensus that popular discourses claiming their origin to be from the continent is groundless. Burakumin have historically engaged in occupations that were shunned by other Japanese, such as animal slaughtering, tanning, and meat processing. A taboo on the slaughtering and eating of animals was deeply linked to the concept of *kegare* (defilement or pollution), which spread among Japanese society when connected with Buddhism during the Heian period (794–1185). When discriminatory practices became strictly institutionalized during the Edo period (1603–1868), Burakumin were pejoratively called "*eta*" by others and governed with tight legal and institutional restrictions on marriage, residence, and nearly all other social spheres. In the modern age, the *mibun kaihō rei* (Emancipation Edict) of 1871 abolished all legal discrimination differentiating them from the rest of the Japanese people. In reality, however, Burakumin continued to suffer discrimination as is evident in the derogatory terms used to refer to them such as eta, *shin-heimin* (new citizens) and *tokushu-burakumin* (special hamlet dwellers), which are no longer in common use today.

This chapter is the first empirical study to examine the experience of Burakumin immigrants within the context of a transpacific history of racism. As many Burakumin were forced to live in poverty, a considerable number of

DOI: 10.4324/9781003266396-4

them left Japan in the modern period in search of new opportunities in new destinations.

The study of the migration of Burakumin provides an exemplar of the historical experiences of various ethnic minorities in the modern world. For example, the government-sponsored migration of Burakumin to Hokkaido, the Korean Peninsula, and Manchuria would unravel an aspect of what Michel Foucault calls "governmentality." The Japanese government promoted migration by telling Burakumin to leave their uncivilized, low-paying occupations and cramped unhygienic dwellings to start a new life earning a stable income from farming. However, what the government gave them was, in fact, "uncultivated land" created by driving away the Ainu, the local indigenous population, as illustrated in Hirano's chapter in this volume. From the viewpoint of settler-colonialism, it cannot be denied that Burakumin can be construed as perpetrators. But, as settlers, they were merely given a ray of hope in the "opportunity" on offer at the expense of others. The reclamation work awaiting them in their settlements consisted of relentless toil and trouble beyond imagination. There was no end to the number of settlers who failed, lost their land and returned to their old home. In the case of the Kutami community of settlers in Manchuria, their venture came to a tragic end when they committed mass suicide upon Japan's defeat in World War II (Takahashi 1995).

The case of Burakumin immigrants to North America, which this chapter focuses on, can be analyzed as historical experiences at the intersection of transatlantic and transpacific racisms. According to Yasuko Takezawa, the idea of "race" has three dimensions, namely, "race" in the lower case, "Race" with a capital-R, and "Race as Resistance"(RR). She emphasizes that it is important to pay attention to how these intersect and interlink with each other (Takezawa 2005). The Burakumin in pre-modern Japan was a marginalized group distinguished by traditional Asian-type institutional discrimination based on a mixture of groundless discourses about the difference in their origin from mainstream society and pollution based on their occupation of slaughtering animals and making leather ("race") (Takezawa 2020). The form of discrimination suffered by the Burakumin was later transformed when it came to be combined with scientific race theories imported to Japan from the West in modern times ("Race") (Sekiguchi 2019).

The history of Burakumin in Japanese communities in the US was even more complex. The historical experience of Japanese Americans on the West Coast of the US around the turn of the twentieth century can be located within a century-long movement that shaped the structure of race relations in America as a whole. As discussed in Tokunaga's chapter in this volume, some European ethnic groups, most notably Irish Americans, who were initially not regarded as "white" in the racial hierarchy on the East coast, came to acquire dominant status as "white" through differentiating themselves from the "yellow," often becoming the initiators of the exclusion movements against Chinese immigrants, then later against Japanese immigrants most of whom arrived on the West coast after the 1882 Chinese Exclusion Act. The Japanese immigrants who were trapped in this white-centric racial hierarchy reacted to various forms of racial discrimination against themselves in two ways. On the one hand, they raised fierce protests against the discriminatory treatment of the Japanese, while at the same time, they advocated giving up their "barbaric and obscurant" cultural practices and customs and assimilating into the American lifestyle (Azuma 2005).

In the latter context, the Burakumin within the Japanese communities were harshly criticized and oppressed as undesirable because they were thought to be a cause of discrimination against the Japanese in American society. Along with the cases of atomic bomb survivors discussed in Uchino's chapter, the study of Burakumin in Japanese society in the US highlights the multilayered nature of oppression generated by the intersectionality of multiple contexts of discrimination. This chapter will bring to light a new aspect of Japanese American history, an aspect that has long remained taboo or not accurately described.

A number of case studies have been conducted on the relocation and emigration of the Burakumin from the viewpoint of state-induced or state-controlled migration, especially imperial Japan's emigration policy in its territories such as Hokkaido and Manchuria. In contrast, there have been no empirical historical studies on the cases of voluntary emigrants to Hawai'i and the Americas.[1] One of the reasons for this is the tendency of historical research to idealize the Burakumin as those who fought discrimination in their homeland. Another reason may be because the movement for Buraku liberation regarded migration as an escape or defeat.

On the other hand, some studies on Japanese American society have pointed to the presence of people from Buraku communities in Japan. *Japan's Invisible Race*, co-edited by George De Vos and Hiroshi Wagatsuma (1966), contains a survey report on the issue of Burakumin in Japanese communities in the US. The report was compiled by Hiroshi Ito (pseudonym) based on a survey conducted by a student at the University of California in the 1950s and highlighted a number of interesting features about Burakumin immigrants in the US. I shall mention a few that are relevant to our discussion here.

First, ten prefectures were identified as places of origin of Burakumin emigrants to the US. These were Hiroshima, Wakayama, Okayama, Fukuoka, Kumamoto, Yamaguchi, Kagoshima, Mie, Kochi, and Fukui, out of which the largest number of emigrants originated from Fukui. Second, the highest concentration of the Burakumin population in pre–World War II America was in and around Florin, Sacramento, California. Third, Burakumin immigrants in the US tended to avoid working in industries such as animal slaughtering, cobbling, and meat and leather processing, that had been their traditional occupations in Japan. Another tendency was to avoid occupations and businesses requiring interpersonal service, such as Japanese restaurants, where they could routinely face overt discrimination (Ito 1966). However, perhaps because of the sensitive nature of the subject matter, the report does not identify the researcher or clearly outline the research process, making it difficult to judge its authenticity and to give it a definitive evaluation.

More recently, Andrea Geiger's *Subverting Exclusion: Transpacific Encounters with Race, Caste, and Borders, 1885–1928*, discusses the history of Burakumin immigrants in Japanese communities in early-twentieth-century America (Geiger 2011). Geiger's work draws important attention to this longtime taboo topic. Her argument, however, has a few serious errors. She repeatedly suggests that most coal miners were Burakumin (Geiger 2011: 66, 68). Her book cover is even decorated with a photo of coal miners. However, historical studies written in Japanese demonstrate that most Burakumin who were engaged in coal mining industry worked only menial jobs serving the miners because they were mostly excluded from coal mining labor in large coalfields which had exclusive rights of mining.[2] Geiger conflates all jobs related to coal mining industry with coal mining.

Geiger also makes an assumed connection between shoemakers in California and Buraku immigrants without giving any historical evidence. Although in Japan, shoemaking and tanning were among the occupations traditionally represented by Burakumin, Buraku immigrants in the US often deliberately changed their occupation as a way of concealing their Buraku backgrounds as will be discussed in this chapter (see also Ito 1966).

In the first section of this chapter, I introduce cases of emigrants from Buraku communities to the US around the late nineteenth century to the early twentieth century to examine the overseas Buraku community at the time in light of interviews with second-generation Japanese Americans.[3] I also argue in this section that Ito's report has a certain level of validity. In the second section, I shed light on the double discrimination Burakumin encountered on foreign land based on reports in the Japanese-language newspapers published in the US at the time and the solidarity between minority groups that was engendered through protests against it.

3.2 Burakumin Emigrants to the US

In this section, I look at cases of Burakumin emigrants to the US in order to elucidate the movement of people, information, and money that developed between Japan and their new home and to examine the lives they led in the new country.

3.2.1 Early Twentieth-Century Buraku Improvement Policy and Emigration Programs

In Japan, various government policies were proposed, and ideas were exchanged about the emigration and resettlement of Burakumin from the late early-modern period under the Tokugawa shogunate (1603–1868). In the Meiji era, the government annexed it as Japanese territory under the name Hokkaido and promoted its development (see Hirano, Chapter 2). In the twentieth century, the government formulated a policy to accelerate the migration of the Burakumin to Hokkaido, which was adopted by prefectural governments and spread nationally (Fujino 1984).

The government's migration policy culminated in the first Saimin Buraku Kaizen Kyōgikai (Conference on the Improvement of Impoverished Communities) in 1912.[4] At the conference, the Home Ministry that organized the meeting proposed migration to Hokkaido as an industrial development strategy for the Burakumin, while attendees reported on some of the efforts made and issues encountered at the regional level. According to the reports, it had already become difficult to offer land to prospective settlers in Hokkaido, despite promotion by the government. The conference records reveal that the actual numbers of migrants from Buraku communities to Hokkaido were very low, as Burakumin had found out about the harsh conditions that they would have to endure.

Many attendees at the conference, however, reported cases of successful emigration to the US. Emigration from Japan to the US was largely restricted at the time under the Gentlemen's Agreement of 1908. Yet, the presenters claimed that emigration to Hawai'i or the US would contribute more to the economic and livelihood improvement of impoverished Buraku communities than migration to Hokkaido. Toshio Takeshima, head of Nagahama village in Agawa County, Kochi prefecture, reported on the experience of a Buraku community in his village as follows:

> The trend of emigration to the US. began seven or eight years ago, and so far, thirteen people from a Buraku community have made the move while there has been hardly any momentum towards migration among regular people. The emigrants have been sending home several thousand yen per year. Their families immediately buy real estate with the money rather than spending it to lead an idle life. This encourages the emigrants to send even more money.

He stressed that the community was highly motivated to improve their lives. For example, a youth association was established to improve living standards in the community, and this news prompted the settlers in the US to send funds to support its activity (Unsigned 1986: 107).

3.2.2 The Migration Project in Mikata County, Fukui Prefecture

Ito points out in the abovementioned report that there is a markedly high number of Burakumin emigrants from Fukui prefecture to the US. Is this true?[5] I looked at statistics compiled by the Chūō Yūwa Jigyō Kyōkai (Central Conciliation Project Association), which the government set up in the pre-war period for the purpose of improving the living standards of Buraku communities and eliminating discrimination against the Burakumin. A comparison of the statistics reveals that the percentage of Burakumin migrants from Fukui prefecture to Hawai'i and North America is 23 percent, more than 20 times

TABLE 3.1 Number of Households and Population in "X" Hamlet (1st Census in 1920)

	The whole Mimi village	"X" hamlet	Ratio
Number of households	1,006	209	20.8%
Population	4,474	946	21.1%

Source: Created from page 27 of Unsigned (2014).

the national average (1 percent) (according to destination based on a national survey of Buraku communities in 1939), indicating that the large number of Burakumin who came to the US were from this prefecture, as Ito mentioned.

At the aforementioned conference in 1912, Shirookawa, head of Mikata county, Fukui prefecture, talked about the case of "X" hamlet within Mimi village in his county as being the pioneer of emigration to the US from that prefecture. "X" hamlet was Fukui's largest Buraku with a population of 946 in 209 households and accounted for just over 20 percent of the total population/households of Mimi village according to the first national census in 1920 (Table 3.1). However, only 102 of the 209 households (roughly half of the hamlet) had primary occupations, and more than 70 percent of them were in farming (Table 3.2). In terms of land ownership, the census figures highlight the very small size of their farming operations, as the area of rice field owned by the residents of "X" hamlet was 0.9 percent of the village total and their horticultural landholdings accounted for just 0.1 percent of the total. Further, their residential landholdings accounted for only 5.5 percent of the village total (Table 3.3).

Shirookawa relayed Burakumin's desire for the relaxation of travel permit criteria, reporting at the conference, "People of that community have been constantly asking to let them travel to America where they would have no trouble finding jobs" (Unsigned 1986: 157), as they could earn around two dollars per day in the US. In 1910, two US dollars were equivalent to approximately four Japanese yen. Considering the consumer price index over 100 years, the wage would have been worth around 14,000 Japanese yen in 2019. It is easy to imagine that working in Hawai'i or North America would be a very attractive prospect for Burakumin with very few opportunities for stable employment in those days.[6]

TABLE 3.2 Occupations of Residents of "X" Hamlet (1923)

	Number of households	Ratio
Agriculture	73	71.6%
Industrial	0	0.0%
Commercial	11	10.8%
Public affairs and freelance	1	1.0%
Other	17	16.7%
Total	102	100.0%

Source: Created from page 61 of Unsigned (2014).

TABLE 3.3 Possession Status of Fields and Residential Land in "X" Hamlet (1921)

	The whole Mimi village	"X" hamlet	Ratio
Rice field (cho; 町)	481.61	4.22	0.9%
Vegetable field (cho; 町)	54.66	0.07	0.1%
Residential land (tsubo; 坪)	124,880	6,929	5.5%

Source: Created from page 23 of Unsigned (2014).

Note: "Cho (町)" refers to a unit of area, approximately equal to one hectare. One "tsubo (坪)" is approximately 3.3 square meters.

Yozaemon Yoshioka, the head of "X" hamlet, set out to improve the Buraku through emigration to the US out of concern about the strained circumstances of the residents. The Yoshiokas were an established family that had produced many headmen and village councilors. Yozaemon had been wanting to raise the living standards of the impoverished residents and promoted emigration to the US as a solution. On his advice, a succession of residents from "X" hamlet emigrated to Hawai'i and the US Emigration to America boomed in the area as non-Buraku residents also began to apply for emigration after seeing the success of emigrants from "X" hamlet.[7]

Remittances sent by the emigrants from "X" hamlet stimulated economic and social activity in their home community. Shirookawa of the aforementioned Mikata county reported the following about emigrants from "X" hamlet of Mimi village to the US.

> From that area, 120 to 130 people have emigrated to work in America or Hawai'i [...] over 100,000 yen have been sent to my prefecture yearly, of which well over 50,000 yen has gone to the Buraku.
>
> *Unsigned 1986 [1912]: 157*

"X" hamlet had been considered problematic due to the low level of education among its residents. It was reported, "It is truly lamentable that the number of those who are not attending elementary school in this village is the highest in this county. The poor showing of the village and the county was due to the presence of a relatively large number of impoverished communities. Poverty is the cause of non-attendance" (Unsigned 1913: 27). In 1919, residents of "X" hamlet revived Kyōfūkai, a pre-existing livelihood improvement group, and renamed it Koshukai (Association of Household Heads) to seek donations from residents who were working overseas, to start special lessons for truants which later developed into a night class held in the hamlet hall with the support of the village's education association (Unsigned 2014: 87).

These activities were initiated by Yozaemon Yoshioka (hereditary name of the son of the aforementioned head of "X" hamlet) in his barn. In 1919, a monument was built to honor his contribution to regional development through the promotion of immigration to North America. In November 1922, he received a commendation from the Home Ministry for his contribution to local development. The "X" hamlet residents, who had long been refused membership of the local parish of Mimi Shrine, raised 5,000 yen from returning residents and donated it to the shrine. They were finally accepted as parishioners in March 1920 (Unsigned 1985: 84).

3.3 The History of Japanese Immigrants in Florin, Sacramento

I now examine surviving records to analyze how the migrant workers from "X" hamlet emigrated to the US. Let us turn to a 1922 publication titled *Zaibei nihonjin jinmei jiten* (Biographical Dictionary of Japanese Names in the US). This dictionary does not contain the names of all Japanese immigrants as it is a "who's who" of Japanese residents in the US who achieved a certain level of economic or social success. With this in mind, we find 69 entries from Fukui prefecture, of which 29 list their birthplace as Mimi village in Mikata county (Table 3.4). With the cooperation of the current residents of "X" hamlet, I found that 22 of these 29 people, or 75.9 percent, most likely came from "X" hamlet based on their names and addresses. According to the listed places of residence, 15 of the former "X" hamlet residents, or just over two-thirds, settled in and around Florin (an area extending from the southern part of Sacramento city to Elk Grove). Further, all former Mimi village residents who settled in the Florin area were from "X" hamlet, suggesting that emigration from that hamlet was of a collective nature. Also, according to this data, none of the immigrants from "X" hamlet were engaged in the traditional occupations of the Burakumin, such as meat processing or leatherworking.

Florin is located on the outskirts of Sacramento, the state capital of California. Large numbers of Japanese immigrants settled there from the end of the nineteenth century, and in the pre-World War II period, it was so prosperous that it was advertised as the "Japanese village" of California. The area became so well-known for its success in farming the vast expanse of land that many famous people from Japan visited. Japanese settlement in Florin began in 1895 when a few dozen Japanese immigrants were hired as laborers by a European American farming family who was growing strawberries. In 1898, a man from Hiroshima prefecture saw the potential of this business and leased 20 acres of land with his younger brother to start strawberry farming. They made a net profit of 15,000 US dollars in three years before returning to Japan. After that, Japanese immigrants cultivated 400 acres of strawberry fields from 1899 to 1900 and reportedly made substantial profits. Hearing these success stories, Japanese settlers in other areas of the US rushed to Florin, and by 1901, the area of farmland cultivated by the Japanese increased to 1,000 acres. White-owned shops near Florin train station boomed, making 50,000–60,000 dollars per year in sales to Japanese customers alone (Ōfu Nippōsha 1909: 30–31).

Let us retrace the footsteps of some of the immigrants to this area from "X" hamlet. As far as I can tell, the first person from "X" hamlet to reside in Florin

TABLE 3.4 List of People from Mimi Village (in *Zaibei nihonjin jinmei jiten* [Biographical Dictionary of Japanese Names in the US], 1922)

1	Denkichi Urokoxxxx	Sacrament, CA	Born in 1873. Traveled to the US in 1906. Agriculture in Florin since 1914. He later moved to the site. He manages 11 acres of strawberries. His family: Wife, the eldest son, and daughter.
2	Iwakichi Okaxxxx	Hermosa Beach, CA	Born in 1879. Traveled to the US in 1904. He runs 3 acres of cut flowers locally. Family: Wife and the eldest daughter.
3	Saburo Kuboxxxx	Los Angeles, CA	Traveled to the US in 1907. Cultivated 70 acres in Hoteiya in collaboration with his cousins. Fukui Kenjinkai officer.
4	Unosuke Koxxxx	Florin, CA	Born in 1900. He has been indigenous to Florin for 6 years. He rents 20 acres of grapes and 1.5 acres of strawberries. Family: Mother, wife, and the eldest son.
5	Kisaburo Goxxxx	Wheatland, CA	Traveled to the US in 1905. He runs a 10-acre vegetable garden. Councilor of the Japanese Association of Melisville. Family: Wife, one son, and one daughter.
6	Shosaburo Goxxxx	Wheatland, CA	Born in 1885. Traveled to Hawai'i in 1903 and to California in 1906. In 1913 he moved to the area and managed a 10-acre vegetable garden. Family: Wife and the eldest son.
7	Otojiro Saxxxx	Watts, CA	Traveled to the US in 1906. He lives near Los Angeles. He runs a farm on 15 acres. Family: The eldest son and his wife, and the second son.
8	Asagoro Saxxxx	Stockton, CA	Born in 1876. Traveled to the US in 1907. After working in San Francisco, settled down the river in Stakton and engaged in agriculture. Family: Wife (Japan), and 3 sons.
9	Denkuro Saxxxx	Los Angeles, CA	Born in 1883. Traveled to the US in 1906. 20 acres of vegetable cultivation in cooperation with Mr. Sugixxxx. Family: Wife, one son, and one daughter.
10	Takazo Shiixxxx	Florin, CA	Traveled to the US in 1896. Florin settled 13 years. Operates 60 acres of vineyards. Family: Wife.
11	Giichiro Sugixxxx	Los Angeles, CA	Born in 1883. Traveled to the US in 1906. He cultivates 20 acres of vegetables locally. Family: Wife, third son, and daughter.
12	Yoshizo Taxxxx	Elk Grove, CA	Born in 1881. Traveled to the US in 1902. After living in San Francisco for 8 years, moved to the site. He cultivates 4 acres of strawberry garden. Family: Wife.
13	Tatsujiro Taxxxx	Stockton, CA	Born in 1882. Traveled to the US in 1905. Returned to Japan after 7 years of radish cultivation in Idaho. Returned to the US in 1921 and cultivated 21 acres of onions. Family: Wife, eldest son and his wife.
14	Tamezo Taxxxx	Elk Grove, CA	Traveled to the US in 1896. Settled in Elk Grove. Engaged in agriculture and owns 20 acres of strawberry garden. Vineyard 65 acres of cash leased. In addition, 40 acres of farm management in Florin. Family: Wife and 5 children.
15	Ikujiro Takexxxx	Florin, CA	Born in 1858. Traveled to the US in 1900. Settled in Florin and engaged in agriculture. He is engaged in the halling industry with several trucks. Family: Wife, one son, and one daughter (returning to Japan).

(Continued)

TABLE 3.4 List of People from Mimi Village (in *Zaibei nihonjin jinmei jiten* [Biographical Dictionary of Japanese Names in the US],1922) (*Continued*)

16	Sankichi Takexxxxx	Florin, CA	Born in 1868. Traveled to the US in 1900. After living in Victoria, Seattle, and Sacramento moved to Florin. Agricultural management for 14 years. Family: Wife (returning to Japan).
17	Hisajiro Toxxxx	Halcyon, CA	Born in 1883. Traveled to the US in 1903. After living in Watsonville, San Francisco, he lived locally. He cultivates 10 acres of strawberries and artichokes. Family: Wife, one son, and one daughter.
18	Isuke Nakaxxxx	Florin, CA	Born in 1887. He went to the US in 1883. Settled in Florin. Engaged in agriculture with his father-in-law. Family: Wife and second son.
19	Yakichi Nakaxxxxx	Florin, CA	Born in 1876. Traveled to the US in 1900. Indigenous to Florin. 20 acres of vineyards and 7 acres of strawberries. Family: Second son.
20	Otojiro Nagaxxxxx	Stockton, CA	Born in 1878. Traveled to Hawai'i in 1907. Lives near Los Angeles. Family: Wife, one son, and one daughter.
21	Chokichi Hayaxxxxx	Elk Grove, CA	Traveled to the US in 1904. 20 acres of orchard grapes. Strawberry 5-acre orchard management. Family: The eldest son and his wife, and the second son.
22	Shosaburo Maruxxxx	Florin, CA	Born in 1876. Traveled to the US in 1900. After living in San Francisco for 10 years, he was indigenous to Florin. Owns 20 acres of vineyard. Family: Wife, second daughter.
23	Shinkichi Maxxxx	Florin, CA	Born in 1885. Traveled to the US in 1902. After studying in San Francisco, settled in Florin for 15 years. He cultivates 25 acres of grapes. In 1918, he returned to the US with his wife. Family: Wife, and second daughter.
24	Kyushichi Morixxxx	Elk Grove, CA	Traveled to the US in 1900. Moved to Florin in 1904. He runs a strawberry garden on 5 acres. 1917 Moved to Elk Grove. Help Mr. Taxxxx (No.14)'s farm business.
25	Munekichi Morixxxx	Los Angeles, CA	Landed in Seattle in 1902. He moved to Los Angeles four years after moving to San Francisco. He has been working as a cook for 10 years. Family living in Japan: Wife and 2 children.
26	Iwamatsu Yamaxxxxx	Auburn, CA	Born in 1886. Landed in Seattle in 1906. Worked at sawmill Hohmann. Moved to the site from 1921 and managed 25 acres of orchards. Family: Wife and the eldest son.
27	Asakichi Yoshixxxx	Florin, CA	Born in 1873. Landed in San Francisco in 1896. Moved to Florin in 1899. Agricultural management on 23 acres of leased land. Grape and strawberry cultivation. Family: Wife, one son, and three daughters.
28	Genjiro Yoshixxxx	Florin, CA	Born in 1879. Arrived in San Francisco in 1905. He ran a hairdressing business there and moved to Florin in 1918 to run the same business. Family: wife, and second daughter.
29	Seikichi Wakaxxxx	Wilmington, CA	Born in 1879. 1898 Landed in San Francisco. After 5 years of commuting to school, worked for SB Railway for 14 years. After that, he runs a grocery store and a Western restaurant locally.

was Shozo Yoshixxxx[8] (born in 1885). He crossed the ocean with his father and arrived in the US. in 1900. After several jobs, including chopping wood in a coal mine, working on the railroad, and farming, he settled in Florin in November 1902. He eventually bought fourteen acres of farmland and immersed himself in a life of cultivating and irrigating the fields by day and planting strawberries by night. As a result, he became a farmer with an annual income of 1,500 dollars by 1907 and was able to pay back his debt in full (Ōfu Nippōsha 1909: 149).

Shuji Yoshixxxx (born in 1885) settled in Florin in the same period. He traveled to the US. in 1898 to live with his father, who had been running a restaurant in San Francisco, and went to elementary school before continuing on to night classes for Japanese people to learn English. After working as a farm laborer in daikon radish fields and then getting a job in a building contractor's office in San Francisco in 1903, he settled in Florin in 1904. He went into strawberry farming in partnership with two other men from his hometown. In October of the same year, he and his father leased 24 hectares of vineyard and 3 acres of strawberry field. He continued to farm there even after his father returned to Japan in 1906 (Ōfu Nippōsha 1909: 150).

Tamezo Taxxxx (born in 1873; No. 14 in Table 3.4) arrived in San Francisco in 1896 and attended a white elementary school for four years to learn English. He saved money while working for a housekeeper placement service before settling in Florin in 1904 and leasing 40 acres of farmland where he grew strawberries and grapes. He married a Japanese woman in 1906, and the whole family worked hard in the farming business, which grew to produce 600 boxes of grapes and 4,000 boxes of strawberries by 1907. He expanded his business further by leasing a 32-acre vineyard in Elk Grove for five years (Ōfu Nippōsha 1909: 158–159).

The above biographies of former "X" hamlet residents who settled in Florin show that there was a close business collaboration between compatriots, evident in the case of Shuji Yoshixxxx, who went into strawberry farming with two others from the same hamlet, and the case of Tamezo Taxxxx who ran a farming business with the cooperation of another person from "X" hamlet (No. 24 in Table 3.4). We can also surmise that the alliance between them would have been strengthened not only by business partnerships but also through family relations. For example, the man listed as No. 18 in Table 3.4 married the younger sister of Shuji Yoshixxxx and engaged in farming with his father-in-law. It seems that the close relationships fostered between people from the same neighborhood were an important lifeline for them in making their livelihood in a foreign land with a foreign language while enduring discrimination from the broader Japanese community in the US, as discussed below.

In the aforementioned survey report, Ito refers to Florin as a place where many Burakumin from Fukui prefecture settled in the pre-war period, stating as follows:

> Fewer than 10 percent of the Fukui people here were judged to be non-outcastes. When Florin was most heavily populated, in the early 1930's,

the total number of Japanese was about 1,800. Some 15 to 20 percent of this number, or 270 to 360 persons were thought to be outcastes. And it is estimated that 90 percent of this population was of the Fukui group.

Ito 1966: 205

It is reasonable to think that the sister community of "X" hamlet in the Florin area was formed through what immigration studies call "chain migration." The first immigrants who leave their homelands have to build their lives from scratch with very little information and spend enormous amounts of time and money in overcoming difficulties. However, once the first wave of immigrants has established a certain standard of living, including work, housing, and education, as in the case of Florin settlers from "X" hamlet, they can assist their family, relatives, and community members who arrive after them with accommodation, job seeking, shopping, finance, and other requirements. This can greatly reduce the financial, informational, and psychological barriers and burdens of emigration for later arrivals. They sent letters and photos to their families back home, telling them about their work and life in Florin (Figure 3.1). Also, returned emigrants shared their experiences with prospective emigrants to give them a greater sense of ease about moving to the sister community overseas. In this way, a feedback loop of information is created between the place of origin and the destination country, and the ties between communities' function as social capital, forming a system that promotes migration (Higuchi 2002).

The aforementioned head of Mikata county reported that many "X" hamlet residents wanted to emigrate because "Going overseas has become [a casual trip] like going to a neighbor's house even when travelling to America" (Shirookawa's remark; Unsigned 1986: 157–158). The high number of emigrants from "X" hamlet and the fact that a majority of emigrants from Fukui in Florin came from that community suggest that chain migration played an important role.

What kind of relationship did the Burakumin have with the rest of the Japanese community in Florin? There is very little information available about this, but some clues can be found in scarce records. Firstly, emigrants from "X" hamlet were not totally isolated from the Japanese community. For instance, Shosaburo Maruxxxx (No. 22 in Table 3.4) was listed as 1 of the 18 initiators of the resolution to build the Buddhist Church of Florin and left his mark on history by becoming the inaugural deputy parish representative in 1917 and the second parish leader in 1918 (Tahara, Shiro, Albert Menda, and Hidemo Kodama 1974: 283). When the Buddhist Church of Florin was built in 1920, they participated in various activities based there (Figure 3.2). This suggests that Burakumin were allowed to take up certain positions as members of the Japanese community in the US and participated in economic and social activities.

However, not all barriers had been eliminated. Ito's report describes the practice of avoidance of Burakumin by the rest of the Japanese community in Florin. The following is Ito's summary of the informants' accounts.

FIGURE 3.1 A Photograph of a Strawberry Harvesting Scene Sent from Florin to "X" Hamlet

When the non-Burakumin Japanese residents interacted with Burakumin, norms observed in Japan were often breached, such as in the case of offering and accepting of freshly brewed green tea and pickled vegetables. When Burakumin offered beverages to non-Burakumin visitors, they would not offer them tea unless they trusted their guests (even if the guests happily accepted their hospitality). In contrast, those who had established a close relationship with the Burakumin did not experience this. If they happened to visit at mealtimes, they might be invited to eat with their Burakumin host. Nevertheless, both those who were trusted by the Burakumin and those who were not mentioned the Shinto concept of *kegare* (defilement or pollution), which defined the Burakumin as impure and dirty beings to be avoided, as the cause of the division between them. By taking this approach, Burakumin avoided the potentially

FIGURE 3.2 Buddhist Church of Florin (Built in 1920)

embarrassing and awkward situation in which visitors were of the belief that what had been prepared by their Burakumin host was unclean according to their religion (Ito 1966: 210–211).

In premodern Japan, there was a widespread folkloric fear that the fire used in daily life would be defiled. Meat preparation, the "black impurity" of a death in the family, and the "red impurity" of blood associated with childbirth or menstruation were seen as potential causes of defilement and were thought to invite calamity and the wrath of the god of the hearth. The hearth of the dwelling had to be kept clean and pure and carefully kept away from the contagion of impurity. For this reason, women lived in a separate hut with a separate cooking fire during menstruation and childbirth, and on the occasion of a family member's death the household would renew the fire in their hearth with fire brought from outside the home (Yanagita 1944). In the same way, it was considered taboo to eat together with the Burakumin (then called "Eta"), and if one did share a meal with them, it was taboo to use the same dishes and utensils. These customs were known as "bekka" (separate fire) and "bekki" (separate dish) (Minegishi 1986). It became an issue in the Japanese community in Florin for Burakumin and the other residents to drink tea together precisely because these premodern racist customs had made their way across the Pacific to the west coast of the US.

In those days, it was customary for the Burakumin families in Florin to hold large house parties on festive occasions with special elaborate Japanese dishes and entertainment provided by amateur performers. These banquets were attended only by Burakumin, with the exception of the local priests. On rare occasions, a few leaders of the Japanese community who were not Burakumin were also invited. They were seated at the top of the table, offered imported liquor or spirits, and served dishes on special trays. In general, however, the weddings, funerals, and banquets of the Burakumin were held within their own community (Ito 1966: 211).

Ito's report indicates the existence of discrimination in the Japanese expatriate community similar to what was found in Japan around the same time. There were barriers separating Burakumin and non-Burakumin groups at the scenes of intimate kinship-centered interaction such as weddings, funerals, and banquets, although the two groups engaged in active interactions in business, education, and religion within the Japanese expatriate community. What was at work behind such discrimination was an aversive feeling based on belief in the concept of *kegare*.

I conducted an interview-based survey on second-generation Japanese residents in Sacramento in May 2018. The following are excerpts of the narratives given by the four interviewees about their memories of people from Fukui prefecture in the pre-war period.[9]

Many residents in the area from southern Florin to Elk Grove were from Fukui prefecture.

Fukui people were discriminated against by others and had their own congregation in their Buddhist practices.

Unlike residents from other prefectures, Fukui people did not form a prefectural association [perhaps to avoid discrimination].

My parents [first-generation] told me not to marry a Fukui person or an Eta [Burakumin].

I had many friends from Fukui at my elementary and middle schools. We often played together.

People from Okinawa prefecture were also discriminated against. My mother told me, "The Eta got swept out to sea and drifted to Okinawa. That's why Okinawa people are Eta."

Fukui people had the same occupations as other Japanese residents and grew strawberries and grapes.

Racism cannot be eliminated as long as the Japanese people discriminate against their fellow Japanese while protesting against discrimination by the white people. It's absurd.

The survey verified that many people from Fukui prefecture formed a community in the area extending from southern Florin to Elk Grove before World War II and engaged in agricultural labor just like other Japanese immigrants. The interviewees suggested that there was persistent discrimination against Burakumin in the pre-war Japanese community in the US, especially among first-generation immigrants, and that immigrants from Okinawa were subjected to similar prejudice. Fukui people did not form a prefectural organization, as is common in the Japanese expatriate community in the US, or set up their own religious center, showing a reluctance and introversion to the outside world in order to avoid being targeted for discrimination.

My assessment of Ito's report after my own research is as follows. It has long been considered that the credibility of his report could not be determined because the sources of information are not identified. However, considering the fact that many of the emigrants from Fukui prefecture to California were Burakumin and that many emigrants from Buraku communities settled in the Florin area, a certain level of validity and accuracy can be attributed to Ito's conclusions according to the relevant Japanese documents on emigration. Further, it is reasonable to think that Ito's description of the Buraku community within the Japanese expatriate community in the US paints at least part of the true picture because the tendency of the Burakumin to pursue active interactions within their own group while taking a more cautious and passive approach to interactions with non-Burakumin Japanese has been corroborated by my survey of second-generation Japanese residents.

The outbreak of war between Japan and the US forced many Japanese residents on US soil into concentration camps and completely destroyed the lives they had built over many years. As a result of their internment, the former inmates lost their jobs and homes and had to wander from place to place in search of a new life after the war. By the end of the war, the Japanese community in Florin had changed greatly, and the settlement area of the Burakumin emigrants from "X" hamlet had disappeared. It is possible that the explicit discrimination of the pre-war era waned gradually in the Japanese expatriate community as a result. As reported by Passin and Isomura (1984), however, discrimination in marriage and other Buraku issues did exist in Japanese American internment camps. In my interview survey, one third-generation non-Buraku Japanese American reported that he had received negative and discriminatory advice against the Burakumin from people of his parent's generation (such as not marrying a Burakumin), but the interviewee commented that such perception was a "mistaken, racist view." This demonstrates that prejudices within the Japanese expatriate community did not disappear entirely after the war.

Very little has been published on settlers from Japanese Buraku communities in the US. I have examined the cases of emigrants from "X" hamlet, a Buraku community in Fukui prefecture, to discover some aspects of their community and lives in pre-war America. From the end of the nineteenth century to the early twentieth century, immigrant workers from the Buraku community in Japan settled on American soil and worked while experiencing discriminatory treatment from the broader Japanese expatriate community. It has become apparent that a chain migration system formed through social networks linking the homeland and its sister community in Florin facilitated travel between the two places. This system allowed people to overcome difficulties, send money to their families back home and support their own lives.

3.4 The Japanese Community in the US and the Burakumin

This section examines the Buraku issue in the US in relation to racism and sheds light on the development of solidarity against it among people across the Pacific Ocean.

3.4.1 Discrimination against Burakumin and Resistance in the US

There was strong discrimination against the Burakumin among the broader Japanese expatriate community in the US, especially among first-generation immigrants in the pre-war era. For instance, a case of marriage discrimination occurred in Reno, Nevada, in 1923, when a man from a Buraku background married a woman without disclosing his Buraku origin. When his wife learned of his origins, she grew to hate him and filed a lawsuit for divorce. In response to the wife's claim that her Burakumin husband had threatened to kill her if she divulged his secret, a newspaper accused her of discrimination, saying, "Isn't it a pity that an innocent man be treated with such contempt even by a wife who has vowed to be with him in this life and the next?" (*Rafu Shimpo*, March 24, 1923).[10]

How did the Burakumin respond to various forms of discrimination? Many Burakumin made heartfelt appeals in newspapers about how they faced the double discrimination of anti-Japanese campaign by white Americans and the prejudice they experienced from Japanese expatriates. For example, in his letter entitled "Shin-heimin[11] no shuki" (A letter from a new commoner), Kakotsusei expressed his sympathy with the Suihei Undō ("Levelers Movement") in Japan and demanded the abolition of both discrimination against the Burakumin and the anti-Japanese movement in American society.

> But look! Now our compatriots in the US. have been branded as international outcasts, and struggle as they are forsaken by all sides. When I look at this situation and think of our people back home struggling for equality, I cannot help but be surprised and saddened by the irony and horror of the comparison. Before the subjects of our empire go abroad to demand racial equality, I cry out to them to liberate their contradictory and irrational society at home and to abolish the traditional discrimination of some of its citizens.
>
> *Nichibei Shimbun, August 12, 1924*

Japan proposed the abolition of racial discrimination during the 1919 Paris Peace Conference at the end of World War I. Kakotsusei argued that Buraku discrimination in Japan was a grave contradiction and that the Japanese were not entitled to call on international society to abolish discrimination while they avoided tackling this issue in their own backyard. For the Burakumin living in the US, the slogan of "racial equality" that had been put to international society by Japan was proof of the legitimacy of their protest against Buraku discrimination in Japanese society.

In 1922, the *Zenkoku Suiheisha* (National Levelers Association) was founded in Japan by a group of Burakumin in protest against their situation. They demanded the elimination of discriminatory practices and pushed for improvements in their social standing and living conditions. Haruji Tahara (1900–1973) was one of the Burakumin who had emigrated from Japan to the US, while studying at Waseda University, Tahara was involved in student activism under the wing of socialists. In 1923, after his graduation from university, he joined his older sister, who had emigrated to the US. He studied journalism at Missouri State University while helping his sister with farming (Koshōji 2004; Tahara 1973).

In a number of essays on life in America he contributed to a Japanese magazine, he stated that none of Burakumin in the US had disclosed their family origin in fear of discrimination (Tahara 1924b). He believed that discrimination against Burakumin in Japanese society had the same roots as racial discrimination in white American society and lamented as follows, "I'm a new commoner in Japan. I'm a new commoner called Jap in the US where I'm doubly excluded." Furthermore, Tahara revealed his disappointment with American society, "It is shallow and shameful to see America as a Christian country or a land of freedom. Marx definitely did not think of Japanese workers in the US or black workers when he said, 'Workers of the world. Unite!' His theory was all about the white man and limited to white people" (Tahara 1924a).

After graduation, Tahara worked for the local newspaper *Colorado Shimbun* and became aware of the activity of Marcus Garvey, who led the Black Liberation Movement and had a strong influence on African Americans. In 1928, Tahara headed for New York shortly before his return to Japan. He had hoped to meet Garvey and exchange views as minorities subjected to the same racial discrimination in American society but was unable to do so as Garvey was being held in detention due to a government crackdown on the movement at the time. Nonetheless, Tahara addressed Garvey's fellow activists and called for solidarity between Black and Japanese (Tahara 1929).

Upon returning to Japan, Tahara joined the National Levelers Movement and worked extensively as a Diet member in the pre- and post-World War II periods. He was a passionate advocate of Japanese-language teaching for overseas Japanese and second- and third-generation Japanese emigrants after the war. He repeatedly asked questions in the Diet to persuade the government to allocate a budget for emigrants who lived in isolation and insecurity. Today, Tahara is remembered as a unique politician who endeavored to provide support for emigrants despite the fact that they could not bring him votes (Yamamoto 2014: 39–44).

Tahara's efforts to connect anti-discrimination social movements with support for emigrants were based on his empathy for those who shared his background and solidarity with those who experienced discrimination. When we look at the transnational historical experience of people who traveled across the Pacific, Tahara cuts a particularly brilliant figure as a social activist and politician.

Another leading figure among Burakumin emigrants to the US, Mamoru Okamura from Yamaguchi prefecture, became the instigator of the Levelers

Movement in the Japanese community in Hawai'i. In 1930, he published a pamphlet entitled *Aku inshū wo zetsumetuseyo* (Eradicate evil customs and practices) that highlighted the severity of the discrimination against Burakumin in the local community. He wrote about instances of discrimination, including discriminatory remarks exchanged between children as well as marriage discrimination, which pointed to the presence of a large Burakumin population in Hawai'i and the extreme discrimination they faced. In his arguments, he put forward the idea that Buraku discrimination was racism, protesting, "Japan emphasized racial equality to the world through Ambassador Makino in the Peace Conference at the end of the world war some time ago. How can the nation step out on the world stage again when it hasn't been able to achieve the liberation of its three-million Buraku people among its own people today?" (Tsurushima 1987: 112). Although it is unclear what activities he was able to organize in the name of the Levelers Movement, it is worth noting the existence of these Buraku activists in the US mainland and Hawai'i.

3.4.2 Anti-Racism in the Japanese Expatriate Community in the US

The Japanese expatriate community that discriminated against Buraku minorities was itself a minority group looked down upon as ignorant and uncivilized savages by white-centric American society. Japanese community leaders were outraged by the discrimination and persecution they were receiving from American society and began to protest against racism. In doing so, they acknowledged the Buraku issue in Japan and in their own community as a serious problem that could not be ignored. Japanese-language newspapers in early-twentieth-century American society published numerous reports on shifts in the Japanese government's Buraku policy and on the activities of the Buraku liberation movement conducted by Zenkoku Suiheisha.

Let us consider an example from the *Rafu Shimpo*, a Japanese-language newspaper published in Los Angeles. In August 1918 during World War I, when the Japanese government decided to send troops to Siberia to intervene in the Russian Revolution, rice merchants, anticipating a sharp rise in the price of rice, were reluctant to sell, and food riots broke out all over Japan in protest (Rice Riots of 1918). On its front page, the *Rafu Shimpo*, published a special dispatch from Tokyo stating that the first riot broke out in a Buraku in Toyama prefecture (11 August). The report that the Burakumin had started the rice riots was also published in Japanese domestic newspapers (Fujino 1988). However, the *Rafu Shimpo* criticized policy-makers and the wealthy who suddenly launched relief work, claiming that the riots would "grow into a huge and irreparable problem unless they change their mindset," and defended those at the bottom of the social scale by stating, "It is obvious that they have come to the stage where they are prepared to resort to violence in order to survive; This trend is terrifying but inevitable" (20 August).

Press articles on the Buraku issue were not limited to sections on political or social news. Yūshio Wagai's novel, *Kien* (Serendipity) (March–July 1918), and Shinto Numata's play, *Shin heimin no ko* (A new commoner's child) (April 1925), were published in the literary section of newspapers. Both works use storylines that are similar to Tōson Shimazaki's *Hakai* (The broken commandment) (1906) and explore the Burakumin's fear of their family background being exposed to people around them and their psychological struggle in overcoming that fear. Numata's story, in particular, is set in America and shows the author's criticism of the discrimination against the Burakumin that exists in Japanese society in the US and his appeal to overcome it. We can surmise that these works were published in newspapers because the oppressed psychology of Burakumin under discriminatory circumstances was a subject matter that attracted the sympathy of many people.

Public opinion against Buraku discrimination was formed in the Japanese expatriate community in the US through these press reports. In March 1923, a non-Burakumin made offensive remarks when he witnessed a Burakumin bridal procession in Nara prefecture. This incident resulted in a violent clash between Zenkoku Suiheisha and the Kokusui Kai (Patriotic Society), an ultra-nationalist organization of outlaw groups that had been mustered by the government involving around 2,500 people, many of whom were injured. (Suikoku Incident). The *Nichibei Shimbun* (Japanese American News) published an editorial entitled "Nihon no kaikyū sen to byōdō taigū, Zaibei no nihonjin ha eta no taigū nari" (Class war and equal treatment in Japan: Eta treatment for Japanese in the US) in relation to this major riot and argued, "Just as it is justifiable for Japanese nationals in the US to demand an end to discriminatory treatment, it is also justifiable for Burakumin to receive equal treatment in Japan; Japan should implement racial equality on its own land before calling out racial equality to the world" (March 21, 1923).

The newspaper immediately began to receive letters about the incident from its readers. Kōhasei compared his own situation as an expatriate Japanese to that of the Burakumin and denounced discrimination by saying, "When I think of the current circumstances of my compatriots living [in the US], I am deeply saddened by the string of blatant and tragic events" ("Nara no tokushu Buraku, Hana no naka no nejiro" [Buraku community in Nara: Sanctuary among flowers], *Nichibei Shimbun*, March 23, 1923). Noboru Shōsonmon called for people to protest against discrimination.

> We expatriate Japanese are subjected to humiliating treatment just as the Eta people are back home. …, it would be foolish for us to continue to endure this treatment until racial prejudice disappears from the minds of all Americans.
>
> When we think of the atrocious situation in Japan in which a contemptuous attitude towards the Eta still exists over half a century after the imperial order of equality for all classes was issued, anyone who expects that

Americans' racial prejudice will be replaced with racial equality within the next fifty or hundred years is as foolish as someone who believes that the sun will go cold in one hundred years from now.

"Eta sōdō to zaibei nihonjin" [The Eta riot and Japanese in the US.],
Nichibei Shimbun, March 28, 1923

In this way, Japanese residents in the US who were subjected to racial discrimination in a white-dominated society during this time expressed their sympathy as they saw a strong resemblance between their fate and the situation of the Burakumin in Japan and perceived it as a social problem that could not be ignored. We can also confirm that they engaged in a protest in solidarity with their fellow targets of discrimination. As Tokunaga shows in Chapter 4 of this volume, in response to the increasing exclusion of Mexicans in the US during the latter half of the 1920s, the Japanese, who had long experienced the same kind of ostracism, used their newspapers to voice dissent and argue against such actions. Thus, solidarity across borders and racial barriers for fighting discrimination was important in the history of this period.

3.4.3 The Search for Solidarity: Japanese US Residents and the Burakumin

Sympathy for the Burakumin in their home country, who shared the same predicament can be found in the social activism of Japanese residents in the US. Following the report of the Suikoku Incident, the Portland Nihonjin Kai (Japanese Society of Portland) received a proposal from a committee member named Yamada at a meeting in April 1923 "to adopt a resolution to abolish the name 'special class Burakumin' and give them equal treatment, and to deliver the resolution to the people" (*Shin sekai* [New world], April 23, 1923). In July 1924, after the passing of the Immigration Act, the Taiheiyō Engan Nihonjin Kinen Kyōkai (Pacific Coast Japanese Memorial Church) in San Diego called for the launch of a campaign to abolish discrimination against the Buraku and other racial groups as follows:

> Our fellow countrymen in the US. have long been suffering from discriminatory treatment based on racism. [...] On reflection, the past treatment of the so-called special communities and other races in Japan is the most deplorable betrayal of what we stand for. On this occasion, it is the wish of we the Nihon Kirisuto Kyōkai [Japanese Christian Church] that a new movement to redress these evil customs and practices will be initiated.
>
> *Rafu Shimpo*, July 21, 1924

Most prominent among this activism were the activities of Motomitsu Matsumoto, who lived in Los Angeles. In order to denounce the Buraku discrimination in Japan and the anti-Japanese movement in the US, Matsumoto formed the Hokubei

Suiheisha (North American Levelers Association) and published a weekly newspaper named *Suihei Jihō* (Leveler Times).[12] In his message in the first edition, Matsumoto urged readers to not allow Japan's racial equality proposal to the League of Nations to become an empty request, stating, "Japan and the Japanese people must wake up and make a major change to their social system, otherwise what authority is there to shout to the world about racial equality?" ("Sekai ni uzumaku warera no suihei undo (Kashū hōjin no sengen)" [Our levelers movement causing a stir in the world (a declaration by Japanese in California)], *Jiyū* [Liberty] No. 3, October 1924). Matsumoto's North American Levelers Association accepted the Burakumin and non-Burakumin sympathizers equally and its activities were also reported in Hawai'i (*Rafu Shimpo*, February 14, 1925; *Hawaii Hochi*, March 9, 1925).

Matsumoto's call for solidarity was welcomed as the "internationalization of the levelers movement" by the Levelers Movement in Japan, which commented, "We must say that the promotion of the Levelers Movement on the eastern and western shores of the Pacific form a curious contrast, or rather, a heartbreaking contrast" ("Suihei undo no sekaika" [Internationalization of the levelers movement] *Dōai* [Comradery], No. 18, December 1924). Upon reading the article, Shōken Hirano, a founding member of the Zenkoku Suiheisha, lamented the Buraku discrimination that existed in the Japanese expatriate community in the USS. and appealed to his overseas compatriots as follows:

> When we think of how people of our ilk feel while living and working among Japanese immigrants in America four thousand miles away, our heart feels heavy, and our eyes are filled with tears. [...] We say to our brothers in California: Do not hold back; tell the world loud and clear about the truth of this unreasonable discrimination, persecution and oppression. For the sake of humanity, win liberty, equality and happiness on a foreign land. We do so not for personal happiness; we do so for the happiness of all mankind.
>
> *"Kisha mōsu" [A reporter's opinion], Jiyū, No. 3, October 1924*

In Japan, Zenkoku Suiheisha took various actions such as appeals and protests to the international community in relation to Japan's proposal for the worldwide abolition of racial discrimination as well as the anti-Japanese campaign in the US. They did so because they perceived Buraku discrimination in Japan as part of the racism that was tormenting minorities all over the world and considered their activity as a social movement advocating anti-racism.

Zenkoku Suiheisha had called for solidarity with the oppressed peoples of the world at its national conferences every year since its founding in 1922. Today, the prevailing view is to regard Buraku discrimination as a feudal legacy of Japanese society, and it may not be common to see it as racism. Yet, a considerable number of early activists in this social movement described themselves as descendants of ancient, conquered peoples, oppressed by racism like other ethnic minorities around the world. For example, participants shouted, "Eta minzoku banzai" (A cheer for the Eta nation) at the closing of Zenkoku

Suiheisha's inaugural conference and at a subsequent council meeting in 1922 (Sekiguchi 2010).

In September 1923, a message from the chairman of the Zenkoku Suiheisha Central Committee appealing to the proletariat all over the world for solidarity was published in a US magazine *The Nation*. Its opening statement read, "After one thousand years of oppression and humiliation in the far eastern corner of the globe, we the Buraku community appeal to all of you who are bravely fighting in the last class struggle [in history] against blood-thirsty capitalism!" The message went on to pronounce, "We the Burakumin are the Jews of Japan. If there is any difference between the Jewish people and our people, we are probably more miserable than they are in most cases. Our community is a relic of slavery in ancient Japan and has been deprived of any freedom of choice in employment to this day. We have been forced to work in limited industries such as animal slaughtering, tanning and footwear repairs"[13] (Haessler 1923).

Zenkoku Suiheisha convened an interim national conference in the Tennōji municipal hall in Osaka on 27 April 1924, shortly after the passage of the anti-Japanese immigration law in the US (Hirohata 2005). It was the only interim national conference in the history of the association and was reportedly attended by around 1,300 people to denounce the legislation. The day before the conference, association officials visited Cyrus Woods, the US Ambassador to Japan in Tokyo and delivered a written resolution. The meeting received extensive coverage, including a photograph, in newspapers. The conference adopted a resolution to dispatch a "manifesto" to the Hyeongpyeong Movement in Korea, the Swaraj India, and the Shanghai Greater Asia Association, as well as a message of solidarity to the Universal Esperanto Association.

Six activists among the top echelons of Zenkoku Suiheisha delivered speeches at the conference. One of them, Rikizō Izuno, argued as follows:

> Our cries are outpourings of the blood and tears we have shed in our experience of oppression for so many years. For we of the Levelers Association, [our protest against the US is] a righteous course of action for the benefit of vulnerable minority peoples in the world.

The situation in which Japanese are being ostracized by Americans bears a strong resemblance to the way we have been oppressed in Japan. Our movement is not for imperialism or militarism; it is a march toward the liberation of oppressed peoples.

Izuno's argument defined the activity of Zenkoku Suiheisha as a racial rights movement and resonated with the circumstance of the Japanese community in the US[14] (Nakagawa 2006).

Burakumin activity that emphasized anti-racism subsequently ceased to be the mainstream of collective social movements. Zenkoku Suiheisha's proposal for solidarity with other minority social movements across national borders also came to a halt in the 1930s. While there were multiple reasons for this, such as government crackdowns, one major factor was the growing Marxist understanding of history that became dominant from the mid-1920s and led to an eventual rejection of understanding Buraku discrimination through the lens of racism. The post-war Buraku liberation movement, and the paradigm of research into the history of the Levelers Movement that started in close connection with it, were both influenced and led by Marxist historical materialism. For this reason, the fact that Zenkoku Suiheisha convened an interim national conference and protested against the passage of the anti-immigrant law in the US has been rejected and forgotten as an action based on fallacies such as "nationalism" and "Asianism."

Despite the failure of this endeavor to make substantial progress, it should not diminish the significance of Zenkoku Suiheisha's aspiration to form solidarity with fellow minorities who were suffering under the same circumstances and to speak out collectively against the racist rule at the time. Today, this activity warrants a fresh examination from the viewpoint of global history and a reassessment of its significance.

3.5 Conclusion

In this chapter, it became clear that through the exchange of people, information and money, strong ties were formed between their hometowns in Japan and the communities to which they moved, and that these ties played a role in supporting their survival in American society. It was this social network that enabled them to survive and overcome the discrimination that persisted in their new home.

When the anti-Japanese Immigration Act was promulgated in 1924, the Japanese residents in American society had no choice but to conform to the white-centric social norms of the US in order to maintain their livelihood (Azuma 2005). Calls for solidarity between minority groups and protest against racism faded away in the Japanese expatriate community in the US.

Japanese Consul-General Kaname Wakasugi told Japanese expatriates in the US that the only way to escape discrimination was through the betterment of the race and argued that for this reason, they should not become an isolated uncivilized group like the Burakumin. He said, "[The Japanese community should] be guided to think and act scientifically because it will face the same fate as the Chinese if it continues to increase its resemblance to a Buraku that is isolated from American society; particularly in view of the recent trends in the US, where national unity and racial consciousness have become increasingly intense since the end of the world war, we must make a great effort to secure the future interests of our people" ("Nihonjin kai ni taisuru ryōjikan no taido" [The attitude of the Japanese consulate toward the Japanese association], *Rafu Shimpo*, 10 February 1925.) He stressed the need for the assimilation of Japanese residents into white-American society and criticized the Burakumin as a symbol of those who deviated from this path.

The movement against anti-Japanese discrimination in American society often used the Burakumin as a metaphor for ignorant and uncivilized outcasts in their demand for equal treatment on the grounds that the Japanese were a civilized race. In other words, the underlying logic here justifies discrimination against "uncivilized" races. Even those Japanese who demonstrated sympathy and solidarity with the Burakumin in Japan did not, whether consciously or unconsciously, make the discrimination against the Burakumin in their own Japanese American community an issue. From this perspective, it can be said that the Japanese in American society was a group with a contradiction between advocating anti-racism externally and being unable to overcome discrimination against Burakumin internally.

These transnational emigrants were forced to create their own mode of existence in a new order of governance in a strange land. Much like other minority groups, the Japanese described in this chapter who came to America at the beginning of the twentieth century, and especially the Burakumin among them had no choice but to work, live and manage their social identity in the face of a host of difficulties. As with the hibakusha in Japanese American society described in Uchino's chapter, it was difficult for the Burakumin, as a minority within the Japanese community, to raise their voices against discrimination. In the hierarchicalized, asymmetrical power relationships where white American society treated the Japanese as an inferior race and the Japanese community treated the Burakumin likewise, it took a long time for people to face the pain of discrimination and rise up in protest.

When we consider the racial nationalism in the US that was built and sustained by people's acceptance of discrimination, the fact that solidarity and resistance to domination were explored across the Pacific, however briefly, is significant. It is interesting to reflect on the alternative histories that people have sought, even if their dreams have failed. In today's world, where globalization is accelerating and the movement of people has become the norm, there is an ever-increasing need to retell and develop this dream.

Notes

1 When we look at the general trend of emigration from *buraku* communities, we find that during the Meiji era, the main destinations were Hokkaido, Hawai'i and North America. Emigration shifted to South America and Manchuria in the Taisho and pre-war Showa periods. Studies on migrants in Hokkaido include a broad discussion by Ōyabu (2005, 2006) and detailed case studies by Ōyabu (2007) and Shiraishi (2009). For emigration to Manchuria, case studies by Maekawa (2005) and Takahashi (1995) are informative. It is difficult to get a concrete picture of emigration to Brazil as no studies are available except an analysis of local newspaper reports by Noguchi (2013). There is little prior research on migration to other regions.

2 The following are the sources Geiger lists in footnote 42 of Chapter 3 in her book: Shigesaki Ninomiya (1933), Regine Mathias (1993), Midge Michiko Ayukawa (1996), Toshiji Sasaki (1987), and Mikiso Hane (1982). Ninomiya's statement in a short footnote of his work, "In the coal mines of Fukuoka prefecture, the majority of miners are the eta people" (Ninomiya, 1933:113), misquoted Sadaki Takahashi's 1924 influential book *Tokushu Buraku Issen-nen-shi* (A 1,000-year history of Burkau hamlet). Takahashi mentions that "in the northern coal mining region of Fukuoka Prefecture, most of the laborers engaged in *such jobs as classifying coal and carrying coal*

with minecarts were Burakumin" (Takahashi, 1924: 208, emphasis added). Mathias states that when the demand for workers increased in northern Kyushu, "*A significant minority* belonged to the discriminated minority of the Burakumin" in the late nineteenth century northern Kyushu (Mathias, 1993: 106, emphasis added), but not "*a significant percentage* of the those working in the coal mines in northern Kyushu during the second half of the nineteenth century" (Geiger 2011: 228, emphasis added). In addition, Ayukawa and Sasaki's studies contain no references to Burakumin being among the Japanese coal miners who migrated to America (Ayukawa 1996; Sasaki 1987). Geiger's quote of Hane, "even some mining companies in Japan refused to employ 'eta' until well into the Meiji period because they believed they would pollute the miners; others forced them to wash in water that was first used to wash horses" does not support her claim (Hane 1982: 242). Consequently, none of the citations listed in Geiger's note 42 support her assertions.

Furthermore, as the scholar of Buraku history Tatsuo Aso points out, Burakumin did not by any means occupy the mainstream of coal mining labor: "After the Meiji twenties [Meiji 20=1887], many burakumin started working in jobs related to coal mining. They first entered the industry as workers who transported coals. As time went on, they were displaced when railroads came to service the large mines, and they were forced to work in medium and small mines" (Aso 1989: 177). And Nagasue mentions that "such mines [large mines that discriminatorily refused to hire Burakumin] on the other hand relied heavily on Buraku labour for the subcontracting of transporting coal outside their mines, as well as classifying coals (mainly done by women)." Geiger conflates coal mining—the mainstream occupation in mines—with the entirety of all jobs related to the mining industry, many of which were relatively marginalized. Thus, her unsubstantiated statement claiming that Burakumin constituted the majority of coal mining labourers and the cover photograph of her book both create a distorted impression of those Japanese migrants to North America whose roots lie in Buraku identity or the mining industry.

3 Even in the field of history, which is based on empirical evidence, the role of testimony is being re-evaluated as a way to compensate for the lack of data and to ensure the credibility of the data, especially in the fields of popular history, social history and the history of events, where data are difficult to preserve. The interview-based survey in this chapter was conducted at the Florin Buddhist Church and other venues in May 2008 with four second-generation and three third-generation Japanese Americans who grew up in Sacramento suburbs. Most of the interviewees were gathered by asking for help from an organizer of a community activity group with Japanese Americans among its core members. At the start of each interview session, I informed them that the purpose of the survey was to ascertain the lifestyle of the Japanese residents and racial prejudices they were subjected to by mainstream society in Florin before World War II, as well as the lives and whereabouts of emigrants from Fukui prefecture there. The interviewees were asked to state their name, age, and personal history and answer some prepared questions before moving on to an unstructured question and answer segment where I tailored questions according to the participants' responses. On several occasions, when they told me their recollections before or after the interview session or while traveling in a car, I also recorded these as valuable testimonies. Although the interviews were conducted through an interpreter, most of the second-generation subjects understood my Japanese and often responded in Japanese. The names of the people who appear in this chapter are all pseudonyms for privacy reasons.

4 One case of emigration to the town of Honbetsu in Oyochi, Hokkaido, in this period involved a group settlement of a few dozen Buraku people from the Tanaka hamlet in Kyoto. Despite the investment of hard-won funds and exhausting efforts by the settlers, the group settlement came to a brutal end after a series of tragedies, including desertions and suicides, had led to its effective collapse and the departure of a majority of settlers (Ōyabu 2007; Shiraishi 2009).

5 Ito made the following statement about emigrants from the Fukui buraku communities: "There was information that a majority of emigrants from Fukui prefecture were Burakumin while the population of former Fukui residents accounted for only 1.9 percent of the total Japanese population in southern California in 1920. Indeed, the informant was unable to name any non-buraku family from Fukui prefecture to the researcher" (Ito 1966: 205).

6 The conversion was made using the "Nihon en kahei kachi keisanki" (Japanese yen currency value calculator) website at https://yaruzou.net/hprice/hprice-calc.html (accessed July 2020).

7 In 1919, a stone monument was erected to honor Yozaemon Yoshioka's contributions to regional development through the project for emigration to North America. See Sekiguchi (2020) for a detailed history of emigration to America from "X" hamlet.

8 In this chapter, xxxx is used in their names to protect the privacy of the individuals.

9 The four interviewees were "E" (born in 1931), "T" (1926), "W" (1920), and "G" (1930). The interview was conducted in English through an interpreter. I was impressed by the dignified manner in which they all pronounced that the discrimination of the past was clearly wrong. I would like to express my gratitude to them for providing me with their valuable testimonies.

10 The Hoover Institution at Stanford University has an extensive collection of Japanese-language newspapers published in Hawai'i and North America during this period. I have utilized information from its digitized version which is available online as The Hoji Shinbun Digital Collection (https://hojishinbun.hoover.org/).

11 A euphemism for Burakumin. It is used by a Burakumin here in a self-deprecatory manner.

12 See Hirohata (2008) for a discussion of Matsumoto's activities. I have not seen this newspaper, but I can confirm that the publication continued until around April 1927 before it was renamed *The Showa Times* (*Rafu Shimpo*, April 10, 1927).

13 See Komai (2008) for the full text of the manifesto.

14 The arguments made by the activists on the day, including those of other speakers, can be summarized in four points: (1) Exclusion of Japanese people in the US is the same as discrimination against Buraku people in Japan, the US; (2) Suiheisha must raise a voice in protest as politicians are unreliable; (3) since exclusion of Japanese is exclusion of Asians, all Asians should unite to fight against it; and (4) Japan should reduce its dependence on the US in international trade and acquire new markets.

References

Aso, Tatsuo. 1989. "Chikuhō ni okeru Hisabetsuburaku to sekitan [Buraku and Coal in Chikuho]." In *Fukuoka no Burakukaihōshi, jō: Burakukaihōshi* kenkyūsōsho 3 [Buraku Liberation History in Fukuoka, Vol. I: Buraku Liberation History Research Series 3], edited by Fukuoka Burakushi Kenkyūkai, 144–177. Fukuoka: Fukuoka Burakushi Kenkyūkai.

Ayukawa, Midge Michiko. 1996. *Creating and Recreating Community: Hiroshima and Canada, 1891–1941*, UMI Dissertation Services.

Azuma, Eiichirō. 2005. *Between Two Empires: Race, History, and Transnationalism in Japanese America*. New York: Oxford University Press.

Chūō yūwa jigyō kyōkai. 1939. *Yūwajigyō kankei chiku jinkō/shigen sonota no gaikyō* [Summary of Population, Resources, etc. in Areas Related to the Reconciliation Project], 99–103. Tokyo: Chūō yūwa jigyō kyōkai.

Fujino, Yutaka. 1984. *Dōwa gyōsei no rekishi* [History of Dōwa Administration]. Osaka: Kaihō shuppansha.

Fujino, Yutaka, Takashi Tokunaga, and Midori Kurokawa. 1988. *Kome sōdō to hisabetsu Buraku* [Rice Riots and the Burakumin]. Tokyo: Yūzankaku.

Geiger, Andrea. 2011. *Subverting Exclusion: Transpacific Encounters with Race, Caste, and Borders, 1885–1928*. New Haven: Yale University Press.

Haessler, Gertrude. 1923. "Japan's Untouchables" *The Nation* 117 (3035): 249–251.

Hane, Mikiso. 1982. *Peasants, Rebels, and Outcastes: The Underside of Modern Japan*. New York: Pantheon.

Higuchi, Naoto. 2002. "Kokusai imin no soshikiteki kiban [Organizational Basis of International Migration: Toward a Comparative Analysis of Migration Systems]." *Soshioroji* 47 (2): 55–71.

Hirohata, Kenji. 2005. "Hainichi iminhō to suiheisha [Anti-Japanese Immigration Law and Suiheisha]." *Suiheisha hakubutsukan kenkyū kiyō* 7: 1–50.

Hirohata, Kenji. 2008. "Kanada kara suiheisha ni todoita rentai messēji [Solidarity Message Sent to Suiheisha from Canada]." *Kaihō kenkyū* 21: 151–174.

Ikeo, Masayori. 2008. "Fukuiken kindai Burakushi [Modern History of the Buraku in Fukui Prefecture]." *Suiheisha hakubutsukan kenkyū kiyō* 10: 1–29.

Ito, Hiroshi. 1966. "Japan's Outcastes in the United States." In *Japan's Invisible Race: Caste in Culture and Personality*, edited by George De Vos and Hiroshi Wagatsuma, 200–221. Berkeley: University of California Press.

Kodama, Masaaki. 1992. *Nihon iminshi kenkyū josetsu* [Introduction to the Study of Japanese Migration History]. Hiroshima: Keisuisha.

Komai, Tadayuki. 2008. "Kaigai de hōjirareta Buraku mondai to suihei undō [Buraku Issues and the Suihei Movement as Reported Overseas]." *Suiheisha hakubutsukan kenkyū kiyō* 10: 31–61.

Koshōji, Toshiyasu. 2004. "Buraku kaihō to shakaishugi: Tahara Haruji wo chūshin ni [Buraku Liberation and Socialism with a Focus on Haruji Tahara]." In *Shakaishugi no seiki* [The Century of Socialism], edited by Naoki Kumano and Haruhiko Hoshino, 101–129. Kyoto: Hōristu bunkasha.

Maekawa, Osamu. 2005. "Hyōgoken seiwakai to manshū imin [The Hyogo Seiwa-kai and Migrants to Manchuria]." *Kiyō* 1: 119–138.

Mathias, Regine. 1993. "Female Labor in the Japanese Coal-Mining Industry." In *Japanese Woman Working*, edited by Janet Hunter, 98–121. New York: Routledge.

Minegishi, Kentarō. 1986. Hōkoku Kinsei niokeru Buraku sabetsu no Shūzoku teki Keitai Buraku sabetsu no Yōtai to Sono Henka. (Report: Customary Forms of Anti-Buraku Discrimination in Early Modern Japan—The Changing State of Anti-Buraku Discrimination), Buraku Studies no. 87.

Miyatake, Toshimasa. 2007. *"Hakai" hyakunen monogatari* [Hundred Years of "The Broken Commandment"]. Osaka: Kaihō shuppansha.

Nagasue, Toshio. 1986. "Chikuhō ni okeru Buraku no keisei: Sekitankōgyō to Burakumondai [The Formation of a Buraku Hamlet in Chikuhō: Coal Mining Industry and Buraku Issues]." In *Ronsyū Kindai Buraku mondai* [Anthology: Modern Buraku Issues], edited by Buraku Kaihō Kenkyūjo, 86–110. Osaka: kaihō shuppansha.

Nakagawa, Nozomu. 2006 "Tokuhi dai 7508 gō, Taibei mondai suiheisha taikai no ken [Strictly Confidential No. 7508, Policy Towards the United States Concerning the General Meeting of Suiheisha]." In *Senzenki keisatsu kankei shiryōshū, Dai 1 kan* [Collection of Materials Related to Prewar Police, Volume 1], edited by Kenji Hirohata, 283–288. Tokyo: Fuji shuppan (originally published in 1924).

Nichibei Shimbunsha. 1922. *Zaibei nihonjin jinmei jiten* [Biographical Dictionary of Japanese Names in the US]. San Francisco: Nichibei Shimbunsha.

Ninomiya, Shigeaki. 1933. "An Inquiry Concerning the Origin, Development, and Present Situation of the Eta in Relation to the History of Social Class in Japan," *The Transactions of The Asiatic Society of Japan*, Second Series, Vol. X, 47–154. Tokyo: Kyo Bun Kwan.

Noguchi, Michihiko. 2013. "Burajiru Nikkei koronia to Buraku mondai: Buraku mondai wa donoyōni katararetekitanoka? [Buraku-Mondai and Japanese Colonies Brazil]." *Jinken mondai kenkyū* 12 (13): 97–110.

Ōfu, Nippōsha. 1909. *Sakuramento-heigen nihonjin taisei ichiran* [The State of Affairs of the Japanese in Sacramento Valley]. no. 2. Sacramento: Ōfu Nippōsha.

Ōyabu, Takeshi. 2005. "Meiji/Taishōki hisabetsu Buraku e no Hokkaido ijū shōrei/jigyō ni tsuite no shiron 1 [Study on the Incentives and Projects for the Burakumin to Migrate to Hokkaido in the Meiji and Taisho Periods 1]." *Buraku kaihō shi/Fukuoka* 120: 17–42.

Ōyabu, Takeshi. 2006. "Meiji/Taishōki hisabetsu Buraku e no Hokkaido ijū shōrei/jigyō ni tsuite no shiron 2 [Study on the Incentives and Projects for the Burakumin to Migrate to Hokkaido in the Meiji and Taisho Periods 2]." *Buraku kaihō shi/Fukuoka* 121: 52–90.

Ōyabu, Takeshi. 2007. "Hokkaido ijū to Ueda Shizuichi [Migration to Hokkaido and Ueda Shizuichi]." *Osaka jinken hakubutsukan kiyō* 10: 67–108.

Passin, Herbart and Eiichi Isomura. 1984. "Sengo 'dōwagyōsei' shi wo iku senryōka no Buraku mondai [History of Postwar Dōwa Administration: Buraku Issues under U.S. Occupation]." *Buraku kaihō* 211: 98–109.

Sasaki, Toshiji. 1987. "Yunion Tanko: Dainiji Keiyaku Imin." In *Kikan Pan* 7 (December 1987), edited by Kazuo Itō, Yōsuke Miyashita, Heika Amano, Shūdan Ahō, 170–195. Tokyo: PMC shuppan.

Sekiguchi, Hiroshi. 2010. "Suihei undō ni okeru 'minzoku' to 'mibun' ['Ethnicity' and 'Status' in Suiheisha]." In *Kindai Nihon no "tasha" to mukiau* [Confronting the "Other" in Modern Japan], edited by Midori Kurokawa, 93–122. Osaka: Kaihō shuppansha.

Sekiguchi, Hiroshi. 2019. "Tōchi Tekunorojī no Gurōbaru na Tenkai to 'Jinshuka' no Rensa [The Global Development of Governance Technology and Chains of 'Racialization.'" *Jinbun Gakuhō* 114: 73–95.

Sekiguchi, Hiroshi. 2020. "Amerika ni watatta hisabetsuburakumin [Buraku People Who Cross to the United States]." In *Kantaiheiyō chiiki no idō to jinshu: tōchi kara kanri e.sōguu kara rentai e.* [Pacific Rim Migration and Race: from Governance to Management, from Encounter to Collaboration], edited by Akio Tanabe, Yasuko Takezawa, Ryūichi Narita, 103–146. Kyoto: Kyoto University Press.

Shiraishi, Masaaki. 2009. "Tanaka shinyū yogakkō to Ueda Shizuichi [Best Friend Night School in Tanaka and Ueda Shizuichi]." *Jinken mondai kenkyū, extra number*: 9–40.

Tahara, Shiro, Albert Menda, and Hidemo Kodama. 1974. "Florin Buddhist Church Sacramento, California." In *Buddhist Churches of America*, 283–287. Chicago: Nobart.

Tahara, Haruji. 1924a. "Nijū ni haiseki sareru mure yori [From a Doubly-excluded Group]." *Dōai* 15: 8–10.

Tahara, Haruji. 1924b "Jibun ni ifu kotoba [Words to Myself]." *Dōai* 17: 19–21.

Tahara, Haruji. 1929. "Harlem no nanokakan: Amerika kokujin undō no chūshinchi inshōki [Seven Days in Harlem: Impressions of the Center of the American Black Movement]." *Yūwajigyō kenkyū* 4: 91–96.

Tahara, Haruji. 1973. *Tahara Haruji jiden* [Autobiography of Haruji Tahara]. Matsudo: Tanaka Hideaki.

Takahashi, Sadaki. 1924. *Tokushu Buraku Issen-nen-shi* [A One Thousand Years History of Burkau Hamlet]. Kyoto: Kōseikaku.

Takahashi, Yukiharu. 1995. *Zetsubō no iminshi* [A History of Migration in Despair]. Tokyo: Mainichi shinbunsha.

Takezawa, Yasuko. 2005. "Transcending the Western Paradigm of the Idea of Race," *The Japanese Journal of American Studies* 16: 5–30.

Takezawa, Yasuko. 2020. "Racialization and Discourses of 'Privileges' in the Middle Ages: Jews, 'Gypsies,' and Kawaramono." *Ethnic and Racial Studies* 43 (16): 193–210.

Tsurushima, Setsurei. 1987. "Hawai nihonjin imin no Buraku sabetsu to suihei undō [Buraku Discrimination and Suihei Movement Among Japanese Migrants to Hawai'i]." *Buraku kaihō* 269: 92–113.

Unsigned. 1913. *Fukuiken Mikatagun Mimimuraze* [Mimimura, Mikata County, Fukui Prefecture]. Mimimura: Unknown publisher.

Unsigned. 1985. "Fukui tsūshin [Fukui Newsletter]." *Shakai kaizen kōdō* [Road to Social Improvement] 17. (In *Kindai Burakushi shiryō shūsei, Dai 9 kan, Suiheisha sōritsu zenya I* [Collection of Modern Buraku History, Vol. 9, The Eve of Establishment of Suiheisha I], edited by Yoshikazu Akisada and Natsumi Ōgushi, 84. Tokyo: Sanichi shobō. (Originally published in 1920).

Unsigned. 1986. "Saimin Buraku kaizen kyōgikai sokkiroku [Shorthand Record of Committee for Improvement of Impoverished Buraku]." In *Kindai Burakushi shiryō shūsei, Dai 5 kan, Yūwa undō no tenkai I* [Collection of Modern Buraku History, Vol. 5, Development of Reconciliation Movements I], edited by Yoshikazu Akisada and Natsumi Ōgushi, 79–161. Tokyo: Sanichi shobō (originally published in 1912).

Unsigned. 2014. *Mihama bunka sōsho IX: Mimimurashi* [Mihama Cultural Series IX: History of Mimimura]. Mihamachō: Mihama bunka sōsho kankōkai (originally compiled in 1923).

Yamamoto, Saeri. 2014. *Sengo no kokka to Nihongo kyōiku* [The Postwar State and Japanese Language Education]. Tokyo: Kuroshio shuppan.

Yanagita, Kunio. 1944. *Hi-no-Mukashi (Ancient Fires)*. Tokyo: Jitsugyō no Nihon sha.

4

FROM ANTI-JAPANESE TO ANTI-MEXICAN

Linkages of Racialization Experiences in 1920s California

Yu Tokunaga

4.1 Introduction

Located on the West Coast of the US, California is the site of the most in-depth encounters and interactions between Asian and Latin American immigrants and their descendants in any region across the country.[1] Southern California faces East Asia across the Pacific Ocean and Latin America across the US-Mexico border. In the first half of the twentieth century, Japanese and Mexican immigrants encountered each other in Southern California, merging their respective histories of immigration into transnational US history. At the same time, many immigrant groups in California have faced an intense history of racial discrimination. More importantly for this study, Japanese and Mexicans did not experience racial discrimination in isolation, but their experiences were mutually linked while being affected by anti-Black racism with deep roots in US history. Further, racism in California entailed a logic unique to the history of the Pacific Rim region in that it developed through linkages between the racialization experiences of Japanese and Mexican immigrants. Highlighting this transpacific aspect of racism in California, this chapter analyzes debates about the so-called "Mexican Problem" and explores the mechanism of racialization in Southern California, particularly Los Angeles County, in the late 1920s.

In the 1920s, US immigration policy strongly reflected racism based on Anglo-Saxon white supremacy. Debates surrounding the "Mexican Problem" between those who wanted to exclude Mexican immigrants and those who wanted to maintain the inflow of Mexican workers reached a crescendo in the late 1920s, with California as a central battleground. Many scholars have studied anti-Mexican racism in the 1920s US in detail. David G. Gutiérrez has carefully analyzed debates over Mexican immigration in Congress and the industrial

DOI: 10.4324/9781003266396-5

circle and argued that not only exclusionists but also advocates for the use of Mexican labor employed racist explanations about Mexicans (Gutiérrez 1995, 44–56). Matt Garcia mentions that agribusiness leaders resorted to anti-Black sentiment ingrained in US society and emphasized the necessity of accepting Mexican workers because they were not Black (Garcia 2001, 89–106). Yuki Oda has also highlighted the relationship between anti-Mexican nativism and the reinforcement of border control in the late 1920s (Oda 2006). Previous studies, however, focus mainly on anti-Mexican exclusionists, leaving room for further research on advocates for the use of Mexican labor.

Natalia Molina argues that there are limits to understanding racism by looking at a single minority group in a racially diverse society such as California. Molina highlights the impact of the anti-Japanese movement on anti-Mexican nativism based on "a theoretical understanding of race as socially constructed in relational ways, that is, in correspondence to other groups" (Molina 2014, 3, 53–58). This chapter, by adopting Molina's approach, reconsiders the process in which racism developed in California by analyzing the still understudied racism of pro-Mexican labor advocates. It focuses on industrial and agribusiness organizations that advocated for unrestricted Mexican labor in the 1920s in order to understand the logic of the racism hidden within their advocacy, particularly in terms of the relationship between this logic and anti-Japanese racism. It also explores how Mexican and Japanese immigrants perceived the nationwide debates over the "Mexican Problem." This study is the first attempt to explore the "Mexican Problem" in a trilingual approach using English, Spanish, and Japanese documents.

There has yet to be a comprehensive study of the racism embraced by pro-Mexican labor advocates through comparison with the racialization experience of Japanese immigrants, another major nonwhite minority group in California. Drawing on the Los Angeles Chamber of Commerce documents, records of congressional hearings, and ethnic Mexican and Japanese newspapers, this chapter attempts to capture the moments that clearly demonstrate linkages between the racialization experiences of Japanese and Mexican immigrants, especially when both groups of people were referenced within the same documents. How can we understand, beyond the binary framework between the majority and a minority, the processes in which racism developed in an immigrant society where various groups of people from different ethnoracial backgrounds live? In addition, how has racism ingrained in such an immigrant society affected immigrant groups? As Yasuko Takezawa explains by employing the concept of "minor transnationalism" in Chapter 10, these questions point to important themes of our own time when increasing numbers of people move beyond national borders. Taking this into consideration, this chapter regards Southern California as a major site of transpacific history and demonstrates the process in which the racialization experience of one immigrant group became linked with that of another immigrant group.[2]

4.2 Immigration Policy and Racism against Japanese and Mexicans

Los Angeles County saw a rapid increase in Japanese and Mexican immigrants in the early decades of the twentieth century. According to the 1920 census, the county population reached 936,455, including 19,911 ethnic Japanese (counted as a racial group) and 33,644 Mexicans (counted as foreign-born whites). If we include the Mexican population as a nonwhite population along with African Americans, Asians, and Native Americans, ethnic Japanese and Mexican-born people combined formed 70.8 percent of the county's nonwhite population. By 1930, the county population had reached 2.2 million and embraced the largest ethnic Japanese and Mexican communities in the mainland US (US Census Bureau 1922, 1932).[3] These immigrant groups interacted with each other as Japanese farmers hired many Mexican farmworkers, thus making considerable contributions to agriculture, one of the region's main industries, until the Pacific War. Modernization policies implemented in both Japan and Mexico in the late nineteenth century resulted in the increase of Japanese and Mexican immigrants to the US. After the Meiji Restoration of 1868, many Japanese peasants faced economic difficulties due to the imposition of a land tax and the plummeting price of rice caused by the deflation policy following the Satsuma Rebellion or Seinan War, a rebellion of former samurai. As Katsuya Hirano mentions in chapter 2, the same economic difficulties led to the involuntary migration and mobilization of prison labor in Hokkaidō, too. On the other side of the Pacific Ocean, Porfirio Díaz implemented a land policy that facilitated large-scale land ownership and pushed many Mexican peasants off their land during his long-term rule from 1876 to 1910, while the Mexican Revolution (1910–1920) brought political and economic unrest which severely crippled their livelihood (Camarillo 1990, 32–35; Ichioka 1988, 42–43, 50–56; Kodama 1992, 11–18; Sánchez 1993, 17–37).

Meanwhile, California's economy developed dramatically from the mid-nineteenth century when gold mines were discovered, and the state would later absorb immigrant workers from Japan and Mexico attracted by the booming economy. Observing the economic growth of California in 1880, Karl Marx wrote, "California is very important for me because nowhere else has the upheaval most shamelessly caused by capitalist centralization taken place with such speed" (McWilliams 2000, 56). The dramatic transformation of California continued into the twentieth century and made the state a major site of global capitalism that encompassed Japanese and Mexican immigrant workers. Although the US Census Bureau declared the demise of the frontier in 1890, from the perspective of an immigration history that foregrounds human migration, California became a new frontier of globalization from around 1890, in which immigrants from Asia and Latin America began to have deeper interactions with each other. At the same time, we should remember that this rapid development of global capitalism in California took place after American settlers subjugated and committed massacres against Native American tribes who had lived there for centuries. While each tribe had different experiences of population decline, the Indian population in California dramatically decreased from about 150,000 in 1846 to 25,000 or 30,000 in 1865 (Madley 2008, 304). White business leaders hired nonwhite foreign workers as an indispensable and, in principle, deportable labor force for the development of California's economy while neglecting the historical presence of Native Americans. Hirano explains that Meiji Japan learned from the American Western expansion and that Japanese policy-makers regarded Japanese prisoners as an expendable but indispensable labor force for Hokkaidō's settler-colonial development while deeming the Ainu as a "vanishing race." That is, even after the westward territorial expansion of the US came to an end in North America, the Western expansion of the racial ideology that justified American settler colonialism did not stop there and moved across the Pacific Ocean to serve Japanese settler colonialism in Hokkaidō. California's transformation was part of this historical trajectory of settler colonialism in the Pacific world.

During the period between 1880 and 1921, the US received more than 23.5 million immigrants (Kraut 2001, 2–3). While the vast majority were from Eastern and Southern Europe, large numbers of Japanese and Mexicans also arrived in the US during this period. The massive influx of immigrants stimulated the development of racial nationalism centered on the Anglo-Saxon population and led to the enactment of the 1924 Immigration Act, which strictly restricted or prohibited the entry of newly arriving immigrants. The 1924 Act introduced national origins quotas to considerably lower the number of Eastern and Southern European immigrants, who were not Anglo-Saxon, and prohibited Japanese immigration altogether by banning the immigration of "alien[s] ineligible to citizenship." The Japanese were legally deemed as aliens ineligible for naturalization due to the Naturalization Act of 1790 that allowed only "free white person[s]" to become American citizens and the Supreme Court decision on the Ozawa case of 1922 that confirmed the ineligibility of Japanese to naturalize. As a result, the 1924 Act was denounced as the Japanese Exclusion Act or *hainichi imin hō* in the Japanese immigrant community in the US as well as in Japan across the Pacific Ocean (Daniels 1968; Gerstle 2001; Higham 1981; Iino 2000; Kurashige 2016; Minohara 2002; tenBroek et al. 1970; Yamakura 1994). The anti-Japanese movement developed first in California but had become a national issue by the 1920s. Since the beginning of the twentieth century, anti-Japanese campaigns expanded in California due to various local and international factors, as white workers became antagonistic toward the increase of competitive Japanese workers, and Japan's victory over Russia in 1905 reinforced the fear of the yellow peril (Minohara 2006, 12–16). Growing anti-Japanese campaigns resulted in the California Alien Land Law of 1920, which prohibited the purchase and lease of land by Japanese at the local level while empowering anti-Japanese voices in their push to enact the so-called Japanese Exclusion Act.

On the other hand, the 1924 Immigration Act did not impose national origins quotas on the countries of the Western hemisphere largely because of the economic dependency of the US Southwest, including California, on Mexican laborers. This, however, did not mean that Mexicans could escape the negative impact of the law. The law institutionalized the procedures related to passports and visas with which immigrants needed to enter the US legally and imposed the payment of ten dollars (approximately 151 dollars in 2020) per person to obtain a visa. In addition to the complication of immigration procedures, the US government established the Border Patrol to tighten border control in the same year. The year 1924 marked a turning point in US immigration history, as the US-Mexico border emerged more clearly as a political wall that hampered the free movement of people (Hernández 2010; Ngai 2004, 19; Sánchez 1993, 57, 60–62).

From the mid-1920s, the presence of Mexican immigrants became more salient in the Southwest. As Mexicans became the major target of American nativism against non-European immigrants, the "Mexican Problem" replaced the "Japanese Problem" as a central theme of immigration policy. For instance, the precursor of the California Joint Immigration Committee, an anti-Mexican nativist organization established a year after the enactment of the 1924 Immigration Act, was the Japanese Exclusion League, which played a central role in the anti-Japanese movement (Daniels 1968, 91; Molina 2014, 53–58; tenBroek et al. 1970, 55). Anti-Mexican exclusionists called for a ban on Mexican immigration, who they regarded as a racial and economic threat to the white-centered US society. Congressman from Texas John C. Box was a prominent nativist and emphasized the need for immigration restrictions to prevent "American racial stock from further degradation or change through mongrelization." Box proposed a bill to apply a national origins quota on Mexican immigrants, and in 1928 Congress held hearings on the so-called Box bill (Gutiérrez 1995, 51–56; Hoffman 1974, 26–30).

The surge of anti-Mexican campaigns produced a sense of crisis among California agribusinesses. By 1929, California had become the largest producer of vegetables and fruits in the Southwest, and the state shipping volume accounted for 40 percent of the nation's total (Sánchez 1993, 19). Agribusiness leaders in California believed that Mexican labor was the only way to maintain and develop local agriculture, and thus its exclusion meant the devastation of California's farmland (Figure 4.1). When the "Mexican Problem" began to be discussed in Congress, agribusiness leaders needed to explain the necessity and safeness of Mexican immigrant labor through publicity activities. In 1928, the California Development Association, a major agribusiness organization, compiled a report titled *Survey of the Mexican Labor Problem in California* and submitted it to the congressional hearings. In the survey, the California Development Association emphasized the importance of California agriculture and refuted the exclusionist characterization of Mexicans as a racial and economic threat (California Development Association 1928, 1, 17; US Congress 1928, 295).

Agribusiness advocates for the use of Mexican labor described Mexicans as disposable and racially and economically safe workers compared to other foreigners to counter exclusionists' contrary characterization of Mexicans. Both advocates and exclusionists similarly looked down on Mexicans as an inferior

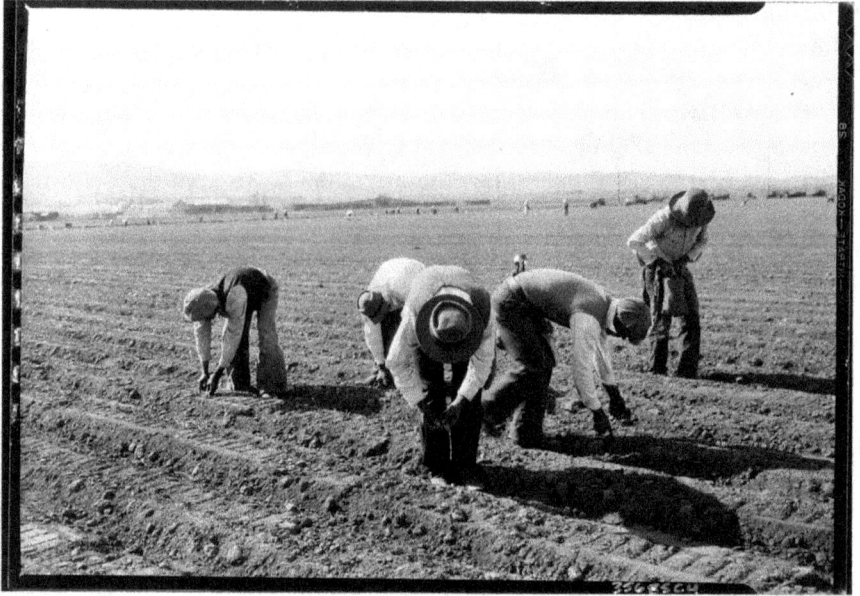

FIGURE 4.1 Mexican Farmworkers in the San Fernando Valley in 1930

Source: California Historical Society Collection, 1860–1960, University of Southern California. Libraries (1930)

race, although the former attempted to replace the alarming image presented by nativists with a comforting image of innocuous Mexicans.

4.3 *Redirecting Racism*: From "Dangerous" Japanese to "Safe" Mexicans

Although pro-Mexican labor advocates provided the positive image of "safe" Mexicans to counter the anti-Mexican argument, their approach had weaknesses because it represented an argument in almost complete opposition to that of nativists. In this standoff between rival sides of the "Mexican Problem," George P. Clements, manager of the Agricultural Department of the Los Angeles Chamber of Commerce, introduced a novel and more adroit way of explaining the necessity of Mexican labor. The Los Angeles Chamber of Commerce played a central role in the development of the Southern Californian economy. At the time, Clements served as the organization's spokesman regarding agribusiness, including the issues related to Japanese and Mexican immigrants working for local agriculture, and boasted "that I thoroughly understand the Mexican people" (California Development Association 1928, 11; Clements 1931; University of California, Los Angeles, Special Collections 1997). While previous studies have mentioned Clements, this chapter highlights his discourse as a premise to explore the linkages of racialization experiences of Japanese and Mexican immigrants (Garcia 2001, 101–103; Gutiérrez 1995, 48–49).

Clements refuted the exclusionist argument that deemed Mexicans as a racial and economic threat by contesting, "We [Americans] class Mexicans as Mexicans. We do not take into consideration that there are three distinct types of Mexican population." According to Clements, Mexicans could be categorized into three distinct types: the first group was the ruling class (about half a million), the second "cholo" or "greaser" in Mexican urban areas (about 1.5 million), and the third "peon[s]" or Mexican farmers in the countryside (about 13 million). Clements emphasized that "a large cholo or greaser class" were "criminal Mexicans" who "should never be permitted to cross the border" and then contrasted them with the safe "Mexican peon." He argued, "[the Mexican peon] are clean, healthy and frugal ... still strongly tribal in their recognition of responsibility," and "It is this class of people who come to the United States to sell their labor for American dollars in the hope of bettering their own conditions" when they would return to Mexico (Clements 1927).

In Clements's categorization, Mexican immigrants were "Mexican peons" with desirable characteristics as foreign workers. In this way, Clements doubled down on the safety of rural Mexican workers in contrast with "cholos" and "greasers" residing in Mexican urban areas by ascribing his argument retroactively to the fact that Mexican immigrants had already come to the US. In his theory, having come to the US was proof of their safety. In chapter 2, Katsuya Hirano argues that the capitalistic inclusion of labor entails a process that differentiates useful labor from useless labor based on racial disparity. Clements racialized Mexican immigrants as useful laborers who were primitive, safe, and industrious by comparing them with "criminal," and thus useless, Mexican urban dwellers.

The Mexican population, however, could not be categorized into Clements' three types. The Mexican majority were mestizos, racially mixed people as the result of Spanish colonization of Mexico since the sixteenth century.[4] Historian George J. Sánchez contends that "[t]he source of most of the emigration to the United States was clearly mestizo/Indian" while carefully explaining that "exactly where 'Indian' ended and 'mestizo' began was as often a function of social definition as it was a boundary set by genetic configuration" (Sánchez 1993, 29–30). In 1929, even Secretary of Labor James Davis, who was in favor of imposing a quota on Mexican immigrants, admitted the difficulty of categorizing the Mexican population, explaining, "The Mexican people are of such a mixed stock [that] it would be impossible for the most learned and experienced ethnologist or anthropologist to classify or determine their racial origin" (Molina 2014, 54–55).

For the sake of California agribusiness, the California Development Association submitted to congressional hearings their survey on Mexican labor that adopted Clements's theory of "three distinct types of Mexican population." In this sense, capitalism and racism together created a new way of categorizing Mexicans in California. This categorization had a discursive role to redirect the eyes of anti-Mexican exclusionists to "cholos" or "greasers" in Mexican urban areas who were deemed "criminal" and thus the most dangerous. By categorizing Mexicans in this way, pro-Mexican labor advocates attempted to distract exclusionist eyes from Mexicans who would come across the border and prove that Mexican immigrants were racially safe. This was the primary defining logic of the racism embraced by advocates represented by people like Clements, a logic that can be called *redirecting racism.*

Importantly, *redirecting racism* became incorporated into pro-Mexican labor advocacy by taking in the experience of Japanese immigrants. In October 1929, shortly after the California Development Association publicized their survey, the Western Divisional Meeting of the US Chamber of Commerce was held in Ogden, Utah. In the meeting, Ralph H. Taylor, the executive secretary of the agribusiness organization called the California Agricultural Legislative Committee, gave a speech entitled "Mexican vs. American Farm Labor" (Taylor 1929). The California Agricultural Legislative Committee, founded in 1919 as an industry organization for California farmers, actively gathered information and secured the passage of agricultural legislation. By 1929, the committee had represented twenty-nine agricultural cooperatives with allegedly about seventy thousand individual members. Taylor served as a spokesperson who advocated for the capitalist development of local agriculture since he was almost the only person in charge of drafting the committee's agricultural policies and thus influential in a wide variety of scenes related to agricultural legislation in the 1920s (Chambers 1952, 54). His central role as a voice of local agribusiness was clear, as evident in his summoning to congressional hearings in 1928 to read a letter from Clements and submit the recently completed survey of the California Development Association (US Congress 1928, 295–329).

In his speech "Mexican vs. American Farm Labor," Taylor insisted that "beyond question the Mexican is the safest source of common labor" until other solutions would be provided, arguing that white Americans could not bear agricultural work in the Southwest as they "have been educated away from hard, physical labor" and that other nonwhite workers were neither suitable nor available for this type of labor. In his argument, Taylor compared Mexicans with Japanese immigrants as a major example of other foreign workers as he added a subtitle "Mexican vs. Japanese etc." to his speech manuscript. Some anti-Mexican exclusionists claimed that Mexicans would compete and take jobs away from white Americans like the Japanese did. Taylor squarely refuted such an exclusionist claim and said, "the Japanese presented an entirely different problem than does the Mexican" for two reasons. First, there was no substitute labor when Mexican workers were excluded from farmland. In contrast, when the 1924 Immigration Act banned Japanese immigration, "there would still remain other sources of common labor to fall back on; viz., the Mexican." Second, unlike Japanese workers who hoped to move up the social ladder to become farmers, "the Mexican did not possess [such] characteristics which made the Japanese objectionable" (Taylor 1929).

The California Alien Land Law of 1920, a product of the anti-Japanese movement in California, prohibited the Japanese deemed as "aliens ineligible to citizenship" from purchasing and leasing land. Nevertheless, many Japanese immigrant farmers continued to farm the lands they leased under the names of their US-born children, who had US citizenship. The Japanese farmland considerably expanded from 62,047 acres in 1905 to 458,056 acres in 1920, although the California Alien Land Law and the economic depression after World War I shrunk the scale of Japanese farms. In 1935, Japanese farmers maintained as large as 307,966 acres of farmland, which was then the economic foundation of the Japanese immigrant community. In Los Angeles County in 1929, Japanese farms were in 605 places totaling 33,730 acres, 98 percent of which were leased lands (Minamikashū Nihonjin Shichijūnenshi Kankō Iinkai 1960, 19, 56, 491; Yagasaki 1993, 51–53). Japanese immigrant farmworkers tended to become tenant farmers to improve their livelihood in California, and many thought it more profitable to lease lands than to purchase them (Iwata 1992, 400). Given this situation, Taylor explained the characteristics of Japanese immigrants, contending, "[I]t is generally understood and believed that the Japanese, while he may come over here as a common laborer to begin with, sooner or later, and usually sooner, becomes ambitious to go into the farming business for himself, and, therefore, purchases land, if a citizen, himself, or if not, in the name of his American born son." As a result, "That not only takes him out of the field as a common laborer, but makes him very definitely a competitor of the American farmer, where his standards of living make it impossible for an American producer to compete with him." Taylor continued his explanation by comparing the Japanese with Mexicans, as he emphasized, "The Mexican, on the other hand, does not have this ambition, and, consequently, is a far more desirable person to have around, for he will work for other people. He is not ambitious, either to own land, to control local, state or national policies, or to displace Americans in those spheres of life where they want to work" (Taylor 1929).

The comparison between Japanese and Mexicans appeared in Taylor's testimony at the congressional hearings in 1928. When Box suggested the potential danger of Japanese immigrants' upward mobility, asking, "[The Japanese] got higher and then got more frightful to you?" Taylor responded to Box and explained, "I am glad you brought up that question. The Mexican has been in our country as long as the Japanese have been there or longer and the Mexican has not shown the characteristics that made it desirable to stop the Japanese from coming in" and then "[t]he Mexican may be easily deported if he does not behave himself properly here" unlike the Japanese (US Congress 1928, 311). Taylor's argument was another example of *redirecting racism* embraced by pro-Mexican labor advocacy as it redirected the attention of anti-Mexican exclusionists from Mexican immigrants to more "frightful" Japanese and thus racialized Mexican immigrants as a relatively safe group of foreigners. As advocates' *redirecting racism* deftly accepted exclusionists' nativism by employing the pre-1924 rhetoric of "dangerous Japanese" developed through the anti-Japanese movement, their advocacy had the uniqueness and dexterity of the racism developed in the immigrant society in the Pacific Coast region where large numbers of the Japanese and Mexicans settled and faced racial discrimination.

Furthermore, behind *redirecting racism* existed anti-Black racism that had persisted since before the independence of the republic and became even stronger nationwide, including in the West Coast, in the 1920s.[5] During World War I, the Ku Klux Klan was reestablished as eugenics came to the forefront of government policy, and in the 1920s, their membership reached five million across the country including the Los Angeles area. In addition, in the 1920s Los Angeles witnessed rapid urban development as well as a heightened sense of anti-Black discrimination because of the increase of African Americans and white Americans from the South, the former fleeing from racism and the latter seeking better opportunities in the West while retaining anti-Black racism (Flamming 2005, 196–200; Painter 2010, 318–325). On the other hand, if Mexican workers were banned from entering the US, alternative nonwhite groups of labor were African Americans, Puerto Ricans, and Filipinos. Puerto Rico and the Philippines became US territories as the result of the Spanish–American War of 1898. In the 1920s, Puerto Ricans had US citizenship, and Filipinos were legally regarded as US nationals, although they did not have US citizenship (Chan 1991, 16–18; Gonzalez 2000, 60–63). Puerto Rico was in the western hemisphere free from the restrictions imposed by the 1924 Immigration Act. Unlike other Asians, who were prohibited from immigration, Filipinos were able to move from the Philippines to the mainland US because of their unique legal status. In his speech in Utah, Taylor raised the question, "The American Negro we all know. Are we Americans, with a full knowledge of the very serious racial problems which he has brought to the South and other parts of America, willing deliberately to spread him over the rest of the country in ever increasing numbers?" Then Taylor continued, "The task of returning negroes is much greater and almost impossible in the case of Porto Ricans and Filipinos" but "The Mexican can be [deported]" and concluded, "beyond question the Mexican is the safest source of common labor" (Taylor 1929).

Around the same time, Clements gave a talk on Mexican farmworkers at a meeting with citrus producers. Rejecting the idea of employing Black workers as out of the question, he said, "I need [to] say nothing [about Black workers]." Regarding Puerto Ricans, he despised them as a mixed-race "Portuguese nigger" and refused the use of Puerto Rican workers, explaining, "They are American citizens and cannot be deported" and "Biologically, they are a serious menace" (Clements 1929). Moreover, Clements's anti-Black racism overlapped with his discriminatory view against the Japanese. Around 1921 when the anti-Japanese movement was active, Clements problematized the situation in which Japanese immigrants turned from workers to tenant farmers and became influential in the production and circulation of several crops such as strawberries. Further, Clements considered that Japanese farms should eventually be handed over to European or American farmers, and, embracing the emerging yellow peril discourse, insisted that "[t]he real struggle is for yellow world supremacy." Even when he mentioned Mexicans and the Chinese as temporary workers, Clements revealed his strong anti-Black racism, saying, "The negro is out of the question and we do not want him." Clements deemed the increase of Japanese farmers as a racial and economic threat and explained, "Our Japanese question is very similar at the present moment to what the Negro question was at the end of the Civil

War with this exception—we were responsible for the Negro, since we brought him here against his will, but the Japanese came to America of his own free will." And he emphasized, "We would like to enucleate this Japanese wart before it becomes a malignant cancer as the Negro is in the South today" (Clements 1921, ca. 1921). As detailed above, Clements supported the exclusion of Japanese immigrants by deeming them as dangerous as Black Americans. Following the enactment of the 1924 Act, in contrast, he advocated for the importation of Mexican workers by describing them as a safe source of labor in comparison with Black workers. Historically deep-rooted anti-Black racism, therefore, formed the basis of the agribusiness discourse regarding foreign workers in 1920s California, no matter which group they discussed, Japanese or Mexican workers.

California's agribusiness leaders forged a strategy to advocate for Mexican labor by comparing Mexican immigrants with other racial and immigrant minority groups instead of presenting them through a simple dichotomy between a Mexican minority and a white majority. As shown in this chapter, the histories of racial discrimination experienced by African Americans, Japanese, and Mexicans converged through the movements and interactions of people in Southern California and clearly linked with one another in the discourses and activities of Taylor and Clements. Moreover, we can further deepen our historical understanding of this linkage by considering the treatment of Irish immigrants and their descendants in the nineteenth century. Initially treated as an inferior race and as like African Americans by many native-born white Americans on the East Coast, by the end of the Civil War, they had gained the status of white Americans and then became a major force of anti-Chinese agitation in the West Coast with their newly acquired whiteness (Painter 2010, 132–150, 201–211; Roediger 2007, 3–17, 133–163; Takaki 1998, 115). By the 1870s, the anti-Chinese movement had spread not only among labor unions but also among the press and politicians in California. Those who called for Chinese exclusion equated Chinese workers with former Black slaves and thus regarded them as antithetical to a nation of republicanism and free labor. Further, the anti-Chinese movement provided a sociopolitical basis for the anti-Japanese movement of the twentieth century. Anti-Asian leaders included Irish Americans such as Denis Kearney, a naturalized citizen and leader of the anti-Chinese Workingmen's Party, and James D. Phelan, a prominent anti-Japanese politician, who played major roles in promoting the anti-Asian movement in California (Daniels 1968, 16–30; Kurashige 2016, 86–138; Saxton 1995, 113–137; Takaki 1998, 99–112). Therefore, the racialization of Mexicans in late 1920s California was a historical product of the century-long experiences of various ethnoracial groups in changing racial relations across the US, which connected the history of racism in the Atlantic world with that of the Pacific world.

In other words, anti-Black discrimination strengthened by the white majority across the country and anti-Asian discrimination first launched in the American West came together to generate the undercurrent of nativism in the 1920s, which helped provide the basis for pro-Mexican labor advocacy that racialized

Mexicans coming from the South of the border as "safe" and "deportable" foreign workers. The racism embraced by the pro-Mexican labor advocates in the late 1920s entailed a unique logic that emerged in a transpacific process as manifested in the linkage of the racialization experiences of Mexican and Japanese immigrants coming respectively from the South and the West. At the same time, the way agribusiness leaders utilized their racist explanations of Mexican workers reveals a process in which the transatlantic history that racialized Black Americans through the slave trade and slavery merged with the transpacific history of Mexicans and Japanese immigrants in California in the first decades of the twentieth century.

4.4 Mexican Immigrant Ambivalence and Japanese Immigrant Empathy

After analyzing how white agribusiness leaders racialized Mexicans in the historical context of 1920s California, it is important to explore how Mexican and Japanese immigrants perceived contemporary debates about the "Mexican Problem." The analysis of ethnic Mexican and Japanese newspapers in relation to other primary sources is fruitful in understanding the Mexican and Japanese immigrant communities, as historian Sally M. Miller writes, "The press is the best primary source for an understanding of the world of non-English-speaking groups in the United States" (Miller 1987, xii). In fact, Mexican and Japanese immigrants in Los Angeles County acquired the latest news, in Spanish or Japanese, respectively, regarding their home countries, international affairs related to their own countries, and local incidents and accidents in the Los Angeles immigrant society.

Spanish language newspapers played an important role in providing Mexican immigrants with national and international news in the Los Angeles region when the booming economy attracted and depended on an increasing number of Mexicans. One of the major papers for Mexican immigrants in 1920s Los Angeles was *La Opinión*, which is still widely read today. The founder Ignacio Lozano left Mexico when the revolution began in 1910 and moved to San Antonio, Texas, where he succeeded in selling his Spanish-language newspaper *La Prensa*. Later, Lozano found an economic opportunity in rapidly developing Los Angeles and launched *La Opinión* in 1926 for Mexican residents, which reached a circulation of about 12,000 copies in 1928 (Lozano 1993; Tovares 2009, 481). *La Opinión* was, therefore, a newly emerging ethnic paper that began publication at the very time that anti-Mexican nativism was surging in the Los Angeles region.

The publication and growing audience of the new Spanish-language press reflected the establishment by the 1920s of Mexican immigrant communities in Los Angeles County and larger Southern California. While anti-Mexican exclusionists warned that the settlement of Mexicans would pose a racial threat to the white-centered American society, pro-Mexican labor advocates countered by arguing that Mexicans would not settle because of their "migratory character." According to historian Camille Guerin-Gonzalez, 40–60 percent of Mexican immigrants were permanent residents in the US in the 1920s, although most of them returned to Mexico at some point in time (California Development Association 1928, 10; Camarillo 1990, 43; Garcia 2001, 88; Guerin-Gonzalez 1994, 45).

As the "Mexican Problem" began to be discussed in Congress in the late 1920s, *La Opinión* carefully observed the debates. It reported that Box presented letters from citizens that claimed, "If California has the right of restricting immigration from Japan and China, Texas has the same right to restrict the Mexican immigration" and "the American Culture will disappear eventually as the United States is falling as Greece and Rome fell." And the press also wrote that the Chamber of Commerce of the US had sent a letter to the House Committee on Immigration and Naturalization emphasizing that it was inappropriate to place a national origins quota on Mexican immigrants and any restriction on Mexicans could have severe consequences for agribusiness in the US Southwest (*La Opinión* 1928a, 1928b).[6]

Nevertheless, their coverage did not squarely oppose the restriction on Mexican immigration but rather reflected an ambivalent feeling among Mexican residents in Los Angeles regarding the "Mexican Problem."[7] *La Opinión* explained, in the editorial in March 1928, that exclusionists deemed Mexicans as "an inferior race," workers that could bear "minimum salaries," and "prone to sickness and crime." On the other hand, pro-Mexican labor advocates, whom the paper regarded as the majority, "scorn the prejudice, use the concrete data and, based on it, we prove to be strong and intelligent for work and obedient to the laws." And it stated, "We will obtain a moral triumph because the defeat of the 'quota' will mean that in the balance of discussions the plate of our utility weighs more than that of our harm to the American life." But it called for more efforts from the Mexican immigrant community, writing that this "triumph" is nothing but "an encouragement" and that "the difficulties that confront the [Mexican] *colonia* have to be overcome by the *colonia* itself." Then the editorial showed a concern that the influx of newly arriving Mexicans would have a negative impact on the employment of Mexican residents already residing in the US and concluded, "Don't confuse the moral triumph with the economic prosperity" (*La Opinión* 1928c). In short, *La Opinión*, based on their observation of the debates in the congressional hearings, kept in step with exclusionists by taking an unfavorable attitude toward the entry of newly arriving Mexicans while protesting against the exclusionists' racial discrimination toward Mexicans. It thus clearly displayed the real concerns and ambivalent feelings of Mexican residents in the US who understood the nativism of their host country as well as their compatriots' strong desire to migrate to the US.

La Opinión also published articles on the history of immigration restrictions in the US. In May 1929, Arthur E. Cook, a former assistant staff of the Labor Department with expertise in immigration policy, contributed a series of four consecutive articles. His first article, entitled "The evolutionary process of the law of immigration," explained about the tax on the importation of slaves imposed by the Constitution, the Chinese Exclusion Act of 1882 that excluded Chinese immigrants who "became competitors of the white race," and immigration policies implemented in the 1920s. While Cook did not write about

Japanese exclusion by the 1924 Immigration Act, he mentioned, "In the United States, there are grave injustices against foreigners, because its people think that [foreigners] are more criminal than American citizens," and backed this up with statistics that showed that those who committed crimes and faced deportation in 1928 were only 1,211 out of approximately six million foreign residents in the US (*La Opinión* 1929). Through such articles in *La Opinión*, Mexican residents in the US had chances to deepen their understanding of US immigration policy in relation to other ethnoracial minorities including Asian immigrants.

Meanwhile, Japanese immigrants, whose compatriots had already been banned from immigration, were also carefully observing the nationwide debates about the "Mexican Problem." In January 1929, the *Rafu Shimpo*, a major Japanese immigrant newspaper, ran an editorial entitled "Bill to restrict Mexican immigrants" and, just like *La Opinión*, explained the opinions of both anti-Mexican exclusionists and pro-Mexican labor advocates on the Box bill. While exclusionists regarded Mexicans as "generally illiterate, poor in moral concepts, and often subjected to the law enforcement," and further argued that "[b]ecause their standard of life is extremely low, it is not favorable [to accept Mexican immigrants] from a viewpoint of improving society. And they take jobs from white workers because they bear low wages." On the other hand, advocates represented by capitalists and agribusiness leaders emphasized, "It is not difficult to anticipate an economic depression since [without Mexican workers] railroad constructions, road building, and other works in farms will face grave obstacles as we are increasingly aware of the shortage of ordinary workers today" (*Rafu Shimpo* 1929a). The *Rafu Shimpo*'s coverage reflects how Japanese immigrants carefully observed the debates on the "Mexican Problem" as a nonwhite immigrant group residing in the same immigrant society with Mexicans and that they understood the major points of the debates rather accurately.

Although the Box bill was repealed in Congress, anti-Mexican campaigns persisted in California so that a bill to ban the employment of foreign workers in public works that targeted Mexicans was proposed at the California State Legislature. In April 1929, in an editorial entitled "Foreign workers exclusion act," the *Rafu Shimpo* strongly criticized the anti-Mexican movement in California and showed sympathy toward Mexican immigrants. Countering exclusionists' claim that Mexicans took jobs from Americans, the *Rafu Shimpo* offered a totally opposite viewpoint by contending that any law to ban the employment of Mexican workers would "take jobs away from Mexicans and bring difficulties to their lives as a result, and could eventually generate a negative impact on US-Mexico diplomatic relations." Then it touched upon the fact that the Box bill's call for placing a national origins quota on Mexicans had been repealed without being sent to the floor and asserted that the foreign workers exclusion bill in the State Legislature "goes against the tide" (*Rafu Shimpo* 1929b). While anti-Mexican sentiment remained strong in California, as the *Rafu Shimpo* anticipated, the bill was voted down in the lower house of the California State Legislature (*San Bernardino Sun* 1929a).[8]

More important for the present study are the two rationales the *Rafu Shimpo* editorial presented regarding the relationship between Japanese and Mexican

FIGURE 4.2   Celery Field in the Venice Area in 1927. Japanese Farmers Were the Major Producer of Celery in Los Angele County and Employed Many Mexican Workers

Source: California Historical Society Collection, 1860–1960, University of Southern California. Libraries (1927)

immigrants. First, it argued that the exclusion of Mexican immigrants could affect the lives of Japanese immigrant farmers who relied on Mexican farmworkers (Figure 4.2). Second, the bill to exclude Mexican workers bitterly reminded Japanese immigrants of the 1924 Immigration Act that had targeted them for exclusion. Since the Mexican exclusion law could have reduced the number of Mexican workers in public construction works and agriculture if enacted, the editorial explained, "We should prepare for not a little damage not only to builders and contractors but also to our fellow compatriot farmers" (*Rafu Shimpo* 1929b). It was impossible for Japanese farmers in Los Angeles County to manage their farms without employing Mexican farmworkers because Japanese immigration had already been prohibited (Minamikashū Nihonjin Shichijūnenshi Kankō Iinkai 1960, 53). After mentioning Japanese farmers' dependency on Mexican farmworkers, the editor of *Rafu Shimpo* deplored the situation in which some state legislators were promoting anti-Mexican campaigns under the influence of white labor organizations. Further, the editor showed understanding and empathy to Mexicans based on his own experience of being discriminated against in California by stating, "I cannot help but feel full sympathy for Mexican workers because I have experienced the same situation in the past" (*Rafu Shimpo* 1929b). In chapter 3, Hiroshi Sekiguchi mentions that Japanese immigrants reflected empathetically on their experiences of being discriminated in the US as something like the experiences of Burakumin discriminated in Japan and expressed such a feeling externally, although they maintained a self-contradictory attitude since they could not overcome discrimination against the Burakumin internally. As shown in this chapter, in the 1920s, Japanese immigrants felt empathy not only toward Burakumin in Japan but also toward Mexicans living along with them in Los Angeles. This can be understood as part of the historical process in which different groups of people in the immigrant society shared similar experiences of being racially and economically oppressed; some of them thus realized the possibility of solidarity while recognizing their mutual differences. In the case of Los Angeles Japanese, their experience as a racially discriminated minority developed a transpacific imagination and empathy for other minority groups in the US and Japan.

At the beginning of the twentieth century, most Japanese residents in California were farmworkers and shared a similar class position with Mexicans. For instance, Japanese and Mexican farmworkers went on strike together during the Oxnard Strike in 1903. Although their bi-national coalition was successful in the strike, the American Federation of Labor continued to reject the membership of Asian workers on the grounds that they were not white (Mexicans were legally regarded as white). The notion of whiteness eventually led to the dissolution of Mexican-Japanese labor solidarity (Almaguer 2009, 183–204). Japanese immigrants, however, moved up the social ladder to become tenant farmers who hired Mexican farmworkers, and class tension between the two groups developed by the 1920s. Although some Mexican workers preferred working in Japanese farms, in the larger picture, the relationship between the two groups deteriorated and Mexican farmworkers would launch large-scale strikes against Japanese farmers in the 1930s (Cady ca. 1928, 27; Tokunaga 2022; Wollenberg 1972). In other words, the empathy shown in the *Rafu Shimpo* toward Mexicans was not one based on commonality in class but rather in the experience of being discriminated against as a racial other in the US, an experience shared by both Japanese and Mexican immigrants. While Japanese immigrants regarded Mexican immigrants as a different race in a different position in their labor-management relationship, they came to embrace cross-racial empathy as nonwhite foreigners, which was an unintended consequence of the anti-Mexican nativism of the late 1920s. The "Mexican Problem," therefore, was not only about Mexican immigrants but part of a series of debates on Mexican immigration in relation to other nonwhite groups, in which the experiences of Mexican immigrants merged with those of Japanese immigrants and helped forge cross-racial empathy.

Predicted in the *Rafu Shimpo* criticism of California's anti-Mexican bill as a policy that "goes against the tide," anti-Mexican campaigns strengthened after the enactment of the 1924 Immigration Act did not result in the application of a national origins quota on Mexican immigrants.[9] But the racist thinking that marginalized nonwhite racial minorities as undesirable aliens who could, if necessary, be excluded from the country was the very "tide" of 1920s US society. Such racist logic became visible in the Mexican Repatriation executed mainly in the 1930s. During the Great Depression, initiated by the stock market meltdown of October 1929, Mexican workers came to be seen as competitors of white American workers as well as a financial burden for American taxpayers. Reinforced anti-Mexican sentiment resulted in the massive repatriation of Mexicans, 138,519 of whom were sent back in the peak year of 1931 and presumably at least 350,000 in the decade from 1929. As the anti-Mexican voice was strong, particularly in Los Angeles, the Los Angeles County government promoted repatriation by paying traveling expenses to Mexicans leaving the US, while the Mexican government cooperated with the project in the hope that returnees could contribute to the development of the Mexican economy (Balderrama 1982, 15–35; Gutiérrez 1995, 71–74; Hoffman 1974, 83–115).

At the time, Clements expressed reluctance to support the massive repatriation of Mexicans in his correspondence within the Los Angeles Chamber of Commerce, stating that "unemployment has nothing whatsoever to do with certain types of agricultural labor." But he continued to deem Mexicans as ignorant foreigners easy to handle as he described, "These men are drawn from tribes all over Mexico, and the majority of them have no real knowledge of their own government or their governmental workings" (Clements 1931). As described previously, the pro-Mexican labor advocacy of California agribusiness represented by Clements had been racializing Mexicans as "deportable" and thus "safe" foreign workers. Although Clements expressed reluctance, the massive repatriation of Mexican immigrants eventually gave a post-factum justification to the logic of agribusiness advocates' racist explanation about Mexicans and also met the expectations of anti-Mexican exclusionists who had deemed Mexicans as a racial and economic threat.

4.5 Conclusion

This chapter has demonstrated the following two points based on an analysis of the "Mexican Problem" of the late 1920s. First, the racism embraced by pro-Mexican labor advocates represented by California agribusiness leaders was a form of *redirecting racism* that targeted and compared Mexicans with other ethnoracial minorities. The logic of their *redirecting racism* was that it diverted the attention of anti-Mexican exclusionists from Mexican immigrants to "criminal Mexicans" residing in urban areas in Mexico, more "frightful" Japanese, and Black Americans, and by doing so, racialized Mexican immigrants as a relatively safe group of foreigners. *Redirecting racism* entailed a unique logic rooted in Southern California, an important site of the Pacific Rim region because it merged the experiences of racial discrimination faced by Japanese, Mexicans, and Black Americans within the pro-Mexican labor discourses of the late 1920s, which were also intersected with the racial experiences of Irish and Chinese immigrants in the nineteenth century. Second, Japanese immigrants in Los Angeles carefully observed the debates on the "Mexican Problem" and demonstrated their understanding and empathy for Mexican immigrants based on their own experience of being racially discriminated against. Their empathy was based on the commonality between Japanese and Mexican immigrants' experiences of racialization and was rooted in the history of Southern California, where the two groups of immigrants interacted with each other in their daily lives. In California, Japanese and Mexican immigration histories converged through their experience of living in the same multiethnic society. In such a unique region, debates on the "Mexican Problem" in the late 1920s connected the history of racism in the Atlantic world with that of the Pacific world, thus generating a new form of racism whose discourse merged the racialization experiences of Japanese and Mexican immigrants. Equally important is that it helped nurture cross-racial empathy to resist racism in the white dominant society. As demonstrated in other chapters of this book, we can better understand the transpacific mechanism of racialization and resistance against it by thinking beyond the simple dichotomy between the majority and one minority group and looking at the experiences of various minority groups around and within the Pacific Ocean.

Racism and racialization of nonwhite minorities can occur in both cases of exclusion and inclusion in US immigration history. At the same time, an ethnoracially diverse immigrant society can nurture cross-racial empathy among different groups who have experienced racial discrimination. This process regarding racism and empathy against racism teaches an important lesson to people not only in the US but also in other countries such as Japan. Before World War II, for example, Japanese workers migrated abroad to places including California, while many non-Japanese workers arrived at the Japanese archipelago mainly from the colonized Korean peninsula. In the post-war period, the number of foreign residents in Japan increased, especially from the 1990s, and reached 2.73 million in 2018. Their countries of origin are increasingly diverse (Ministry of Justice of Japan 2019). In 2019, Japan's amended immigration control law came into effect and began to accept more foreign workers. Although the coronavirus pandemic temporarily stopped the global flow of migrant workers, it remains meaningful to observe how racism and racial nationalism would play out in increasingly diverse societies around the world, how different marginalized groups could forge a sense of empathy among each other, and how waves of empathy can spread across society and help form bonds of solidarity that not only connect minority groups but also engage those in the majority. To think deeply about such questions, it will be increasingly important for us to shed light on the common historical experiences of different ethnoracial groups and their interactions in daily life.

Acknowledgments

I would like to thank Daniel Milne for helping me improve the chapter.

Notes

1 The total population of California in 2020 was 39.5 million. California's population reflects its history of immigrants coming from diverse backgrounds, as its Hispanic or Latino population accounts for 40.2 percent, its Asian alone counterpart 15.9 percent, and its foreign-born 26.6 percent. See US Census Bureau (2022), online at https://www.census.gov/quickfacts/fact/table/CA/POP010220, accessed July 31, 2022.

2 This chapter takes the approach of transpacific history to explore the processes in which the racialization experiences of Japanese and Mexican immigrants overlapped and helped develop a new form of racism uniquely rooted and developed in California. Lon Kurashige, Madeline Y. Hsu, and Yujin Yaguchi contend that the emerging field of transpacific history sees people's struggles within and around the Pacific Ocean "as not simply national problems, but as articulations of transpacific processes and circumstances that have produced new relationships and modes of explanation" (Kurashige et al. 2014, 187–188).

3 In 1930, 78 percent of the nonwhite population in Los Angeles County was composed of approximately 35,000 ethnic Japanese and 167,000 ethnic Mexicans (US Census Bureau 1932).

4 Kelley R. Swarthout has analyzed the historical development of mestizaje (Swarthout 2004).

5 David Gutiérrez and Matt Garcia have pointed out that Clements' advocacy for the importation of Mexican workers was based on anti-Black discrimination (Garcia 2001, 101–103; Gutiérrez 1995, 48–49). This chapter further explores the role of anti-Black racism in the pro-Mexican labor advocacy in relation to Japanese immigrants.

6 *La Opinión* edited and translated the remarks of the congressional debates in Spanish, although they did not change the general meaning and intent of such remarks. According to the congressional hearings' records, Box presented a letter from an American citizen in Texas who claimed that "if California had a right to stop the Chinese and Japanese from coming to their State, that every Southern State has a hundred times more reasons for stopping the Mexicans from coming to our State than California had from stopping the Chinese or Japanese." Box also presented a statement from an anti-Mexican organization named the California Immigration Study Commission that exclaimed, "Thus American culture will disappear. Greece and Rome both decayed through not grasping this biological law about such differential birth rates" (US Congress 1928, 86, 92).

7 The author has previously explored how Mexicans responded to the "Mexican Problem" in late 1920s Los Angeles by focusing on the transnational role played by the local Spanish-language media and correspondences across the border between Mexican immigrants and the Mexican government (Tokunaga 2019).

8 The *San Bernardino Sun* insisted on the need to restrict Mexican immigration, regretfully stating, "The fact that the bill [to exclude foreign workers] was defeated in the assembly will be disappointing to those who earnestly believe California must revise its ideas of citizenship responsibilities and a higher standard of living for workers" (*San Bernardino Sun* 1929b).

9 Although no national origins quota was applied to Mexican immigration, the US government reinforced the border control based on a new law passed in March 1929 that deemed illegal entry to the US as a misdemeanor and the attempt of illegal reentry after deportation as a felony (Hoffman 1974, 32–33).

References

Almaguer, Tomás. 2009 [1994]. *Racial Fault Lines: The Historical Origins of White Supremacy in California*. Berkeley, CA: University of California Press.

Balderrama, Francisco E. 1982. *In Defense of La Raza: The Los Angeles Mexican Consulate and the Mexican Community, 1929 to 1936*. Tucson: University of Arizona Press.

Cady, George L. ca. 1928. "Report of Commission on International and Interracial Factors in the Problems of Mexicans in the United States." Box 62, George Pigeon Clements Papers, Special Collections, University of California, Los Angeles, Los Angeles, California (hereafter as Clements Papers).

California Development Association. 1928. *Survey of the Mexican Labor Problem in California.* Box 63, Clements Papers.

Camarillo, Albert. 1990 [1984]. *Chicanos in California: A History of Mexican Americans in California.* Sparks: Materials for Today's Learning.

Chambers, Clarke A. 1952. *California Farm Organizations: A Historical Study of the Grange, the Farm Bureau and the Associated Farmers, 1929–1941.* Berkeley, CA: University of California Press.

Chan, Sucheng. 1991. *Asian Americans: An Interpretive History.* Boston, MA: Twayne Publishers.

Clements, George P. 1921. Box 63, Clements Papers.

Clements, George P. ca. 1921. Box 63, Clements Papers.

Clements, George P. 1927. December 2, Box 62, Clements Papers.

Clements, George P. 1929. Before Lemon Men's Club, October 2, Box 80, Clements Papers.

Clements, George P. 1931. To W. G. Arnoll, June 11, Box 80, Clements Papers.

Daniels, Roger. 1968. *The Politics of Prejudice: The Anti-Japanese Movement in California and the Struggle for Japanese Exclusion.* New York: Atheneum.

Flamming, Douglas. 2005. *Bound for Freedom: Black Los Angeles in Jim Crow America.* Berkeley, CA: University of California Press.

Garcia, Matt. 2001. *A World of Its Own: Race, Labor, and Citrus in the Making of Greater Los Angeles, 1900–1970.* Chapel Hill, NC: University of North Carolina Press.

Gerstle, Gary. 2001. *American Crucible: Race and Nation in the Twentieth Century.* Princeton, NJ: Princeton University Press.

Gonzalez, Juan. 2000. *Harvest of Empire: A History of Latinos in America.* New York: Penguin Books.

Guerin-Gonzalez, Camille. 1994. *Mexican Workers and American Dreams: Immigration, Repatriation, and California Farm Labor, 1900–1939.* New Brunswick: Rutgers University Press.

Gutiérrez, David G. 1995. *Walls and Mirrors: Mexican Americans, Mexican Immigrants, and the Politics of Ethnicity.* Berkeley, CA: University of California Press.

Hernández, Kelly L. 2010. *Migra!: A History of the U.S. Border Patrol.* Berkeley, CA: University of California Press.

Higham, John. 1981 [1955]. *Strangers in the Land: Patterns of American Nativism, 1860–1925,* 2nd edition. New York: Atheneum.

Hoffman, Abraham. 1974. *Unwanted Mexican Americans in the Great Depression: Repatriation Pressures 1929–1939.* Tucson: University of Arizona Press.

Ichioka, Yuji. 1988. *The Issei: The World of the First Generation Japanese Immigrants, 1885–1924.* New York: Free Press.

Iino, Masako. 2000. *Mō hitotsu no nichi-bei kankeishi: Hunsō to kyōchō no naka no nikkei amerikajin* [Another history of Japan-US relations: Japanese Americans in conflicts and cooperation]. Tokyo: Yūhikaku.

Iwata, Masakazu. 1992. *Planted in Good Soil: A History of the Issei in United States Agriculture, 2 vols.* New York: Peter Lang Publishers.

Kodama, Masaaki. 1992. *Nihon iminshi kenkyū josetsu.* Hiroshima: Keisuisha.

Kraut, Alan M. 2001 [1982]. *The Huddled Masses: The Immigrant in American Society, 1880–1921.* Wheeling: Harlan Davidson.

Kurashige, Lon. 2016. *Two Faces of Exclusion: The Untold History of Anti-Asian Racism in the United States.* Chapel Hill, NC: University of North Carolina Press.

Kurashige, Lon, Madeline Y. Hsu, and Yujin Yaguchi. 2014. "Introduction: Conversations on Transpacific History." *Pacific Historical Review* 83 (2): 183–188.

La Opinión. 1928a. "2 diputados de E.U. iniciaron una ofensiva contra la cuota a la inmigración de Mexicanos." *La Opinión*, February 24, 1928. Available at: https://news.google.com/newspapers (Accessed September 20, 2019).

La Opinión. 1928b. "Envió ayer un memorial a la Cámara." *La Opinión*, February 28, 1928.

La Opinión. 1928c. "Probable fracaso de la 'cuota'." *La Opinión*, March 7, 1928.

La Opinión. 1929. "Una documentada plática sobre los problemas de inmigración en los E.U." *La Opinión*, May 20, 1929.

Lozano, Monica. 1993. Interview with Shirley Biagi. Washington Press Club Foundation website, December 13. Accessed September 12, 2018. http://beta.wpcf.org/oralhistory/loz.html.

Madley, Benjamin. 2008. "California's Yuki Indians: Defining Genocide in Native American History." *Western Historical Quarterly* 39 (3): 303–332.

McWilliams, Carey. 2000 [1939]. *Factories in the Field: The Story of Migratory Farm Labor in California*. Berkeley, CA: University of California Press.

Miller, Sally M. 1987. *The Ethnic Press in the United States: A Historical Analysis and Handbook*. Westport, CT: Greenwood.

Minamikashū Nihonjin Shichijūnenshi Kankō Iinkai [Publishing Committee of Japanese in Southern California: A history of 70 years], ed. 1960. *Minamikashū nihonjin shichijūnenshi* [Japanese in Southern California: A history of 70 years]. Los Angeles: Nanka Nikkeijin Shōgyō Kaigisho.

Ministry of Justice of Japan. 2019. Immigration Service Agency. "Heisei 30 nen matsu genzai ni okeru zairyū gaikokujin sū ni tsuite [The number of foreign residents as of the end of the year 2018]." March 22.

Minohara, Toshihiro. 2002. *Hainichi imin hō to nichi-bei kankei* [The Japanese Exclusion Act and Japan-US relations]. Tokyo: Iwanami Shoten.

Minohara, Toshihiro. 2006. *Kariforunia shū hainichi undō to nichi-bei kankei: Imin mondai o meguru nichi-bei masatsu, 1906–1921* [The anti-Japanese movement in California and Japan-US relations: Japan-US conflict over immigration issues, 1906–1921]. Tokyo: Yūhikaku.

Molina, Natalia. 2014. *How Race Is Made in America: Immigration, Citizenship, and the Historical Power of Racial Scripts*. Berkeley, CA: University of California Press.

Ngai, Mae M. 2004. *Impossible Subjects: Illegal Aliens and the Making of Modern America*. Princeton, NJ: Princeton University Press.

Oda, Yuki. 2006. "1924 nen iminhō ni okeru Mekishikojin: 1920 nendai ni okeru Mekishikojin imin kunibetsu wariate ronsō to beiboku kokkyō kanri mondai [Mexican under the US Immigration Act of 1924: Mexican quota debate and border control policy in the 1920s]." *Amerika taiheiyō kenkyū* [Pacific and American Studies] 6: 261–272.

Painter, Nell Irvin. 2010. *The History of White People*. New York: W. W. Norton & Company.

Rafu Shimpo. 1929a. "Bokukoku imin seigen an" [Bill to restrict Mexican immigration]. *Rafu Shimpo,* January 12, 1929.

Rafu Shimpo. 1929b. "Gaikoku rōdōsha haisekihō" [Foreign workers exclusion act]. *Rafu Shimpo*, April 24, 1929.

Roediger, David R. 2007 [1991]. *The Wages of Whiteness: Race and the Making of the American Working Class*, revised edition. New York: Verso.

San Bernardino Sun. 1929a. "Alien Labor Ban Fails to Get Passage." *San Bernardino Sun*, April 25, 1929. University of California, Riverside, California Digital Newspaper Collection website. Accessed September 20, 2019. https://cdnc.ucr.edu.

San Bernardino Sun. 1929b. "California Jobs for Americans." *San Bernardino Sun*, April 25, 1929.

Sánchez, George J. 1993. *Becoming Mexican American: Ethnicity, Culture, and Identity in Chicano Los Angeles, 1900–1945*. New York: Oxford University Press.

Saxton, Alexander. 1995 [1971]. *The Indispensable Enemy: Labor and the Anti-Chinese Movement in California*. Berkeley, CA: University of California Press.

Swarthout, Kelley R. 2004. *"Assimilating the Primitive": Parallel Dialogues on Racial Miscegenation in Revolutionary Mexico*. New York: Peter Lang.

Takaki, Ronald. 1998 [1989]. *Strangers from a Different Shore: A History of Asian Americans, updated and revised edition*. New York: Little, Brown and Company.

Taylor, Ralph H. 1929. "Mexican vs American Farm Labor." October 1, Box 62, Clements Papers.

tenBroek, Jacobus, Edward N. Barnhart, and Floyd W. Matson. 1970 [1954]. *Prejudice, War and the Constitution: Causes and Consequences of the Evacuation of the Japanese Americans in World War II*. Berkeley, CA: University of California Press.

Tokunaga, Yu. 2019. "'Mekishikojin mondai' to imin media: 1920 nendai rosanzerusu ni okeru haigai shugi to Mekishikojin imin no teikō [The 'Mexican Problem' and immigrant media: Mexican immigrants' resistance against nativism in 1920s Los Angeles]." *Amerikashai kenkyū* 42: 3–18.

Tokunaga, Yu. 2022. *Transborder Los Angeles: An Unknown Transpacific History of Japanese-Mexican Relations*. Oakland: University of California Press.

Tovares, Paul D. 2009. "*La Opinión* and its contribution to the Mexican Community's Adaptation to Life in the US." *Latino Studies* 7 (4): 480–498.

University of California, Los Angeles, Special Collections. 1997. "Finding Aid for the George Pigeon Clements Papers, 1825–1945." Online Archive of California website. Accessed September 12, 2018. https://oac.cdlib.org/findaid/ark:/13030/tf2q2nb1h7/.

University of Southern California. Libraries (digital). 1927 and 1930. California Historical Society Collection, 1860–1960. Accessed November 6, 2021. https://digitallibrary. usc.edu/.

US Census Bureau. 1922. *Fourteenth Census of the United States: 1920, Population*. Washington, DC: GPO.

US Census Bureau. 1932. *Fifteenth Census of the United States: 1930, Population*. Washington, DC: GPO.

US Census Bureau. 2022. QuickFacts California. US Census Bureau website. Accessed July 31, 2022. https://www.census.gov/quickfacts/fact/table/CA/POP010220.

US Congress. 1928. House. Committee on Immigration and Naturalization. Immigration from Countries of the Western Hemisphere: Hearings before the Committee on Immigration and Naturalization, 70th Cong., 1st sess. Washington DC: GPO. HathiTrust Digital Library website. Accessed September 12, 2018. https://www.hathitrust.org.

Wollenberg, Charles. 1972. "Race and Class in Rural California: The El Monte Berry Strike of 1933." *California Historical Quarterly* 51 (2): 155–164.

Yagasaki, Noritaka. 1993. *Imin nōgyō: Kariforunia no nihonjin imin shakai* [Immigrant agriculture: The Japanese immigrant society in California]. Tokyo: Kokonshoin.

Yamakura, Akihiro. 1994. "'National Humiliation': Anti-American Reactions in Japan to the Immigration Act of 1924." *Tenri University Journal* 45 (2): 95–116.

PART II

Empire and Effects of Categorization

5
COLONIAL RULE AND "CATEGORY"

Policing in Colonial Singapore

Takeshi Onimaru

5.1 Introduction

Since its founding in 1819, British Malaya and the Straits Settlements, including Singapore, were colonies that had developed through the labor of mostly Chinese immigrants accepted into the territories as workers.[1] In Singapore, people of Chinese descent accounted for over half of its population from the middle of the nineteenth century. This was because Singapore was a frontier city that was premised on the presence of immigrants and formed one of the important intersections in the flow of Chinese immigrants across the Pacific Rim region. Because of this demographic and social reality, Singapore's colonial government and law and order enforcement found it necessary to treat Chinese immigrants and residents of Chinese descent as an important target group to bring under their rule. As the number of Chinese immigrants grew, some turned to crime or joined what Westerners called "secret societies" to cause disturbances in the streets or organized political and labor movements to mount strikes and anti-British and anti-colonialist campaigns. Identifying these "troublemakers" as a threat to their control and economic advancement in British Malaya, of which Singapore formed a part, the colonial authority devised a system of policing these people and containing such disturbances. How did the colonial government in Singapore implement this system?

In order to answer this question, this chapter examines how Chineseness itself came to be labeled as "problematic" and how "the Chinese" became "racialized" as a distinct group with inherent characteristics as their "secret societies," and communist activities became the target of surveillance by the British colonial administration. In doing so, it elucidates the formation of "categories" with which the colonial ruler tried to screen out and clamp down upon such immigrants in this highly mobile frontier island city.

DOI: 10.4324/9781003266396-7

Categories of "race" and "ethnicity" were only introduced during the colonial period in Southeast Asia. As Benedict Anderson and Takashi Shiraishi point out, in the colonial states of Southeast Asia, the "ethnic" categories used in the census were initially insubstantial, but these "ethnic" categories became gradually "substantial" from the later nineteenth century through to the early twentieth century, as a consequence of the imposition of colonial rules and regulations on places of residence, education, and customs which were implemented on these "ethnic" categories (Anderson 2006; Shiraishi 2000). As this process of substantialization went on, group-based discrimination could be seen in the Southeast Asian region, and it was the population categorized as "the Chinese" who were targeted the most. They were labeled with terms such as "outsiders," "troublemakers," "communists," and "Jews of the Orient." Some of these labels are still utilized when anti-Chinese sentiments become heightened in post-independent Southeast Asia.

In Singapore, like many other societies in Southeast Asia, "race" as a concept introduced from the West is linked with differences in observable physical appearances between groups, whereas the term "ethnic group" is preferred to designate groups whose phenotypical differences are not immediately perceived. However, this chapter employs the concept of racialization, as defined in the Introduction of this volume, as the process of differentiation and discrimination on the basis of people's belief in "inheritable" characteristics, whether phenotypically visible or invisible. From this perspective, it will shed light on a colonial, modern development of the category of "the Chinese" in Singapore as the target of law-and-order enforcement by paying attention to the process of visibilization of inherent characteristics of "the Chinese."

5.2 Colonial Singapore and the Chinese

Singapore was founded in 1819 by Sir Thomas Stamford Raffles, an officer of the British East India Company, and was added to the Straits Settlements along with Penang and Malacca in 1826. In 1832, Singapore became the administrative center of the Straits Settlements, which had been ruled by the British East India Company and then the government of British India before becoming a Crown Colony under the direct control of the British Colonial Office in 1867.

Since its founding, Singapore had always been expected to function as a British trading post in the Southeast Asian region (Turnbull 1989: 20). Singapore was designated as a "Free Port" with no customs or trade-related impositions, and its trade steadily grew, as shown in Table 5.1. From the 1820s, it thrived as Southeast Asia's intraregional trade hub as it expanded commerce with its major trading partners in the region (Kobayashi 2013; Wong 1991).

Singapore is a city-state situated off the southern tip of the Malay Peninsula and on the southeastern end of the Straits of Malacca—a vital waterway connecting South and East Asia. Today it has become one of the financial and economic centers of Asia and Southeast Asia. Singapore is a multicultural, multilingual,

TABLE 5.1 Trade in Singapore (1824–1938) ($ million)

Year	Imports	Exports	Total
1824	6.6	5.0	11.6
1833	9.1	7.6	16.7
1843	13.1	11.5	24.6
1853	15.5	13.4	28.9
1863	29.8	25.7	55.5
1873	47.9	41.8	89.7
1883	79.2	68.2	147.4
1893	124.0	108.5	232.5
1903	299.3	257.7	557.0
1913	349.7	272.4	622.1
1923	573.0	402.7	975.7
1933	261.7	251.1	512.8
1938	369.6	320.2	689.9

Source: Wong (1991: 51).

and multiethnic society. English, Standard Chinese (Mandarin), Malay, and Tamil are Singapore's official languages.

According to the *Yearbook of Statistics Singapore 2018*, published by the Singapore Department of Statistics, the total population of the country at the end of 2017 was approximately 5.6 million, of which 3.43 million were citizens, 0.52 million were permanent residents, and the remaining 1.64 million were temporary residents in Singapore for work or other purposes. The combined 3.95 million citizens and permanent residents comprised 2.94 million Chinese (75 percent), 0.53 million Malays (13 percent), 0.35 million Indians (9 percent), and 0.12 million people of other ethnicities (3 percent) (Singapore Department of Statistics 2018).

While the cultural and linguistic diversity is palpable in the range of people and languages one encounters in the streets, it is evident from the data that the Chinese form the dominant group in the multiethnic state. They came to comprise a majority of the country's population when Singapore was part of the British Straits Settlements in the mid-nineteenth century (Table 5.2). The large presence of the Chinese traces its history back to the mid-nineteenth century, as Singapore was also a major transfer point for Chinese immigrants to Southeast

TABLE 5.2 The Population of Singapore in the Nineteenth Century

Year	Total	Chinese	Ratio of Chinese (%)
1824	10,683	3,317	31.0
1834	26,329	10,767	40.8
1849	52,891	27,988	52.9
1860	81,734	50,043	61.2
1871	97,111	54,572	56.1
1881	139,208	86,766	62.3
1891	141,300	100,446	71.0

Source: Makepeace et al. (1991: 355–359).

Asia. Immigrants from South China arrived in Singapore and journeyed on to the Malay Peninsula or the Dutch East Indies in search of livelihoods. The number of immigrants from South China to Southeast Asia increased due to the rising demand for a workforce to support the development of the tin mining industry in the Malay Peninsula from the 1850s and the deregulation of migration from China under the 1860 Convention of Peking (Yong 1994: 2). Southeast Asia was not the only region that experienced a rise in the number of Chinese immigrants during this period. As Takeshi Hamashita points out, the abolition of the African slave trade in the middle of the nineteenth century led to the expansion of demand for Chinese and Indian immigrants in Southeast Asia, Africa, and America (Hamashita 2013: 277). For Chinese immigrants, however, Southeast Asia was the primary destination because colonization by Britain, the Netherlands, and France had turned Hong Kong, Singapore, Batavia, and Saigon into major destinations and transit points for migration (Hamashita 2013: 277–279). In other words, the influx of Chinese immigrants into Southeast Asia was the main source of the expansion of Chinese migration to the Pacific Rim region, including the Americas, and Singapore was the colony that played an extremely important role in this current.

The population of Singapore continued to grow along with its commercial expansion, dramatically increasing from an estimated 1,000 at its founding in 1819 (Gillis 2005: 15) to over 10,000 in 1824. By 1891, the population of Singapore exceeded 140,000. Chinese immigrants from mainland China drove this population growth. They had become the largest ethnic group in Singapore by 1827 and continued to proliferate partly because the Straits Settlements actively promoted the intake of Chinese immigrants as a workforce for further development of the colony (Shiraishi 2000: 62–63; Turnbull 1989: 36). The presence of Chinese immigrants was thus integral to the development of the frontier colony of Singapore.

The population growth of Singapore over a short period of seventy-odd years was rapid. While a majority came from mainland China, Singapore was a frontier city inhabited by immigrants from all corners of the Southeast and South Asian regions. How did Britain, its colonial ruler, try to classify and govern these immigrants? How did Chinese residents live, and what kind of communities did they form?

Two Mass Rapid Transit (MRT) stations, Bugis MRT station and Chinatown station, can be found in present-day Singapore. Bugis station, named after the group of people who lived in the southwestern part of Indonesia's Sulawesi Island and became active in the Southeast Asian maritime world from the fifteenth century (Tachimoto 2008: 377–378), is situated on the left (northern) bank of the Singapore River past the current City Hall, which used to be the administrative center of colonial Singapore. Chinatown station is located on the right (southern) bank of the river. The reason behind the locations of these two MRT stations stems from the city planning devised by Raffles and others at the founding of Singapore in the early nineteenth century.

Raffles planned the new city by segregating residential communities on the basis of "ethnic" categories such as European, Chinese, Malay, Arab, and Bugis. In his plan, government offices, churches, and the military post were first established on the left bank of the Singapore River, and the European residential district was placed next to this center, followed by the Arab and Malay Sultan communities. The Bugis settlement was constructed further away from the center. On the right bank of the river, the commercial district was established near the river mouth, and a community of South Indian immigrants called Chulia was settled a little further up the river, while the Chinese town was built a short distance away from the river (Shiraishi 2000: 95–98; Turnbull 1989: 12).

As Shiraishi points out, these all-encompassing ethnic categories, including the "Chinese" category, did not correspond to reality at the time (Shiraishi 2000: 93–94). The Chinese immigrant community in colonial Singapore was divided into five subgroups on the basis of their place of origin and topolects, namely, Hokkien, Teochew, Cantonese, Hakka, and Hainanese. Almost ninety percent of the Chinese residents in Singapore were new immigrants, called "newcomers" (*xin ke*), and relied on connections based on their hometown, topolect, and kin relationship when seeking work and protection. Such care and protection were provided by organizations called *kongsi*, *hoey*, and *huidang* (Lee 1991: 23–24; Shinozaki 2017: 102; Shiraishi 1975: 77; Turnbull 1989: 52–53).

These were multifaceted organizations that functioned as business entities that operated plantations and tin mines, mutual-help associations that assisted immigrants in looking for work or housing, protected immigrants in dire circumstances, and organized funerals and repatriation of remains and crime syndicates involved in labor management, the transportation and management of immigrants, protection racketeering with opium dens, brothels and gambling houses, and violence used to resolve organizational or financial conflicts (Lee 1991: 30; Shinozaki 2017: 57, 102; Shiraishi 1975: 78–80, 82–83).

The Chinese community in colonial Singapore was also economically stratified. As mentioned earlier, a great majority of Chinese residents were impoverished immigrants who engaged in physical labor with the top echelon in this community occupied by a small number of wealthy merchants and industrialists. They made their fortune through Southeast Asian regional trade and retail business operations, management of or investment in plantations and tin mining, and tax farming to collect taxes on opium and spirits under contract with the colonial government. Some of them had been living in Southeast Asia well before the foundation of Singapore, married locally, and built their economic bases there. Because of their wealth, they were called "headmen" (*taukeh*) and respected within the Chinese community, where they acted as community leaders (Shiraishi 1975: 77–78; Turnbull 1989: 13–14; Yong 1994: 3–4).

These Chinese community leaders were deeply involved in the organizations *kongsi*, *hoey*, and *huidang.* They were managers of, or investors in, plantations and tin mines, but the actual operation of these businesses was conducted by the said organizations. These organizations played a significant role in tax farming and also in the prevention of smuggling, maintenance of distribution networks, and sale of opium and alcohol to coolies. The *taukeh* even mobilized the members for violence within these organizations in order to protect their own economic interests (Lee 1991: 28–29; Shiraishi 1975: 78–80).

In short, the Chinese community in colonial Singapore, especially in the nineteenth century, was not a monolithic group that converged under the ethnic category of "Chinese"; it was divided into the Hokkien, Teochew, Cantonese, Hakka, and Hainanese subgroups based on topolect grouping and stratified with headmen in the upper echelon and a large number of new immigrants in the lower tier. *Kongsi, hoey,* and *huidang* played a significant role in this community but were described as "secret societies" by the colonial administrators.

5.3 Secret Societies and Colonial Rule until 1867

In the nineteenth century, "secret societies" was the primary category used as almost equivalent to the Chinese "ethnic" category. In the early twentieth century, it shifted to political movements, especially the communist movement. The colonial rulers identified both secret societies and communist movements as troublemakers and targeted the Chinese.

The *kongsi, hoey,* and *huidang* organizations were accessible institutions for Chinese residents and not at all secret and hidden. In times of trouble, new immigrants sought help from these organizations rather than turning to government agencies (Lee 1991: 30). Given this fact, why did authorities call them "secret societies"?

The answer to this question largely lies in the fact that the colonial administration did not have any officers who understood the Chinese language and its topolects. Many of these organizations had memberships of young single men bound by oaths of brotherhood (Shiraishi 1975: 80; Trocki 1990: 3). It is not surprising that government officials regarded these organizations as "secret societies" because they had no idea about the rites and discussions of these organizations.

Another reason was their frequent use of violence. The violent aspect of *huidang* soon became apparent after the founding of Singapore. For instance, it was noted in *The Story of Abdullah,* which recorded the early days of colonial Singapore, that the *huidang* organization Tian Di Hui had established its base in the inland jungle from which its members mounted raids on surrounding towns (Abudurrā 1980: 2–6). These organizations played a central role as the apparatus for violence in the 1854 clan war[2] between the Hokkiens and the Teochews and the frequent Hokkien-Teochew clan wars that erupted between 1871 and 1873 (Lee 1991: 35–39).

These organizations even used violence against the colonial government when it attempted to impose regulations on the Chinese community or moved to infringe upon its economic interests. In October 1872, a riot broke out in opposition to the Contagious Diseases Ordinance to regulate brothels for the purpose of controlling venereal diseases and in response to regulations on street vendors. In 1876, a riot and a shopkeepers' strike took place against the establishment of the Chinese Post Office, which was set to take the money remittance service for Chinese residents out of the hands of the mostly Teochew operators and place it under government control. In both cases, *huidang* members were mobilized and led the riots (Lee 1991: 38–43; Shiraishi 1975: 79).

From the viewpoint of the Singaporean government and resident Europeans, organizations such as *kongsi, hoey,* and *huidang* were regarded as secret societies due to their "secrecy" and "violence," even though they were common and offered accessible services to Chinese residents. So, what measures did the Straits Settlements administration take to deal with the secret societies which posed a significant threat to law and order enforcement in Singapore?

Little was done to control secret societies while Singapore was under the jurisdiction of the British East India Company or British India. For example, in 1843, residents, including the Chinese, held a public meeting demanding that the government enact a law to suppress secret societies. The administrators drafted an ordinance in response, but it was rejected by the Bengal office of the British East India Company. Another ordinance, modeled on one already in operation in Hong Kong, was drafted in 1854 to establish a registry of residents, give the governor-general the power of deportation, require secret societies to register, and appoint headmen as officials in charge of maintaining public order. Once again, this attempt was unsuccessful due to opposition from British India. In both cases, legal control was not implemented based on the argument that the problem should be solved by expanding police forces (Blythe 1969: 63–67, 80–82; Shinozaki 2017: 56–57).

However, the police were unable to adequately control the situation. The colonial government did not recruit Chinese inhabitants into the police force in fear of infiltration by secret societies. Consequently, police officers could not exert sufficient control as none of them spoke the Chinese language and topolects. Moreover, the power of the police was limited to the urban area until around the 1860s, and the inland headquarters of secret societies were largely untouched. Even though the police force did not recruit Chinese police officers, it was infiltrated by secret societies. For example, the interpreters hired by the police to assist in their inquiries often turned out to be members of secret societies (Blythe 1969: 2–3; Jarman 1998: Vol. 1: 208, 464; Lee 1991: 35).

Since there was no law to regulate secret societies and the police force was ineffective in controlling them, the only way for the colonial government to deal with the disturbances was to seek cooperation from the headmen who presided over the Chinese community or to suppress them by the use of military force.

Gaining the headmen's cooperation was essential not only to exert a measure of control over secret societies but also to achieve effective governance of the Chinese community. The colonial officers referred to some headmen as "respectable Chinese" those able to speak English, those who had their economic bases in Singapore or the rest of Southeast Asia, or those who had trade and commercial relationships with Europeans—and made use of their influence in governing the Chinese community by giving them official positions such as Justice of the Peace (JP). The colonial state relied on its powers over secret societies to resolve problems when secret societies engaged in disorderly conduct (Shiraishi 1975: 76–79; Yong 1994: 13–14, 293–294).

When a violent confrontation between the Hokkiens and the Teochews broke out in 1854, for instance, Superintendent of Police Thomas Dunman declared that the police did not have the capacity to deal with the situation and called for military intervention. The administration asked Teochew headman Seah Eu-chin and Hokkien headman Tan Kim-seng for their cooperation in bringing the situation under control. In the disturbance of 1857, the authorities were assisted by Hoo Ah-kay of the Cantonese and Tan Kim-ching of the Hokkien in restoring order (Lee 1991: 35–37; Yong 1994: 13–14).

Another reason behind the colonial administration's continued tolerance of the existence of the secret societies was the important role they played in tax farming, especially for opium and spirits. *Kongsi, hoey,* and *huidang* carried out the work of controlling smugglers and protecting distribution networks that were needed to secure tax farming revenues. The consumers of opium and spirits were coolies, especially the Chinese immigrant laborers who worked on inland plantations. And the business operation, labor management, and sale of opium and spirits to the workers were controlled by secret societies. The colonial government had no choice but to rely on secret societies while the inland part of Singapore was covered in dense jungle with no road access, as it was difficult to send in officials to collect taxes directly from the inland plantations (Song 1967: 34; Trocki 1990: 48, 70, 77; Wong 1991: 54; Yen 1986: 115, 122).

In Singapore, the secret societies enjoyed the status of *imperium in imperio* because the police were unable to control them effectively due to a prolonged absence of laws to regulate them and because the colonial government was forced to rely on them for tax collection even though they were recognized as a threat to law and order (Shiraishi 1975).

5.4 Illegalizing Secret Societies

The situation started to change in the late 1860s after the control of Singapore was transferred from British India to the Colonial Office, making it part of a British Crown Colony in 1867 that included Penang and Malacca.

In 1867, an ordinance was enacted to give the Governor of Singapore the power to deport anyone who threatened law and order in the colony upon declaration of a state of emergency. Two years later, in 1869, another ordinance was passed for the purpose of regulating the secret societies by making registration and notification of meetings compulsory for organizations with ten or more members and enabling justices of the peace or police officers to attend such meetings. This ordinance also decreed that secret societies were obligated to pay for any damage caused in clan wars. These ordinances were initially passed as temporary measures to be in force for a single year, but in 1872 they were made permanent (Blythe 1969: 151–152; Jarman 1998: Vol. 2: 141; Lee 1991: 57–60).

The above two ordinances used deportation and registration as means to exert control over secret societies. The threat of deportation turned out to be effective in this regard. For the leaders of secret societies, expulsion from the colony meant a loss of their personal wealth, prestige, and power base, and, moreover, deportation to mainland China might lead to death by beheading (Shiraishi 1975: 87; Turnbull 1989: 88).

From 1871 to 1873, Singapore was frequently beset by clan wars and anti-government riots. In particular, the clan war between the Hokkiens and the Teochews that broke out in December 1872 was the most violent since the Hokkien-Teochew conflict of 1854 and prompted the Straits Settlements administration to proclaim a state of emergency. This state of emergency was not lifted until 1885 (Blythe 1969: 155–156, 198; Jarman 1998 Vol. 2: 137; Lee 1991: 35–41; Yen 1986: 197), and the Chinese Post Office Riot of 1876 erupted during this period.

The Chinese Post Office Riot was mainly led by Teochew merchants involved in the remittance business who saw the opening of a Chinese Sub-Post Office by the government as an infringement of their vested rights. During the riot, Singapore was paralyzed entirely for four days as the Sub-Post Office was burned down and shopkeepers went on strike. The government initially asked local headmen to help quell the disturbance and requested that the shopkeepers end their strike, but to no effect. It was rumored that Tan Seng-poh, a Teochew headman, had aligned himself with the authorities in suppressing Chinese residents. In light of the headmen's failure, the colonial administration adopted a strategy of isolating the Teochew merchants and secret-society leaders who had been in detention since the onset of the riot by keeping them on a ship off the coast of the island. This approach proved effective, and the town regained calm that night. After the riot was quelled, the colonial administration expelled the leaders of the secret societies from Singapore. The government's resolute actions in this situation had a significant bearing on the subsequent development of countermeasures against secret societies (Blythe 1969: 202; Lee 1991: 43–46; Shiraishi 1975: 86).

In this way, the anti-secret societies policy of the Straits Settlements administration changed from non-intervention to aggressive control and policing after 1867. What was the reason behind this policy shift?

The placement of the Straits Settlements under the rule of the Colonial Office in 1867 was undoubtedly a factor behind this policy turnaround. In addition, a shift in Singapore's socio-economic condition and a change in the nature of secret societies were essential elements.

Let us consider socio-economic change first. The number of inland plantations began to fall from the second half of the 1860s due to soil degradation. A government report in 1868 states that a majority of Singapore's pepper and gambier plantations were being abandoned due to soil degradation and relocated to Johor on the other side of the Johor Strait (Jarman 1998: Vol. 1: 36). Secondly, access to the inland part of Singapore had improved. The clearing of the jungle by the development of plantations and the expansion of road networks improved transport to the island's outskirts and inland areas. As a result, the government was able to collect land taxes outside of the city and reported an increase in land-tax revenues during the 1870s. These changes began to reduce the level of the government's dependence on the tax farming carried out by secret societies. The improved access to the outskirts and the inland also promoted urbanization and made administrative control easier than before (Jarman 1998: Vol. 2: 106; Trocki 1990: 149; Wong 1991: 53).

Further, there was a change in the nature of secret societies. In the aftermath of the suppression of the Taiping Rebellion in mainland China, many outlaws and criminals were driven out of the country and migrated to Singapore and the rest of Southeast Asia from around 1870. These were professional combatants called "*samseng*" who had been trained in martial arts. When they joined secret societies, the level of violence escalated, and even the Chinese community leaders were unable to control them (Lee 1991: 34–35, 42; Trocki 1990: 159–160).

It is reasonable to conclude that the colonial government changed its policy toward secret societies because these socio-economic shifts reduced its tax collection dependence on them and made it difficult to exert indirect control through community headmen on the increasingly violent and criminal organizations.

The next anti-secret society measure adopted by the Straits Settlements government was the establishment of the Chinese Protectorate in 1877, designed to take over the tasks of managing Chinese immigrants and protecting them from secret societies. The first Protector of Chinese was William A. Pickering.

Pickering had learned to speak Mandarin, Hokkien, Hakka, Teochew, and Cantonese while working in the Chinese Maritime Customs Service in mainland China from 1862 to 1871. He began to work at the Straits Settlements government in 1871 as a translator. Pickering was the first European official in the colony who was fluent in the Chinese language and its topolects and conducted research into secret societies and immigration issues even before he was appointed Protector (Blythe 1969: 157–158; Shinozaki 2017: 105; Turnbull 1989: 85).

As the Protector of Chinese, Pickering was tasked with managing and checking the employment contracts of Chinese immigrants to ensure that their interests were protected as well as administering the re-registration of secret societies. The latter task was undertaken in cooperation with Samuel Dunlop, Inspector-General of Police, from 1877 and involved identifying the local leaders of each secret society and the registration of its members. The re-registration process was completed ten years later in 1887 (Blythe 1969: 205–207; Lee 1991: 71, 75–80; Shinozaki 2017: 105–106; Shiraishi 1975: 86).

The Protector's work was significant in two respects. One was to make newcomers to Singapore understand that they should rely on the government rather than secret societies. The other was to establish a system to keep secret societies under the control of the Chinese Protectorate using means such as deportation and the re-registration process through which secret societies became more "visible" (Shinozaki 2017: 10; Shiraishi 1975: 86).

In line with the strengthening of control over secret societies by the Chinese Protectorate and the police, legal regulations were also tightened. In 1882, the law was amended to ban any secret society with British nationals or natural-ized British subjects among its membership and to enable the government to declare a secret society illegal if it was considered dangerous. This amendment was introduced because the deportation of British citizens was not possible under the earlier deportation ordinance of 1867. In 1885, the government was given the power to expel people without the proclamation of a state of emer-gency (Blythe 1969: 213; Lee 1991: 97).

From the 1880s, a new system[3] was set up under which cadet officers who spe-cialized in Chinese affairs in the colony were sent to Amoy, Swatow, or Canton to learn Hokkien, Teochew, or Cantonese. The police force was also strength-ened in terms of human resources and organizational upgrades. A police training school was opened in 1881, a criminal investigation section was created in 1884, and a number of Sikh and European ex-army officers were employed as inspec-tors and constables (Turnbull 1989: 84, 88).

The final step in the anti-secret societies policy of the Straits Settlements government was the passing of an ordinance in 1889 to make secret societies illegal and the implementation of complete prohibition upon the enforcement of the ordinance on January 1, 1890. However, this was not what the Protector of Chinese had wanted.

Before he was appointed as Protector of Chinese, Pickering had been in favor of the immediate outlawing of secret societies. In 1878, after his appointment, however, Pickering expressed the view that secret societies should be utilized in managing the Chinese community. He claimed that it was difficult to control the Chinese community through the rule of law and that it would be easier to do so using the framework of the secret societies because they were deeply rooted in the community. He developed an understanding of the role secret societies played in the Chinese community and became acquainted with their leaders through his work as the Protector of Chinese and through the re-registration of secret societies. In order to control the Chinese community through the secret societies and eventually integrate it into the rule of law, Pickering planned to persuade the leaders of secret societies to see the benefits of siding with the colo-nial government. For this reason, he considered it dangerous to expeditiously disempower secret societies and hence strip them of their ability to control the Chinese community (Shiraishi 1975: 8; Lee 1991: 92–98).

Nevertheless, the move toward prohibition gathered momentum after a secret society's failed assassination attempt on Pickering in July 1887 and further accel-erated upon the appointment of Cecil C. Smith as the Governor of the Straits Settlements in October that year.

Smith began his career in colonial administration in Hong Kong in 1862. He specialized in dealing with Chinese residents in Hong Kong and adopted a rather heavy-handed approach toward them. When the Colonial Secretary of Hong Kong retired in 1878, John Pope Hennessy, the Governor, refused to appoint Smith to the position. Smith instead assumed the office of Colonial Secretary in the Straits Settlements and, after a posting in Ceylon in 1885, returned to the Straits Settlements as its Governor (Holdsworth and Munn 2012: 398–399; Lee 1991: 151).

In 1888, Smith drafted a bill to prohibit secret societies completely. This move was opposed by Pickering and Dunlop, who feared that the government would lose the means to monitor and control the vast number of Chinese immigrant workers managed by secret societies with the supervision of the Chinese Protectorate's registration system if it implemented a complete ban without establishing an alternative body to take over the function these organizations performed in the Chinese community. Despite their opposition, Smith tabled the bill in the Legislative Council and secured its passage with some alterations in 1889. The ordinance was promulgated on January 1, 1990, and the complete prohibition of secret societies became a reality (Blythe 1969: 233; Lee 1991: 135–144, 150: Straits Settlements Government 1898: 1106–1111).

Along with the outlawing of secret societies, Smith set up the Chinese Advisory Board. It comprised the Protector of Chinese and seventeen representatives from the Chinese community—six from the Hokkiens, five from the Teochews, and two each from the Cantonese, Hakkas, and Hainanese—and was responsible for providing advice on various issues and legislative proceedings in relation to the Chinese community in response to requests from the colonial administration. As advocated by Pickering and Dunlop, this body was intended to take over the function of secret societies and constituted the first step in the move to govern the Chinese community by the rule of law rather than via secret societies through cooperation between the colonial administration and Chinese community leaders (Lee 1991: 150; Shiraishi 1975: 93).

The complete prohibition of secret societies did not mean that they were eradicated. However, it marked the end of the frequent occurrence of large-scale disturbances led by secret societies that had vexed the Straits Settlements administration until 1890 (Turnbull 1989: 89).

5.5 Policing Communist Movement

After the problem of the secret society was settled at the end of the nineteenth century, another threat emerged to jeopardize public order in the colony. This new threat to stability emerged in the form of political movements that upheld such goals as reforming political frameworks and achieving liberation from colonial rule. A wave of political movements was experienced across Asia from the end of the nineteenth century to the early twentieth century, including the Philippine Revolution seeking independence from Spain in 1898, a series of uprisings in China led by Sun Yat-sen and others from the end of the nineteenth century, the Dong Du Movement in French Indochina at the start of the twentieth century, and the Swadeshi Movement in British India. These political movements became the targets of policing and suppression as they posed a major threat to the establishment.

In colonial Singapore, around the turn of the twentieth century, the Straits Settlements government was concerned about several political movements: the Chinese nationalist movement, the Indian nationalist movement, and the communist movement.

The nationalist movement had been gathering momentum among Singapore's Chinese inhabitants in step with political shifts in mainland China since the opening of a diplomatic mission in Singapore by the Qing Dynasty in 1877. More specifically, the colonial government targeted political movements concerning their financial support for the late Qing reforms and Sun Yat-sen's revolutionist movement against the Qing Dynasty, the activities of the Kuomintang (KMT) in Singapore, and the rest of British Malaya after the 1911 Xinhai Revolution and the proclamation of the Republic of China (Lee 1991: 203–249; Onimaru 2014: 124).

The government increased its vigilance against the nationalist movement among the Indian inhabitants in response to the Singapore Mutiny staged by Punjabi Muslim soldiers of the 5th Light Infantry on February 15, 1915, during World War I. The event sparked the strengthening of Singapore's intelligence gathering systems as the rebellion was suspected to originate in a conspiracy devised by the Ghadar Party based in the Ottoman Empire and on the West Coast of the US to help Indian independence with support from hostile Germany. After this incident, Singapore was on high alert for Ghadar Party activities and the influences of the nationalist movement in British India on its Indian residents (Comber 2009: 530–536; Onimaru 2014: 124; Popplewell 1995: 258–262).

As for the communist movement, communism was first introduced to British Malaya by Chinese anarchists around the time of World War II. In 1921 after the war, agents from the Chinese Communist Party (CCP)'s organizations in Shanghai and Guangdong and Chinese communists who immigrated in search of jobs as teachers and editors began to organize students and workers by creating communist cells at night schools spreading propaganda through classes and magazines. Another wave of communists arrived from Shanghai, Guangdong, and Hainan from 1925 to 1926 and set up the Nanyang Communist Youth League, the Nanyang General Labor Union, and the Nanyang Regional Committee of the Communist Party of China (Yong 1997a: 9–10, 17–28, 41–44, 53–54, 62–63, 67, 69, 71–72).

The dissolution of the First United Front between the KMT and the CCP and the launch of the White Terror by Chiang Kai-shek in 1927, together with the failure of the Guangzhou Uprising in December the same year, prompted many communists to flee mainland China to the Southeast Asian region. They became the leaders of the communist movement in British Malaya from mid-1929. The Malayan Communist Party was formed in 1930, and the Nanyang General Labor Union was re-formed as the Malayan General Labor Union in the same year. From then on, the communist movement in British Malaya was to evolve under the guidance of these two organizations (Yong 1997a: 68, 85–86, 91, 101, 113–114, 121, 130–131, 156).

The Straits Settlements government attempted to deal with these political movements by setting up the Political Intelligence Bureau. In 1919, the Criminal Intelligence Department was established within the Straits Settlements police force to handle political movements. The establishment of the political intelligence apparatus realized that Singapore's intelligence gathering capacity needed to be improved following the aforementioned Mutiny of the 5th Light Infantry in 1915 (Onimaru 2014: 118–120). From the end of the nineteenth century, both the Indian nationalist movement and the Chinese nationalist movement remained major targets of the Political Intelligence Bureau into the 1920s to 1930s. However, at the top of its list during this period was the communist movement.

The reason for the raising of the highest level of alarm against the communist movement was primarily due to its potential to spread beyond ethnic boundaries. By their very nature, the Chinese and Indian nationalist movements waged within their respective ethnic groups calling for their independence, whereas the communist movement was meant to cross ethnic lines for the liberation of the proletariat. However, the communist movement in British Malaya during the interwar period was dominated mainly by Chinese communists. Attempts to go beyond ethnic divisions were made, albeit to a limited extent, when members of the Communist Party of Indonesia from the Dutch East Indies tried to indoctrinate Malays into communism in the 1920s, and in the early 1930s, there were reportedly around 1,000 Malay and Indian communists (Cheah 1992: 8–12; Hara 2001: 23).

The development of the communist movement beyond ethnic categories was under the directive of the Third International (the Comintern), whose presence was a second reason for the Political Intelligence Bureau's high level of alertness toward the communist movement. The Comintern was formed in Moscow in 1919 to support communist campaigns across the world to achieve a world revolution. It also advocated liberation from colonial rule as part of its endeavor. The Comintern set up liaison offices in different parts of the world from which it dispatched agents to provide instructions and finance to various communist movements (Onimaru 2014: 30–31, 36–37).

In other words, if authorities wanted to counteract the communist movement in Singapore and the rest of British Malaya, they needed to take a three-pronged approach—suppressing the movement itself that was largely driven by Singapore-based Chinese communists, preventing its spread beyond ethnic boundaries and clamping down on Comintern agents who exerted influence on the local movement from outside of the territory.

Intelligence gathering was the first weapon in the Political Intelligence Bureau's armory against not only the communist movement but also all political movements. The main sources of intelligence it used included informers, spies, and postal surveillance (Onimaru 2014: 123–128). The gathered information was used to identify movements' members and operational bases, leading to raids on their hideouts and the arrest and imprisonment or deportation of activists. The process of intelligence gathering, detention, and deportation were precisely the same as the countermeasures used against secret societies by the colonial administration in the nineteenth century.

The first countermeasure against the activities of Singapore-based Chinese communists involved the closure of the night schools used by the activists and the suppression of their publications. A crackdown was implemented during two periods, from 1922 to 1923 and from 1926 to 1927, resulting in the arrest and deportation of the leaders and the closure of many night schools. Next came the suppression of communist organizations such as the Malayan Communist Party and the Malayan General Labor Union. In the Straits Settlements alone, 1,704 people were arrested between 1932 and 1935 for their alleged involvement in communism. The number of communists who were exiled from the colony over the six years from 1930 to 1935 reached 882 (Yong 1997a: 33, 36, 57, 74–75, 169).

Secondly, the countermeasure against the spread of the movement out of the Chinese community was implemented mainly through the arrest and deportation of the activists of the Communist Party of Indonesia from the Dutch East Indies and the arrest of Malay communist leaders. The activity of Malay communists subsided after 1929 due to the rigorous crackdowns, the limited effort made by Chinese communists to overcome language barriers, and the indifference of Malay inhabitants toward the movement itself (Cheah 1992: 6–12; Hara 2001: 19–23; Yong 1997a: 139). However, the Straits Settlements government did not lower its guard against the spread of the movement. In 1930, a standing committee was set up to share intelligence on the political movements of all ethnic groups in British Malaya as well as to examine the influence of the political activities of Chinese inhabitants, especially their communist movement, over the "subversive" activities of other ethnic communities in the territory (Yong 1997b: 135).

The Political Intelligence Bureau made the political movements in the British Malayan territory "visible" by using intelligence obtained from informers and spies to clamp down on their activities. Its greatest success on this front was the recruitment of a spy named Lai Teck. He joined the Central Executive Committee of the Malayan Communist Party in 1936 and became the party's Secretary-General in 1939 (Akashi 1994: 63–64; Yong 1997a: 145, 169, 194). For the Political Intelligence Bureau, this source of intelligence at the center of the movement rendered it "visible" and no longer a threat.

The final point in this matter is that the colonial authorities needed to institute measures to stop the infiltration of Comintern agents into British Malaya. The Straits Settlements' Political Intelligence Bureau regularly exchanged intelligence with its counterpart in the British Empire, British diplomatic missions overseas, and relevant departments in French Indochina and the Dutch East Indies to keep a close watch on agents' movements. One of the outcomes of that effort happened in June 1931 when a French agent, who had been sent by the Far Eastern Bureau of Comintern in Shanghai, was arrested in Singapore. Information obtained through this arrest led to the detainment of Nguyen Ai

Quoc[4] in Hong Kong as well as the arrest of the agent in charge of international liaison at the Far Eastern Bureau in Shanghai. From a dossier seized during these arrests, it was discovered that the Comintern had planned to use Singapore as the liaison point in Southeast Asia and was taking steps to strengthen its partnership with the communist movement in British India (Onimaru 2014).

The colonial authorities were able to make the series of arrests in 1931 only because they had shared intelligence on the French agent obtained in France and Shanghai and spread a dragnet on this basis. It was extremely difficult to catch agents on the move in the absence of accumulated and shared intelligence. In 1934, the Straits Settlements Police Special Branch received information that an agent from Comintern's Far Eastern Bureau in Shanghai had arrived in Singapore on board a train from Bangkok. The effort made by the Special Branch to identify this agent while he was in Singapore was unsuccessful, and he subsequently departed for the Dutch East Indies (Straits Settlements Policce 1934: No. 4, 6, 10, 11).

Although there were limitations on policing agents on the move, the communist movement in the Straits Settlements during the interwar period was well controlled. There were no incidents reminiscent of the series of armed revolts driven by the Communist Party of Indonesia in the Dutch East Indies from 1926 to 1927 or those that formed the liberated zones in French Indochina in the early 1930s. Policing the communist movement was inherently difficult because it was impossible to judge whether people were communists or not by their outward appearance. For this reason, policing was carried out by drawing links between the communist movement and more concrete and specific organizations such as night schools, labor unions, the communist party, and the Comintern. In doing so, the Political Intelligence Bureau utilized informants and spies as lenses through which to make the movement more "visible."

5.6 Conclusion

The following statement was made in the memoir of René Onraet, who played a significant part in policing the political movements in British Malaya as the Chief of the Criminal Intelligence Department of the Straits Settlements Police during the interwar period.

> From the very outset, subversive activities in Malaya were due to outside influences. There was no irritant within Malaya to give rise to such a reaction. There was no organisation within Malaya which was capable of producing such clever, political propaganda. All of it came from China.
>
> *Onraet 1947: 109*

As expressed in Onraet's statement, the view of Chinese immigrants as the root of the problem or as outsiders reflected the challenge that faced the colonial government in Singapore from the nineteenth century onward of how to control the Chinese immigrants and residents—in other words, how to identify and regulate the troublemakers among them. However, the reality of colonial rule cannot be understood by this simple schematization alone.

To begin with, categories such as "secret societies" and "the communist movement" were applied to "invisible" targets of law and order enforcement whose inner workings were not easily apprehensible by the government. On the frontline of policing these "invisible" targets, however, efforts were made to make these organizations "visible" through meticulous intelligence gathering. As a result, it became apparent that secret societies were not simply violent gangs but that they performed various functions in the Chinese community and that their members were not limited to new immigrants. This realization led the colonial government to establish new agencies to take over the role played by these organizations in the Chinese community—such as the Chinese Protectorate and the Chinese Advisory Board—and to outlaw secret societies simultaneously.

As to the communist movement, the Political Intelligence Bureau knew that those involved were not limited to Chinese communists but were from various ethnic backgrounds, such as Malayan Communist Party members from the Dutch East Indies and Comintern agents. The Political Intelligence Bureau used informants and spies to identify those with connections to communist parties, labor unions, and the Comintern and implemented countermeasures such as arrest and deportation.

In short, the frontline personnel in the colonial government made continuous efforts to make "secrecies" of the Chinese community "visible" and identify targets that had been causing trouble, monitor them closely, and understand them before taking countermeasures. However, as the aforementioned remark by Onraet suggests, if the targets of law and order enforcement were associated exclusively with particular ethnic categories, finer points of difference and circumstances that were perceived on the ground level would be ignored, and only the simplified logic of "Chinese immigrants/residents were the root of the problem" would be perpetuated. This was the very process of racialization of "the Chinese" by which invisible but inherent characteristics of the target group were made visible and substantialized. The categorized population of the Chinese as a whole became the target of control, suppression, and discrimination.

Further, the argument in this chapter may be relevant to the question of racial representations of the Ainu people as a mode of domination in the development of Hokkaido from the Meiji era onward discussed by Hirano in Chapter 2. Colonial rule by making "invisible" targets "visible" in order to control them, as discussed in this chapter, can be regarded as one of the historical origins of the modes of "control" that uses biometric and individual authentication systems to identify and control "individuals" in contemporary India as discussed by Tanabe in Chapter 6.

Notes

1 An earlier version of this chapter was translated by the Transpacific Press.
2 "Clan war" refers to an armed conflict between different topolect groups or societies over clashing interests.

3 A similar system had already been introduced in Hong Kong in 1862 (Onimaru 2003: 515).
4 The pseudonym of Ho Chi Minh, who later became the first President of the Democratic Republic of Vietnam.

References

Abudurrā. 1980. *Abudurrā monogatari—Aru Marējin no jiden* [Tales of Abdullah: An Autobiography of a Malay Man]. Translated by Michiko Nakahara. Tokyo: Heibonsha.

Akashi, Yoji. 1994. "Lai Teck, Secretary General of the Malayan Communist Party, 1939–1947." *Journal of the South Seas Society*, 49: 57–103.

Anderson, Benedict. 2006. *Imagined Communities*. London: Verso.

Blythe, Wilfred. 1969. *The Impact of Chinese Secret Societies in Malaya: A Historical Study*. London: Oxford University Press.

Cheah Boon Kheng. 1992. *From PKI to the Comintern, 1924–1941: The Apprenticeship of the Malayan Communist Party*. Ithaca, NY: Southeast Asia Program Publications, Cornell University.

Comber, Leon. 2009. "The Singapore Mutiny (1915) and the genesis of political intelligence in Singapore." *Intelligence and National Security*, 24(4): 529–541.

Gillis, E. Kay. 2005. *Singapore Civil Society and British Power*. Singapore: Talisman Publishing.

Hamashita, Takeshi. 2013. *Kakyō kajin to chūka mō: Imin kōeki sōkin nettowāku no kōzō to tenkai* [Overseas Chinese, Ethnic Chinese and Chinese Networks: The Structure and Development of the Migration, Trade and Remittance Networks]. Tokyo: Iwanami shoten.

Hara, Fujio. 2001. *Maraya kakyō to Chūgoku: Kizoku ishiki tenkan katei no kenkyū* [Overseas Chinese in Malaya and China: A Study of the Transformation in the Sense of Belongingness]. Tokyo: Ryukei shosa.

Holdsworth, May, and Christopher Munn (eds.). 2012. *Dictionary of Hong Kong Biography*. Hong Kong: Hong Kong University Press.

Jarman, Robert L. 1998. *Annual Reports of the Straits Settlements, 1855–1941*, Vol. 1, 2. Slough: Archive Editions.

Kobayashi, Atsushi. 2013. "The role of Singapore in the growth of intra-Southeast Asian trade, c. 1820s–1852." *Southeast Asian Studies*, December, 2(3): 443–474.

Lee, Edwin. 1991. *The British as Rulers: Governing Multiracial Singapore 1867–1914*. Singapore: Singapore University Press.

Makepeace, Walter, Gilbert E. Brooke, and Roland St. John Braddell (eds.). 1921. *One Hundred Years of Singapore*, Vol. 1. London: J. Murray.

Onimaru, Takeshi 2003. "Ahen, himitsu kessha, jiyū bōeki: 19 seiki Shingapōru, Honkon deno Igirisu shokuminchi tochi no hikaku kenkyu [Opium, secret societies, free trade: A comparative study of British Colonial Rule in nineteenth century Singapore and Hong Kong]." *Japanese Journal of Southeast Asian Studies*, 40(4): 502–519.

Onimaru, Takeshi 2014. *Shanghai "Nūran jiken" no yami: Senkanki Ajia ni okeru chika katsudō no nettowāku to Igirisu seiji jōhō keisatsu* [The Noulens Affair in Shanghai: The Network of Political Underground and the Activities of British Political Police in interwar Asia]. Tokyo: Shosekikobo Hayayama.

Onraet, René. 1947. *Singapore: A Police Background*. London: Dorothy Crisp & Co.

Popplewell, Richard. 1995. *Intelligence and Imperial Defence: British Intelligence and the Defence of the Indian Empire 1904–1924*. London: Frank Cass.

Shinozaki, Kaori 2017. *Puranakan no tanjō—Kaikyō shokuminchi Penan no kajin to seiji sanka* [The Birth of the Peranakans: Ethnic Chinese and political participation in the Straits Settlement of Penang]. Fukuoka: Kyushu University Press.

Shiraishi, Takashi 1975. "Kamin goeisho no setsuritsu to kaitō: 19 seiki Singapōru no kakyō shakai no seijiteki henka [The Establishment of the Chinese Protectorate and secret societies: Political change in overseas Chinese society in nineteenth-century Singapore]." *Aziya Kenkyu [Asian Studies]*, 22(2): 75–102.

Shiraishi, Takashi. 2000. *Umi no teikoku* [Empire of the Seas]. Tokyo: Chuo Koron Shinsha.

Singapore Department of Statistics. 2018. *Yearbook of Statistics Singapore 2018*. https://www.singstat.gov.sg/publications/reference/yearbook-of-statistics-singapore/yearbook-of-statistics-singapore-content-page (Last accessed on October 3, 2018.)

Straits Settlements Government. 1898. *The acts and ordinances of the Legislative Council of the Straits Settlements, from the 1st April 1867 to the 7th March 1898*. London: Eyre and Spottiswoode.

Song Ong Siang. 1967. *One Hundred Years' History of the Chinese in Singapore*. Singapore: University Malaya Press.

Straits Settlements Police. 1934. Straits Settlements Police Political Intelligence Journal (SSPPIJ). Centre des Archives d'Outre-Mer, Aix-en-Provence, France. Indochine, Government G1 Indo, 65560, 65561.

Tachimoto, Narifumi. 2008. "Bugisu [Bugis]." In *Shinban Tōnan Ajia wo shiru jiten* [Encyclopedia of Southeast Asia new edition], edited by Shirō Momoki et al., 377–378. Tokyo: Heibonsha.

Trocki, Carl. 1990. *Opium and Empire: Chinese Society in Colonial Singapore, 1800–1910*. Ithaca, NY: Cornell University Press.

Turnbull, C. M. 1989. *A History of Singapore 1819–1988* (second edition). Singapore: Oxford University Press.

Wong Lin Ken. 1991. "Commercial growth before the Second World War." *In A History of Singapore*, edited by Ernest C.T. Chew and Edwin Lee, 41–65. Singapore: Oxford University Press.

Yen Ching-hwang. 1986. *A Social History of the Chinese in Singapore and Malaya 1800–1911*. Singapore: Oxford University Press.

Yong, C. F. 1994. *Chinese Leadership and Power in Colonial Singapore*. Singapore: Times Academic Press.

Yong, C. F. 1997a. *The Origin of Malayan Communism*. Singapore: South Seas Society.

Yong, C. F. 1997b. "Law and order: British management of Malayan communism during the interwar years, 1919–1942." In *Empires, Imperialism and Southeast Asia*, edited by Brook Barrington, 126–148. Melbourne: Monash Asia Institute.

6

THE VIRTUALIZATION OF RACE

Data Governance and Racialization in Modern India

Akio Tanabe

6.1 Introduction

This chapter will trace the history of racialization mechanisms in the governance of modern India.[a] Over the course of time, from the British Raj (1858–1947) to the present, the unit of governance has shifted from the population to the individual body. We can see this change as the gradual disappearance of the existing imperial/colonial racial order. At the same time, fingerprinting as a system/technology for controlling individual bodies on the move has been developing in India since the late colonial period, leading eventually to the creation of Aadhaar, the world's largest biometric ID system. Even as the (post-)imperial/colonial racial order is publicly repudiated, data governance linked to biometrics has given birth to a new form of racialization under globalization.

Throughout modern history, India has been the testing ground for cutting-edge systems and technologies of governance, from its imperial/colonial racial order based on religion, caste, and race—and the fingerprinting system that spawned as a means for identifying individual bodies—to the current Aadhaar system. In order to classify and control its diverse population, India has become a laboratory, so to speak. Aadhaar, initiated in 2010, is the world's most ambitious and largest biometric ID system. A thorough examination of the new racialization this enormous experiment has produced is vitally important for understanding racism today.

The concept of "race" as an objective indicator of differences between groups of people was at the root of governance under the British Raj. The distinction between "white rulers" and "Indian ruled," that is, the racialized "rule of colonial difference" (Chatterjee 1993), was one of the pillars of colonial rule. The British

---

a   An earlier version of this chapter was translated by Daniel Joseph.

DOI: 10.4324/9781003266396-8

came to India around the Cape of Good Hope and across the Indian Ocean, so the encounter accompanied long-distance travel on the part of Europeans. The racial order formed by this transoceanic encounter between groups, who recognized one another as physically and visibly very different, was similar to the racism formed in transatlantic experiences (see Introduction). After clearly distinguishing between the rulers and the ruled, the British Raj classified, counted, and governed the population under rule according to categories of religion, caste, tribe, and race. This policy of "divide-and-rule" formed another pillar of colonial rule, contributing to the creation of an order that classified various populations according to their attributes, optimally positioned them within the system, and allocated state resources accordingly. Since "the ordering of difference"[1] via classification of the population was held to derive from innate and immutable attributes, it can be said to be based on "race" in a broad sense. This colonial racial order did not only employ imported "scientific" racial theories but also utilized the existing local architecture of social classifications.[2] The British thus created hybrid categories of rule and organized the racial order by complex intertwining of scientific "Race" with pre-existing "race" categories. In that sense, the new racial order in India that appeared during the colonial period is similar to the transpacific racial order (see Introduction).[3]

One of the reasons the British were able to rule the enormous Indian Empire was that, by combining their imported scientific racism with the pre-existing racism, they succeeded in constructing a racial order that both legitimized British rule and brought about an architecture of control which accorded with the actual state of affairs on the ground. We should note, however, that this colonial racial order presumed a sedentary population as its object. For individual "bodies on the move" including non-sedentaries and criminals, the colonial authorities could not rely on the autonomous function of the racial order, and so beginning in the late nineteenth century, they used fingerprints as a means to identify and control individual bodies.[4]

The concurrent rise of Indian nationalism around the end of the nineteenth century challenged the racial order the colonial authorities had established. In the face of an imperial/colonial order based on a hierarchy rooted in racial theory—the colonialist attribution of difference between whites and Indians and a divide-and-rule approach to governing the various population groups within the empire—Indian nationalism advocated for equality both between nations and for citizens within the nation. In other words, the Indian nationalist movement was an anti-racist democratization movement aimed not just at the achievement of independence for the nation-state but at the realization of individual equality through the eradication of all discriminatory orders both at domestic and international levels (Tanabe 2014).

Thus, the Indian nationalist movement held that the individual, and not the population group, should be the political subject. However, discrimination and violence based on differences in caste and religion did not disappear in post-independence India (Tanabe 2019). Post-colonial studies have shown that the racial order constructed in India during the colonial period—a political order based on inborn and immutable attributes including caste, tribe, race, and religion—was carried over to some degree even after independence (Dirks 2001). This observation is correct in and of itself, but now, over 70 years after independence, we cannot say that all discrimination in present-day India derives from the colonial political order. Past historical descriptions have used a progressivist framework to describe the development from an imperial racial order to the civic order of the nation-state. And they have discussed how the realization of the ideal civic order of the nation-state has been impeded by traditional structures of discrimination and (post-)colonial structures of power. If we are to understand contemporary racial discrimination, however, it is insufficient to simply combine critiques of tradition and colonialism while taking this progressivist schema for granted. Rather, we must seek to comprehend whatever forms of racialization are occurring within the current political order.

Globalization has relativized the framework of the nation, and with an upsurge of transboundary movement comes an increase in the importance of identification of individual bodies as "a technology for controlling people on the move" (Takano 2016; Watanabe 2003, 333). The key to governance is not "the population" and the ascription of a racial order to it but the direct apprehension of the identity of the "individual body." In present-day India, the logic of the state's direct guarantee of individual rights and the advance of technologies for the control of individual bodies are connected. This connection is enforced by an anti-colonial democratic discourse that repudiates a divide-and-rule approach to governing population groups. The spread of the democratic system has propagated the idea that it is the individual who is the subject of rights and politics and that the state must guarantee these rights. As a result, while the direct connection between the individual and the state was held as instrumental to democracy, insufficient attention has been paid to the significance of intermediate groups, be they caste-related or religious, civic organizations or NGOs. As a result, in the name of safeguarding democratic rights, India has ironically arrived at the creation of Aadhaar, the world's largest biometric ID system, which has enabled the state to apprehend the individual bodies of every one of its residents. Aadhaar purports to be the foundation for individuals to assert their rights vis-à-vis the state, and registration is not compulsory, though it is pragmatically necessary in order to receive administrative and financial services. While, on the one hand, the direct connection between individual bodies and the state via Aadhaar has clarified the rights of the individual, on the other, it has in practice weakened the function of intermediate public domain as state control of the individual and majoritarianism in politics and society are simultaneously strengthened.

Now that the identity of individual bodies can be distinguished at the physical level and their attributes stored as massive amounts of data, racial categories like caste and religion no longer serve to form an explicit and fixed public order. This does not mean, however, that such racial categories, deeply linked as they are to sense and affect, have lost their influence. Race as a category that marks and excludes minorities continues to exist tacitly, in a virtual or latent phase, operating affectively and arbitrarily. So, what new mechanisms of racialization operate in a political order founded on biometrics and the control of individual bodies rather than on population or discipline? We will begin with an explanation of the Aadhaar and then go on to examine the history of the racial order in modern India that has culminated in this system of overt biometric data governance.

6.2 Biometrics and Data Governance—India's Aadhaar

From the use of fingerprints to the current Aadhaar system, India has long led the world in the use of biometrics in governance. Generally speaking, biometrics refers to the technology or process of identifying individuals using information from their physical and/or behavioral characteristics. Such information can include fingerprints, iris patterns, vein patterns, voiceprints, facial features, handwriting, gait, body odor, and so on.

Social control through biometric ID systems places the emphasis not on indirect control via "population" groups, nor on discipline and training of the "subject," but on the direct control of "individual bodies." This means determining simple biological identity and enacting control at the physical/informational level, irrespective of the subjectivity (will, morality) a given individual body possesses. Control is based on biological/physical identity and on the personal history, attributes, and entitlements of the individual body attached thereto. In other words, the individual body is managed and controlled based on a plethora of electronic data tied to it as a biological organism. This is data governance linked to biometrics.

China is often cited as the archetypal example of biometrics and data governance. This is because people envision state control through biometrics as a facet of authoritarian regimes. While straightforward, this model is also misleading. Biometrics and data governance are not necessarily connected to authoritarian regimes in today's world; more and more, democracies are also putting such systems into place under the guise of basic infrastructure for delivering efficient government services and guaranteeing the rights of the individual. Under the intensification of biopolitics, the actual form of governance is becoming more similar across so-called authoritarian and democratic regimes. Control through biometrics and data governance exhibits its primary function not in the ostensible imposition of a specific order—typically a racial one—but in circumstances where freedom and diversity appear at first glance to be more broadly tolerated. The essence of contemporary control society lies in the unseen, unnoticed control of the physical body within a state of freedom. Aadhaar is the world's largest biometric ID system, but the majority of the massive population of India—a democracy—accepts it or even welcomes it. What does this imply? By taking up the case of Aadhaar, we analyze the characteristics of contemporary control society and the new type of racialization therein.

FIGURE 6.1 The Aadhaar Logo. A Combination of the Sun and a Fingerprint

Source: Wikimedia Commons

So, what is Aadhaar? Aadhaar refers to a 12-digit unique identity number (UID) that residents of India can obtain based on biometric and personal information (Figures 6.1 and 6.2). As of August 2021, 1,303,334,958 people had registered, making it the world's largest biometric ID system.[5] Aadhaar is open to all residents of India who wish to register regardless of nationality, including foreigners and those without clear citizenship; it does not certify Indian citizenship.

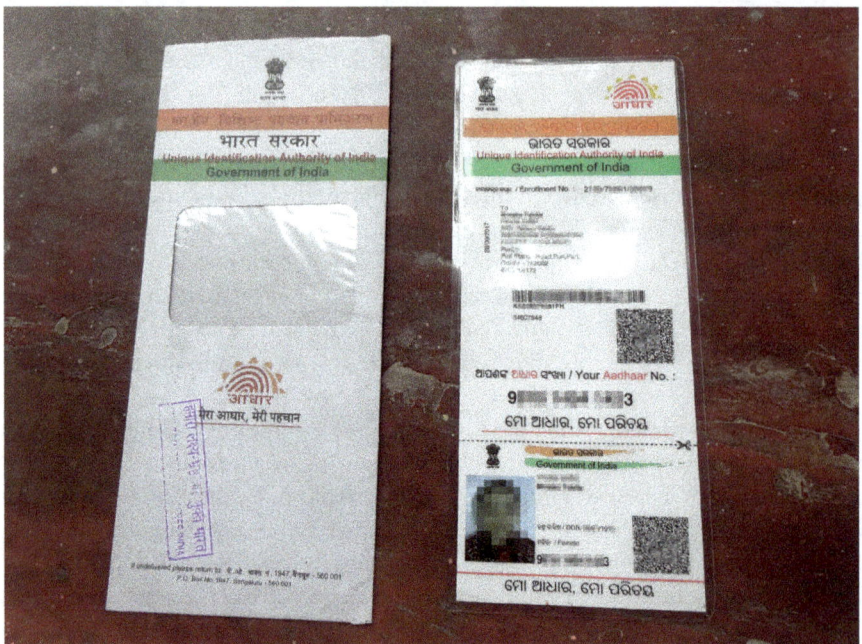

FIGURE 6.2 Aadhaar Card (lower right). Issued in Odisha State

Source: Photograph by the Author

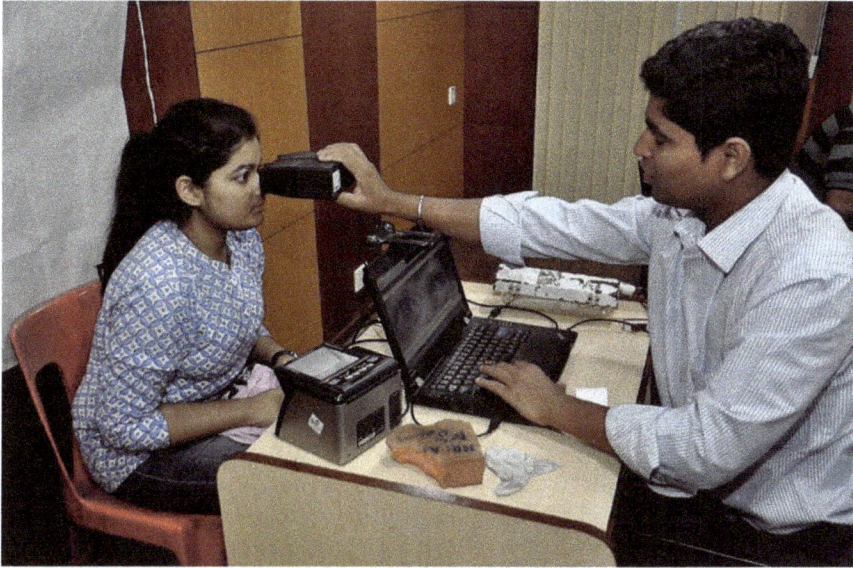

FIGURE 6.3 Recording Iris Data for Aadhaar. March 18, 2015, Kolkata

Source: Wikimedia Commons

Conversely, non-resident Indians (NRI) who live outside the country are ineligible, even if they are Indian citizens. Aadhaar's predecessor, the Indian Unique Identification Project, began in 2009, and in 2016 the Aadhaar Bill was passed. Along with personal information—full name, date of birth and/or age, address (including cell phone number and optionally email), gender (male, female, transgender), and the name of either a father, mother, husband, wife, or guardian (optional for adults)—Aadhaar uses biometric information from the irises of both eyes, all ten fingerprints, and a photograph of the face (Figure 6.3).

Aadhaar is the Hindi word for "foundation" or "base." The original slogan for the program was "Aam Aadmi ka Adhikar" (the right of the common man) but was changed after the emergence of the Aam Aadmi Party, and since 2016 it has been "Mera Aadhar, Meri Pehchaan" (My foundation, my identity). This slogan implies that Aadhaar is the foundation for guaranteeing the rights of the individual.

6.3 From British Territory to Global India

6.3.1 The Colonial Racial Order—Caste, Tribe, Religion

Let us trace the history of how such a large-scale biometric ID system came to be. We will begin with an overview of the changing face of the racial order from the British Raj (1858–1947) to present-day global India. This can also be construed as the historical shift of the unit of governance from population to individual body.

In order to assemble soldiers loyal to the empire, the British Indian Army categorized those who had remained loyal to Britain during the Indian Mutiny of 1857—including the Punjabi Sikhs and the Nepalese Gurkhas—as "martial races," preferentially recruiting them into their ranks. Thus, caste, religion, and ethnicity or race became crucial when enlisting a soldier (Fujii 2003, 115–129; Omissi 1991; Streets 2004). Those who did not apparently obey the British authority were legally designated "criminal tribes" and subjected to strict regulation (Fujii 2003, 130–137; Radhakrishna 2001).[6]

The advancement of colonial knowledge on Indian society underpinned these new classifications (Cohn 1968; Fujii 2003, Chapter 3). W. Hamilton's *A Geographical, Statistical, and Historical Description of Hindustan and the Adjacent Countries* (Hamilton 1990 [1820]), published in 1820, was "the first serious attempt to create a geography of India" (Cohn 1987, 232). Beginning in the mid-nineteenth century, many administrative reports, land settlements, census reports, and the *Caste and Tribe* series built on these early geographies, describing various regions of India. These represented one facet of the colonialist and Orientalist attempt to acquire intellectual and practical control of Indian society (Breckenridge and van der Veer 1993; Cohn 1987; Inden 1986, 1990).

The first Indian national census was conducted in 1872, and in it, we discern the British officials' desire for "power-knowledge" in their attempts to objectify and classify Indian society (cf. Foucault 1978; Said 1978). As part of the project of colonial rule, the British categorized and counted the Indian population largely along religious and caste lines. For Hindus, the 1872 census recorded caste, while for those who belonged to other religions, it recorded class (i.e., their social position within the group; for Muslims, this included Sayyid, Sheikh, Pathan, etc.). The 1881 census recorded caste and sect (denominations within religions other than Hinduism: Shia and Sunni for Muslims, Catholic and Presbyterian for Christians, etc.); the 1891 census recorded caste and race (the group to which non-Hindus declared themselves as belonging, such as Bamar, European, Eurasian, etc.); the 1901 and 1911 censuses recorded caste for Hindus and Jains, and tribe or race for all others; and from 1921 through 1941, the census recorded caste or tribe for Hindus, Muslims, Jains, and Sikhs, and race (Anglo, Indian, Goan, Turkish, etc.) for all others.

Categories such as caste, class, sect, tribe, and race are extremely vague, and the British administrators more or less abandoned any attempts to define them. The director in charge of the 1931 census, J.H. Hutton, wrote, "the term 'caste' needs no definition in India; the tribe was provided to cover the many communities still organized on the basis in whose case the tribe has not become a caste; it was likewise determinate enough, and no attempt was made to define the term race which was generally used so loosely as almost to defy any definition." The term race was included to "obtain a return of Indians to whom the terms like 'caste' and tribe are inapplicable" (Hutton 1986, 425; quoted in Bhagat 2006, 122). Regardless of these unsystematic and seemingly chaotic categories, the colonial authorities consistently maintained the presumption that distinctions of religion and caste were fundamental to Indian society.

Religion and caste became public keywords representing the Indian order for the power-knowledge of the ethnographic state. By classifying people according to religion and caste, the colonial government affixed their identities to group affiliation. This kind of classification was necessary for the colonial rulers to control the ruled as quantifiable objects (Appadurai 1993; Cohn 1987). In Chapter 2 of this book, Hirano observes that "racism, one of the most virulent ideologies in modern times, is such an extra-economic force that directs how labor power is subsumed under capital" (p. 27). Human life includes externalities that cannot be reduced to the logic of capital, but the category of race, along with other extra-economic forces such as law, politics, ideology, and social values, subsumes these and transforms them into objects that can be controlled and manipulated.

The colonial administration's desire to understand and manage the population of Indian society as an agglomeration of quantifiable categories like religion and caste ended up heightening the Indian people's sense of belonging to those very categories, in turn giving rise to a colonial civil society (Dirks 2005). The latter half of the nineteenth century saw a rise in the formation of religious organizations (van der Veer 2001) and caste associations (Carrol 1978), with a concomitant boom in socio-economic and political activities by these intermediate groups. Caste associations were created with the aim of improving the socio-economic status of their own caste group. They arose in response to the colonial government's policy of social positioning and granting autonomous entitlement or educational and professional opportunities according to caste.

The political importance of religious organizations was further amplified by the Morley-Minto Reforms of 1909, which introduced separate electorates for Muslims in the legislatures. The early twentieth century saw the successive formation of social movement organizations and political organizations divided by religious affiliation, including the Muslim League (founded 1906), the Hindu Mahasabha (founded 1915), and the Rashtriya Swayamsevak Sangh (or RSS, lit. "National Volunteer Organization," founded 1925). During the same period, Hindu reform organizations like Arya Samaj started a movement to reconvert tribals and Dalits who had converted to Islam. This was clearly tied to a "politics of population" that advocated the distribution of resources according to the number of members in a given group (Gill 2007; Guha 2003).

Thus, the colonial government identified these various religions and castes as groups possessing clearly defined attributes and boundaries, to which the Indians responded by actually forming groups based on their own religions and/or castes. The British government adopted a policy of non-intervention in Indian society's religions and traditional customs, while they left matters of caste to "caste autonomy" (Kotani 1994; Kotani, Yoshimura and Awaya 1994; Yoshimura 1994). This was not rooted in the principles of liberalism but in the clear intention to exploit Indian society's autonomous order-formation capacity for the sake of state control. Far from being non-interventionist, this policy of controlling the population via ethnographic objectification and autonomous order-formation, in fact, had a considerable impact on Indian society (Dirks 2001).

6.3.2 Control of Individual Bodies on the Move—The History of Fingerprinting

The racial order of the British Raj, centered around caste, tribe, and religion, was targeted at sedentaries, as the capturing of population groups was well suited to controlling such people. Population was ill suited to be the unit of control for people on the move, however, and in those cases, it was necessary to directly apprehend the individual body. To accomplish this, the British authorities turned to fingerprints.

Scientific fingerprinting as a means for identifying individual bodies first became a topic of debate in the academic world with the publication of Henry Faulds' "On the Skin-furrows of the Hand" in the journal *Nature* in 1880. Faulds went to Japan as a member of a Scottish medical missionary group, and while visiting the Ōmori shell mound in the company of Edward Morse, he noticed fingerprints which had been left on the surface of some Jōmon pottery; the scientific study of fingerprints stemmed from this observation (Figure 6.4). However, in the very next issue of *Nature*, senior Indian civil servant William Herschel asserted that he had already been using finger marks for the purpose of identifying individual bodies for 20 years (Herschel 1880).

At the same time, Francis Galton (Charles Darwin's cousin) had conceived an interest in fingerprints from the standpoint of eugenics, becoming acquainted with Herschel through *Nature*. In 1892, he wrote *Finger Prints*, which demonstrated both that no two people have the same fingerprints and that our fingerprints remain unchanged throughout our lifetime (Galton 1892). Herschel sent this book to his former assistant Henry Cotton, who passed it on to Edward Henry.

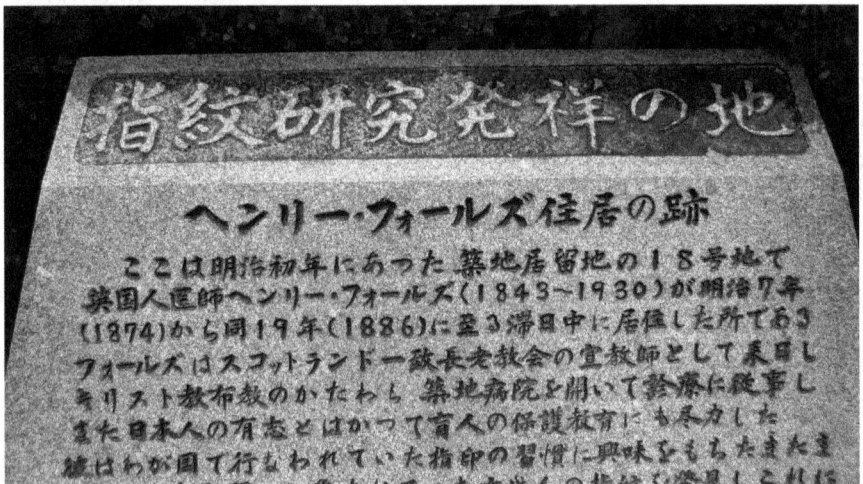

FIGURE 6.4 Site of Henry Faulds' Residence in the Tsukiji Foreigner Settlement. The "Birthplace of Fingerprinting Research"

Source: Photograph by the Author

As a senior official in India, Edward Henry was tasked with controlling the "criminal tribes." The Criminal Tribes Act was used against people on the move, such as nomadic traders or pastoralists, who did not conform to the colonial image of settled agriculture and wage labor. Henry was appointed Inspector-General of Police of Bengal in 1891, and in order to control the individual bodies of a criminal tribe called the Magahiya Dom, he tested out an anthropometric methodology known as the "Bertillon System," which measured 11 parts of the body (Yang 1985). The Bertillon System was a method for identifying individual bodies which had been officially adopted in France in 1885, but the results were unsatisfactory. Working from Galton's research, Henry set out to create a method for identifying individual bodies, eventually devising the "Henry System" for sorting and searching fingerprints. His system for identifying criminals by their fingerprints was adopted throughout India in 1897. In 1900 Henry introduced this fingerprinting method to the British colony of South Africa, and in 1901 it was adopted in Britain itself (Breckenridge 2014; Maguire 2009; Takano 2016; Watanabe 2003). These accomplishments led to Henry's appointment as Commissioner of Police of the Metropolis in 1903 (Figure 6.5).

Technologies and systems for the control of individual bodies sat beside systematic racial discrimination at the core of colonial power. Indeed, the catalyst for Gandhi's satyagraha (holding firmly to the truth) movement in South Africa was the 1906 Asiatic Registration Act, which mandated compulsory fingerprinting. In that sense, Gandhi's non-violent protest movement was a protest against both racial discrimination and the control of individual bodies. Ironically, however, there has been insufficient consideration of the implications of Gandhi's non-violent protest movement in post-colonial India, to the point that the government has introduced the identification of individual bodies as a means to guarantee the people's rights and empower the underclasses.

6.3.3 From Post-Colonial India to Global India

During World War II, the British formulated a system of total war to capitalize on India's labor potential. The state allotted ration tickets to every household, creating a system of control wherein it assembled data on each individual and household. As Kamterkar has demonstrated, the wartime system created in 1942 was carried over into post-independence India (Kamterkar 2002).[7]

From independence in 1947 through to 1970, post-colonial India carried out its democratization project and the development of state leadership in the name of modern progress. The goal was the formation of an enlightened nation, and the various social groups that were not part of the mainstream became targets of education and development. In order to identify those targets, however, the state employed constitutional frameworks which had clear continuities with the colonial period, such as "Scheduled Castes," "Scheduled Tribes," and "Other Backward Classes." Despite the high idealism of Ambedkar, the chief architect of

FIGURE 6.5 Caricature of Edward Henry from the October 5, 1905 Issue of British Entertainment Magazine *Vanity Fair*. Captioned "Fingerprints." By "Spy" AKA Leslie Ward (1851–1922)

Source: Wikimedia Commons

the Constitution of India and a Dalit, the Indian nation the majority envisioned was tacitly centered around the Hindu high-caste middle class, racistly marking the "backward" groups that did not fit this norm/standard and designating them as targets of education and development.

The 1980s was a period of transition, after which India made a hard turn toward economic liberalization. This marked the turning point from post-colonial India to global India. Amid the insecurity and dissatisfaction stemming from the fluidity of globalization, various minorities have been blamed for caus-ing disturbances, becoming the targets of exclusion and violence (Appadurai 2006). It is not the groups' characteristics that are deemed problematic, however, but their perceived probability of danger to society. Diversity is seen as a good thing, but for the sake of the common welfare (public order, the environment, sanitation, efficiency), perceived risk groups (Muslims, tribes, slum residents, immigrants) must be controlled. For example, the state of Maharashtra forcibly deports Bengali Muslims charged with being illegal Bangladeshi immigrants, even though the majority of them are, in fact, Indian citizens. The Citizenship Amendment Act (CAA) of 2019 offers a pathway to Indian citizenship to reli-gious minorities who have migrated from Pakistan, Bangladesh, and Afghanistan but excludes Muslim immigrants from eligibility.[8] And in the state of Odisha, state power colludes with multinational corporations to violently remove tribes who resist the expansion of forestry and mining, labeling them violent Maoist revolutionaries (Tokita-Tanabe and Tanabe 2014).

Risk groups, whether they be Muslims, immigrants, or tribals, are designated with the social category of "other"—not "us." These "others" who precipitate the dangers of terrorism, disease, social unrest, and economic burden must be excised in order to protect "our" society. This is indisputably one form of racism that occurs within Michel Foucault's biopower. Racism is "primarily a way of introducing a break into the domain of life that is under power's control: the break between what must live and what must die" and establishes a positive rela-tionship between life and death in which "the death of the other" makes our lives "healthier and purer" (Foucault 2004, 254–255). Power thus protects society through the logic of this kind of racist risk management.

There are differences, however, between the nineteenth- and early twentieth-century imperial and national racism Foucault discusses—a stable racial order in which specific groups are fixed as categories—and the new racism that has emerged amid globalization. The latter does not necessarily involve the othering of specific racial groups. Instead, power arbitrarily determines who or what is dangerous to society in response to the exigencies of the moment. In order to mitigate risk, power by control (power in control society, as opposed to power in disciplinary society) and/or social power supplants the judicial system to carry out ad hoc preemptive measures of excluding dangerous others. As what is seen as problematic shifts, the axis of exclusion shifts with it. As Hindus, Dalits attack Muslims, while at the same time, as members of the bourgeoisie, middle class Muslims and Hindus collaborate to exclude slum residents (a majority of whom are Hindu Dalits and/or poor Muslims) from their living spaces. There is no fixed group order. With a plural axis of ascription of difference that includes factors such as religion, caste, income, movement history, and area of residence, anyone can be named a minority at any time. In the face of such uncertainty, people increasingly attempt to position themselves within the nation's majority and attempt to designate others as minorities. This rampant majoritarianism creates the constant anxiety that one will be designated a dangerous minority oneself.

This new racialization occurring amid globalization is deeply linked to technologies and systems for the identification of individual bodies. The Indian election commission began issuing photo IDs to enfranchised individuals in 1993. Twenty years later, in 2003, the government decided to issue Multipurpose National Identity Cards (MNICs) to all Indian citizens in order to "provide a credible individual identification system and simultaneous use for several multifarious socio-economic benefits and transactions within and outside the Government" as "the basis of more efficient e-Governance."[9] Behind this lies the further progression of biopolitics. As globalization allows state power to infiltrate every corner of the lifeworld alongside the market economy, power has attempted to apprehend and control every single individual body.

6.4 The Indistinct Realm between Law and Life

Giorgio Agamben (2005) argues that in our contemporary age, the exception becomes the norm. Human beings in the contemporary world are compelled—like *homo sacer*, who was placed outside the law—to live "bare life" (life whose *bios* has been taken away, leaving only *zoe* on a political level and which exists in the space between *bios* and *zoe*), their human rights suspended as if under a state of emergency even in normal everyday life. Biopolitics makes bare life its target. These observations are correct, but we should note that placement outside civil society and the suspension of human rights were a matter of course under colonialism. The state of exception, therefore, needed no normalization, as it was already the usual experience for a great many people in India; it was, in fact, the possession of human rights as a member of civil society that was an exceptional privilege. The focus of politics in such colonial circumstances was not on rights but on rule and governance.

Governmentality may be purely mechanical. Various categories are constructed through interaction with existing social factors, and these categories become the foundation for special consideration, as well as for people's own political subjectification. For example, the various population categories related to caste and religion in India—"Scheduled Caste," "Scheduled Tribe," "Other Backward classes," and "religious minority" (a common euphemism for Muslims in India)—are the foundation not only for rule from above, but for the various demands from below rooted in their particular positions and histories: rectifying discrimination, welfare measures and the elimination of poverty, respect for the autonomy of religious communities, and so on. This place where the encounter between "those who govern" and "the governed" takes place is a heterogeneous space in which the universal technologies, systems, and values of those who govern interact with the particular social realities of the governed (Chatterjee 2004). Within colonial reality, "population" categories placed the majority of people in the colony outside of civil society while at the same time including them in intermediate groups, and so did not turn them completely into bare life. In other words, caste and religion performed the role of one form of "colonial civil society" (Dirks 2001, 12).

On the other hand, bodies on the move individually controlled using fingerprints *were* treated as true "bare life" under Indian colonial rule. Since then, these technologies/systems for controlling individual bodies, originally implemented for criminal tribes on the move, have come to be used more subtly and on a much grander scale for the populace at large. In the control of individual bodies, our particular mode of life (*bios*) as human beings is not at issue—the living body itself (*zoe*) is directly surveilled and controlled. What makes this kind of direct scrutiny of the individual body necessary? As movement becomes more frequent, the sedentary racial order of the past is no longer sufficient. There is an increased need to thoroughly apprehend the entitlements and attributes of individual bodies wherever they may go and to carry out governance appropriately tailored to those individual bodies.

This is also related to the space between legal and illegal, citizen and noncitizen. On this point, Takano Asako makes the following incisive observation: "The important thing here is the fact that we are approaching a kind of turning point with regard to increasing control of movement. First, control of cross-border movements is transcending the current framework of legal/illegal, and the discourse of risk management has created increased interest in future illegality contained within current legality (risk); second, this has resulted in the demand that a continuous gaze be leveled at these bodies even before they cross national borders" (Takano 2013, 98). I would add that as the space between legal and illegal becomes more indistinct, it is not only interest in future illegality contained within current legality (risk) that is increasing; but there is also a demand to guarantee the life of (and at the same time a pressure to exclude) those who are held to be within illegality—squatters and illegal immigrants—as well as a move toward exploiting them as a resource of capital or the state. So, while being illegal does not mean unconditional exclusion, there is a push to fully surveil and investigate the attributes and abilities of the individual bodies in question for the sake of ascertaining the legitimacy of humanitarian claims and the political or economic utility. In this way, all bodies become the object of the gaze of control regardless of their legal/illegal status and whether or not they move and what kind of bodies they are becomes the object of intense scrutiny.

In contemporary Indian politics, what is legally correct is less of a concern than whether or not the people feel their life is improving and the government feel they have a better control over its people. In any case, the political focus is on individual lives. The important question is whether or not a given life can be appropriately dealt with outside the law (in the form of exclusion or special attention). This frequently gives rise to ethical and political negotiations around how a person's life should be politically and socially treated, even if they have no legal rights.

Partha Chatterjee (2004) provides a case of land acquisition as an example of political consideration conducted outside the law. Around the year 2000, New Town was under construction in Rajarhat, the northeastern part of Calcutta (officially renamed Kolkata in 2001). In the course of only two or three years, the area transformed from a rural farming district to an effective extension of the metropolis. The site procurement committee carried out land acquisition and price negotiations for the construction of New Town, and while legally, land payments could only be made to the land's owners, this would have caused hardship for the people who lived and worked on the land. The actual negotiations took a more pragmatic approach, not bound solely by the letter of the law. The local consensus was that part of the compensation, which legally should have gone to the owners of the land be distributed to the leaseholders and laborers who were losing their livelihoods.

Lest this looks all nice, we must keep in mind that this kind of political consensus tends to benefit the dominant parties and to ignore the interests of marginalized minorities. Such consensus is also often socially conservative, with a lack of sensitivity toward issues related to gender and religious minorities. Political society is not desirable for the entire populace, and this is where the laws of civil society and the stipulations of human rights can play an important role.

Next, let us consider events surrounding Bangladeshi immigrants in the state of Odisha in the years since 2005 (Chhotray 2017). This case shows the widening of the indistinct realm between citizen and non-citizen. Many immigrants have come to India from eastern Pakistan and Bangladesh since the partition of India in 1947 and Bangladeshi independence in 1971, a great many of whom have settled in Odisha. The government treats them as ordinary citizens, issuing them official documents recording property rights, the right to vote, the right to receive rations, and so on. In 2005, however, based on a directive from the high court, the Odisha state government suddenly produced a list of 1,551 people who had entered the country illegally. Since they had done so after 1971, the state declared that their citizenship would no longer be recognized. In 2007 they were removed from the public distribution system (PDS) list, losing their right to receive necessities like rice and kerosene at reduced prices. However, a Bengali village headman convinced dealers to distribute 1 kilo of kerosene per household for humanitarian reasons. Furthermore, while these people were struck from the government's old-age pension and home construction subsidy lists, they were allowed to continue using public schools and infant healthcare centers, and some also got work through the National Rural Employment Guarantee Scheme. In some villages, they even voted in local elections. So, there was tacit approval of their continued presence even if they no longer had citizenship, and they continued to use a number of public services.

The above examples demonstrate that administrative and judicial authorities can suddenly strip people of the rights they had enjoyed up to that moment, while at the same time, people who have lost their citizenship can obtain some measure of entitlement through negotiation with local government and/or the people of the locality. Citizenship is not consistent or fixed; its substance is, in fact, negotiable.[10]

In the modern nation, we imagine the distinction between the law and its outside to be relatively clear. For instance, immigrants and refugees are seen as "beyond human rights" (Agamben 2000). The law and human rights are applied to the citizen, while immigrants and refugees are outside that protection. The framework of the nation-state is clear here, and in situations where control of people on the move is strictly enforced, this may be a valid distinction. Where it is essentially impossible to control who moves where when, however, as in the case of South Asia (especially as regards movement between India, Bangladesh, and Nepal), the space between citizen and non-citizen as well as legal and illegal expands. This space is precisely the indistinct territory that in a different context Agamben (1993) has called "the space between law and life," and it seems appropriate to say that the bases for rights which people can obtain in that space are currently up for negotiation. It is a heterogeneous space in which the technologies, systems, and values of law and governance become entangled with the realities of life. As membership in a given population or citizenry becomes less and less clear in societies on the move (Sadiq 2008), the question of what entitlements and bases for rights each person has (should have) comes under scrutiny.

In such a context, India has opted to try and register the biometric information of all residents regardless of whether or not they are citizens rather than attempt to clarify who is a member by virtue of citizenship (which would be virtually impossible). This brings us to Aadhaar, the biometric ID system launched in 2010.

6.5 The Creation and Development of Aadhaar

6.5.1 The Creation of Aadhaar

The Indian government began issuing Multipurpose National ID Cards to citizens in 2003, but this necessitated determining who was and was not a citizen. To that end, the Ministry of Home Affairs decided to create the National Population Register (NPR) based on the Citizenship Act 1955 and the Citizenship (Registration of Citizens and Issue of National Identity Cards) Rules, 2003.[11] In the face of increasing terrorist activity and other such factors, the goal was to clearly distinguish between citizens and non-citizens for the sake of public order. People moved around and across India frequently, however, and the government's ability to govern was at a low ebb, making it difficult to determine who was a citizen.

Furthermore, mass migrations took place around the time of both the partition of India in 1947 and Bangladeshi independence in 1971, making it extremely hard to determine who had been living where and for how long. In 1960, India had the second largest population of immigrants in the world after only the US, comprising 9.41 million people, or 12.20% of the world immigrant population (total 77,110,000). Pakistan was third with 6,350,000 immigrants, and India and Pakistan alone accounted for 20.44% of the world immigrant population. By 2005, India had fallen to 8th on the list with 5,890,000 immigrants, or 3.02% of the world immigrant population of 195,250,000 (UNDP 2009, 145). Looking at internal migration within India, 28.5% of the total population moved in 2007–2008. The population at that time was 1,150,000,000, which means that a full 328,000,000 people were living on the move (National Sample Survey Organization 2010, H-vi). Within that group, 42,300,000 people (4% of the total population) migrated across state borders (UNDP 2009, 145). With both international and internal migration occurring in such great numbers, it was difficult to create the NPR and little progress was made.

In the face of these problems, Infosys co-founder Nandan Nilekani offered a blueprint for a system linking state and individual through an information network in his book *Imagining India* (Nilekani 2008). Unlike NPR, this network would not be limited to citizens and would be open to all residents. Nilekani argued that the proper delivery of state services would ensure the livelihoods of India's inhabitants, and the country as a whole would flourish. There were many welfare schemes in India, but rampant corruption meant that the funds often did not reach their intended recipients. To combat this, Nilekani envisioned an information system free of corruption and duplication. As Lawrence Cohen has pointed out, the image of human beings in this system is that of "bare life" (Agamben 1998; Cohen 2016). It is an existence in which human beings do not construct their own lives; instead, their biological life is ensured through the distribution of material resources. Nilekani's proposal resonated with a nation fed up with corruption, and the government moved to adopt it. The State Planning Commission established the Unique Identification Authority of India (UIDAI) in 2009, and the Aadhaar project went forward with Nilekani appointed as its head. As a result, Aadhaar and the Home Ministry's NPR proceeded in tandem.[12]

The government began issuing Unique Identification Numbers in September 2010. Nilekani set the following six goals: (1) Assign an ID number to every individual; (2) Eliminate corruption; (3) Create an inclusive register (provide ID to as many residents as possible by including transgender as an option, not requiring proof of address or age, etc.); (4) Ensure credibility through deduplication; (5) Ensure privacy; and 6() Ensure transparency of administrative processes (Nilekani 2018). Through Aadhaar, "biometric attributes of the residents are going to be used as the basic signature for deduplication and to ensure uniqueness" (UIDAI 2010, 13). The loanword "duplicate" is used frequently in Indian languages with regard to corruption. As a result, "deduplication" does not simply mean removing duplicates but carries an implication of eliminating all corruption, reflecting the people's desire for a society in which state services properly reach the intended individuals. Indian residents' biometric attributes hold the decisive key to this elimination of corruption. The notion is that it is precisely the direct connection of the bodies of individuals to the state that enables those individuals to assert their rights. Nilekani argues that "Aadhaar is not a surveillance tool by the state, on the contrary, it is an assertion of your individual identity vis-à-vis the state" (Nilekani 2018).

6.5.2 The Development of Aadhaar

Today's expanded Aadhaar is the combination of two different lineages. First, the Home Ministry's NPR, implemented in 2003, which represented a centralized authoritarian model of data management for the sake of governance and public order. This register, which aimed at registering "usual residents" of India, sought to clarify membership in the national community based on "usual" residential status and thus the possession or lack of citizenship, in the end clearly distinguishing between citizen ("usual residents") and non-citizen (immigrants) with the goal of excluding the latter. By contrast, the Department of Electronics and Information Technology's Aadhaar employs a decentralized model of data management with the goal of social welfare.[13] Aadhaar is a platform linking innumerable information repositories, constituting a data ecosystem (Cohen 2016).

On July 1, 2015, Prime Minister Narendra Modi presented his Digital India initiative (with the goal of "Making India a stronger knowledge economy society through digitalization"). One of the core elements of this initiative is the "JAM trinity" (combining bank account, ID number, and cell phone).[14] The expectation is that this will allow the government to reliably ensure the people's standard of living by providing cashless services, and furthermore, that Aadhaar will develop as a platform for the spread not only of government services but of diverse services provided by private capital as well.

With the JAM trinity, the distinction between centralized information networks like the NPR and decentralized networks like the shared platform of Aadhaar no longer holds. This expanded Aadhaar unites the state goal of efficient governance represented by Modi with Nilekani's dream of an information system through which individuals can receive appropriate services thanks to the elimination of corruption and duplication (Cohen 2016).

While there are privacy concerns in some quarters regarding increases in efficiency and elimination of corruption thanks to the use of electronic data in India, the overall impression seems to be largely positive. For example, the hero of the hit 2018 Tamil-language film *Sarkar* (Government) decides to take on the thoroughly corrupt state administration by selecting candidates for the coming election who will selflessly work to make social welfare a reality for the people. He says there is no need for an interview or an announcement of candidacy to select candidates: with an internet search, one can find out a person's email address, message history, purchase history, payment history, school attendance record, health status, academic record, whether they have ever paid any fines, even how they have treated their parents, and thereby determine whether or not they have the integrity to be a candidate. The protagonist then selects candidates based on this online information and convinces them to run in the election. This reflects the idea that it is precisely in the "objective" electronic data that peoples' real selves appear. This way of imagination and thinking serves as an endorsement of data governance and has the unfortunate effect of legitimizing the inclusion or exclusion of people based on electronic data.

By connecting the individual's various attributes and entitlements to biometric data, the data governance of expanded Aadhaar creates de-territorialized e-borders (or electronically controlled physical borders) everywhere, which become a means of controlling people's possible actions (access to resources and spaces). This is what Nikolas Rose calls "the securitization of identity." As he points out: "The image of control by totalizing surveillance is misleading. Control is better understood as operating through conditional access to circuits of consumption and civility: constant scrutiny of the right of individuals to access certain kinds of flows of consumption goods; recurrent switch points to be passed in order to access the benefits of liberty" (Rose 2000, 326; see also 1999, 243).

In contrast to the census's objectification of race and population in (post-)colonial India (Appadurai 1993; Cohn 1987), expanded Aadhaar brought about the "datafication" (digitalization) of daily life and the individual. Unlike the management and control of population and race using categories and numbers, data governance works directly on (bank accounts and cell phone numbers connected to) the individual's data via electronic space. And the individual can electronically access money and services through the mediation of data linked to biometric identification. For the government, objective facts lie in electronic data, of which physical reality is nothing more than a reflection. The age of "governing the population" through the central concept of "race" based on group attributes and physical difference is over; we are now in an age of "governing individual bodies," where biometric identification and electronic data are linked, and activities of bodies on the move can be controlled anywhere they go either physically or digitally.

6.6 Biometric Identification and Data Racism in the Control Society

When data governance at the level of the individual body becomes dominant, the borders of citizenship become ambiguous. In the old national order, you either had citizenship (nationality) or you didn't. But when a control on the level of the individual body becomes possible, so too does finer control over who is afforded what rights. This is because the individual body's biometric information itself becomes a passport to various spaces and entitlements (a baseline for granting rights). Behind this ambiguation of citizenship and the new necessity for control at the level of the individual body lies increasing trans-border movement and the relativization of the framework of the nation-state. In a globalizing society on the move, Foucault's "biopolitics of the population" (rule by classifying and counting groups) or "anatomo-politics of the human body" (rule by disciplining the bodies of individuals) no longer apply. Unlike the racist mechanisms tied to the logic of the modern state—normalization and standardization stemming from the disciplining authority—here, the focus is very much on the "control and governance of moving bodies" (Takano 2016) and the identification of individual bodies thus becomes decisively important. People are not required to belong to a group or internalize discipline. There would be cyber-physical control of each body according to its attributes and entitlements. It is no longer population groups but the individual bodies that become the basis of control (Deleuze 1992; Foucault 1978).

We can view the rise of contemporary data governance as the shift "from a disciplinary society to a control society" (Deleuze 1992). The disciplinary society had two poles: the signature that designates the individual and the number that indicates the position of the individual within the mass. The disciplining authority assembled people into masses (groups), then forced each individual to fit the mold. What is important in the control society, however, is no longer a signature or a number but a code. Whereas the disciplinary society was regulated by watchwords (words of command and discipline), in a control society, this code functions as a password, through which access to given spaces or information can be controlled. Here the distinction between the mass (group) and the individual no longer has meaning. The individual body is no longer a consistent, indivisible "individual" but manifests as a "dividual," fragmented into various data (Deleuze 1992, 296). The present control society no longer requires subjectification based on discipline (the judgment of "good/evil") nor a divide-and-rule approach based on population groups. The lives and bodies of individuals are encoded as a collection of fragmentary data—fingerprints, iris patterns, IQ, place of birth, movement history, academic record—and the behavior of the individual body is controlled through these "objective" indices. The individual body is no longer an individual with an inner life (bios) but a bundle of information codes (zoe reduced to information), and it is these codes, rather than the individual, which are the object of surveillance (Mima 2003, 192). And these codes are collected and controlled via an information network which transcends borders.

In the contemporary control society, it has become possible to control the individual body's access and behavior based on ad hoc categorizations deriving from the acquisition and analysis of information at the micro level (DNA and other molecular-level information), the mezzo level (fingerprints and iris patterns), and the macro level (population, epidemiology). The essence of power in a control society lies in the use of data to physically and informationally control "the possibility of action" itself. This kind of power is clearly evident in so-called non-traditional security safeguards like anti-terrorism and COVID-19 control and prevention measures. This is perhaps easiest to grasp through examples like the restriction of freedom of movement via incarceration or hospitalization, or the control of access to particular spaces (stadiums, buildings, or countries), in the name of health and public safety. Such measures are based on personal data collected without the knowledge of the people in question. Classifying this accumulated information according to specific risks allows the creation of risk group categories, in turn enabling the direct control of the masses of bodies that come under those categories (Mima 2003, 193). This suggests the birth of a new "data racism" in contemporary society—discrimination based not on visible differences but on electronic data inside an invisible black box. "Race" in this context is a category of dividuals, constructed around a specific axis of difference extracted from a bundle of data rather than around a uniform group based on a stable order. The problem is that the categories distilled from these data get superimposed onto past notions of race based on vague affective and emotional structure, becoming a framework for exclusion and the assignment of qualitative difference.

In contemporary Indian data racism, the axis used to assign difference and the question of who is considered a risk group depends on the issue at hand, be it public safety, health, and sanitation, disease prevention, the environment, etc. Furthermore, the groups distilled from the data differ fundamentally from the pre-existing group framework of the imperial/colonial racial order. In most cases, however, the category terms of caste, religion, and tribe are nevertheless used as shorthand when naming these groups, who are then racialized by virtue of a latent, unconscious sense of collective differences attached to those categories, thereby becoming targets of discrimination and exclusion. Race lies dormant, so to speak, inside the colossal databank, manifesting at times as one link in the chain of management and control. As populist nationalism is tied to the push for efficient governance, exclusion of and violence toward "others" such as Muslims, immigrants, and slum dwellers continues unabated. We must keep a close and watchful eye on expanded Aadhaar so that data racism does not produce a dystopia in which majoritarianism and efficient governance proceed hand in hand.

We find the overt exclusion of Muslims in India involving data racism in the Indian government's policies on census and immigration. In December 2019, the cabinet decided to update NPR across the country (except Assam) from April to September 2020. NPR was seen by its critics as a move to construct the National Register of Citizens (NRC). Also, in December 2019, the parliament passed the CAA. CAA is an amendment of the Citizenship Act 1955 offering possibilities of attaining Indian citizenship to religious minorities—Hindus, Sikhs, Buddhists, Jains, Parsis, and Christians—from Afghanistan, Bangladesh, and Pakistan who came to India before the end of December 2014. Muslims were excluded on the pretext that they are not minorities in these countries. Thus, the marking of Muslim minority as the "other" for Indian majority was actualized by law. We can see this as an actualization and legalization of the latent sensual and affective discrimination toward Muslims by the Hindu majority and its allies. The massive wave of protests against both CAA and NRC inside and outside India that followed the passing of the law, as well as the callousness of those who support the law, demonstrates peoples' differing sentiments over the issue.

As the form of power changes with the shift "from a disciplinary society to a control society," our strategy must change along with it. Disciplinary power was concerned with the individual's internalization of the norm, and so opposition based on civil liberties of the individual was well-suited as response to intrusion of governance in human life. In order to protect personal liberty of the individual, it was imperative that state power not be permitted to invade a person's privacy. At the stage of power by control, however, individual bodies have already been dividualized, and are in a state of pre-individual molecular relation. Critiquing power by control from the standpoint of the protection of personal privacy is irrelevant, at least on a theoretical level.[15] This kind of power does not attempt to control each individual's inner self but to control the entire molecular relation. Power here refers to something which contains the workings of multifarious and diverse forces rather than to a monolithic and decisive sovereign power (Connolly 2005, 145). "When power becomes completely biopolitical, the entire social body is constructed by the machine of power and developed within the latency of that machine. This is an open relation, something qualitative and affective. Society that has ended up subsumed inside power that has arrived at the core of social construction and its process of development more or less responds to the sole body" (Hardt and Negri 2005, 18–19).

In a society where individuals are dismantled into dividuals and the whole molecular relation responds affectively as a single body, racist discrimination also develops in a latent phase. Power by control and social power engage in a "politics of affect" (Massumi 2015) surrounding race, wherein latent sense and affect regarding various differences crystallize seemingly out of nowhere in the form of real political acts of designating and excluding "others." In these processes of racialization and differentiation, data governance bestows "objective" indices. Even as the fixed "racial" categories of the past are rejected as prejudiced, they are replaced by a self–other dichotomy based (supposedly) on objective fact in the form of data. In other words, here, we have not just the "objective subjectification" described by Osawa Masachi (2013, 163–167) but an "objective othering" as well. This new racialization in the form of data racism is set in motion by the arbitrary and fluid connection between electronic data and latent affect, both of which are invisible.

6.7 Conclusion—The Virtualization of "Race"

Indian colonial rule was centered around the concept of "race." The rulers and the ruled were divided into "white and Indian," and the ruled were further placed in a racial order based on religion, caste, tribe, and race. India began to use fingerprinting for the individual identification of bodies on the move around the end of the nineteenth century. A racial order based on religion, caste, tribe, and race was, to some degree, carried over into post-colonial independent India, and fingerprinting developed into the governance technology of Aadhaar, a system for controlling the bodies of individuals through biometric identification. As a unique identification number, Aadhaar began as a neutral platform for the identification of individual bodies, but as that ID has become linked to various databases through bank accounts and cell phone numbers, each individual body has become inextricably linked to the myriad data related to it. Hence, indirect governance in the form of control of "population" groups through the category of race is no longer necessary. Through the state's apprehension of data on bodies on the move, there is direct control of "individual bodies." Where large numbers of people are on the move, Aadhaar's goal is the individual control/management of every single person residing in India. During the colonial period, the control of individual bodies was applied to peoples on the move, who were then the exception, but in contemporary India, we see the exception becoming the norm (Agamben 2005).

In an order based on the identification of individual bodies, whether or not a given body can access certain resources, information, and spaces is decided using "objective" criteria based on data about that body. What is important for order in a control society is neither the discipline of the "individual" nor the attributes of the "group." Each body manifests as neither an individual nor a group but as a "dividual" fragmented into various data. These data about each person's life and body are encoded, and access is controlled using those codes. In this type of data governance, supposedly innate and hereditary "racial" categories like caste and tribe are used in tandem with acquired, non-hereditary, "non-racial" categories like class, income, gender, education, academic record, movement history, and purchase history. With increasing control of individual bodies, the space between "citizen and non-citizen," "legal and illegal," becomes more indistinct even as the distinction between "racial differences and non-racial differences" begins to break down. Within trans-border information networks, all codes are used under the guise of a balanced objectivity, and all bodies are assigned difference and controlled in accordance with risk and possibility.

The old racial order based on distinctions of caste and religion, important though it was in post-colonial India, is no longer fixed or self-evident. In contemporary India, the politics of governance operate not on population groups but on individual bodies. Outside the law, the authorities can accord special political consideration to the life of a given body one day and steal its citizenship without warning the next. The political and administrative decisions about individual bodies are no longer based on explicit racial categories but stem from scrutiny of the various data concerning that individual body within an invisible black box.

The dissolution of the fixed and self-evident imperial/colonial racial order does not mean that racial discrimination has disappeared, however. The sense and affect of racial discrimination based on distinctions of religion, caste, and tribe persist in an unofficial and often latent phase, frequently transforming into real violence or sometimes into legal code in the form of designation and exclusion of the "other" when some catalyst triggers their resurgence. Risk groups distilled through data governance appear to be categorized from an objective, neutral standpoint, but they are often, in fact, designated using "racial" categories that are deeply linked to latent sense and affect regarding differences between people. This is precisely what makes the connection between contemporary data governance and the politics of affect such a thorny problem.

The virtualization of race in contemporary India has been two-fold: race has become an index of electronic data in the digital cum virtual realm while also lying dormant at the not-yet-actualized virtual level in the operation of latent sensual and affective differentiation. The (post-)imperial/colonial racial order has disappeared from center stage, but that does not mean race itself has disappeared. Rather, it has gone virtual and continues to be activated affectively, fluidly, and arbitrarily by both governments and people, giving rise to populist and majoritarian exclusion and discrimination. It is undeniable that opposition to racial discrimination has become more difficult under these circumstances. We must fully comprehend the process by which the latent sense and affect of racial discrimination get connected to the racial categorizations in the territory of data racism and become a political reality in the form of real exclusion and violence. This is the site of the generation of persistent racism in the present world.

In our continuing consideration of latent sense and affect, the performances, literature, and art discussed by Narita, Tsuchiya, and Takezawa in Chapters 7, 9, and 10 of this book, respectively, provide important media for becoming more keenly attuned to the questions at hand. In order to resist the deeply rooted racism of the present, we must not only thoroughly analyze and rationally critique the technologies, systems, and values of contemporary politics—including data governance—but also change the very way we feel things and imagine others within our bodies, minds, and hearts. This is also a way for us as dividuals in the age of globalization to train our imaginations for a new form of solidarity.[16] The anti-racist politics of the future must extend the range of its discourse and praxis from the real world to virtual dimensions and must transcend every border to alter the entire molecular relation in which we find ourselves situated.

Notes

1 The "civilizing mission" and "the ordering of difference" were important to the ideology of the British Raj (Metcalf 1994). In the early stages of the colonial period, "the civilizing mission" carried more weight, but after the great rebellion in 1858, the authorities became keenly aware of how difficult it would be to change Indian society and culture, and "the ordering of difference" became the dominant ideology. Difference here includes both the difference between British and Indian, and differences between various groups within India.

2 It is debatable whether the architecture of social classifications that existed in local society—caste, for example—can be called a pre-existing "race" in India. There has never been a clear distinction between biological and cultural bases for caste, and even before the modern period, it was entirely possible to change caste through marriage or by gaining a new post or social position. However, because the caste system is hierarchical and has a (very strong) innate character, we can at least consider it something close to "race" (Robb 1995). In this chapter, when the pre-existing architecture of social difference has a hierarchical and innate character, it will be included in the discussion of "race."

3 However, it is also true that under British colonial rule from the middle of the nineteenth century on, scientific theories of race had an extremely close relationship with Indian sociology and theories of caste. Indian sociology and theories of caste were not simply Orientalist. While they contain many fallacies when viewed from the

perspective of our current knowledge, they were also deeply connected to what were at the time cutting edge theories of race, social evolution, and ethnography, and were developed as part of the search for universal truths (Robb 1995).

4 On the question of governance and control of people on the move, see also Onimaru's discussion of Singapore in Chapter 5 of this book.
5 From "AADHAAR dashboard." https://uidai.gov.in/aadhaar_dashboard/ (Last accessed on August 23, 2021).
6 From the Criminal Tribes Act, 1871.
7 The "1940 system" (Noguchi 1995) and "total war system" (Yamanouchi and Sakai 2003; Yamanouchi et al. 2015) in Japan also discuss how the wartime system was carried over into post-war Japan.
8 On the history of governance of immigrants leading to CAA, see Sato (2020).
9 https://censusindia.gov.in/Vital_Statistics/MNIC/MNIC.html (Last accessed on 18th August 2021).
10 However, in this example, there was likely more room for negotiation because the immigrants in question were Hindu. Muslims, whether immigrants or not, sometimes become sudden targets of violent exclusion by the government or society.
11 Office of the Registrar General & Census Commissioner, India, Ministry of Home Affairs, Government of India. https://censusindia.gov.in/2011-Act&Rules/notifications/citizenship_rules2003.pdf (Last accessed on August 18, 2021).
12 On the relationship between NPR and Aadhaar and their history, see Sato (2020) and Venkataramanan (2019).
13 The Department of Electronics and Information Technology had been part of the Ministry of Communications and Information Technology, but it was elevated to become a ministry in its own right in June 2016.
14 J stands for Jan Dhan Yojana (people's wealth scheme, a project to ensure everyone in India has a bank account), A for Aadhaar, and M for Mobile phone.
15 However, it is conceivable to *strategically* develop the politics of privacy protection.
16 In response to the rampant "predatory dividualism" of global finance capitalism, Appadurai proposes a politics of "progressive dividualism," in which we share the wealth of life through the trans-border solidarity of dividuals (and all various energies and agencies in the world) (Appadurai 2016, 145–148). Appadurai's idea echoes my suggestion to include the biomoral interactions—fluid exchanges between the self and the other—as an ethical facet of biopolitics, so that the major agenda for democracy becomes how to bring about socio-political conditions that will enable people (and all beings in the world) to pursue their own way of life in symmetrical interactions and exchanges with others. This is a proposal for a "vernacular democracy" with the biomoral consideration for multiple ways of life, as an attempt to live together diversely and equally (Tanabe 2021: 267–268).

References

Agamben, Giorgio. 1993. *The Coming Community*. Translated by Michael Hardt. Minneapolis, MN: University of Minnesota Press.
Agamben, Giorgio. 1998. *Homo Sacer: Sovereign Power and Bare Life*. Translated by Daniel Heller-Roazen. Stanford, CA: Stanford University Press.
Agamben, Giorgio. 2000. *Means without End*. Translated by Vincenzo Binetti and Cesare Casarino. Minneapolis, MN: University of Minnesota Press.
Agamben, Giorgio. 2005. *State of Exception*. Translated by Kevin Atell. Chicago: University of Chicago Press.
Appadurai, Arjun. 1993. "Number in the Colonial Imagination." In *Orientalism and the Postcolonial Predicament: Perspectives on South Asia*, edited by Carol A. Breckenridge and Peter van der Veer, 314–339. Philadelphia, PA: University of Pennsylvania Press.

Appadurai, Arjun. 2006. *Fear of Small Numbers: An Essay of the Geography of Anger.* Durham and London: Duke University Press.

Appadurai, Arjun. 2016. *Banking on Words: The Failure of Language in the Age of Derivative Finance.* Chicago: The University of Chicago Press.

Best, Kirsty. 2010. "Living in the Control Society: Surveillance, Users and Digital Screen Technologies." *International Journal of Cultural Studies* 13 (1):5–24.

Bhagat, Ram B. 2006. "Census and Caste Enumeration: British Legacy and Contemporary Practice in India." *Genus LXII* 2: 119–134.

Breckenridge, Keith. 2014. *Biometric State: The Global Politics of Identification and Surveillance in South Africa, 1850 to the Present.* Cambridge: Cambridge University Press.

Breckenridge, Carol A., and Peter van der Veer 1993. "Orientalism and the Postcolonial Predicament." In *Orientalism and the Postcolonial Predicament: Perspectives on South Asia,* edited by Carol A. Breckenridge and Peter van der Veer, 1–19. Philadelphia, PA: University of Pennsylvania Press.

Carrol, Lucy. 1978. "Colonial Perceptions of Indian Society and the Emergence of Caste(s) Associations." *Journal of Asian Studies* 37 (2): 233–250.

Chatterjee, Partha. 1993. *The Nation and Its Fragments: Colonial and Postcolonial Histories.* Princeton, NJ: Princeton University Press.

Chatterjee, Partha. 2004. *The Politics of the Governed: Reflections on Popular Politics in Most of the World.* New York: Columbia University Press.

Chhotray, Vasudha. 2017. "Nullification of Citizenship: Negotiating Authority without Identity Documents in Coastal Odisha, India." *Contemporary South Asia* 26 (2): 175–190. doi: 10.1080/09584935.1303445.

Cohen, Lawrence. 2016. "Duplicate, Leak, Deity." *Limn* website. https://limn.it/articles/duplicate-leak-deity/ (Last accessed on August 23, 2021).

Cohen, Lawrence. 2017. "Duplicate." *South Asia: Journal of South Asian Studies* 40 (2): 301–304.

Cohn, Bernard S. 1968. "Notes on the History of the Study of Indian Society and Culture." In *Structure and Change in Indian Society and Culture,* edited by Milton Singer and Bernard S. Cohn, 3–28. Chicago: Aldine.

Cohn, Bernard S. 1987. "The Census, Social Structure and Objectification in South Asia." In *An Anthropologist among the Historians and Other Essays,* edited by Bernard Cohn, 224–254. Delhi: Oxford University Press.

Connolly, William E. 2005. *Pluralism.* Durham: Duke University Press.

Deleuze, Gilles. 1992. "Postscript on the Societies of Control." *October* 59: 3–7.

Dirks, Nicholas B. 2001. *Castes of Mind: Colonialism and the Making of Modern India.* Princeton, NJ: Princeton University Press.

Dirks, Nicholas B. 2005. "The Ethnographic State." In *The State in India: Past and Present,* edited by Masaaki Kimura and Akio Tanabe, 229–254. New Delhi: Oxford University Press.

Faulds, Henry. 1880. "On the Skin-furrows of the Hand." *Nature* 22 (574): 605.

Foucault, Michel. 1978. Vol. I of *The History of Sexuality.* Translated by Robert Hurley. Harmondsworth: Penguin.

Foucault, Michel. 2004. *Society Must Be Defended: Lectures at the Collège de France, 1975–76.* Translated by David Macey. Edited by Mauro Bertani and Alessandro Fontana. London: Penguin Books.

Fujii, Takeshi. 2003. *Rekishi no naka no kāsuto: Kindai indo no "jigazō"* [Caste in History: Self-Portrait of Modern India]. Tokyo: Iwanami Shoten.

Galton, Francis. 1892. *Finger Prints.* London: Macmillan.

Gill, Mehar Singh. 2007. "Politics of Population Census Data in India." *Economic and Political Weekly* 42(3): 241–249.

Guha, Sumit. 2003. "The Politics of Identity and Enumeration in India c. 1600–1990." *Comparative Studies in Society and History* 45 (1): 148–167.

Hamashita, Takeshi. 2013. *Kakyō kajin to chūka mō: Imin kōeki sōkin nettowāku no kōzō to tenkai* [Overseas Chinese, Ethnic Chinese and Chinese Networks: The Structure and Development of the Migration, Trade and Remittance Networks]. Tokyo: Iwanami Shoten.

Hamilton, Walter. 1990. Vol. 1 and Vol. 2 of *A Geographical, Statistical, and Historical Description of Hindostan and the Adjacent Countries*. Delhi: Classical International Publishers. First published 1820.

Hardt, Michael, and Antonio Negri. 2005. *Multitude: War and Democracy in the Age of Empire*. London: Penguin Books.

Herschel, William J. 1880. "Skin Furrows of the Hand." *Nature* 23 (578): 76.

Hutton J. H. 1986. Vol. 1 of *Census of India*. New Delhi: Gyan Publishing House. First published 1931.

Inden, Ronald B. 1986. "Orientalist Construction of India." *Modern Asian Studies* 20 (1): 1–46.

Inden, Ronald B. 1990. *Imagining India*. Oxford: Basil Blackwell.

Kamterkar, Indivar. 2002. "A Different War Dance: State and Class in India 1939–1945." *Past & Present* 176 (1): 187–221.

Khilnani, Sunil. 1999. *The Idea of India*. 2nd edition. New Delhi: Penguin.

Kotani, Hiroyuki. 1994. "'Kāsuto no jichi' seisaku to kāsuto shūdan: Jūkyū seiki zenhan no bonbei kanku o chūshin ni [The Policy of 'Caste Autonomy' and Caste Groups: A Focus on Bombay Presidency in the Early Nineteenth Century]." In *Kāsuto seido to hisabetsumin 2: Seiyō kindai to no deai* [The Caste System and the Discriminated People, Vol. 2: Encounter with the Modern West], edited by Hiroyuki Kotani, 129–158. Tokyo: Akashi Shoten.

Kotani, Hiroyuki, Reiko Yoshimura, and Toshie Awaya. 1994. "'Kāsuto no jichi' seisaku no tenkai [Explication of the Policy of 'Caste Autonomy']." In *Kāsuto seido to hisabetsumin 2: Seiyō kindai to no deai* [The Caste System and the Discriminated People, Vol. 2: Encounter with the Modern West], edited by Hiroyuki Kotani, 159–198. Tokyo: Akashi Shoten.

Maguire, Mark. 2009. "The Birth of Biometric Security." *Anthropology Today* 25 (2): 9–14.

Massumi, Brian. 2015. *Politics of Affect*. Cambridge: Polity Press.

Metcalf, Thomas R. 1994. *Ideologies of the Raj*. Cambridge: Cambridge University Press.

Mima, Tatsuya. 2003. "Shintai no tekunorojī to risuku kanri [Technology of the Body and Risk Management]." In *Sōryokusen taisei kara gurōbarizēshon e* [From Total War System to Globalization], edited by Yasushi Yamanouchi and Naoki Sakai, 168–201. Tokyo: Heibonsha.

Nair, Vijayanka. 2018. "An Eye for an I: Recording Biometrics and Reconsidering Identity in Postcolonial India." *Contemporary South Asia* 26 (38): 1–14. doi: 10.1080/09584935.2017.1410102.

National Sample Survey Organization. 2010. *Migration in India 2007–2008*. National Sample Survey Office, Ministry of Statistics & Programme Implementation, Government of India.

Neyazi, Taberez Ahmed, Akio Tanabe, and Shinya Ishizaka (eds). 2014. *Democratic Transformation and the Vernacular Public Arena in India*. London: Routledge.

Nilekani, Nandan. 2008. *Imagining India: The Idea of a Renewed Nation*. New Delhi: Penguin.

Nilekani, Nandan. 2018. "We're All in This Together: Aadhaar Isn't Building a Surveillance Dystopia, It Asserts Your Individual Identity vis-à-vis the State." *The Times of India* website, January 17. https://timesofindia.indiatimes.com/blogs/toi-edit-page/were-all-in-this-together-aadhaar-isnt-building-a-surveillance-dystopia-it-asserts-your-individual-identity-vis-a-vis-the-state/ (Last accessed on August 23, 2021).

Noguchi, Yukio. 1995. *1940 nen taisei: Saraba "senjikeizai"* [The 1940 System: Farewell to the "Wartime Economy"]. Tokyo: Tōyōkeizai shinpōsha.

Omissi, David E. 1991. "'Martial Races': Ethnicity and Security in Colonial India, 1858–1939." *War and Society* 9 (1): 1–27.

Osawa, Masachi. 2013. *Seikenryoku no shisō: Jiken kara yomitoku gendai shakai no tenkan* [Philosophy of Biopolitics: Deciphering Transformation of Modern Society through Analysis of Incidents]. Tokyo: Chikuma Shinsho.

Radhakrishna, Meena. 2001. *Dishonoured by History: "Criminal Tribes" and British Colonial Policy*. New Delhi: Orient Longman.

Raheja, Gloria G., and Ann G. Gold. 1994. *Listen to the Heron's Word: Reimaging Gender and Kinship in North India*. Berkeley, CA and Los Angeles: University of California Press.

Robb, Peter (ed.) 1995. *The Concept of Race in South Asia*. Delhi: Oxford University Press.

Rose, Nikolas. 1999. *Powers of Freedom*. Cambridge: Cambridge University Press.

Rose, Nikolas. 2000. "Government and Control." *British Journal of Criminology* 40: 321–339.

Sadiq, Kamal. 2008. *Paper Citizens: How Illegal Immigrants Acquire Citizenship in Developing Countries*. Oxford: Oxford University Press.

Said, Edward W. 1978. *Orientalism*. New York: Pantheon Books.

Sato, Hiroshi. 2020. *Indo ni okeru iminhaijohōsei no tenkai: Indo hokutō chiiki o chūshin ni* [The Development of Immigration Exclusion Legislation in India: A Focus on the North-East Region]. IDE Technical Report. Tokyo: Institute of Developing Economies, Japan External Trade Organization (IDE-JETRO).

Streets, Heather. 2004. *Martial Races: The Military, Race and Masculinity in British Imperial Culture, 1857–1914*. Manchester: Manchester University Press.

Takano, Asako. 2013. "Teijū to idō no yōkai: Idō suru shintai/imizukerareru shintai [The Dissolution of Settlement and Mobility: Mobile Bodies/Bodies Attached with Meaning]." In *Idō toiu keiken: Nihon ni okeru "imin" kenkyu no kadai* [The Experience of Mobility: Issues in "Migrant" Studies in Japan], edited by Toshio Iyotani, 97–115, Tokyo: Yūshindōkōbunsha.

Takano, Asako. 2016. *Shimon to kindai: Idō suru shintai no kanri to tōchi no gihō* [Fingerprinting and Modernity: Control of Moving Bodies and Technology of Governance]. Tokyo: Misuzu Shobō.

Tanabe, Akio. 2014. "Indo minzoku undō no tenkan [Transformation of the Indian National Movement]." In *Gendai no kiten: Daiichiji sekaitaisen, Daiikkan, Sekaisensō* [The Starting Point of Our Times: World War I. Volume 1: The World War], edited by Shinichi Yamamuro, Akeo Okada, Takashi Koseki, and Tatsushi Fujihara, 101–124. Tokyo: Iwanami shoten.

Tanabe, Akio. 2019. "Dokuritsugo indo no shakai to bunka [Society and Culture in Post-Independence India]." In *Minami ajiashi 4* [History of South Asia 4], edited by Nobuko Nagasaki, 290–316. Tokyo: Yamakawa shuppansha.

Tanabe, Akio. 2021. *Caste and Equality in India: A Historical Anthropology of Diverse Society and Vernacular Democracy*. London: Routledge.

Tokita-Tanabe, Yumiko, and Akio Tanabe. 2014. "Politics of Relations and the Emergence of the Vernacular Public Arena: Global Networks of Development and Livelihood in Odisha." In *Democratic Transformation and The Vernacular Public Arena in India*, edited by Taberez Ahmed Neyazi, Akio Tanabe, and Shinya Ishizaka, 25–44. London: Routledge.

Unique Identification Authority of India (UIDAI). 2010. *UIDAI Strategy Overview: Creating a Unique Identity Number for Every Resident in India*. New Delhi: Government of India.

United Nations Development Programme (UNDP). 2009. *Human Development Report 2009: Overcoming Barriers: Human Mobility and Development*. New York: UNDP.

van der Veer, Peter. 2001. *Imperial Encounters: Religion and Modernity in India and Britain.* Princeton, NJ: Princeton University Press.

Venkataramanan, K. 2019. "Explained: What Connects the NPR, NRIC and Census?" *The Hindu*, December 22, 2019. https://www.thehindu.com/news/national/what-connects-the-npr-nric-and-census/article30368465.ece (Last accessed on August 23, 2021).

Watanabe, Kōzō. 2003. *Shihōteki dōitsusei no tanjō: Shimin shakai ni okeru kotai shikibetsu to tōroku* [The Birth of Judicial Identity-Registration and Identification in the Civil Society]. Tokyo: Gensōsha.

Yamanouchi, Yasushi, and Sakai, Naoki (eds.). 2003. *Sōryokusen taisei kara gurōbarizēshon e* [From Total War System to Globalization]. Tokyo: Heibonsha.

Yamanouchi, Yasushi, Toshio Iyotani, Ryūichi Narita, and Minoru Iwasaki (eds). 2015. *Sōryokusen taisei* [Total War System]. Tokyo: Chikuma Gakugei Bunko.

Yang, Anand A. 1985. "Dangerous Castes and Tribes: The Criminal Tribes Act and the Magahiya Doms of Northeast India." In *Crime and Criminality in British India*, edited by Anand A. Yang, 108–127. Tucson: The University of Arizona Press.

Yoshimura, Reiko. 1994. "'Kāsuto no jichi' to shimin teki kenri ['Caste Autonomy' and the Right of Citizens]." In *Kāsuto seido to hisabetsumin 2: Seiyō kindai to no deai* [The Caste System and the Discriminated People, Vol. 2: Encounter with the Modern West], edited by Hiroyuki Kotani, 199–241. Tokyo: Akashi Shoten.

7

RACISM IN IMPERIAL AND POST-IMPERIAL JAPANESE LANGUAGE LITERATURE

Ryuichi Narita

7.1 Introduction

This chapter focuses on racism in literary representation. I discuss the cross-national genre of literature referred to as "Japanese-language literature" in conjunction with imperial-colonial and post-imperial-colonial issues and highlight the ways in which the discourse on national origin generates and regenerates the concept of race.

The concept of race in East Asia first spread as a form of racism that accompanied growing migration across the Pacific Ocean and proliferated in colonies during the nineteenth and twentieth centuries. It created a race-based ranking system as a way of discriminating against people under colonialism or colonial systems in order to legitimize imperialist rule. At the same time, however, colonialist governments used racial equality as a pretext for assimilation. One such example is the slogan *isshi dōjin* [All subjects are equal under the Emperor's benevolence], which the Japanese empire used to expand its territories and subsume alien populations under its sovereign power. Racism embodied the contradictory components (discrimination and assimilation) of imperial Japan's colonial rule.

Generally speaking, Japan's colonial rule required the "cooperation" or proactive involvement of the local people to successfully sustain its governance, but there was only a fine line between "cooperation" and "disobedience." When two parties interacted under an asymmetrical relationship, the dominant party often maintained asymmetry through prejudicial attitudes.

This type of relationship continued even after the war and the demise of imperialism. When the asymmetrical institutional framework was removed in the decolonization process after 1945, the relationship between the imperialist ruler and the colonial populations was reorganized in a new environment. The seeds of the current fallacy that racism does not exist in Japan developed there.

DOI: 10.4324/9781003266396-9

I will use Japanese-language literature as a guide to analyze this process from a racial perspective.

The creation of the genre of Japanese-language literature was part of a broader move to reflect on racism that evolved when nineteenth-century academic classifications began to align with the idea of a "nation-state." It was also created to rename existing academic fields such as national literature and national history. There were two stages in the creation of this new genre.

The first stage was driven by the fact that knowledge in pre-war Japan had been mobilized as imperialist learning and used for domination. It involved looking into the use of national integration for the control of Japan's colonies in the name of national history as well as national literature and a transition from post-war "learning" in the name of national history and national literature under lingering nationalism, even after Imperial Japan's defeat and loss of its colonies. At that stage, the fields were renamed Japanese history and Japanese literature. This shift took place around the turn of the twenty-first century. It was an attempt to make people aware of the unconscious unification of education and race as well as the propagation of racism in education in the past.

However, Japanese literature underwent the second stage of transformation into Japanese-language literature based on the perception that names such as "Japanese literature" and "Japanese history" still had a residue of nationalism and might breed a new kind of racism (despite this, Japanese history has yet to be renamed).

Thus, the academic field of Japanese literature has come to be called Japanese-language literature after a long period of being called national literature. Accordingly, the departmental name at universities has transitioned from national literature to Japanese literature and now Japanese-language literature. The new designation of Japanese-language literature has been proposed because it demonstrates that categories such as "Japan," "Japanese language," "Japanese national," and "Japanese literature" are neither objective nor naturally given.

In order to break down the idea that Japanese literature is a genre of literature written by the Japanese national in the Japanese language in Japan, the term "national literature" was relativized and renamed "Japanese literature." Thus, the distinction between "Japanese literature" and "Japanese language literature" was made so that the meaning of "Japan" was defined and the concept clarified.

In other words, literary works that have been presented and accepted as Japanese literature were presumed to have been written by ethnically Japanese authors inside the national borders of Japan. Considering that, are the works of Zainichi Korean (Koreans living in Japan) authors or Japanese-Brazilian authors classified as Japanese literature? Can Ainu folktales be included in Japanese literature? These questions have been raised and prompted the creation of the field of Japanese-language literature that covers literary works that are written in the Japanese language. The category includes the works of authors who live outside of Japan and write in the Japanese language (ranging from those who lived in pre-war overseas colonies to the contemporary author Yoko Tawada) and authors with foreign citizenship (e.g., Ian Hideo Levy and Yuju On, who are discussed later).

The above problematic has been articulated by Masahiko Nishi, a comparative literature scholar, in his *Gaichi junrei* [*From an Outland to Another*] (2018). The book deals with: (1) the subject of imperialism and colonialism; and (2) literary works that have been produced in relation to migration. The subtitle is *"Ekkyōteki" Nihongo bungaku ron* [*Migratory Study of Japanese Literature*]. Nishi's work discusses race within the written word as well as a race created by the written word—racialization by the politics of text generation.

In short, Nishi's book focuses on diverse manifestations of Japanese-language literature and explores the relationship between Japanese nationals and colonized peoples in the outlands: the "Japanese-language literature of Japanese nationals living in outlands" and the "Japanese-language literature of non-Japanese nationals."[1]

In his book, Nishi also discusses: (3) the inherent problem of Japanese-language literature, that is, further border-crossing by Japanese-language literature. While Japanese-language literature has relativized Japan, Nishi's study goes on to question Japanese-language literature itself.

Nishi's study also examines issues pertaining to imperialism and language. In his earlier book, *Bairingaru na yume to yūutsu* [*Image of Bilinguals in Hyphenated Japanese Literatures*] (2014), Nishi writes:

> [It was] a historical process by which colonialism with the "colonial master's language" violently interfered with the language environment of its colony, molded local-language speakers into bilingual (or trilingual) speakers, reduced these multilinguals to "second- or third-class" citizens, and eventually turned them into "monolinguals" who used the "language of other."

In this chapter, I share Nishi's awareness of the issue and examine the cunning way in which the concept of race embedded in Japanese language literature produces colonial consciousness and hierarchies.

This chapter has two parts. The first examines a series of racial issues created by imperial Japan as it vied for supremacy in the Asia-Pacific region in the mid-twentieth century. The second focuses on migration during the post-imperial period after World War II, particularly the asymmetrical human movements brought on by past imperial-colonial relationships and migration.

7.2 Imperial Literature: Literature about Japanese-Indigenous Resident Relations in the Empire

First I will examine some literary works that address the relationship between the Japanese and native residents in the empire. Race manifests at the interface between them. Let me divide Japanese migrants (α) into two groups: (A) those acting as imperialist rulers and (B) those who emigrated to foreign lands such as Brazil as settlers. Their relationship with native residents (β) varies depending on whether they lived in (A) or (B). In colony (A), (α) belonged to a dominant group with power (although small in number) and prevailed over (β). In place (A), Japanese is the language of the ruler and the native residents must use Japanese as the "language of other" (Derrida 1989). On the other hand, the Japanese migrants are a minority who use a minority language in overseas settlements (B).

7.2.1 The Colonialist's Viewpoint

I examine the case of Nobuo Ishimori (1897–1987), who was active in both the homeland and outland of Japan before and after World War II, as an example of the imperialist ruler (A).

Ishimori was a scholar of children's literature and a Japanese-language educator who was born in Hokkaido and worked as an educator in pre-war Manchuria. He epitomized a colony-dwelling Japanese migrant (α). He is well known as the author of *Kotan no kuchibue* [*Whistle in My Heart*], a story of Ainu siblings, which he wrote after World War II (1957).

My analysis of Ishimori begins in the Manchuria phase of his life after the installation of a puppet regime by Japan. Ishimori collected local folk tales and wrote some children's stories set in Manchuria (e.g., *Sungari no asa* [*Morning on the Sungari*] (1942)). One of them, *Nihon ni kite* [*Coming to Japan*] (1941), was published as part of the Shōnen bunka sōsho [Juvenile culture series]. It is the story of a boy named Jiro who travels to Tokyo with his mother, leaving his surgeon father behind in Manchuria. Narrating Jiro's journey from Manchuria to Tokyo appears to be the primary intent of Ishimori's book. However, Jiro, who is supposed to go to a middle school in Tokyo, exhibits an unusually strong interest in nationality and race during his journey. He asks about people he sees on the ship, saying, "Which country is that person from?" Jiro is defined as a character who has a heightened awareness of national origin and racial identity because he has grown up in the multiracial (*gozokukyowa*) state of Manchuria.

To begin with, the story is titled *Coming to Japan*: Ishimori's story is told from the viewpoint of a Manchuria-raised boy going to Japan. In the story, Jiro converses with a painter ("Mister") on the ship traveling from Manchuria to Korea:

> Mister, do you know which country that foreigner is from?
> I do.
> How do you know? The hair?
> No.
> The color of the eyes?
> No.
> The height of the nose?
> No.

Jiro's inquisitiveness regarding nationality and race is rather abrupt, but we can interpret this scene as evidence that: (1) Ishimori thinks that people of Japan are less cognizant of nationality and race; (2) he wants to encourage his readers in Japan to be more aware of racial differences. However, the matter becomes rather convoluted. After his conversation with Mister, Jiro believes that he can tell Koreans and Manchus apart, but he's still unsure of the difference between Manchus and Chinese because he infers the difference between Koreans and Manchus only by the language they speak. In other words, Jiro considers so-called ethnic traits (here, language) as a matter of racial difference (i.e., a phenotypic difference).

More importantly, Ishimori himself confuses ethnicity and race. The confusion manifests in the next part of dialogue between Jiro and Mister. Jiro continues to quiz Mister on how he can tell which country someone is from.

Mister answers, "It's easy—I can tell as soon as I hear the language spoken by the person." Jiro is satisfied with the answer, but there are numerous occasions of mutual misunderstanding in their exchange which Ishimori does not properly handle.

In his initial question, Jiro uses the expression "Which country" to ask about the race of a foreigner in terms of distinguishing physical characteristics. Mister switches the question to one of ethnicity and offers language (a cultural distinction) as a marker. Moreover, he shows Jiro a painting of a Russian farmer's daughter who lives in the outskirts of Harbin and lectures about Russian culture and how culture defines ethnicity.

The dialogue about race and ethnicity continues in a similar fashion. Jiro encounters a boy (Chon-i) and a girl (Shin-li) on the ship. Jiro says, "Those two children must be Korean." Mister agrees: "They look that way. They are wearing lovely clothes."

Then, Chon-i speaks in Japanese: "This girl (Shin-li) is Korean. But I'm not. I'm Chinese." Chon-i was raised by Shin-li's mother (a Korean woman) after his mother died shortly after giving birth to him. He says that he finds it "easier to speak Korean." Ishimori adds, "Mister understood that it would be natural for him because the first language he learned after birth was Korean."

Again, Mister observes ethnicity on the basis of cultural parameters as he uses language as the primary indicator of racial identity while emphasizing the boy's self-identification as Chinese. Chon-I dresses like a Korean and speaks Korean as his mother tongue, but Ishimori depicts him as someone who sees himself as Chinese.

After arriving in Tokyo, Jiro asks himself if he can be a true Japanese child when imitating the West as many Japanese do. This is the moment he consciously begins to seek the unique identity of a Japanese person. Because of his upbringing in the multicultural and multiracial environment of the Manchurian State, his longing for nationalism intensifies through the fantasy of an innate identity.

Jiro looks for "something Japanese, something born in Japan, something born of Japan, on Japanese soil, in Japan, not introduced from another country." Nationality is defined by cultural factors and linked with identity, with land (Japan) thrown into the mix. Jiro says to his mother that people there are "all Japanese, aren't they?" and his mother responds, "Yes, we are at home in Japan."

In Ishimori's mind, Manchuria is perceived as one version of a nation-state in which a distinction among Koreans, Manchus, and Chinese is made according to language and ethnic culture. When Jiro hears that there is an "American-born friend" among his brother's classmates, he responds, "He is still Japanese even if he was born in America, isn't he?" The brother answers, "Of course, he's a second-generation," thus bringing up the idea of using bloodline as an identifier.

According to Jiro's awareness, this means that racial distinction based on physical features has collapsed into ethnicization based on clothing and language. In nationalization under imperialism, language-centric culture is grafted onto identification by blood and land.

Ishimori's post-war attention was shifted to the story of the Ainu people in Hokkaido, but his perspective formed by his Manchurian experience was kept intact. His post-war publication, *Kotan no kuchibue*, is a story of siblings named Masa and Yutaka who were born to an Ainu father and a *Wajin* (Japanese) mother. Ishimori depicts the way they are seen as Ainu and racially discriminated against by the Japanese and turns it into a story of compromise and reconciliation. The Japanese discriminate against them by pointing out their physical characteristics, customs, and manners that they deem different from their own.

These differences are described through the eyes of Yutaka, who differentiates himself from the Japanese and includes cultural differences such as the Ainu's custom of tattooing in his description. Yutaka identifies himself as Ainu and points out physical features that differ from typical Japanese features: "We are hairier than Japanese." In this scene, Ishimori seemingly criticizes discrimination, but it is hard not to feel that these differences are given meaning and ranked. Against the backdrop of a shared national culture, Yutaka's words highlight physical differences that point to Japanese superiority, affirming Ishimori's beliefs.

Moreover, Yutaka thinks that the sleeping face of his father Ion "looks like an old Russian man with curly and wavy hair, a white bushy beard" and observes his older sister Masa as having "somewhat Slavic facial features" in comparison with "the flat and smooth Japanese face." Yutaka is portrayed as a boy who is curious about human physical characteristics and targets both Ainu and Japanese for relativization.

Cultural characteristics are superimposed upon physical characteristics. The lyrics of *Yaisama*, an Ainu folk song sung by Ikante, an elderly woman next door, are written down. Ishimori's sympathy for Ainu Indigenous culture is apparent, but his constant reference to the physical features of the Ainu leads to the substantiation of ethnic culture. Yutaka sees Ikante's "dark blue tattoos around her lips" and thinks, "She wouldn't look the same without her tattoos." This is one instance of invoking Ainu cultural stereotypes.

Ishimori's gaze is paired with something that forces (the asymmetrical) "other" out in the open. *Kotan no kuchibue* depicts social discrimination against the Ainu people and adopts a critical tone toward it. However, old stereotypes—concerning their physical characteristics and distinct culture—define the Ainu and reinforce Ishimori's sense of Japanese identity.

Ishimori writes about Yutaka's "righteous anger" toward a sightseeing show that uses "an elderly couple who claim to be Ainu tribal chiefs" and displays a critical stance against unjust discrimination. Yet, it is undeniable that Ishimori's perception of racial stereotypes was preserved in his continuous fascination with ethnic identity after Japan's defeat and the collapse of the Japanese Empire in 1945. Thus, Ishimori acted as a Japanese migrant (A) (Japanese (α)) in Manchuria and maintained his sense of superiority over Indigenous residents (B) (non-Japanese (β)) as he reproduced racial categorizations of social relationships in post-war Japan.

This also means that the perception of race did not change after the war and post-war Japanese society was still underpinned by the blood lineage principle and nationalism. The GHQ (General Headquarters) draft of the Japanese Constitution prepared by the Supreme Commander for the Allied Powers (commonly referred to as GHQ in Japan) provided that "all natural persons" are equal before the law "on account of race, creed, sex, social status, caste or national origin" (Koseki 1989). The term "natural persons" was subsequently replaced with "Japanese nationals." Post-war Japanese society was supposed to proclaim equality for all natural persons (unlike in imperial Japan), but the term "nationals" narrowed the scope down to those who had Japanese citizenship. Borders were set up around the idea that nationals were the true Japanese instead of natural persons who lived in the dominion of Japan (even in the Japanese Constitution).

The pull of the notion of nationality was so great that it sustained the concept of race with some modification, even in post-war Japanese society. Japan's "honorary white" status throughout the pre-war to post-war period underpins this mindset that has roots in imperialism. Naoki Sakai, who teaches social theory in the US, points out that imperialist nationalism is a form of racism that continues in post-war Japan as it is intertwined with overseas imperialism (Ukai et al. 2012). There is no doubt that this situation has resulted from the influence of the US Empire on post-war Japanese society.

From the perspective outlined in this chapter, another important argument arises on the subject of *Kotan no kuchibue*: the insouciant and uncritical way Ishimori depicts a phenomenon in which Indigenous residents (β) in the imperial colony (A) come to live in the language of other (Derrida 1989). The Ainu people have also been forced to use the Japanese language and live in Japanese as the "language of other," but Ishimori does not exhibit any awareness of this point.

One example relates to the aforementioned *Yaisama* scene in *Kotan no kuchibue*. It is explained that the song lives in Ikante's heart as she can sing sadly when she is feeling sad and joyously when she feels joyous, but the lyrics in the text are written in Japanese, with no explanatory note about this from Ishimori. Even though the inside cover of the Tōto Shobō edition carries the lyrics of an Ainu dance song in Romaji and Japanese, Ishimori himself makes no mention of it.

Both the speech and inner thoughts of Yutaka are written in Japanese. Readers of *Kotan no kuchibue* also take this for granted and do not question it. It is the historical fact that the Japanese language (national language) functions as a form of violent ideology, that is, the sole use of the "language of other," and eventually becomes the mother tongue (or part of it) of neighboring peoples (Nishi 2014, *op. cit.*). The book makes no mention of history, which Hirano's chapter thoroughly demonstrates in this volume, and treats the depiction of Yutaka and other characters as Japanese speakers as self-explanatory.

7.2.2 The "Language of Other"

In the case of Brazil (B), an outland for Japanese settlers, a new situation arose during the post-war era. Literary works of Japanese-Brazilians (β) are collectively called "Colonia literature." This genre emerged in the 1950s and "blossomed outside of Japanese literature rather than inside" (Nishi 2018, *op. cit.*).

In short, the Japanese-language literature of post-war Brazil no longer saw Brazil as an outland. The authors redefined themselves as Japanese-Brazilian instead of Japanese and called their community Colonia. They shifted their standpoint from that of Japanese (α) to the vicinity of that of native residents (β) on the land of (B) and adopted a new identity in their transition from (α) to a different existence (γ).

During World War II, Brazil banned the use of the Japanese language, considering it an enemy language, and treated Japanese settlers as a minority group. For this reason, there were conflicts after Japan's defeat between a group of Japanese who believed Japan was victorious and a group who recognized Japan's capitulation. Against this backdrop, post-war Japanese-Brazilians (γ) chose to put down roots in Brazil. They abandoned their outland Japanese identity and went on to redefine their existence as permanent settlers of Brazil (B). Colonia literature was the product of this awareness and change in identity.[2]

Colonia literature is understood as another genre of Japanese-language literature produced outside of Japan. When pre-war emigrants to Brazil continued to live there throughout their experience of Japan's defeat in Asia and the Pacific, their self-identity transformed from temporary residents to Colonia. Their self-identification as Colonia was the result of their search for a new identity that didn't fit into traditional colonial terms (assuming their eventual repatriation) nor complete assimilation into Brazilian society. Colonia literature was produced in this particular context.

A major work of a Colonia author named Ricardo Ueki, *Hana no hi* [*Flower Monument*] (published online at http://www.100nen.com.br/ja/ueki/), is a historical novel comprising three parts: Part 1, "Shin imin no ichi nōnen" [*A Farming Year of a New Immigrant*]; Part 2, "Katta maketa no daisōdō" [*The Controversy over Winning or Losing*]; and Part 3, "Ryūko no uitasekusuarisu" [*Ryūko's Vita Sexualis*]. It is a story of a girl who emigrated to pre-war Brazil and lived as a member of the Colonia both during and after the war. It is a search for her identity based on her experience of living in Brazil.

This story stands in sharp contrast with Nobuo Ishimori's as a piece of post-war literature. Immigrants in Brazil (B) redefined their identity as minorities who chose to live as an integral part of a foreign land, whereas Ishimori, as an imperial ruler (A), stubbornly held onto his belief in Japan's dominant position and superiority. For Ueki, identity was not a way to dominate others but a way of survival, a way that enabled settlers to make new lives as immigrants.

One important issue created by present global circumstances lies beyond the scope of this chapter. The difference between contemporary migrants and refugees is defined by whether they enter a new country as nationals of a state more than whether they are leaving their home country voluntarily or fleeing from it. In other words, immigrants carry their passports, whereas refugees do not. For this reason, immigrants have the ability to change their position according to circumstances (as members of the Colonia could). In contrast, refugees cannot make such a change. Receiving countries often categorize, isolate, exclude and racialize refugees.

7.3 "Post-Imperial" Literature

7.3.1 Absence of Awareness of Imperialist Consciousness

The collapse of Japan's imperialism passed into the post-war phase without any self-reflection on the part of many of the rulers (α) in the colonies (A). The unchanged mindset is exemplified with the Japanese term *hikiage* (repatriation). Although their migration from the outland back to the homeland upon the fall of the Japanese empire was actually a banishment/expulsion from the colony (A), they used the more innocuous term "repatriation," and they took it for granted that they were returning to their country of origin.

Repatriation literature is seen as the literature of migration from colonies. One such work is *Nagareru hoshi ha ikiteiru* [The Floating Stars Are Alive] by Tei Fujiwara (1949), which depicts the difficulty of returning home after Japan's defeat. Returnees are depicted as victims who completely disregard their previous status as colonists (Narita 2003). It is a self-involved work which tells of their repatriation (expulsion) while maintaining the position of (α)–(A), taking the Japanese language and Japanese nationality as a given, and disregarding all connections with the colony.

On the other hand, what did (β) in Japan have to say after the war? Nishi analyzes *Kinuta wo utsu onna* [The Cloth Fuller] by Lee Hoe-seong (1972). Written by a Zainichi Korean (a Korean national living in Japan), it tells the story of the narrator's mother, who died young. She had migrated from the Korean Peninsula to Japan, where she married a man from Korea, then migrated to Sakhalin and died there. She had encountered hardship during her migration and her last message to her husband on her death bed was "Don't be swept away."

> In essence, *Kinuta wo utsu onna* is a story of men who were faced with the death of a Korean woman. A story of men who continued to be "swept away" despite the fact that the woman's voice told them "Don't be swept away."

Nishi went on to proclaim:

1. It is highly likely that Japanese readers (the main readership of the book) took the woman's words "Don't be swept away" as her dying wish.
2. Lee Hoe-seong used the genre of Japanese literature as a "devise to let the Japanese people read surreptitiously" "the story of family bonds between Koreans."
3. The Japanese literary world created the subgenre of Zainichi Korean literature to segregate works such as this and brought it under the umbrella of Japanese literature.

(Nishi 2014, op. cit.)

Nishi argues that the Japanese/Japanese literary circles who maintain the position of (α)–(A) have failed to understand Lee's message (β).

In addition, Nishi calls attention to the fact that a senior writer made a "misguided comment" in a round-table discussion of literary writers that included Lee shortly after his debut, saying that they "should rather disregard the fact that he is Korean."

7.3.2 "Post-Imperial" Japanese-Language Literature I

In *Gaichi junrei*, Nishi frequently refers to Ian Hideo Levy and Yuju On as "cross-border Japanese-language authors." Let us look at Levy in relation to post-imperial Japanese-language literature. Levy was born in California, USA, in 1950. His father was a Jewish-American diplomat and his mother was a daughter of Polish immigrants. In his youth, he lived in Taiwan (1956–), Hong Kong (1960–), and the US (1962–).

Levy completed his undergraduate and postgraduate studies in Japanese literature at Princeton University. After teaching at Princeton and Stanford Universities, he became a writer. According to his own chronology, he frequently traveled between Japan and the US from 1967 onward.

Levy has been interested in the issue of using Japanese as an American-born author. His first collection of essays was titled *Nihongo no shōri* [*A Victory of the Japanese Language*] (1992) and he later published another collection of essays entitled *Nihongo wo kaku heya* [*A Room for Writing in Japanese*] (1992).

Levy's self-analysis was set off by his transition from a scholar of Japanese literature to a Japanese-language writer. It began with the publication of *Seijōki no kikoenai heya* [*A Room Where the Star-Spangled Banner Cannot Be Heard*] in 1987. The story is told from the viewpoint of a son of an American diplomat who "grew up as a white child living in Asia."

In Yokohama, people stared at the protagonist along with his bald father, his stepmother, who was fluent in Shanghainese, and his younger brother with long blond hair. Faced with the stares, which were the product of "the anxiety of white women living in Asia," his father spit out in English: *Christians*. When the father was with Japanese people, he let out "loud" laughter, which he chose not to do when he was surrounded by his "white family." The protagonist felt "embarrassed" by this behavior. In these scenes, Levy introduced the transpacific relationship between American imperialism and racism.

The portrayal of the protagonist and his tall and paternalistic father, who took his superiority over Asians for granted and lived in the "house of white supremacy" protected by "Japanese security guards," is closely associated with racism and behavior that is the incarnation of racism itself. Levy narrates this part in Japanese.

In the story, Levy uses the word "race" to say that the protagonist was not unaware of hatred between different races. He talks about being Jewish and the enmity he attracted from "Blacks" as he was regarded as "white" in the US. However, the protagonist got the biggest shock when he encountered "four black eyes" of the Japanese in Shinjuku. The protagonist, who was not unaware of "hatred between different races," describes the scene of his encounter with "frosty glare:"

> The four black eyes were telegraphing a sense of alarm that one would feel when something unknown wandered into one's field of vision as well as the audience's irritation at a sudden appearance of a *blot* [emphasis in original] on the cinema screen.

In this incident that befell him, the protagonist encountered the gazes of "others" who were total strangers to him. He describes his confusion in meeting complete "others"—"others among others"—rather than "others (such as African Americans) among white people." The "black eyes" blatantly expressed a censure for "the appearance of something that should not be there" (just like a blot on the screen). The protagonist felt "dizziness" when he was subjected to discriminatory taunts such as "*gaijin*" (foreigner) and "go home, go home." Here, the protagonist is presented as both racist and suffering from racism.

Thus, Levy had to grapple with the complexity of writing a novel in Japanese on the subject of racial issues. When Westerners deal with Japanese literature, they stand outside of literature to study it. If they are writing a literary piece, however, they are stepping inside of it. They create a rift as they break into the strong concatenation of nationality, language, literature, and country. While it is considered part of Japanese-language literature, it ends up aggravating the old school of Japanese literature.

As mentioned earlier, Levy was preceded by a deluge of Zainichi Korean literature and he began his writing career fully aware of his position as a foreigner writing in the language of the other. Here, Levy becomes aware of his own Western origin. He writes:

> If I wrote an account of one's odyssey of travelling from the West to Japan and infiltrating its language as the wicket gate to the 'inside' of its culture—you might call it an act of 'border crossing'—in English, it would

be nothing more than an English translation of a Japanese novel. That was the major reason for my thinking that I'd better write the Japanese *original* [emphasis on original] from the start. ('Boku no Nihongo henreki [*My Japanese Journey*]', first published in 2000; in *Nihongo wo kaku heya, op. cit.*)

While the Japanese literary circles treated the question posed by Zainichi Korean literature as a matter of cultural difference, that is, "ethnicity," Levy revealed that the question was fundamentally about race.

Nevertheless, Levy chose to continue to illuminate this issue in the context of East Asia. His recent work, *Mohankyo* (2016), is a novel about his visit to his former family home in Taiwan. It is written in the style of an I-novel, which is perceived as characteristically and exclusively Japanese, with an appearance by Yuju On under her real name (discussed below). He lets it be known that his work resonates with the works of Kōbō Abe and Yangji Lee.

7.3.3 "Post-Imperial-Colonial" Japanese-Language Literature II

Yuju On, born in 1980, belongs to the younger generation of authors who consciously work in the Japanese-language literature genre. The title of her collection of essays is *Taiwan umare Nihongo sodachi (Born in Taiwan, Raised in Japanese)* (2016). The use of "Japanese" instead of "Japan" is refreshing and signifies her stance on identity.

On was born to Taiwanese parents who spoke "Chinese mixed with Taiwanese" and was thrown into "a new language called Japanese" when she arrived in Japan at the age of three. She reflects on her own process of language acquisition and recalls that she replied to her parents in Japanese "Wakatteru" (I know) instead of "我知道/Wozhidao" or "我知啦/Wazaila") when she understood what her parents told her. She acknowledges that she "grew more like a Japanese" in the manner of speech, gesture, and movement as she became more fluent in Japanese.

In her supple writing style, On tells of three forms of politics. The first is politics instituted by Japan—the existence of the alien registration certificate (to control foreign nationals living in Japan) that defines On as an alien (other). In the nationality section of her certificate, it is written *China (Taiwan)*. On says that it is a reminder that she is a *gaijin* and she would not try to forget the fact that she "had been a Taiwanese once" even if she obtained Japanese citizenship.

The Alien Registration Act was abolished in 2012 and a residence certificate was issued to On. However, she was given the status of "mid-term resident" and noted, "This expression sounds like they assume I will go home eventually."

On the other hand, she wants to "be a Japanese and a Taiwanese at the same time"—she wishes to retain her Taiwanese nationality and writes about the circumstances surrounding voting in Taiwan's presidential election. She exhibits ambivalence toward her own political stance in response to her situation in which she has been categorized as other by Japanese politics and therefore tried to participate in Taiwanese politics.

The second form is politics vis-a-vis China. On travels to the Matsu Islands in the Taiwan Strait, On contemplates (in Japanese) "a division of the Chinese language"—into mainland Chinese and Taiwanese. And she refers to Ying-tai Lung, an author who was born in Taiwan to "immigrants from mainland China," studied in the US and married a German. Lung narrates the lives of individuals who were "tossed about by national borders" in her novels.

In one story, a woman traveled to Fuzhou in mainland China to meet the parents of her husband-to-be, but a sea blockade began in the afternoon on the day of her arrival. She has forgotten her native Taiwanese after so many years, but she sings *Kimigayo* (Japan's national anthem) to Lung as a "Taiwanese song."

On expresses her empathy toward Lung, who writes these novels and says, "The Chinese language is my passport." The Japanese language intervened again and On became absorbed in reading the Japanese translations of Lung's books.

The third form is politics created by the mother tongue/language of one's mother country. One is drawn to the works of Zainichi Korean writer Yangji Lee. She recognizes in Lee's works the state in which one vacillates between one's "language of the mother country" and "mother tongue" because they are different, and notes that "the language which is supposed to be one's own does not feel like one's own." Again, On writes that she was "engrossed in reading *Japanese* [emphasis in original]" written by Lee.

On states:

> I have a relationship with a language as if it were the language of my native country although it could have been a foreign language to me. When I realized that this was my reality, I began to feel that there were many I's swirling inside myself, too many to be contained by the first person 'I.'

She recasts the problem of identity as the question of language and affirms her position as *"I am not Japanese but I live in Japanese"* [emphasis in original]. And this situation leads her to *Nihongo*—the Japanese language interwoven with Chinese. She demonstrates that history is carved into language and reflects on her inner process that took her to reassess the point at issue from the perspective of language.

When On's works are transposed onto race, there are already signs of appropriation of this new insight. Let us look at a conversation between On and Levy, her former university teacher and fellow author, on the topic of "Why do I write in Japanese?" (*Bungakukai* [Literary world], November 2017).

On tells Levy that she wanted to write her version of *Yuhi* (Yangji Lee's major work). Yuhi is the protagonist of the Zainichi Korean author's novel, who explores her own identity using language (Hangul and Japanese) as a clue. Lee relativizes Yuhi's attempt while she empathizes with it.

In the conversation, On advances her point of argument further by stating that "Circumstances surrounding the mother tongue and the language of the mother country are very different in Taiwan and Korea." She continues, "When I considered the case of Taiwan, it gradually dawned on me that the mother tongue itself was actually plural," and advocates for the separation of identity and "mother tongue."[3]

At the same time, I cannot overlook the rising social pressure to push her work as identity politics as On deepens her analysis. Even though she argues for her identity to be separated from Japan, the introduction to their conversion in *Bungakukai* states, "Hideo Levy left an American university to live in Japan permanently and Yuju On migrated to Tokyo as a child with her parents."

In the introduction, the respective inner conflicts of On and Levy have been converted to conflicts (associated with national borders) between America and Japan, Japan and Taiwan, and China and Japan. The narrow path of constructing an identity-based argument is secured by one's origin and defines one's inner conflict as conflict over one's origin. The situation wherein the act of writing in Japanese is separate from the nexus of Japanese literature, Japanese nationality, Japanese culture, and the Japanese language is again tied to one's country of origin. Hence the introduction states that Hideo Levy from America and Yuju On from Taiwan express themselves in Japanese.

This is why On herself makes a remark that dwells on origins: "The way I wrote conveyed that a daughter with a very Japanese sensibility was overwhelmed or irritated by her mother who was Taiwanese in the way she lived, using multiple languages as her own with equal ease."

Levy questions On's explanation and recasts her argument as conflict over otherness. He points her away from the narrow path of origin by stating, "Other looks like just a Chinese or a Japanese. This level of egoism is awful. The other does have 'I', too."

However, even Levy himself recalls that he was once told, "You couldn't know because you are a Westerner." Points of discussion become entangled as the politics of origin are deep-rooted.

7.4 In Closing

I have examined Japanese-language literature from the imperialist to the post-imperialist eras and discussed the works of (a) Nobuo Ishimori, (b) Colonia literature, (c) Hideo Levy, and (d) Yuju On in terms of how they have used Japanese-language literature as an avenue to express or confront racism in the past. Ishimori's approach did not change throughout pre-war and post-war imperialist Japan. And Japanese readers gave a favorable reception to his post-war work imbued with racism (*Kotan no kuchibue*). In Brazil, Colonia literature attempted to search for a new identity through writing in the new genre of Japanese-language literature. Levy and On engaged in Japanese-language literature from a new standpoint and opened up new aspects, such as the multiplicity of identities. All of their works were created in the trans-Pacific and post-colonial contexts.

In short, the works of Colonial literature, Levy and On constitute a similar attempt to eliminate cultural essentialism and therefore express a strong criticism of racism. Nevertheless, the resistance and cunning of racism are very persistent in their unconscious dwelling on their origins.

Unfortunately, racism continues to attack those who speak out against it more than half a century later. When On was nominated for the Akutagawa Award (*Mayonaka no kodomotachi*, 2017), one of the judges commented: "The theme of confronting one's identity may be close to the heart of the people concerned but to Japanese readers it is a fire on the other side of the river and difficult to empathize with. I understood that some people would encounter such a problem but I found it boring to read an endless story about someone else's problem" (*Bungeishunjū*, September 2017). Further, the panel of judges failed to distinguish the words *bogo* (mother tongue) and *bokokugo* (language of the mother country). One expressed her displeasure on Twitter and asked whose language Japanese was.

Moreover, the cunning of racism tries to absorb the discourse on Japanese-language literature into essentialism and exhibits an excessive fixation on the origins of Levy and On.

Race or racism refuses to leave and stirs up a new argument under new circumstances. We need to cut open its narrow path and deepen the debate by engaging in dialogue. Further discussion on racism of the twenty-first century is needed.

Acknowledgments

This chapter was translated by Transpacific Press. Special thanks go to Katsuya Hirano for giving me constructive and concrete suggestions and for copyediting the entire text.

Notes

1 The works of "outland literature" of the empire include works produced by Japanese migrants (A) in overseas settlements and native (non-Japanese) residents (B) in colonies. Here, (A) and (B) live in completely different environments. They face one another asymmetrically and create asymmetrical relations within their ruler-colony relationship. The push factor for (A) is poverty and their inability to achieve success in their homeland. By contrast, their relationship with (B) is based on capitalism.

2 This also contrasts with "permanent residents" of Japanese descent in Japan. Among many Brazilians living in Japan, Japanese descendants and their family members have been recognized as "permanent residents of Japanese descent." The initial criteria required four grandparents to be Japanese nationals, but the 1990 revision of the Immigration Law gave resident status to third-generation Japanese-Brazilians and recognized the spouses of the second- and third-generations as permanent residents. The definition of "Japanese descent" was legally and institutionally determined. A race was created statutorily.

3 Yuju On calls herself a "writer of Japan." While "writer of Japanese" may be more in line with the context, she intentionally uses the former and proclaims, "With this self-awareness, I intend to keep writing in the belief that my issue is not 'someone else's issue' for Japanese literature." Her practice is based on the separation of "Japanese" and "Japan."

References

Derrida, Jacques. 1989. *Tasha no Gengo: Derida no Nihon Koen* [Language of Others: Derrida's Lecture in Japan]. Tokyo: Hosei University Press.

Fujiwara, Tei. 1949. *Nagareru hoshi ha ikiteiru* [The Floating Stars Are Alive]. Tokyo: Hibiyashuppansha.

Koseki, Shōichi. 1989. *Shinkenpō no tanjō* [The Birth of the New Constitution]. Tokyo: Chūōkōronsha.

Lee Hoe-seong. 1972. *Kinuta wo utsu onna* [The Cloth Fuller]. Tokyo: Bungeishunjū.

Levy, Hideo. 1992. *Seijōki no kikoenai heya* [A Room Where Stars and Straps Cannot Be Heard]. Tokyo: Kōdansha.

Narita, Ryuichi. 2003. "'Hikiage' ni kansuru joshō [An Introduction on Return]." *Shisō* 953: 149–174.

Nishi, Masahiko. 2014. *Bilingual na yume to yūutsu* [Bilingual Dreams and Melancholy]. Kyoto: Jinbunshoin.

Nishi, Masahiko. 2018. *Gaichi junrei: "Ekkyōteki" Nihongo bungakuron* [Overseas territories: On "Transnational" Japanese Language Literature]. Tokyo: Misuzushobō.

On, Yuju. 2016. *Taiwan umare Nihongo sodachi* [Born in Taiwan and Raised in Japanese]. Tokyo: Hakusuisha.

Sasanuma, Toshiaki. 2011. *Levy Hideo: "Hina" no kotoba toshite no Nihongo* [Levy Hideo: Japanese as a Language of Hina]. Tokyo: Ronsōsha.

Ukai, Satoshi, Naoki Sakai, Tessa Morris=Suzuki, and Hyoduk Lee. 2012. *Racism studies josetsu* [An Introduction to Racism Studies]. Tokyo: Ibunsha.

PART III

Minor Alliance, Memory, and Affect

8

A JAPANESE AMERICAN CRITIQUE OF THE ATOMIC BOMB AND ITS UP AGAINSTNESS

Crystal Uchino

On June 28, 1995, *Enola Gay,* an exhibition featuring the fuselage of the Enola Gay—the infamous B29 Superfortress bomber that dropped the bomb on Hiroshima—and several photographs of its crew, opened at the National Air and Space Museum (NASM). Dramatically different from the (canceled) original planned exhibit that would have presented the warplane alongside artifacts borrowed from Hiroshima and Nagasaki, the installation represented an attempt to preserve the threatened legitimacy of the narrative of America's heroic past.

One month later, the exhibition *Latent August: The Legacy of Hiroshima and Nagasaki* opened at Pier One, Fort Mason Center in San Francisco. Pictures from the opening day depict a large crowd overflowing out of the exhibition space representing the over 400 attendees who visited the exhibition that day; an installation centered around the experiences of Japanese American *hibakusha;*[1] numerous art pieces; and a performance by drummers from the Korean Youth Cultural Center honoring the tens of thousands of Korean victims of the atomic bomb.

These two exhibitions that opened in the summer of 1995 were notable for the disparate ways that each addressed the memory of the atomic bombings of Hiroshima and Nagasaki. The *Enola Gay* exhibit, and the public controversy that surrounded it, highlighted American exceptionalism by rendering invisible the violence of US militarism. In contrast, the *Latent August* exhibition, which commemorated the 50th anniversary of the atomic bomb(s) from a Japanese American perspective, inclusive of the violence enacted on Japanese colonial subjects, directs our attention to the initiatives and interactions of Asian/Americans[2] on both sides of the Pacific and the ways they confronted complicated layers of meaning and uneven

DOI: 10.4324/9781003266396-11

power relationships amidst contentious war memories in the 1990s. As the title, *Latent August,* suggests, Japanese American counter memories of the atomic bomb had been present but relatively imperceptible for nearly 50 years.

Although there exists a considerable body of literature on the *Enola Gay* exhibition controversy,[3] the significance of the *Latent August* exhibit, and its place within the larger historiography of contested memories of war and the nuclear Pacific, has yet to be examined. This chapter explores Japanese American initiatives in 1995 to remember the atomic bomb—who its victims were, whose lives are worth grieving, and how its violence can be understood in relation to issues of colonization and imperialism. In doing so, it attempts to elucidate a number of possibilities and limitations of "Race as Resistance" (see the introduction to this volume for the definition of "Race as Resistance"; Takezawa 2011) in a transpacific context. It will pay attention to the multi-directional ways that Japanese American remembering and critiques of the atomic bomb in 1995 were constructed across borders in ways that not only countered dominant narratives in the US and Japan but also contemplated war memory and nuclear history in a "minor transnational" (Lionnet and Shi 2005) way that emphasized horizontal relationships to other minority populations.

Throughout this chapter, I locate the Japanese American intervention in the memoryscape of the atomic bomb within the frames of Asian American and transpacific critique. According to Lisa Lowe, Asian American critique emerges in response to the process of Asian racialization and, like Asian American culture itself, is "a site that shifts and marks alternatives to the national terrain by occupying other spaces, imagining different narratives and critical historiographies, and enacting practices that give rise to new forms of subjectivity and new ways of questioning the government of human life by the national state" (Lowe 1996, 29). Extending beyond the American sphere, transpacific critique, as outlined by Lisa Yoneyama, is constituted by a "conjunctive critique" of American and Japanese imperialism (Yoneyama 2017). As other chapters in this anthology articulate, racialization did/does not happen in isolation. Transpacific critique underscores the point that neither should liberation.

Phanuel Antwi (2018) suggests that doing transpacific work necessitates thinking through Judith Butler's "ethics of cohabitation." Originating in the context of Palestine/Israel, Butler's ethics of cohabitation directs us to how histories of migration, colonization, imperialism, and processes of globalization produce "up againstness—the result of populations living in conditions of unwilled adjacency" (Butler 2012). It is in the reflexive consideration of what we are "up against" (connoting a relational proximity as much as it does opposition) that opportunities for "solidarity across space and time" (Butler 2012) emerge. With these insights in mind, I argue that the productive possibilities and limitations of race as resistance found in the Japanese American remembering and especially critique of the atomic bomb in 1995 are intricately linked to the ways that Japanese Americans negotiated tensions and solidarity with other minority communities (and their histories) as they came up against dominant narratives of the nuclear bombing(s) as well as growing Asian/American demands for the redress of Japanese colonial violence, Indigenous critiques of US "nuclear colonialism," Black struggles for freedom and other calls for minority rights.

The Japanese American critique of the atomic bomb in 1995 is anything but uniform. It was formed by voices of Japanese Americans of various backgrounds, each with a different relationship to the event and memory of the atomic bomb, including Japanese American hibakusha and their supporters; activists who had worked to bring about redress for the mass removal and incarceration of Japanese Americans during World War II; historians; veterans; peace activists; writers; and artists. In other words, it was comprised of a multiplicity of people, each with their own personal stories, analyses, visions, and frustrations informing their ideas about how the atomic bomb should be remembered, each contributing one marginal view to a broader provisional critique of the atomic bomb. What they shared was a history of being racialized as others in the US, which led them to draw connections between the marginalization of the experiences and stories of Japanese Americans and those of other marginalized communities affected by nuclear radiation in the US, Japan, Korea, and the Pacific Islands. I contend that the Japanese American critique(s) of the atomic bomb in 1995 offers a compelling intervention in dominant narratives via a minor transpacific historical imagination that attempted to reckon with issues of racialization, colonization, and war both domestically and across the Pacific.

7.1 Transpacific Subjectivities, Long-Time Silence, and Early Activism

A disproportionate number of early Japanese immigrants to the US emigrated from Hiroshima prefecture. During the "first wave" of Japanese emigration between 1885 and 1894, Hiroshima produced 38 percent of all government contract migrants (Sakata 2015, 18), many of whom were recruited to work on sugar plantations in US-occupied Hawai'i. By 1929, there were 46,596 overseas Japanese from Hiroshima living in Hawai'i or the continental US (Hiroshima-ken 1991, 625). Prior to 1941, patterns of reverse migration to Japan, both temporary and permanent, were common among first- and second-generation migrants. This resulted in a large number of Japanese Americans living in Hiroshima Prefecture before the outbreak of the war. Hiroshima prefectural records placed 11,317 Japanese Americans in the prefecture in 1932 (Hiroshima-ken 1991, 703). While the tragic loss of life in Hiroshima has captured the imaginations of scholars and ordinary people around the world, many are not aware that victims of the atomic bomb included those possessing what Naoko Wake has called "cross-national identities" (Wake 2017). The significance of cross-national ties to Hiroshima among the Japanese immigrant population and the impact the atomic bomb had on both individuals and families has been largely unexamined.

In the aftermath of the war, as many in the US rejoiced at the news of the bombing, most in the Japanese American community kept quiet about any possible connections to the atomic-bombed cities and their anxiety about the status of their kin who had resided there. Even within the Japanese American community, the experiences, grief, and trauma of transnational families and survivors were suppressed and self-censored for decades. Underlying the abjection of Japanese American experiences and memories of the nuclear bombings from American, Japanese, and Japanese American historiographies is the Cold War construction of several prevalent narratives. These include the dominant American and Japanese national narratives of the war and its end, as well as the narrative of Japanese American loyalty, which has been significantly informed by the psychological force of concentration camp memory and the conditions of inclusion under white supremacy.

Dominant national narratives produced about the atomic bombing of Hiroshima and Nagasaki in the US and Japan—justifiable events in the final episode of a so-called "good war," or conversely, symbolic sites of horror and redemption—delineated post-war national identities and their distributions of power in the Pacific during the Cold War period. On the one hand, America's victory "for democracy" led to its increased economic and military power in Asia during the subsequent Cold War. But, as scholars such as Robert J. Lifton and James Mitchel (1996) have pointed out, understanding the atomic bombings as part of a story in which hundreds of thousands of American soldiers were saved, and democracy brought to the world required the subjugation of narratives recalling the horror and indiscriminate destruction of hundreds of thousands of Japanese lives. On the other hand, Japan's post-war emergence as an economic superpower has been linked to the construction of a narrative of collective national victimhood whereby Japanese wartime victimization told through Hiroshima's suffering works to obscure knowledge about Japanese wartime atrocities in Asia (Dower 1995; Yoneyama 1999; Igarashi 2000).

In the American domestic sphere, the narrative of Japanese American loyalty aimed to secure Japanese American belonging in American society by assuring white nationalists that there was no threat of "yellow peril" within US borders. It was demonstrated by calling to mind Japanese American support for the war effort and the sacrifices of Japanese American veterans in order to stress their Americanness. Up against the discourse of Japanese American (masculine) patriotism, however, were the divergent ways that Japanese Americans had experienced World War II that complicated the narrative of loyalty. The transpacific experiences of Japanese American hibakusha were particularly illegible and troubling. Hibakusha could not fit into the loyalty narrative because they were not fighting for "American democracy"—they were in places like Hiroshima and Nagasaki. The proliferation of a Japanese American civil rights consciousness seemed to only compound the problem. The Japanese American redress movement had been inseparable from Americanization (Takezawa 1995). As a result, even at the height of Japanese American civil rights activities, Japanese Americans themselves became complicit to the silencing of hibakusha experiences. Japanese American hibakusha were even warned by community leaders not to rock the

proverbial boat. As one hibakusha recalled in an interview in 2006, when hibakusha activists in California first tried to make their plight known, they were
warned: "You talk about A-bombing and radiation, the whole Japanese community [is] going to be discriminated against" (Goren and Cox 2006). Thus, while
silence may have been an important part of the healing process for many survivors (Wake 2021), silence was also reinforced by the oppressive force of racism in
the US that served as an additional deterrent for Japanese Americans to disclose
their experiences. Kazue Suyeishi, a Japanese American hibakusha residing in
Los Angeles, likened the act of breaking the silence about her experience to
"talking to a wall, with echoes coming back saying 'Remember Pearl Harbor'"
(Nakayama 1995b, 1). Mary Teruyo Fujita, an organizer of the Seattle hibakusha group, reported being visited by the FBI for speaking about her experiences
(Hokubei Hochi 1995).[4] Significantly, fearing more anti-Japanese discrimination, many hibakusha who returned to the US in the post-war years were told
by their communities and even their families not to talk about their troubled
transpacific experiences (Sodei 1998). Like the *burakumin* immigrants discussed
by Sekiguchi in Chapter 3, hibakusha became a double minority in the Japanese
American community, whether they were American-born or more recent immigrants. They were subject to American racism and fear of racism against Asians,
as well as the discrimination/fear of being discriminated against in their own
community for their status as atomic bomb survivors. As a result, for many, being
Japanese American made the already difficult act of talking about the experience
of the atomic bomb even harder.

It would be inaccurate to say that there had been no effort prior to 1995 to
break the silence surrounding Japanese American experiences of the atomic bomb
or its memory and meaning among Japanese Americans. In fact, in the 1970s and
1980s, the organizing efforts of two groups of activists radically challenged the
paradigm of Japanese American silence on the atomic bomb. The first was the
Committee of Atomic Bomb Survivors (CABSUS) and their supporters, most
notably the Friends of Hibakusha (FOH). The other consisted of Japanese (and
other Asian) Americans active in the early stages of the Asian American movement (AAM). Although they differed in demographics, tactics, and goals, the
activism of these two groups sowed a seed of critique in the Japanese American
consciousness that would gain heightened visibility in 1995.

Between 1972 and 1979, CABSUS engaged in a lengthy legal struggle that
sought to secure supplemental medical assistance from the US government for
hibakusha residing in America. Unlike in Japan, where hibakusha activism
throughout the 1950s and 1960s resulted in significant relief and compensation
measures from the Japanese government, hibakusha activism in the US was met
with little more than ignorance, suppression, and racist backlash. The title of
Rinjiro Sodei's book, *Were We the Enemy: American Survivors of Hiroshima* (1998),
captures this phenomenon well. Among the experiences detailed in the book is
how a number of Japanese American hibakusha reported receiving intimidating
mail and phone calls after going public with their experiences. Reminiscent of

the wartime racialization of Japanese Americans, these included being called "the enemy," a "Jap," or being told to "go back to Japan" (Sodei 1998).

While CABSUS generally avoided getting involved in the activities of the anti-nuclear and anti-war movements out of fear that being too political might hinder their campaign for medical assistance, the memory of the atomic bomb played a significant role in the radical political imaginary of AAM activists in the early 1970s, functioning as an apparatus of pan-ethnic and transborder solidarity. Tangible and imagined connections to the atomic bomb both constructed and gave legitimacy to their Asian American place in US domestic social movements such as the anti-war movement and in the global anti-colonial moment. Through art and protest, AAM activists recast the memory of Hiroshima and Nagasaki alongside the more protracted events of cultural and biological genocide, such as slavery, colonialism, and the US war in Southeast Asia, critiquing both American imperialism and domestic racisms (Oyagi 2013; Uchino 2019). Despite these breaches of silence by AAM and CABS in the 1970s and 1980s, the atomic bombings would remain a dissonant issue for most Japanese Americans into the early 1990s.

7.2 Entitled to Debate

A diverse body of literature has developed on the *Enola Gay* exhibit controversy. Some interpreted the dispute as an example of "competing strategies of remembrance" (Hubbard and Hasain 1998) or as an example of the disparity between popular memory and historical scholarship (Boyer 1996). Others have made comparisons to the lack of Japanese accountability in addressing its wartime victimization of others (Sodei 1995; Dower 1996) or emphasized how it brought up the need to reconsider the ways the past is, or should be, mediated by the present (Thelen 1995). More recently, Lisa Yoneyama (2016) and Rika Nakamura (2017) have highlighted the uncritical transnational elements of the controversy surrounding issues of American and Japanese wartime violence. For example, Yoneyama points out that when former Japanese colonial subjects came forward with their stories of being brutalized by Japanese military violence in the 1980s and 1990s, their calls for redress worked to disrupt overly simplistic narratives of Japan's victimization. Yet, when Asian critiques of Japanese violence (meant to be dissenting and oppositional) were mobilized by conservative American interests, they served as a justification for American wartime violence and to reinforce the problematic narrative of American exceptionalism. According to Yoneyama, "one of the most valuable outcomes of the mid-1990s Smithsonian dispute is that the incident generated a sense of urgency for envisaging transpacific and transnational—or more precisely post-Statist—public spheres in which diverse memories of historical violence might intersect and be shared coalitionally" (Yoneyama 2016, 200). In this section I revisit the debate from a bottom-up perspective focusing on the voices of Japanese Americans. Similar to Tsuchiya in Chapter 9, I highlight the work of racialization in disciplining the politics of memory and ask: what new image of history is possible when we foreground minority voices and perspectives?

At the height of the *Enola Gay* debates, aside from a few Japanese American veterans who expressed support for the American Legion in demanding that the Smithsonian cancel the exhibit on the allegation that it depicted the US as an aggressor, few Japanese Americans risked public comment, especially dissenting ones. Naomi Hirahara—who at the time was the English section editor of the *Rafu Shimpo*, the largest Japanese American daily newspaper—admitted that she had avoided getting involved in the *Enola Gay* controversy because she "didn't want to be accused of being a Japanese apologist" (Hirahara 1995a, 3). Even James Yamazaki, a prominent opponent of nuclear weapons and the author of *Children of the Atomic Bomb: An American Physician's Memoir of Nagasaki, Hiroshima, and the Marshall Islands* (1995), declined to comment directly on the controversy (Nakayama 1995a, 1). On the periphery of the dispute, however, discord had been growing in the Japanese American community. As I will show, throughout 1995, more and more Japanese Americans would take an active interest in thinking through the meaning and memory of the atomic bomb as well as the justificatory premise of the bomb's first (and second) use. And as the fifty-year anniversary approached, a formidable critique began to coalesce in the broader Japanese American society.

In many ways, the Japanese American critique of the atomic bomb in 1995 was a product of its time. From the mid-1980s to the early 1990s, many contentious war memories were brought into the public eye as calls for redress permeated the political landscape across the Pacific. In Asia, campaigns by victims of Japan's colonial and military violence altered the memoryscape of the Pacific War. This led to Japanese Prime Minister Hosokawa Morihiro's 1991 acknowledgment of Japan's military aggression inflicted on its neighbors. In the US, the redress movement concerning the wartime internment of Japanese Americans successfully culminated in the 1988 Civil Liberties Act, unarguably a monumental turning point in Japanese American political precarity. Just fifty years prior, Japanese Americans had been forced into segregated carceral spaces under a politics of anti-Japanese racism, but when the post-redress era brought multicultural ideologies center stage in the American political landscape, the general public seemed to embrace Japanese American citizenship (albeit through the trope of the model minority). Without doubt, the struggle for redress politicized and made activists out of ordinary and even conservative-leaning Japanese Americans (at least in the contiguous US)[5] who increasingly made use of racial justice frameworks and insights developed in the Black civil rights movement as they championed for Japanese American civil liberties and redress.

Among those shaping the critical Japanese American discourse on the atomic bomb in 1995 was Asian American historian Ronald Takaki. A trailblazer in Asian American history, Takaki had made a name for himself by retelling US history through stories about people of color, raising uncomfortable questions about race, and insisting on the Americanness of multicultural experiences as well as the importance of their inclusion in the historiography. In 1995, Takaki had just completed his book, *Hiroshima: Why America Dropped the Atomic Bomb*. In it, he asserted that anti-Japanese racism motivated policy-makers' decision to use the atomic bomb and influenced public opinion afterward—an argument based on his examination of recently declassified documents. In the book's introduction, Takaki situated the US atomic attacks on Japan within a long genealogy of US racism. He wrote: "Ever since the first contact between the English settlers and the Powhatans in Virginia in 1607, and then the arrival of Africans in 1619, race has been significant in our history. Hiroshima, as it turns out, was no exception" (Takaki 1995, 7). Building on John Dower's thesis in *War Without Mercy: Race and Power in the Pacific War* (1986), Takaki argued that "racialized rage" against the Japanese that intensified after Pearl Harbor was an extension of nineteenth-century anti-Asian prejudice (for example, the many Asian exclusion acts)[6] built into the fabric of pre-war American culture.

The release of Takaki's book in 1995 placed it squarely within the hot topic of debate over how to remember the atomic bomb, most fervently represented in the *Enola Gay* controversy. Taking a multicultural approach, Takaki's position on the *Enola Gay* debate challenged the idea that it was unpatriotic to seek understanding of the atomic bomb beyond the dominant [white] American narrative: "we are entitled to this debate, as Americans committed to our constitutional right of free speech—one of the 'four freedoms' for which Americans bravely fought and died during World War II" (Takaki 1995, 11). Takaki called for historical accuracy and a "serious and substantive debate." He asserted that "institutions of culture and knowledge have the responsibility to make facts available to the American public" and stressed that these institutions should "serve as forums for discussions, even disagreements, conducted with civility" (Takaki 1995, 11). Takaki also insisted on the need for individuals to "examine critically as many of the facts as possible and consider differing viewpoints … All of us owe it to ourselves" (Takaki 1995, 11). Handwritten by Takaki in my copy of *Hiroshima* is a quote: "'I don't want to touch the past,'" by an anonymous atomic bomb survivor, whose scars Takaki described as a permanent reminder of the atomic blast, and Takaki's words: "We need to touch that past in order to understand why it happened."

Japanese Americans in California responded to Takaki's call to action enthusiastically. By the time the Smithsonian exhibit opened in June, the voices of Japanese Americans from diverse backgrounds seemed to come together in a resonating frequency, penetrating the metaphoric silencing wall that had surrounded the memory of the atomic bomb in the Japanese American community for so long. What started out as sporadic opinion pieces in the Japanese American newspapers grew into near daily articles depicting a plurality of individual views on the *Enola Gay* controversy as well as a milieu of transpacific memories and critical perspectives of the US atomic bombings. Japanese American critique(s) of the atomic bomb appeared in the pages of California's Japanese American newspapers and other publications in public forums, counter exhibitions, memorial services, poetry, and art.

In Southern California, historical silence surrounding the bomb was confronted in events such as a panel discussion at Centenary United Methodist Church. Organized by Phil Shigekuni, who had been a prominent redress activist and had served as JACL chapter president, the event centered Japanese American Christian perspectives on the atomic bomb. According to Shigekuni, pressure to prove loyalty to the US in the face of racialization had stifled dialogue about the atomic bomb among Japanese Americans. During the forum, he highlighted the historical difficulty of engaging in critical dialogue about the atomic bomb, explaining: "If the government's justification for the dropping of the bombs was that it saved American lives, that kind of brought all discussion to a screeching halt. How was anybody going to disagree with something like that?" (*Rafu Shimpo* 1995b). Two months earlier, in a letter to the editor published in the *Rafu Shimpo*, Shigekuni had articulated that the issue of the atomic bomb was one of "cultural conflict" for him:

> We all went to camp to "prove" our loyalty. Our men fought and died to tell the world we were 100 percent loyal American citizens, and not one of "them," the enemy. Yet, to completely buy the American line does not feel right. My relatives came from Hiroshima. For me to dismiss the annihilation of 200,000 men, women, and children as merely an unfortunate but justifiable part of war without trying to fathom the depth of the loss to the surviving relatives and to Japan, tears at who I am as a Japanese and as a Christian.
>
> *Shigekuni 1995, 3*

In his column for the *Rafu Shimpo*, Brian Niiya wrote, "Fifty years after the bombing of Hiroshima and Nagasaki, the Japanese American community [had] seemed to finally come to grips with the impact of the war and the camps in many ways. After years of silence, the stories of the war years have come pouring out" (Niiya 1995, 3). What is more, Japanese American dailies in California seemed to eagerly seek out the perspectives of Japanese American hibakusha, who finally had sympathetic ears in their community. A number of outspoken hibakusha activists readily shared their experiences and opinions about nuclear weapons. Francis Tomozawa, an outspoken Japanese American survivor, told the *Hokubei Mainichi*: "I did not say this prior to this year, but I must say it now. The dropping of the atomic bomb was absolutely wrong no matter what the reason is" (Yamamoto 1995b, 1). Kazue Suyeishi, the hibakusha mentioned above, described her nightmarish experience of the atomic bomb for readers of the *Rafu Shimpo*: "I became sick, from the radiation—nausea, skin disease and bleeding from everywhere—and when I came out, I saw many dead people, burned bodies. My whole family was sick and homeless" (Nakayama 1995b, 1). Still, perhaps "pouring out" was not exactly the right way to describe the willingness of all to share their wartime experiences. Some, like Ben Okumura, who as a sixth grader saw his friends burned, understandably "[didn't] like to go back to those memories." Instead, Okumura hinted at the enduring injustice he experienced as an uninsured hibakusha who could not afford the high cost of medical insurance in the US. He said: "I'm an American and the United States tried to kill me, so I wish the US government would take care of me" (Nakagawa 1995b, 1).

Although Naomi Hirahara had been reluctant to comment on the *Enola Gay* controversy, by June she found other ways of publicly engaging the memory of the atomic bomb. In her column for the *Rafu Shimpo* she declared: "This year, Hiroshima will come to us." Literally speaking, she was referring to an upcoming visit by her grandmother, Chiyoko Mukai, a Hiroshima hibakusha. Metaphorically, Hirahara's statement alluded to her overdue confrontation with the personal impact of the atomic bomb on her family history and perhaps more broadly reflected a belief that speaking about what happened in Hiroshima was important. As the daughter of cross-national hibakusha, this reckoning was as corporeal as it was cultural for Hirahara. Hirahara discussed what it had been like for her two years earlier when she had participated in a medical exam for first- and second-generation hibakusha residing in America conducted by Hiroshima physicians.[7] Part of her had felt "strange and embarrassed" for taking part in the exams because, in her own words, she "wasn't a survivor" (Hirahara 1995a, 3). But, when the test results revealed an elevated white blood count, she wondered how she should interpret them. Were the results the reflection of a temporary immune condition, a cold perhaps? Or could they be connected to the atomic bomb? Hirahara described the haunting and intergenerational presence of the atomic bomb in her family as a "screen that colors our eyes" (Hirahara 1995a, 3).

For her, the 50th anniversary of the atomic bomb was not simply a news story, but it was also deeply personal. While her grandmother was visiting California that summer, Hirahara interviewed her about the war and surviving the bomb. The interview would become the base of a story that described Chiyoko's search for her husband, Kazuso Mukai, in the aftermath of the bomb. Published as part of a *Rafu Shimpo* special series, the story concluded with a message of the providential potential of sharing memories about the bomb (Hirahara 1995b, 1). One year later, Hirahara left her position at the *Rafu Shimpo* to become a creative writer. Her first novel, *Summer of the Big Bachi* published in 2004, explored the transpacific memory of the atomic bomb through her Japanese hibakusha characters—a theme she would continue to explore throughout the seven books comprising her Mas Arai mystery series.

Powerful as these personal reckonings were, what stands out in the memorialization of the atomic bomb by Japanese Americans of various backgrounds in 1995 was the boldness of the challenge posed to the dominant US narrative. Hiroshi Yamaguchi, who had spent the war years in Japan, renounced any justification of the atomic bombing, stating, "The manufacture of atomic bombs and dropping of those bombs on human people is a crime" (*Rafu Shimpo* 1995b, 3). When asked to comment on the NASM exhibit, Suyeishi told the *Rafu Shimpo*: "If they are going to destroy the whole (exhibit), we are going to have to work even harder" (*Rafu Shimpo* 1995a, 1).

Many echoed Ronald Takaki's critique of racism as a motivating factor for the use of the atomic bomb and the limitations of the discourse produced about it. While participating in the panel discussion at Centenary United Methodist Church, Paul Tsuneishi, a long-time member of the JACL (former chapter president, district chair, and National Board member), expressed his belief that the critical views of the atomic bomb were oppositional to white-American values—something he had been indoctrinated into. He recalled that in his early life, "The dropping of the atomic bomb never created a problem" for him, stating, "All of my values were White, I was an Anglo in values" (*Rafu Shimpo* 1995b, 3).

By 1995, however, Tsuneishi was not only vocal about his stance in opposition to nuclear weapons and the dominant (white) American discourse surrounding the bombings, but his critique of the bomb also included an indictment of JACL's politics of Americanization. This Americanization, he argued, had not only led to a tragic lack of support for hibakusha but equated to a kind of complicity to US racialized hegemony, as JACL's relative silence on the issue had left the dominant narrative unchallenged. Contrary to more positive depictions of JACL support for US hibakusha (Sodei 1998; Wake 2021), several months earlier, Tsuneishi had also authored a scathing opinion piece in the *Rafu Shimpo* lamenting that while the JACL identified a need to support the plight of Japanese American hibakusha in the 1970s, the organization failed to follow through. He opined that "Nisei hibakusha are not important to the JACL and have no standing with JACL today."[8] Denouncing what he saw as conservative posturing of the JACL, he went on: "The record is clear that from the beginning: JACL was co-opted by Nisei who had bought into the Anglo American vision of minorities of color, with the same Western/European value system and mentality as the Anglos" (Tsuneishi 1995, 3). Tsuneishi attributed his critical stance on JACL's apathy regarding the plight of hibakusha to his observations during his four-year tenure as the self-proclaimed lone JACL liaison to CABS in the 1970s.

In another opinion piece in the *Rafu Shimpo* titled "Radioactive Colonization," Ryan Masaaki Yokota, a community activist living in West Los Angeles whose father and grandparents survived the Hiroshima bombing, wrote:

> The recent controversy over the planned Smithsonian Institute exhibit has shown that historical inaccuracy and blind patriotism have gained the upper-hand in failing to address the true horror of the atomic bombs ... If all the facts surrounding the bombings were truly addressed, then the racism that guided the decision to bomb Japan would be revealed in its truest light ... A common thread links the incarceration of my great-grandfather in an Arkansas concentration camp—along with 120,000 other Americans of Japanese ancestry—with the bombings of Hiroshima and Nagasaki. That connection is the thread of racially based decision-making on the part of our government.

Yokota 1995, 3

Pointedly, Yokota's critique also moved beyond the frame of anti-Japanese racism as he connected to the struggles of Indigenous nations impacted by the violence of the US nuclear industry:

> Even beyond the actual use of nuclear weaponry on non-White peoples, the presence of nuclear waste in America has disproportionately impacted non-White populations here in the U.S. The Native American population for example, has consistently been a victim of environmental racism. Native American reservation lands and water supplies have been continually contaminated by radioactive tailings left by uranium mines and nuclear contamination disposed of on reservation land.
>
> *Yokota 1995, 3*

Similar to the solidarity expressed between Indigenous people and the artist discussed by Takezawa in Chapter 10 of this volume, it was important for Yokota to articulate in his critique how nuclear issues impacted not only the Japanese across the ocean but Indigenous people who are also victims of US settler colonialism. Yokota placed his critique of the atomic bomb within a complex web of racial domination, exploitation, and *nuclear colonialism*. A term that emerged in the 1990s through the work of Indigenous scholars and activists, nuclear colonialism describes a form of environmental racism present in the way that nuclear weapons testing, mining, and dumping disproportionately occurs on Indigenous land under colonialism (Churchill 1993; Smith 2005). In addition to the issue of mining and dumping[9] brought up by Yokota, scholars, and activists have highlighted how communities in two regions—Islands located in the Southeast Asia-Pacific and the American Southwest—have been disproportionately impacted by nuclear "testing."[10] For example, there have been over 928 American and 19 British nuclear explosions at the Nevada Test site, a US installation occupying a portion of unceded Western Shoshone territory known as Newe Sogobia. These explosions have been classified by the Western Shoshone National Council as bombs, not tests, leading many Indigenous leaders and activists to call the Western Shoshone nation the most heavily bombed nation in the world (Kuletz 2001, 237).

Of course, not all Japanese Americans shared these critical views (indeed, they may have been a minority). However, these examples demonstrate how Japanese American critiques of the atomic bomb were intricately connected to their own domestic understandings of anti-Japanese racism, the limits of Americanization, and US nuclear colonialism in ways that sought to disorder, unsettle, and disturb the facile American narrative of the atomic bomb.

7.3 Latent August

This section discusses the efforts to commemorate the atomic bombing(s) by Japanese Americans in Northern California who spearheaded a coalition called the Hiroshima/Nagasaki 50th Anniversary Committee. Members included the

FOH (mentioned above), the National Japanese American Historical Society (NJAHS), and the Asian Pacific Environmental Network. Their efforts resulted in nearly one hundred different programs and events spanning from July through September 1995. At the heart of the commemoration events was a three-month long exhibit (July 22 to September 30, 1995) entitled *Latent August: The Legacy of Hiroshima and Nagasaki* (mentioned in the introduction), which confronted the meaning of the bomb through "history, memory, and art." Heralding the opening of the exhibition at Pier One, Fort Mason Center in San Francisco. *Hokubei Mainichi* staff writer J.K. Yamamoto wrote: "In contrast to the Smithsonian Institution's current exhibit—which sought to avoid controversy by displaying without commentary the plane that dropped the bomb on Hiroshima—'Latent August,' produced by the National Japanese American Historical Society, explores the decision to drop the bomb and the experiences of those who survived the nuclear holocaust" (Yamamoto 1995a).

Heeding the call by Ronald Takaki for institutions to make facts available, the *Latent August* exhibit (and associated programming) defied the 1995 political challenges to institutions concerning the representation of the atomic bomb.[11] Not only was it the product of constructive and critical collaborations between veterans, atomic bomb survivors, and "revisionist" historians, but *Latent August* explored several taboo issues that had been dropped from the Smithsonian's *Enola Gay* exhibition. Specifically, it included the perspectives of hibakusha and underrepresented historical evidence meant to unsettle the heroic rendering of the American narrative of the atomic bomb. In doing so, it engaged uncomfortable memories while contending with the tenuous nature of inclusion and representation for racial minorities.

While *Latent August* was not the only exhibition to counter the narrative set by the Smithsonian exhibition (the exhibition at American University in Washington DC is a notable example),[12] it was distinctive in that it attempted to rethink the meaning of the atomic bomb from a Japanese American perspective. Notably, rather than depicting the stories of faraway victims, part of the NJAHS exhibition centered on the intimate memories of Japanese Americans from the local community including Japanese American hibakusha as well as Japanese American military officers who witnessed the aftermath of the atomic bomb after traveling to Hiroshima as part of the occupation forces. In a press release that would have been almost unthinkable two and a half decades before, NJHAS proudly announced: "A special feature of the exhibit is the wartime experience of Japanese Americans from California. As Americans of Japanese ancestry stranded in Japan during the war, they offer insight into the complex nature of how Americans view the legacy of the atomic bomb 50 years later" (Tonai 1995).

After twenty-five years of sustained activism by hibakusha and their supporters, their experiences that had so troubled the narrative of Japanese American loyalty were now center stage in a major Japanese American institution. Consequently, *Latent August*—both the exhibit and its associated programs—not only brought attention to the traumatic stories of survivors but also highlighted the dilemma of recognition for survivors with nationalities that had historically fallen outside the assumed bounds of the hibakusha neologism. This included many who were victims of both Japanese and US wartime violence, specifically Korean hibakusha. Comprising the second largest demographic of victims, many Korean hibakusha were exposed to the bomb as a direct result of being forcibly conscripted by the Japanese colonial government as labor for the Japanese Imperial Military in the 1930s and 1940s. Despite this, Korean survivors were subjected to exclusion from hibakusha relief laws and to this day continue to face unequal treatment in measures by the Japanese government enacted to support hibakusha.[13] As was mentioned in the introduction to this chapter, drummers from the Korean Youth Cultural Center occupied a prominent place in the opening ceremony. Additionally, on more than one occasion, *Latent August* program director Rosalyn Tonai brought media attention to the controversy over the memorial dedicated to Korean hibakusha in Hiroshima that was placed in an area outside of the official Peace Park—a matter considered by some to be symbolic of the erasure of Japanese colonialism from Hiroshima's dominant narrative.[14]

Just as Japanese Americans in Southern California had drawn attention to the ways that minority populations have been victimized by US nuclearism, the acknowledgment of Korean experiences of the atomic bomb was important to Japanese American organizers. In acknowledging the transnational particularities of Japanese American and Korean survivor experiences in the decades since the atomic bomb, the Japanese American critique called attention not only to the continuity of US wartime racialization of Japanese and Japanese Americans but also to that of Japanese colonial racialization of Koreans and the respective suffering and injustice that remained unredressed. This functioned as an act of local and transnational solidarity with victims of Japanese wartime imperialism, and it also showed that they were sensitive to how certain aspects of Hiroshima's peace narrative and the focus on Hiroshima and Nagasaki as victims might work to cover up Japanese colonial violence which may have worked to legitimize Japanese American perspectives to an American audience.

Significantly, the main actors responsible for the exhibition were not simply a fringe group of leftist thinkers (though they too were involved), but the majority were authoritative figures in the mainstream Japanese American community—prominent Japanese American veterans, established and influential community leaders, and respected Japanese American scholars. Two such figures were Clifford Uyeda, former redress chair of JACL, who took up the demanding role of *Latent August* exhibition chair; and Chizu Iiyama, co-founder of the JACL's redress Women's Concerns Committee, who served as the vice president of programs. Thus, in contrast to the marginalized critique of the atomic bomb by the radical AAM activists in the 1970s mentioned above, the critique by Japanese Americans in 1995 blurred the boundaries of dissenting and conventional politics. It is also worth noting here that while Uyeda was an influential leader in the struggle for Japanese American Civil Rights and Redress, he also had a problematic anti-Black history, a fact that draws our attention to the risks of reading race resistance too narrowly in ways that may obscure the complicated layers of migration history, uneven relationships, and assimilation strategies too often complicit in perpetuating the logics of transatlantic racialization.

In a divergent narrative to that of the veterans' groups that obstructed a more balanced presentation of the *Enola Gay* at the Smithsonian, contributions by Japanese American veterans played a vital role in the physical construction and content of the *Latent August* exhibit. For example, the volunteer labor and construction expertise of veterans Shig Iwasaki and Hank Ogawa was credited with transforming the venue's warehouse space into an exhibition space. Donor acknowledgments printed in the 1995 spring edition of *Nikkei Heritage* show that many Japanese American veterans also financially supported the exhibition. Finally, the personal experiences of Harry Fukuhara and Thomas Sakamoto, two Japanese American members of the US military who entered Hiroshima after the bomb was dropped, were prominently featured in the *Latent August* exhibition and associated programming. Against dominant US military accounts of the triumph of the atomic bomb told through the perspective of B-29 bombers, their firsthand accounts spoke of alarm and personal loss.

In 1995, Thomas Sakamoto was a retired US Army colonel active in many community associations and was also the vice president of communications on the NJAHS Board of Directors. Sakamoto was one of the first graduates of a once secret US Army language school at the Presidio of San Francisco in 1941. After serving in active combat in the Pacific, he became the first Japanese American officer to enter Hiroshima on assignment as a language officer to a group of Allied war correspondents on September 9, 1945. Reflecting back to that day, Sakamoto recalled: "As a Japanese American, I was really shaken up" (Sakamoto 1995). He explained:

> What I observed firsthand at the Red Cross Hospital is what I can only describe as gruesome and like "hell." Even after 50 years, it chokes me up and I find it very difficult to fully describe my feeling and emotions of that day. The Red Cross Hospital was overcrowded with atomic bomb victims. Lying in every available space were not combat soldiers, but defenseless women, children, and elderly Japanese. The flash burn effect of the bomb practically and completely peeled off skins and faces. What remained were red fleshy wounds and puss had begun to form all over their bodies.
>
> *Sakamoto 1995*

Harry Fukuhara's connection to Hiroshima was even more intimate. As a linguist with the 33rd Infantry Division of the US Army, Fukuhara had been among those stationed in the Philippines preparing to invade Japan when he heard the news of the bombing. Although the bombing meant that he would not have to participate in the dreaded invasion, the news traumatized him. Fukuhara had lived in Hiroshima before the war, and his mother and three brothers still lived there at that time. The more Fukuhara thought about it, the more he believed his family could not have survived and the more depressed he became. He recalled,

"My thinking degraded to the point that I blamed myself—that they had died because I had volunteered to fight against them" (Fukuhara 1995). After the war, Fukuhara was given a choice to either go back to America or go to Japan—where he had the chance of being reunited with his family. Although he feared the futility of looking for his family, he chose the latter. After landing in Japan in mid-September, he immediately set out for Hiroshima, failing to get there three times.

On October 2, during his fourth attempt to enter the city, he finally succeeded. "I was probably one of the earliest members of the US Occupation Forces to see Hiroshima after the world's first atomic bomb," recalled Fukuhara. "But I was not there to assess damage or report back to intelligence. I was driven by a personal mission. I had come to find my family ... if they were still alive" (Fukuhara 1995). It had been seven years since Fukuhara had seen his family. Their reunion was bittersweet. Although it seemed everyone had survived the war and the atomic bomb, Fukuhara soon realized that it wouldn't be long before his brother, Victor, would die (presumably due to his exposure to the bombs harmful radiation). Fukuhara and his family avoided talking about their complex wartime trauma for decades. But as he disclosed in 1995, the pain of his family's transpacific wartime experiences stayed with him:

> For years, by virtue of a silent mutual agreement, we avoided talking about what happened to our family in Hiroshima [...] It is forty-nine years since Victor died and twenty-seven years since my mother died plagued by unexplainable illnesses. I can talk about what happened in Hiroshima now, fifty years later. I believe that talking about it now, with a purpose, was the medicine I needed.[15]
>
> *Fukuhara 1995*

The transference of traumatic experiences and grief from implicit memory—where it is often stored in fragments—into narrative form is understood to be an important step in healing (Neimeyer 1999; Wheeler 2007). Thus, while talking about his experiences was meaningful for his personal healing, Fukuhara's act of disclosure as the first step to healing can also be read as a metaphor for the *Latent August* exhibition and perhaps for the Japanese American critique more generally.

In centering the experiences and embodied transpacific memories of hibakusha and others like Fukuhara and Sakamoto, the *Latent August* exhibition exposes the hypocrisy of the American national narrative and the insistence by some in the US on remembering the atomic bomb solely in terms of science, technology, and modernity.

7.4 War Responsibility and the Limitations of Remembering Hiroshima and Nagasaki

As momentum accelerated for Japanese Americans to remember the atomic bombings of Hiroshima and Nagasaki on their own terms in 1995, questions about the possible limitations of such remembrances also surfaced. In the larger context of contentious memories of the Asia-Pacific War in the 1980s and 1990s, one concern was the issue of how to consider the memory of the atomic bomb (and corresponding controversies) as one of multiple protracted, entangled, and suppressed Asian/American war grievances. Put a different way, the perils of overidentification with Japan's wartime victimization, without acknowledging Japan's role as a perpetrator of imperial violence in Asia, were put into question. In the context of American imperialism, another concern was the issue of Japanese American war responsibility, or as Victor Bascara has argued in *Model Minority Imperialism*, the importance of reflexively contending with how Asian American culture is both "manifestation and a critique of U.S. global hegemony" (2006). These issues were raised through introspective reflections by Japanese Americans as well as in tension with other Asian Americans on the issue of the atomic bomb.

Emphatically, the issue of Japanese American war responsibility presents a problematic for understanding the Japanese American critique of the atomic bomb as part of an ethic of cohabitation. It presents as its ethical problem the question of how to be Japanese American. In the context of racialization in the transpacific, it asks: If American racism has allowed for the justification of the atomic bomb; if Japanese racism allowed for the suppression of knowledge about Japanese colonial violence in Asia; and if US-Japan complicity to imperial projects in Asia continues to structure both realities, then how can Japanese Americans insist on a memory of the atomic bomb that refuses to reproduce the subjugation of others?

One of the more striking articulations of this problematic appeared in the *Rafu Shimpo* on May 23, 1995, in the form of an opinion piece written by Kevin Uchida, who was living and working in Hiroshima at the time. In it, he cautioned against representations of the atomic bomb, which skip over the history of the US and Japanese imperialism. Problematizing the ways in which Japanese American assimilation had been reconciled with ethnic pride, he alleged that when Japanese Americans "remember the atomic bomb victims of Hiroshima while (remaining?) ignorant of the Asian victims of Japan's aggression, this mirrors the arrogance of Japanese who refuse to recognize their country's accountability for Asian suffering during the war" (Uchida 1995, 3). Uchida believed that Japanese American reckoning with the impacts of historical war needed to go beyond internment and beyond the US-Japan paradigm. For him, this necessitated centering not only a critical understanding of the historical racialized relations between the US and Asian Americans and Asia but an equal consideration of the historical relations of colonialism between Japan and other Asian nations.

In particular, Uchida called for an understanding of the greater context in which both countries participated in the war in the Pacific, a war which he described as an "imperialist struggle to decide which colonizer would rule over the colonized Asians." For Uchida, this was not just about the past; pertinently, it was also about the ways the impact of the Pacific War "continued to intersect and overlap with present day issues." He explained how the refusal of Japan to reckon with its wartime history—exemplified in what he observed as high-level Japanese politicians' belligerent denial of atrocities such as the Nanjing massacre—hindered any true reconciliation in the region. At the same time, he described the *Enola Gay* controversy as an embarrassing incident that demonstrated "how little Americans have learned about ourselves in the last fifty years" (Uchida 1995, 3). Refuting the dominant justificatory premise for US actions in the Pacific Theater, he suggested that "for the US, it was not a fight for freedom and democracy as we are taught to believe, but a war to maintain hold over its own Pacific empire which already included Hawai'i and the Philippines, and to protect White supremacy" (Uchida 1995, 3). Uchida maintained that any Japanese American reckoning with their experiences of war must consider both of these factors, most importantly because they both impacted the relationships that Japanese Americans had with other Asian/Americans. Without dismissing the need for accountability at the national level, Uchida underscored the importance of war responsibility to be taken up at the individual and personal minor transnational level. Extending this minor transnational burden to himself and all Japanese Americans, he posed the problem: "As a Japanese American, how do I address my war responsibility?" (Uchida 1995, 3).

It is worth mentioning, as Uchida did, that by 1995, 61 percent of the Asian American population had immigrated to the US after 1970. Consequently, they did not necessarily have a shared memory of anti-Asian discrimination in America. Instead, as Uchida noted: "The majority of Asian Americans share[d] a collective regional experience of Japanese and/or U.S. imperialism and domination in their countries of origin" (Uchida 1995, 3). Furthermore, several postwar decades had nurtured vibrant inter-Asian "counteramnes(t)ic" movements in Asia (Yoneyama 2016). Committed to making Japanese colonial violence visible, these movements actively called for the redress of its harms. With the flow of more Asian immigrants into the US following the 1965 Immigration and Nationality Act, the idea that certain Japanese war atrocities had not yet been adequately redressed—but still should and could be—also gained traction in Asian/American circles in the 1980s and 1990s (Yoneyama 2016). The influence of these movements on Japanese American political practice can be seen, for example, in the work of former congressional representative Mike Honda in calling for apologies and redress for "comfort women."[16]

Thus in 1995, up against the Japanese American critique that emerged to unsettle the dominant American narrative of the atomic bomb were the growing Asian/American critiques of Japanese colonialism that were also transforming the political landscape of the Asian/American community. At times this led to tensions within the community which raised questions about the incompleteness of certain aspects of Japanese American critique of the atomic bomb. For example, during the panel discussion at Centenary United Methodist Church mentioned above, a Korean minister in the audience responded to the discussion with an impassioned speech condemning the cruelty of Japanese war crimes. Though not always framed as oppositional, the dialectical tension between the memory of the atomic bomb and the memories of other unredressed atrocities in Asia was frequently depicted in the pages of the *Rafu Shimpo*. Several articles drew attention to two provocative exhibitions that invited those in the Asian American community and beyond to reckon with the historical violence of Japanese aggression in Asia: *Comfort Women: Struggling for Dignity in Asia during World War II*, organized and hosted by the Korean American Museum in Los Angeles; and, also in Los Angeles, *The Forgotten Holocaust* exhibition, privately organized and financed by Daniel Kwan and the Northern California-based Alliance for Preserving the Truth of the Sino-Japanese War. Addressing the complicated inter-Asian dynamics stirred by recalling the war, Julie Ha's (1995) article "Fifty Years is Long Enough" discussed the confusing and sometimes conflicting feelings faced by younger generations of Asian Americans, like herself, in reflecting on the history and legacy of the Asia-Pacific War. Critical of Japanese colonialism and its legacy, Ha voiced her support for the comfort women redress movement and asserted the necessity of reckoning with past atrocities but lamented about how the painful issues of the past remained unreconciled and divisive. For Ha, hope for the next generation was the willingness to face the past honestly, both Japanese colonial violence and US military violence in Asia, to disarm resentment.

What does it mean that these perspectives are part of my discussion precisely because they were included in the pages of the Japanese American press? I want to suggest that the placement of these Asian/American war memories alongside the Japanese American memories and critique(s) of the atomic bomb embodied a searching—as opposed to static—relationship to the task of reckoning with questions of the past and the present. And that this inclusion was an attempt, marked by tension and alliance, by both Japanese Americans and Asian/Americans at grappling with what it meant to be Asian American in the 1990s. *Forgotten Holocaust* exhibit organizer Daniel Kwan put it best when he said: "I know we can't talk about healing and all this bullshit until you can acknowledge what it is you are trying to heal" (Nakagawa 1995a, 1).

It was precisely this transnational appeal for healing by inter-Asian activists that Uchida was responding to in his call for Japanese American war responsibility. Significantly, Uchida's consideration of Japanese American war responsibility was inspired by the critical conversations taking place around him during his residency in Hiroshima. In the introduction to his piece in the *Rafu Shimpo*, Uchida explains:

> As a third-generation Japanese American born in the 1960s long after the end of World War II, and as a racial minority whose parents and relatives were unjustly herded into internment camps because of their ethnicity, I would never have thought about the issue of war responsibility as it pertains to me if I were not living in Japan at this time.
>
> *Uchida 1995, 3*

As Akiko Naono (2005) has observed, pressure from former Japanese colonial subjects, their descendants, and other activists who supported them throughout the 1980s shifted the discourse toward recognizing Japan's war responsibility in the Japanese narrative of the atomic bomb. This was reflected in changes made to the narrative presented at the Hiroshima Peace Memorial Museum after it was renovated in 1994. Although the narrative presented at the museum had focused exclusively on Hiroshima's victimization through the 1980s, the newly renovated museum exhibition included descriptions of Hiroshima's involvement in Japan's colonial aggression in Asia before the bombing (Naono 2005).

In addition to putting pressure on mainstream institutions, activists in Japan also created alternative spaces to critically examine Japan's colonial past. In October of 1995, the same year the *Enola Gay* and *Latent August* exhibits were held in the US, the Masaharu Oka Memorial Nagasaki Peace Museum, a private volunteer-run museum dedicated to addressing the issue of Japanese war aggression in Asia, opened in Nagasaki. The museum is named for the late Lutheran minister and grassroots activist Masaharu Oka, who had been active in calling attention to the experiences of Korean atomic bomb survivors since the 1970s. His work included establishing a monument for the Korean victims of the atomic bomb as well as surveying for Korean atomic bomb survivors and their conditions. The Oka Masaharu Museum is arguably the first and only museum to foreground the experiences of Korean and Chinese atomic bomb survivors in Japan.

An excerpt from the museum's mission statement reads in part:

> The victim of Japan's invasion and war have been forgotten. Fifty years since the war, they have received no compensation. This murderous history has been swept under the carpet. The fact that no sincere apology or compensation has been offered by the authorities responsible to the victims shows a blatant disregard for human suffering and an utter betrayal of international trust. This Peace Museum was established by volunteers in the memory of Oka Masaharu and his lifelong fight against Japan's shameful stance, and aims to continue to propagate the truth of Japan's bloody past.
>
> *Masaharu Oka Memorial Nagasaki Peace Museum, 1995*

Inspired by the critical self-reflectiveness of activists in Japan calling for a reckoning with Japan's war responsibility, Uchida also turned inward. His thesis on Japanese American war responsibility held that it involved "accepting responsibility [and] also demanding that the government take responsibility for what it did to us during the war" (Uchida 1995, 3). The successful Japanese American movement for redress and reparations was an important step toward the latter, but the task of facing Japanese American complicity to US and Japanese wars in Asia remained largely untouched. Stressing the importance of understanding the context of Asia, Uchida made the argument that war responsibility necessitated shifting the paradigm of Japanese American war memories from one abstracted and neatly confined within the convenient victim/hero narrative to a consideration of what it might mean to be both a victim and a perpetrator. In a blow to the habitual Japanese American soldier/loyalty/hero narrative—often credited with the rise in Japanese political power and the overturn of a number of racist laws—Uchida stated:

> Like other Americans, Japanese Americans supported and participated in this war [and other U.S. imperial wars]. Thus, we must also bear responsibility for waging a war that killed tens-of-millions of Asians, and for the result of that war: 50 years of an international political and economic structure which continues to exploit countries in the Asian region for the primary benefit of North American and Western European nations.
>
> *Uchida 1995, 3*

To be sure, question 27 of the loyalty questionnaire administered to Japanese Americans in the internment camps (which asked Japanese American men to prove their loyalty/eligibility to be released from the camp through a willingness to serve the US military on combat duty wherever they were assigned), as well as conscription under the 1940 Selective Training and Service Act, complicate any claim that Japanese Americans were simply willing participants in American wars. However, with the exception of a small number of war resisters (who were considered traitors within the Japanese American community until the 1990s), the end result is that Japanese Americans did participate, not only in World War II but in successive American imperial wars in Korea, Vietnam, and Iraq (among others). And their participation has been celebrated within the Japanese American community and remains a hallmark of Japanese American citizenship.

In the discussion here, the issue of Japanese American war responsibility reveals the limit of thinking of race as resistance only in terms of the vertical relationships between minority and dominant populations. It highlights that for race as resistance to be a compelling force in a transpacific context, it must include an examination of the construction and deconstruction of oppressors and oppressed that surround the intersection of Asian American, Asian, Indigenous, Black, and other minority positionalities in the face of both transpacific and transatlantic logics of racialization.

7.5 In/Conclusion

In this chapter, atomic bomb memory is conceived of as both a factual event and an unsettled idea where multiple fields of meaning and remembering come up against each other and connect Japanese Americans in several California communities to the contested memories of war and nuclear history across the Pacific.

In 1995, after nearly 50 years of compulsory silence, the Japanese American community admitted into its historical narrative the discordant wartime stories of local Japanese American hibakusha and the trauma of those transpacific families who were impacted by the atomic bomb. Armed with the confidence of post-redress citizenship and domestic understandings of American anti-Japanese racism, Japanese Americans in the California communities that I examined distinctly and collectively challenged dominant national narratives of the atomic bomb at social and institutional levels. In doing so, they engaged in the process of personal and community healing. Significantly, this process included a confrontation with Asian racialization in the US, a recognition of harms brought on by Japanese colonial violence in Asia, and the US colonization of Indigenous land. And yet, genuine as I believe these gestures were, they are also complicated by the extent to which the Japanese American critique was mediated through the frames of Japanese American loyalty and multicultural America, which can problematically reinscribe complicity to the American myth of exceptionalism and be in opposition to Indigenous critiques by participating in liberal US nationalism. Moreover, as introspective elements of the critique articulated, the Japanese American critique of the atomic bomb also risks complicity to Japanese colonial amnesia when manifested through expressions of ethnic pride. One might also bear in mind that a focus on the visibility of a critique might obscure the continued reluctance of many Japanese Americans in 1995 to raise critical questions about the atomic bomb at all. With these considerations in mind, we are directed to questions about the unrealized potential of the Japanese American critique of the atomic bomb to challenge narratives of war that continue to disavow the oppression of others—questions which are as much about the present and future as they are about the past.

Rather than establishing a linear trajectory for the adaptations of a Japanese American critique of the atomic bomb, I have demonstrated the complexity of its transpacific up againstness. An up againstness that insists on our need to reimagine how we think of the history of an event, or ethnic histories, beyond the confines of geographic, political, or temporal boundaries of knowledge. An up againstness that points us toward alliances across these distances. An up againstness that is constantly being reconfigured.

To commemorate the 75th anniversary of the atomic bomb, the Japanese American National Museum's in Los Angeles collaborated with the cities of Hiroshima and Nagasaki in their exhibit entitled *Under a Mushroom Cloud: Hiroshima, Nagasaki and the Atomic Bomb*. Notably, a special feature of the exhibit was the experiences of Japanese American hibakusha. Yet, amidst escalating tensions over the Japanese government's continued denial of the "comfort women" system, and as Japanese (and other Asian) Americans continue to construct citizenship through complicity to US violence, we are reminded that what is not spoken of is also important. In our contemporary moment, replete with racialized state violence, the Japanese American critique of the atomic bomb in 1995, in its possibilities and limitations, points to the arduous and unfinished work ahead. In our distance and proximity to this history, we are presented with an open-ended possibility for future critique across the Pacific that asks of us: What are we "up against?" (Butler 2012; Antwi 2018).

Acknowledgments

This chapter is modified from a version previously published in Japanese. I would like to thank the editors, as well as Lisa H. Kuroda, Tommy Saburo, Rika Nakamura, and Martha Knauf, for their generous comments on previous drafts.

Notes

1 A postwar neologism originally used to refer to victims of the atomic bombing in Hiroshima and Nagasaki. It has since been extended to other radiation victims.
2 My use of the term Asian/America follows the convention of Lisa Yoneyama (via David Palumbo-Liu) to denote a subjectivity delineated by "the mutually constitutive formation of Asia, the United States and Asian America, with or without hyphenation" (Yoneyama 2016, 268).
3 For an extensive list of books and articles, see http://digital.lib.lehigh.edu/trial/enola/resources/.
4 For more that suggests possible state repression of Japanese American hibakusha experiences, see Sodei (1998, 80–85).
5 The story was different in Hawai'i, where internment had been minimum.
6 For more on Asian exclusion, see Lee (2007).
7 Since 1977 physicians specializing in the effects of radiation from Japan have been conducting biennial medical visits to support hibakusha living in the United States.
8 The term Nisei refers to second-generation Japanese Americans.
9 For more on the ongoing impacts of uranium mining on Indigenous land, see https://cleanupthemines.org/facts/.
10 For more on the impact of US nuclearism in the Pacific, see (Teaiwa 2010).
11 Not surprisingly, Ronald Takaki was cited as a key scholar for the exhibition.
12 For a discussion of the exhibition at American University, see Naono (1997).
13 For more on the plight of Korean hibakusha, see Yoneyama (1999) and Duró (2018).
14 Without disputing the uneven power relationships between exclusion and belonging inscribed in the Hiroshima narrative Il-song Nakamura (2017) points out that although outside of the park, the site had been chosen by the memorial's dedicators because it had been the spot where the body of Prince Lee-Woo, nephew of the last Korean Crown Prince, was found after the bombing.
15 Fukuhara's story has recently been told in more detail in *Midnight in Broad Daylight* (Sakamoto 2016).
16 "Comfort women" is a euphemism to describe women conscripted to perform sexual services for the Japanese Imperial Army, many or the majority of whom were forced to do so against their will under slave like conditions and subjected to repeated acts of sexual violence. For a discussion of the comfort women issue, see Yoshimi (2002). For a discussion of Asian/American engagement with the comfort women issue, see RikaNakamura (2017).

References

Antwi, Phanuel. 2018. "The Risks of Trans-Oceanic Intimacies." In The Minor Transpacific: A Roundtable Discussion," edited by Leung, Helen Hok-Sze, and Christine Kim. "The Minor Transpacific: A Roundtable Discussion." *BC Studies: The British Columbian Quarterly*, no. 198: 13–36.
Bascara, Victor. 2006. *Model-Minority Imperialism*. Minneapolis, MN: University of Minnesota Press.
Boyer, Paul. 1996. "Whose History Is It Anyway? Memory, Politics and Historical Scholarship." In *History Wars: The Enola Gay and Other Battles for the American Past*, edited by Edward T. Linenthal and Tom Engelhardt, 115–139 New York: Holt Paperbacks.
Butler, Judith. 2012. "Precarious Life, Vulnerability, and the Ethics of Cohabitation." *The Journal of Speculative Philosophy* 26, no. 22: 134–151.
Churchill, Ward. 1993. *Struggle for the Land: Indigenous Resistance to Genocide, Ecocide, and Expropriation in Contemporary North America*. Monroe: Common Courage Press.

Dower, John W. 1986. *War Without Mercy: Race and Power in the Pacific War*. New York: Pantheon Books.

Dower, John W. 1995. "The Bombed: Hiroshimas and Nagasakis in Japanese Memory." *Diplomatic History* 19, no. 2: 275–295.

Dower, John W. 1996. "Three Narratives of Our Humanity." In *History Wars: The Enola Gay and Other Battles for the American Past*, edited by Edward T. Linenthal and Tom Engelhardt, 63–98. New York: Holt Paperbacks.

Duró, Ágota. 2018. "Medical Assistance for Korean Atomic Bomb Survivors in Japan: (Belated) Japanese Grassroots Collaboration to Secure the Rights of Former Colonial Victims." *Asia Pacific Journal* 16, no. 2. https://apjjf.org/2018/08/Duro.html

Fukuhara, Harry. 1995. "The Return." *Nikkei Heritage: National Japanese American Historical Society* 7, no. 3: 12–13.

Goren, Jennifer, and Cox, Patrick. 2006. "Hiroshima's Survivors." *PRI's The World in 2006*, Columbia Journalism School: Dart Center for Journalism and Trauma. https://dartcenter.org/content/hiroshimas-survivors.

Ha, Julie. 1995 "Fifty Years is Long Enough." *Rafu Shimpo*, August 9, 1995.

Hirahara, Naomi. 1995a. "Hiroshima Will Come to Us This Year." *Rafu Shimpo*, June 30, 1995.

Hirahara, Naomi. 1995b. "In Search of Kazuso Mukai." *Rafu Shimpo*, August 4, 1995.

Hirahara, Naomi. 2004. *Summer of the Big Bachi*. New York: Bantom Dell.

Hiroshima-ken. 1991. *Hiroshimaken iminshi*. Tokyo: Daiichihoki Shuppan.

Hokubei Hochi. 1995. "Anti-Nuclear Baasan." *Rafu Shimpo*, August 15, 1995.

Hubbard, Bryan and Marouf A. Hasain. 1998. "Atomic Memories of the Enola Gay: Strategies of Remembrance at the National Air and Space Museum." *Rhetoric & Public Affairs* 1, no. 3: 363–385.

Igarashi, Yoshikuni. 2000 *Bodies of Memory: Narratives of War in Postwar Japanese Culture, 1945–1970*. Princeton, NJ: Princeton University Press.

Kuletz, Valerie. 2001. "Invisible Spaces, Violent Places: Cold War Nuclear and Militarized Landscapes." In *Violent Environments*, edited by Nancy Lee Peluso and Michael Watts, 237–60. Ithaca, NY: Cornell University Press.

Lee, Erika. 2007. "The 'Yellow Peril' and Asian Exclusion in the Americas" *Pacific Historical Review* 1 November 76, no. 4: 537–562.

Lifton, Robert Jay, and Greg Mitchell. 1996. *Hiroshima in America: A Half Century of Denial*. New York: Avon Books.

Lionnet, Françoise, and Shumei Shi, eds. 2005. *Minor Transnationalism*. Durham: Duke University Press.

Lowe, Lisa. 1996. *Immigrant Acts: On Asian American Cultural Politics*. New York: Duke University Press.

Nakagawa, Martha. 1995a. "Atomic Bomb Survivors Still Face Obstacles: As Some Hibakusha Still Suffer the Effects of Radiation Exposure, the Question Remains, 'Who Should Pay?'" *Rafu Shimpo*, June 12, 1995.

Nakagawa, Martha. 1995b. "Never Forget." *Rafu Shimpo*, August 2, 1995.

Nakamura, Il-song. 2017. "Tanaka Hiroshi intabyu 'Kyosei' o motomete Dai 4 kai Chosenjin hibakusha." *Buraku Kaiho* 743: 96–106.

Nakamura, Rika. 2017. *Ajiakei Amerika to sensou kioku: Genbaku, ianfu, kyouseishuyou*. Tokyo: Seikyusha.

Nakayama, Takeshi. 1995a. "Smithsonian Cancels A-Bomb Display." *Rafu Shimpo*, January 30, 1995.

Nakayama, Takeshi. 1995b. "50th Anniversary Service Held in Little Tokyo for Atomic Bomb Victims." *Rafu Shimpo*, July 31, 1995.

Naono, Akiko. 1997. *Hiroshima/Amerika: Genbakuten o megutte*. Hiroshima: Keisuisha.

Naono, Akiko. 2005. "'Hiroshima' as a Contested Memorial Site: Analysis of the Making of a New Exhibition at the Hiroshima Peace Museum." *Hiroshima Journal of International Studies* 11: 229–244.

Neimeyer, Robert A. 1999. "Narrative Strategies in Grief Therapy." *Journal of Constructivist Psychology* 12, no. 1: 65–85.

Niiya, Brian. 1995. "The Legacy." *Rafu Shimpo*, August 5, 1995.

Oyagi, Go. 2013. "Over the Pacific: Post-World War II Asian American Internationalism." PhD dissertation, University of Southern California, 2013.

Rafu Shimpo. 1995a. "Scaled-Back Enola Gay Exhibit Opens." *Rafu Shimpo*, June 22, 1995.

Rafu Shimpo. 1995b. "Japanese American Christian Perspectives on 'The Bomb,'" *Rafu Shimpo*, August 7, 1995.

Sakamoto, Pamela Rotner. 2016. *Midnight in Broad Daylight: A Japanese American Family Caught Between Two Worlds*. New York: HarperCollins Publishers.

Sakamoto, Thomas. 1995. "News of the Century: Japan's Surrender & Hiroshima, September 1945." *Nikkei Heritage* Fall: 10–11.

Sakata, Yasuo. 2015. "Migration Statistics." In *Guide to Exhibits*, edited by Japanese Overseas Migration Museum, 12–13. Yokohama: Japan International Cooperation Agency.

Shigekuni, Phil. 1995. "Remembering A-Bombing of Hiroshima, Nagasaki." *Rafu Shimpo*, June 23, 1995.

Smith, Andrea. 2005. *Conquest: Sexual Violence and American Indian Genocide*. Boston, MA: South End Press.

Sodei, Rinjiro. 1995. "Hiroshima/Nagasaki as History and Politics." *The Journal of American History* 82, no. 3: 1118–1123.

Sodei, Rinjiro. 1998. *Were We the Enemy? American Survivors of Hiroshima*. Boulder, CO: Westview Press.

Takaki, Ronald. 1995. *Hiroshima: Why America Dropped the Atomic Bomb*. Boston, MA: Little, Brown, and Co.

Takezawa, Yasuko I. 1995. *Breaking the Silence: Redress and Japanese American Ethnicity*. Ithaca, NY: Cornell University Press.

Yasuko Takezawa, ed. 2011. *Racial Representations in Asia*. Kyoto: Kyoto University Press.

Teaiwa, Teresia K. 2010. "Bikini's and Other S/pacific N/oceans." In *Militarized Currents: Toward a Decolonized Future in Asia and the Pacific*, edited by K. Camacho and S. Shigematsu, 15–32. Minneapolis, MN: University of Minnesota Press.

Thelen, David. 1995. "History after the Enola Gay Controversy: An Introduction." *Journal of American History* 82, no. 3: 1029–1035.

Tonai, Rosalyn. 1995. "Latent August: The Legacy of Hiroshima and Nagasaki." *Nikkei Heritage* Spring: 8.

Tsuneishi, Paul. 1995."Nisei Atomic Bomb Survivors Still Face Obstacles." *Rafu Shimpo*, June 23, 1995.

Uchida, Kevin. 1995. "Japanese Americans and the Issue of War Responsibility." *Rafu Shimpo*, May 23, 1995.

Uchino, Crystal. 2019. "'Born Under the Shadow of the A-Bomb': Atomic Bomb Memory and the Japanese/Asian American Radical Imagination, 1968–1982." *Social Systems: Political, Legal and Economic Studies* 22: 103–120.

Wake, Naoko. 2017. "Surviving the Bomb in America: Silent Memories and the Rise of Cross-National Identity." *Pacific Historical Review* 86, no 3: 472–509.

Wake, Naoko. 2021. *American Survivors: Trans-Pacific Memories of Hiroshima and Nagasaki*. Cambridge: Cambridge University Press.

Wheeler, Kathleen. 2007. "Psychotherapeutic Strategies for Healing Trauma." *Perspectives in Psychiatric Care* 43: 132–141.

Yamamoto, J.K. 1995a. "JA Historical Society's Atomic Bomb Exhibit Opens." Hokubei Mainichi, July 29, 1995.

Yamamoto, J.K. 1995b. "JAs Give First-Hand Recollections of Atomic Bombings." *Hokubei Mainichi*, August 9, 1995.

Yokota, Ryan Masaaki. 1995. "Radioactive Colonization." *Rafu Shimpo*, August 22, 1995.

Yoneyama, Lisa. 1999. *Hiroshima Traces: Time, Space, and the Dialectics of Memory*. Berkeley, CA: University of California Press.

Yoneyama, Lisa. 2016. *Cold War Ruins: Transpacific Critique of American Justice and Japanese War Crimes*. Durham: Duke University Press.

Yoneyama, Lisa. 2017. "Toward a Decolonial Genealogy of the Transpacific." *American Quarterly* 69 no. 3: 471–482.

Yoshimi, Yoshiaki. 2002. *Comfort Women: Sexual Slavery in the Japanese Military During World War II*. New York: Columbia University Press.

9

THE 1992 LA UPRISING AND THE POLITICS OF REPRESENTATION

Multilayered Memories in *Twilight: Los Angeles, 1992*

Kazuyo Tsuchiya

9.1 Introduction

Throughout the twentieth century, LA has attracted successive waves of Latin American, Asian, and European immigrants, as well as African Americans who migrated from the South and developed into one of the most diverse cities in the US and the world. LA has become the place where the Atlantic Rim and the Pacific Rim "meet." Scholars have focused on this LA's multiracial/ethnic dynamics, exploring its interracial political activism (Pulido 2006; Sides 2006; Kurashige 2008; Lipsitz 2010; Bernstein 2011; Kun and Pulido 2014; Rosas 2019; Davis and Wiener 2020).

LA has also drawn attention as a "post-modern city," presaging the future of the American metropolis: it has been represented as a residentially diffuse "city without a center" that cannot be understood within a solely Black/white paradigm, contributing to the view that Los Angeles should be seen as a new urban model differing from cities like Chicago. Researchers who study the city have asserted that LA reflects the future of American society (Scott and Soja 1996; Dear 2002; Soja 2014).

LA, however, has also been a model carceral city (Hinton 2016; Felker-Kantor 2018). The City of Angels has a long history of human caging, leading historian Kelly Lyte Hernández to call the metropolis the "City of Inmates" (Hernández 2017, 1–2). LA had become the "carceral capital of the United States" by the 1950s, having served as a hub of surveillance and mass incarceration since the 1965 Watts uprising. Historian Mike Davis refers to LA as a law-and-order "fortress city" that keeps poor people of color under surveillance so that the wealthy white can safeguard their lifestyles (Davis 1990). Poverty and affluence contrast sharply in LA, and the extreme inequality that exists in the city has given birth to new racialization and discrimination.

DOI: 10.4324/9781003266396-12

The not-guilty verdict rendered on March 29, 1992, in the trial of the police officers indicted for the beating of Rodney King gave rise to one of the largest uprisings in twentieth-century American history. Because this uprising caused enormous damage to Korean-owned shops and also involved Latinx residents, some have called it America's first "multiracial riot." But were the events of 1992 a chaotic "riot" involving only people of color? And what does this rhetoric of a "multiracial riot" obfuscate?

Sociologists and political scientists published a great deal of scholarship on the uprising in the years that followed (Chang and Leong 1993; Gooding-Williams 1993; Madhubuti 1993; Baldassare 1994; Totten and Schockman 1994; Abelmann and Lie 1995; Min, 1996; Hunt 1997). These works primarily relied on newspaper articles and statistical data, however, and many of the documents produced by the administration of Mayor Thomas J. Bradley and the independent commission he established to investigate the Los Angeles police department, as well as by the Webster Commission regarding police response to the 1992 uprising, remain untouched. The first half of this chapter will employ some of these materials to explicate the process that led to the 1992 uprising while showing what racialized representations of the "multiracial riot" tend to obscure. It will demonstrate that the 1992 uprising occurred under rampant economic inequalities brought about by both deindustrialization and reindustrialization and neoliberal policies, constant police brutality, as well as the systematic exclusion of people of color from juries.

The second half (Section 9.5) will examine the play *Twilight: Los Angeles, 1992*, actor and playwright Anna Deavere Smith's attempt to create an unvarnished and multilayered depiction of the uprising through the words of actual "participants." Based on a large number of interviews, the play sheds light on the many facets of the uprising that statistical data alone do not reveal. As such, it has garnered a great deal of scholarly attention in both the performing arts and literary studies (Song 2005; Afary 2009; Smith 2011; Itagaki 2016). Based on this scholarship, I will examine the multilayered memories that Smith draws out from the "multiracial city" of Los Angeles.

Literary and humanities scholars Françoise Lionnet and Shu-mei Shih introduce a framework of minor transnationalism which illuminates the "creative interventions that networks of minoritized cultures produce within and across national boundaries," troubling the "prevalent notions of transnationalism as a homogenizing force" (Lionnet and Shih 2005, 5, 7). While my chapter certainly delves into the topic of inter-minority relations and the "complex and multiple forms" of expressions implemented by marginalized groups, it furthermore scrutinizes how the relationships among these minoritized residents developed in an increasingly polarized urban space: Los Angeles between the years of 1965 and 1992. Studies of minor transnationalism need to be situated within the context of what historians Destin Jenkins and Justin Leroy call the "racialized economic violence of capitalism" in order to untangle the complicated relationships among marginalized groups in South LA before and during the 1992 uprising (Jenkins and Leroy 2021, 14).

My chapter then sheds light on how *Twilight: Los Angeles, 1992,* sought to recover the differentiated yet relational voices of Angelenos against the backdrop of the gross economic and racial inequalities.

9.2 Representations of the 1992 Los Angeles Uprising: "The First Multiracial Riot"

Late on the night of March 3, 1991, the police ordered a 25-year-old African American man named Rodney King to pull over for speeding. He ignored them and fled until he was eventually surrounded by a total of 27 law enforcement officers from the LAPD and other agencies. King was severely beaten by four officers of the LAPD, suffering a laceration requiring 20 stitches, a broken right ankle and jaw, and brain damage. Nevertheless, Sergeant Stacy C. Koon reported that despite having sustained "several facial cuts due to contact with asphalt," the suspect was "oblivious to pain." King was subsequently released, but the entire incident was caught on video by local resident George Holliday. He provided the tape to the local TV station, and CNN subsequently broadcast it worldwide (Independent Commission on the Los Angeles Police Department [Christopher Commission] 1991, 9; Los Angeles Times 1992).

The FBI, Bar Association, and LAPD launched investigations into the incident on March 6. Mayor Bradley promised a rapid indictment of the officers involved and established an independent commission (known as the Christopher Commission) on April 1. The four officers indicted by the LA Bar Association were Laurence M. Powell and Timothy E. Wind, who actually beat King; Koon, who ordered the beating; and their colleague Theodore J. Briseno. No charges were brought against the other officers at the scene, who neither tried to stop the beating nor reported it to their superiors.

On April 2, Bradley publicly called for the removal of LA police chief Daryl F. Gates and suspended him for the duration of the Christopher Commission's investigation. The LA City Council, however, nullified the Commission's decision and reinstated Gates. When the Commission released their report on the King beating in July, criticism of the police increased dramatically. The Commission accused the LAPD of allowing its officers' violence to go unchecked and called for Gates's resignation and drastic reforms within the police department. Bradley supported these findings, but Gates refused to resign.

The trial began on March 4 of the following year. A LA Times survey carried out one week after the beating found that 92% of LA residents thought the police had used excessive force against King. In spite of this, the jury deadlocked on the excessive force charge against Powell, the officer who had beaten King most violently, and found the remaining three defendants not guilty (Los Angeles Times 1992, 35). On that same day, one of the largest uprisings in American history began.

The media quickly disseminated the not-guilty verdict, which shocked the nation. The enraged African American residents of LA's South Central district gathered in protest, and Mayor Bradley also expressed his shock and anger at a press conference held immediately after the verdict: "Today a jury told the world that what we all saw – with our own eyes – wasn't a crime ... My friends, I am here to tell this jury: No."[1] About three and a half hours after the verdict had been rendered, Reginald O. Denny was attacked at the intersection of Normandie and Florence in South Central. Denny, a white truck driver who had entered South Central unaware that the verdict was causing unrest there, was dragged from the cab of his truck by four African American men and severely beaten. The entire incident was broadcast live by a reporter aboard a news helicopter reporting on the "riot." Four African American residents who saw the beating on television rescued Denny and got him to the hospital, where doctors narrowly managed to save his life. This incident lodged in the collective memory alongside the Rodney King beating as a symbol of the dilemma of racial hatred (*Newsweek*, April 26, 1993).

Incidents of arson began around 7:45 pm as the uprising spread throughout South Central, and looting, arson, and destruction of property continued through the night. Mayor Bradley declared a state of emergency and the next day instituted a city-wide curfew from sundown to sun-up. Public facilities were declared off limits, and the uprising spread from South Central to Koreatown, where many Korean-owned businesses suffered damage. Unable to expect aid from the police, residents of Koreatown organized their own defense, constructing barricades and manning them with armed lookouts. In a televised interview on May 1, King made an appeal for peace (Figure 9.1): "I mean, please, we can get along here. We all can get along ... We've just got to, just got to" (Los Angeles Times 1992, 98).

Ultimately, 6,000 members of the California Army National Guard, 4,500 members of the US Army, and 1,000 federal law enforcement officers were deployed to quell the uprising. According to the Webster Commission's investigation into the events, at least 42 people died (the LA Times puts the number at 63), and the total property damage reached an estimated 1 billion dollars (Office of the Special Advisor to the Board of Police Commissioners, City of Los Angeles [Webster Commission] 1992, 23, 26; *Los Angeles Times*, April 26, 2012). The Rodney King beating was later tried in front of a federal grand jury, and on April 17 of the following year, Sergeant Koon and Officer Powell were found guilty of violating King's civil rights.

The demographic breakdown of arrestees reveals some unexpected facts: over half of those arrested during the uprising were Latinx (51%), while 36% were African American and 11% white (Petersilia and Abrahamse 1994, 140–141). A study carried out by the California Department of Insurance found that of the 928 businesses damaged during the riots, 674 were owned by Koreans—just under three quarters (Center for Pacific Rim Studies 1993, 9–10).[2] This formed the basis for discourses describing the 1992 uprising as "the first multiracial/ethnic riot" (*Los Angeles Times*, May 10, 1992).

For example, a RAND Corporation report situates the events as a "minority riot."[3] Demographer P. A. Morrison and Housing and Development Consultant I.S. Lowry state that the "riot" was caused by a turf war between racial and ethnic groups and by the presence of multitudes of young people with too much time

FIGURE 9.1   Rodney King Being Interviewed (May 1, 1992)

Source: Ted Soqui/Corbis via Getty Images

on their hands; that the majority of people who participated did so just for fun or for the purposes of looting; and that to couch the uprising as a "rebellion against the white power structure" would be "misleading" (Morrison and Lowry 1994, 39). Behind these statements lies the knowledge that not just African Americans but also Latinx people were among the "perpetrators" and that Koreans rather than whites were the primary victims.

But were the events of 1992 the work of aimless "minority youth"? Was this "riot" in fact, chaos caused "just for fun"?

9.3 "America, Land of Opportunity"?: Korean Business Owners, the African American and Latinx Communities, and the LA Uprising

9.3.1 Korean Business Owners and the African American Community

What aspects of the 1992 uprising do the narrative of an intra-minority "riot" obfuscate?

The "clash" between Korean business owners and African American residents is one oft-mentioned facet of the uprising. Tensions between Koreans and African Americans had been on the rise since the mid-80s as incidents of arson followed the dramatic rise in Korean-owned businesses opening in South Central, but two subsequent incidents dramatically worsened relations between the groups.

On March 16, 1991, liquor store owner Soon Ja Du accused 15-year-old Latasha Harlins of not paying for a bottle of orange juice. The argument escalated until, finally, Du shot and killed Harlins, who was African American. The entire incident was captured on the store's surveillance camera, and television stations throughout the country repeatedly broadcast the footage. Then, on June 4, another Korean liquor store owner fatally shot Lee Arthur Mitchell during a break-in. This was deemed legitimate self-defense against a robbery, but Mitchell had not been carrying a gun. Protests broke out within the African American community. Bradley said he wanted to ensure that the two groups continued talking to prevent future violence and urged the leaders of a boycott movement against Korean-owned businesses to end it in the name of easing tensions while at the same time appealing to Korean business owners to work at improving relations with the surrounding community (*Los Angeles Sentinel*, August 14–18, 1991; *Asian Week*, August 23, 1991; Los Angeles Times 1992, 37–38).

The November 15 verdict in the Harlins case further widened the rift between the two groups. The jury found Du guilty of voluntary manslaughter, but the Anglo Los Angeles Superior Court Judge Joyce Karlin only sentenced her to five years' probation: no jail time beyond what Du had served prior to her release on bail. Du was ordered to pay Latasha's funeral expenses and complete 300 hours of community service (Stevenson 2015). The fact that Du was not actually punished despite having been found guilty of killing Harlins gave the local community the impression that "the Koreans are being protected by the white system." With the not-guilty verdict in the Rodney King trial coming less than five months later, King's beating and the murder of Latasha Harlins came to be linked in the eyes of the African American residents.

In order to understand the relationship between African American residents and Korean business owners in South Central LA, one needs to take a closer look at the histories of the two minoritized groups. In the early twentieth century, Los Angeles was labeled a city called "heaven" for African Americans. In 1910, Los Angeles showed one of the highest percentages of homeownership for African Americans. While 36.1% of Black Angelenos owned their own homes in the City of Angels, only 2.4% of Black residents in New York City were home-owners. Central Avenue became a "hub" for Black residents, providing space for Black businesses, the offices of Black physicians and dentists, jazz clubs, and the famous Hotel Somerville, later renamed the Dunbar Hotel.

As historian Douglas Flamming argues, however, Black Los Angeles was only "half-free and locked in struggle" (Flamming 2005, 3). Racial discrimination was persistent in the City of Angeles, and in fact, with the large-scale influx of Black and white migrants from the South, residential segregation hardened. In 1926, a local court decided to take no action on a Los Angeles city policy that restricted the use of bathhouses and pools by "colored groups." In 1929, the California Supreme Court declared that residential restrictions were valid, legitimizing restrictive covenants that were widely used to keep people of color out of white neighborhoods (Bunch 1990; Anderson, 1996, 336–364; Sides, 2003, 11–35; Tsuchiya 2014, 60). The 1930s and 1940s saw a massive increase in the African American population in Los Angeles. During the Great Depression, many Black migrants joined in the journey to California, searching for better economic opportunities. In Los Angeles County, the Black population increased from 46,425 (2.1% of the total population) in 1930 to 75,209 (2.7%) in 1940. The number of migrants contin-ued to grow during and after WWII: since Los Angeles was a regional center for defense production, Black workers pursued opportunities there. Between 1940 and 1950, 130,000 Black migrants headed to Los Angeles. In 1950, the number of African American residents in Los Angeles County rapidly increased to 217,881 (5.2%). The African American population in Los Angeles County rose to 461,546 (7.6%) in 1960, with 334,916 people (13.5%) in the City of Los Angeles alone (Los Angeles County Commission on Human Relations 1963, 1–5; Los Angeles County Commission on Human Relations 1974; Bunch 1990, 115–120; Grant, Oliver, and James 1996, 381–382; Sides, 2003, 176–181; Tsuchiya 2014).

Although the Supreme Court found restrictive covenants unconstitutional in 1948, de facto segregation continued thereafter. With limited residential options, the concentration of the African American population in South Central proceeded apace, and as factories moved out of the city center, the continuing deindustri-alization made it harder and harder for African American residents to find work. Unemployment and poverty grew worse: according to 1960 statistics, while the overall unemployment rate in Los Angeles was 5.3%, it reached as high as 11.3% in the southern part of the city. As a result, by 1965, over one-fourth of households (26.8%) in southern LA were living below the poverty line (which at the time represented a yearly income of less than $3,130 for a four-person household). In the Watts neighborhood, the poverty rate soared as high as 41.5% (Tsuchiya 2017).

On August 11, 1965, what was at the time the largest uprising in US his-tory broke out in Watts. Stemming from an incident in which Marquette Frye, a 21-year-old African American man, was arrested for speeding along with his mother and older brother, the uprising lasted for seven days from August 11 to 17 and resulted in 34 dead, 1,032 wounded, and 3,592 arrested. A total of 977 buildings were looted, damaged, or destroyed, with the total property damage exceeding

40 million dollars (The Governor's Commission on the Los Angeles Riots 1969 [1965], sc, sc-15). According to the novelist Thomas Pynchon, the events of 1965 turned Watts from an anonymous locale to the "Raceriotland," which everyone wanted to forget but no one could (*New York Times*, June 12, 1966). The uprising transformed Watts into a "dystopian" symbol of Black resentment.

On the one hand, the Immigration Act of 1965 abolished the National Origins Formula. While limiting visas to 170,000 for the Eastern hemisphere and 120,000 for the Western hemisphere and putting a uniform 20,000-person cap on immigrants from any single country, this new legislation drastically reduced immigration from Europe. In turn, Asians, who had accounted for 4% of totals in 1960, rose to account for 22% of immigration in 1990, while immigration from Mexico and other Latin America rocketed from 9% to 43% over the same period (Budiman et al. 2020). In Los Angeles County, "non-Hispanic whites" (referred to as "Anglos") accounted for 70.9% of the population in 1970 but had shrunk to 40.9% by 1990. On the other hand, "Hispanics" went from 18.3% in 1970 to 37.8% in 1990, while the Asian population expanded from 5.8% to 10.2% between 1980 and 1990 (Gooding-Williams 1993, 112–113; Waldinger and Bozorgmehar 1996).

In 1990, Korean immigrants to the City of Los Angeles numbered 73,000, while for LA County as a whole the number reached 145,431. In addition to the influence of the Immigration Act of 1965, the rapid rise of Korean immigration can be attributed to strengthened military ties in the wake of the Korean War. The close linkages which developed between the US and South Korea during and after the Korean War, as well as American cultural influence within South Korea, have led to a continued influx of Korean immigrants to the US (Min 1996, 28). There were other factors in increased immigration to America as well: Korean industrialization advanced rapidly under the military dictatorship of Park Chung-Hee alongside the collapse of the agricultural economy and an urban population explosion, creating an unemployment problem; the Korean government endorsed overseas immigration in 1962; and they promoted a program to dispatch doctors and nurses overseas for training purposes (Abelmann and Lie 1995, 67; Min 1996, 33–34; Lee 2015, 298–300).

Recent Korean immigration to the US has largely been by the middle class. According to the 1990 census, 34% of those 25 or older held college or graduate degrees, while fully 80% were high school graduates (Min 1996, 30). The majority had held white-collar jobs in their home country. Initially, they hoped to find white-collar or specialized jobs in America as well, but many gave up due to a combination of the language barrier, an inability to leverage their Korean education or work experience, and workplace discrimination (Ong, Park, and Tong 1994, 267).

Many Korean immigrants found a way out through self-employment. In 1990, 34.5% of Korean-born residents of LA between the ages of 25 and 64 owned their own businesses. This number is extremely high in comparison to other groups (Min 1996, 46–48). Because no large-scale businesses existed in the vicinity of South Central, smaller businesses were able to survive, which attracted prospective Korean business owners to the area.

The neighborhood of Koreatown was at the heart of this Southern California Korean community, and it expanded rapidly in the 1970s as the center of business and culture for Koreans in the US. But while the number of Korean-owned businesses in Koreatown had risen to approximately 3,000 by April 1992, 59% of their owners lived elsewhere (Min 1996, 36). The majority of Korean immigrants saw Koreatown, with its concentration of poverty, as a transitional home.

The 1991 murder of Latasha Harlins became even more serious in light of the daily suspicion and dissatisfaction the people of South Central felt toward the immigrant business owners. Residents were disgruntled about the high prices, low inventory, poor selection, and absence of competition—regardless of which liquor stores were disproportionately numerous (Freer 1994, 183, 189; Ong, Park, and Tong 1994, 272). Korean businesspeople, the majority of whom did not live in South Central, invited further criticism for profiting off the African American community while giving "little back to the community," as they rarely employed members of the Black community.

There were reasons, however, that the price of goods in South Central had to be so high. Business owners had to spend money on round-the-clock security and the installation of numerous security cameras to guard against robbery, and insurance was much more expensive than in the suburbs because of hefty insurance premiums against the possibility of "riots." Furthermore, consumption per individual was low in impoverished areas (Freer 1994, 183). Prices were relatively high owing to these circumstances, further inflaming local discontent.

In an attempt to improve relations with the African American community, Korean churches and trade associations created scholarships for Black youth and provided food, clothing, and housing for low-income residents. The Young Nak Presbyterian Church of Los Angeles, for instance, awarded scholarships of $3,000 per year to Black children and provided aid to the poor and homeless in the form of food and clothing. Before the 1992 uprising broke out, Korean and Black chambers of commerce planned a joint project to construct low-income housing for Black residents and promote youth employment (Min 1996, 120, 136–139).

These efforts went unreported, however, while the above incidents were painted by the mass media as "antagonism between Koreans and Blacks." By repeatedly broadcasting the video of the Rodney King beating alongside the murder of Latasha Harlins in the wake of the uprising, ABC television and other channels created the impression that the two were linked, which in turn amplified the damage to Korean-owned businesses. Such broadcasts emphasized "Korean-Black tensions" and highlighted the racial biases harbored by both sides (*Los Angeles Sentinel*, August 22–28, 1991; *Korea Times*, September 1, 1991). Countervailing this emphasis on "racial antagonism" were protests against racial discrimination and violence carried out in Koreatown during the uprising and calls for dialogue (Figure 9.2).

Some Korean business owners and intellectuals felt betrayed by their belief in America as the "land of opportunity."[4] There was a great deal of disappointment and anger at the emphasis on the image of "antagonism between Koreans and Blacks" over the problem of poverty confronting South Central and at the fact

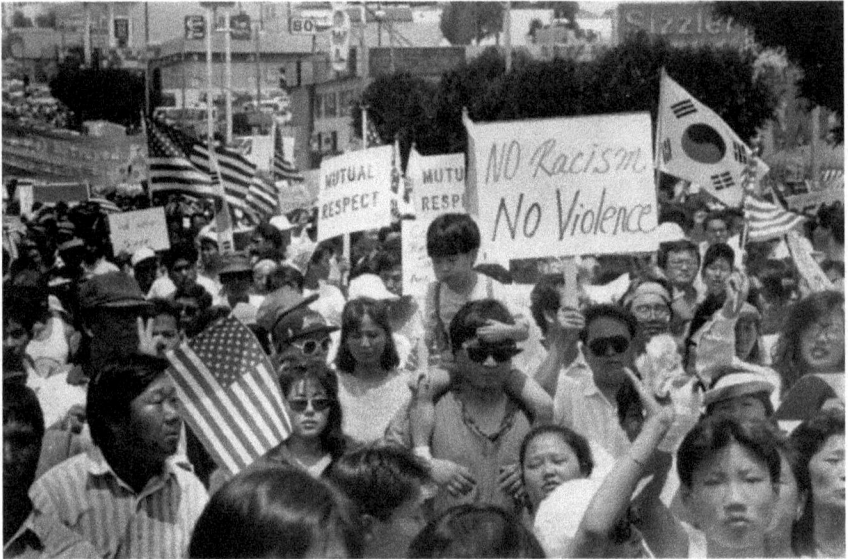

FIGURE 9.2 Rally in Koreatown, Los Angeles (May 1, 1992)

Source: Dayna Smith/*The Washington Post* via Getty Images

that the police had provided no aid during the crisis. For example, John H. Lee, a contributor to *KoreAm Journal*, wrote, "News stories pitted Korean- and African Americans in a zero-sum battle, in which one group is the victim, the other oppressor. The problem with this ethnocentric analysis is it assumes that African- and Korean Americans are the only active agents in the conflict" (*KoreAm Journal* 4, no. 4 (April 1993)). The Korean American Grocers Association issued the following statement: "Korean Americans have been wrongly and unjustly scapegoated for America's societal problems. Many of us came to the U.S. believing in this country's founding principles of democratic government guaranteeing every Americans' constitutional rights to life, liberty, and property. Our confidence has been shattered by the recent violence and inability of our government to protect our rights."[5] Behind this "antagonism between Koreans and Blacks" lay the worsening unemployment and poverty of South Central. Lee and the Korean American Grocers Association point to the fact that Korean immigrants who had found a way out through small business ownership became the scapegoats for the resulting discontent and make clear that the American government's response to the uprising shook their faith in "America as a democratic state."

9.3.2 The LA Uprising and the Latinx Community

The Mexican American population of Los Angeles increased rapidly around the turn of the twentieth century. From 1876 to 1910, under Porfirio Díaz's administration, the wealth disparity in Mexico widened enormously; those who lost their land and were struggling with poverty turned their thoughts to immigration. After 1910, even greater numbers headed north into the US to avoid the chaos of the Mexican Revolution. This migration was bolstered by the establishment of railways in both Mexico and the US; demand for immigrant labor centered around mining and agriculture; the decrease in cheap labor coming from other regions due to the Chinese Exclusion Act of 1882 and the Immigration Act of 1924; and the expanding Mexican community in the US. In the 30 years after 1900, 15 million people came north across the border.

Through the first decade of the twentieth century, the residential center for LA's Mexican immigrant population was the Plaza District, northeast of downtown. Development was rapid, however: City Hall was completed in 1928, and the LA Times building was constructed in 1935, and as rents rose the Mexican community was pushed further east (to East Los Angeles) beyond the reach of developers (Romo 1983; Acuña 1984, 9–10; Sánchez 1993, 71–73; Torres 2005, 24–25; Lewthwaite 2009, 21).

During the Great Depression, Mexicans were forced outside the bounds of "the citizenry." With more than one in four workers unemployed, the Department of Labor (in cooperation with state and local government) was at pains to deport Mexican laborers. From 1929 to 1939, close to 500,000 people were deported nationwide, and even some who had citizenship were deported by the Immigration and Naturalization Service if they were seen as Mexican. As a result, LA lost close to one-third of its Mexican population (Torres 2005, 28–29; Bernstein 2011, 30–31; Molina 2014).

To supplement labor shortages during World War II, the US and Mexican governments instituted the Bracero Program in 1942. In June of 1943, amid the rapid influx of Mexican laborers under this program, a series of violent incidents known as the Zoot Suit Riots broke out, in which Anglo soldiers returning from the war assaulted Latinx and African American youths who were dressed in zoot suits. These riots, along with the Sleepy Lagoon murder the previous year in which 17 Mexican American youths were arrested on insufficient evidence and falsely charged with murder, are inscribed in LA's history as symbols of the rise of anti-Mexican sentiment (Pagán 2003).

After the reform of the immigration laws in 1965, the proportion of immigrants coming from Central America rose rapidly. Immigrants from countries like El Salvador and Guatemala increased dramatically in the 1980s, and by 1990 the Latinx population of the LA area had risen to 12% of the total. Central Americans achieved much lower rates of US citizenship than Mexicans, and since 1965 the majority of the Latinx population has been immigrants. 74% of the Salvadoran population and 70% of the Guatemalan population that lived in LA in 1990 had immigrated during the 1980s. Growing populations and worsening unemployment rates in their native countries, as well as political disorder and economic collapse due to civil wars, drove these people to set their sights on the US, which was increasingly involving itself in the affairs of their homelands (Lopez, Popkin, and Telles 1996, 280–285; Arregui and Roman 2005, 43–49; Gonzalez 2011, 129–148).

As their communities spread westward from East LA, Latinx immigrants began to settle in South Central in large numbers. By 1990, they accounted for 45% of the population of that area (African Americans accounted for 48%). These Latinx immigrants were subjected to crushing poverty as a result of the later deindustrialization and reindustrialization of LA. The average income for a Latinx man born in the US between the ages of 25 and 64 was approximately two-thirds that of an Anglo, while for immigrants born outside the country, it was even lower, no more than 23–43% of the Anglo average (Office of the Special Advisor to the Board of Police Commissioners, City of Los Angeles [Webster Commission] 1992, 36; Lopez, Popkin, and Telles 1996, 299).

The high proportion of Latinx residents among those arrested during the 1992 uprising contributed to their image as "criminals," but the substance of their "crimes" has not been scrutinized. The fact is that many of those arrested were rounded up for curfew violations: 4,200 of the 9,000 arrestees were only charged with misdemeanors (California State Senate Office of Research 1992, 6).

It is important to recognize that the LA uprising was exploited as a means to "crackdown" on undocumented immigrants. According to an ACLU study, the LAPD and LA County Sheriff's Office handed as many as 1,542 people over to Immigration and Naturalization Services, and police continued to carry out raids on "illegal immigrants" in the wake of the uprising (ACLU-SC 1992, 2). The 1992 uprising furthered the criminalization of Latinx immigrants.

Also, little attention was paid to those who were victims. Through June 1, 1992, the "Latino Reconstruction Coalition" fielded consultations from 32 people who had lost their stores to arson or looting, 10 who had lost their homes, 28 who had lost their jobs, and 6 who had been injured.[6] Many hesitated to report these crimes to the police, however, out of fear of deportation. These people viewed the police not as an organization meant to "protect and serve" them but as one that would round them up without legitimate cause and drive them out of the country (ACLU-SC 1992, 8–9).

9.4 Unemployment, Poverty, and Violence: South Central in "Global City" Los Angeles

9.4.1 Increased Discrimination: Deindustrialization and Reindustrialization

Economic inequality became an undercurrent in the heightening of "racial tensions." As poverty and discrimination expanded in South Central, it intensified "racial antagonism." These changes were closely linked to shifts in the structure of American industry and to the rise of neoliberal policies. According to geographer Edward W. Soja, deindustrialization and reindustrialization occurred simultaneously in the city of Los Angeles (Soja 2014, 16–17). The first change was the decline of so-called "frost belt"-type industries. As factories closed and manufacturing shrank or moved from the city center to the suburbs, the south and southwestern parts of the city, or overseas, jobs for unskilled workers with limited education became scarce. This deindustrialization hit the area around South Central particularly hard. Between 1978 and 1982, South Central lost over 7,000 relatively high-paying jobs (heavy industry of the "frost belt" type, with traditionally high rates of unionization: automobiles, tires, glass and steel, etc.), and over 2,000 factories formerly based in LA relocated. These were blue-collar jobs with strong unions and relatively high wages, which employed large numbers of African American and Latinx residents (Soja et al. 1983).

At the same time, LA was also developing so-called "sun belt"-type industries (high tech and related services centered around electronics and aviation/space) at a startling rate. Such sunbelt industries are notable for the disparities they produce: while creating specialist jobs for scientists and technicians, financial managers, lawyers, accountants, and other highly skilled and highly paid workers, they also generate low-skill, low-wage jobs constructing semiconductors and the like—the majority of which go to immigrant laborers and boast extremely low rates of unionization.

LA was also a center for the labor-intensive garment and jewelry industries, made possible by the presence of a low-wage, low-job-security labor force in the form of "illegal immigrants." In the sweat shops of the garment industry, approximately 80% of the work was done by undocumented immigrant women, and 80% of work environments did not meet legal health and safety standards. Furthermore, 80% either paid below minimum wage or force workers to work unpaid overtime. In order to compete with cheap labor in Mexico and Southeast Asia, they conspired to keep labor costs down by bringing in domestic Mexican and Asian immigrants, and because of their tenuous legal position, such undocumented workers were perforce hesitant to lodge complaints about inferior working conditions.

Los Angeles was also a hub for international capital, having developed into the financial center of the Western US. In 1980, total bank deposits reached 194 billion dollars, second only to New York in the nation. This status as a global city also contributed to increasing polarization. Alongside an increase in high-paying jobs requiring high levels of specialized knowledge (banking, securities, insurance, real estate; engineering; architecture; software development and data processing; accounting and bookkeeping, legal services, etc.), and in addition to the massive number of low-wage jobs required to maintain LA's function as a major city (traffic, telecommunications, building maintenance, security, administration, etc.), the rise of LA as a financial hub created a raft of service jobs necessary to maintain the cosmopolitan lifestyles of its top earners (Soja 1987).

Along with the decline of traditional manufacturing, the creation of low-skill, low-wage jobs alongside these newly generated and highly paid specialized occupations widened the gap between rich and poor. This change in the structure of industry had a particularly outsized effect on South Central. Around 321 factories closed in the 15 years following the Watts uprising in 1965, and 22,000 jobs were lost during the 80s alone. As a result, living conditions in South Central degraded rapidly. According to the 1992 census, 30.3% of households in the area were living below the poverty line. This was twice the rate for LA in general and three times the average for the nation as a whole. The African American population of the area declined (it was 55.5% in the 1992 census), and in their place, immigrants from Latin America ballooned to 45.1%, but there was no housing put in place to account for this rise in population. Rents rose, while 3 in 4 houses had been built over 40 years ago and were in a state of dilapidation. The lack of large supermarkets and a limited number of smaller stores also made life inconvenient. LA County as a whole had a ratio of 1 store for every 203 people, but in South Central, the ratio was 1:415. While grocery stores were few and prices were high, liquor stores were numerous: in the affluent city of Santa Monica, there was only 1 per 4,648 people, but in the Watts neighborhood, the number stood at 1 per 1,568 people, a much greater density (ACLU-SC 1992, 1–6).[7]

This widening disparity was exacerbated by the tax revolt in the second half of the 1970s and by federal cuts to welfare in the 1980s. In 1978, California voters approved Proposition 13, which limited property taxes to 1% of market value to be assessed at 1975–1976 rates with a 2% growth limit and established a requirement for a two-thirds majority to approve any future tax increases (US Congressional Budget Office 1978). The adoption of this voter initiative reduced California property tax by 45% in a single year, from $10,300,000,000 to $5,600,000,000. This caused a significant drop in municipal tax revenue and led to a retreat from welfare programs (O'Sullivan, Sexton, and Sheffrin 1995, 94–120).

Furthermore, the Reagan administration saw government intervention as a wrench in the gears of American society's development. The line of thinking was that, rather than solving the problem of poverty, welfare made things worse by encouraging reliance on government assistance. The Reagan administration also drastically reduced taxes on wealthy investors and corporations, enacted a significant shift from domestic programs to the defense industry, transferred power from federal to state and local governments, and put its faith in the private sector. The President's National Urban Policy Report (1982) concluded that the best mechanism to increase employment and stimulate community revitalization was to leave everything to the free market (US Department of Housing and Urban Development 1982, 57). As a result, federal disbursements to state and local governments decreased drastically from 11.7% in 1978 to 6.2% in 1985, forcing communities to back off from employment, education, and welfare programs (Morial, Barry, and Meyers 1986, 2).

It was Thomas Bradley who helmed LA's municipal government through these harsh economic conditions, serving as mayor for 20 years beginning in 1973. Confronted with the "flight" of the affluent to the suburbs, the adoption of Proposition 13 in 1978, and the drop in federal support, Bradley poured his energy into promoting economic growth. The crux of this effort was the redevelopment of downtown LA. He worked to increase LA's status as a "global city" through the opening of the Westin Bonaventure Hotel in 1976, the completion of Crocker Tower (now the Wells Fargo Center) in 1983, construction of condominiums for the wealthy, and a successful bid to host the 1984 Summer

Olympics. At the same time, the lack of low-income housing and the rising rents that accompanied this redevelopment further exacerbated the housing crisis (Payne and Ratzan 1986, 140–142; Sonenshein 1993, 164–171). The people left behind by LA's development into a "global city" lost their safety net even as de- and reindustrialization widened the gap between rich and poor. Economic inequality—caused and exacerbated by urban restructuring processes and federal/local neoliberal policies—was deeply embedded in the development of so-called "racial tensions" among minoritized groups.

9.4.2 Persistent Police Brutality and Problems with the Jury System

The discourse of "racial antagonism" surrounding the 1992 uprising obfuscates its direct cause: the Rodney King beating. By extension, it conceals the persistent police brutality that continues to this day and the problems of the criminal justice system, which "operates at the expense of African American communities and society as a whole" (Taylor, 2016, 3). Amnesty International's investigation into the incident found that the LAPD's use of excessive force had become normalized (Amnesty International 1992, 2–3). The independent commission set up in the wake of the King beating also made clear that this incident was merely the tip of the iceberg. First, it pointed to the LAPD's high arrest rates despite the fact that it had the lowest ratio of officers to population in the country and to the fact that the LAPD had garnered high praise for being "efficient, sophisticated, and free of corruption" (Independent Commission on the Los Angeles Police Department [Christopher Commission] 1991, ix, 23). According to its own internal regulations, the LAPD only allowed its officers to use whatever force was "reasonable and necessary to protect others or themselves from bodily harm." In the five years from 1986 to 1990, however, there were over 2,500 complaints of property damage or injury at the hands of the LAPD. In particular, routine stops of young African American and Latinx men, seemingly without "probable cause" or "reasonable suspicion," were common (Independent Commission on the Los Angeles Police Department [Christopher Commission] 1991, x, 26, 36, 55–56, 75–77). In a survey carried out after the King beating, 68% of LA residents (87% of African Americans and 80% of Latinx people) responded that police brutality was widespread. The commission's report also found many instances of police comparing African American and Latinx residents to animals or mocking their origins—"Sounds like monkey slapping time," "I would love to drive down Slauson with a flamethrower … we would have a barbecue" (Independent Commission on the Los Angeles Police Department [Christopher Commission] 1991, xii, 69, 72).

The commission also found institutional and systemic problems above and beyond the personal racial biases of individual officers. First, while the proportion of African American, Latinx, and Asian officers was on the rise, most were stuck in subordinate posts. In June of 1990, 13.4% of officers were Black, and 21% were Latinx, but the numbers for supervisors were only 8% and 10.4%, respectively (Independent Commission on the Los Angeles Police Department [Christopher Commission] 1991, 71, 81–82). A citizen's commission had been established to monitor the LAPD, but in practice, its power was severely limited. It is also important to note that the LAPD poured its resources into training high-tech riot squads and special forces who cultivated the animosity and distrust of the local population by repeatedly rounding up and arresting local residents. This confluence of circumstances laid the groundwork for an increased criminalization of African American and Latinx communities, along with the use of excessive force against them.

In addition to the problem of continuing police brutality, the Rodney King beating also threw the issue of the warped jury system into stark relief. In order to select an impartial and representative jury, prospective jurors undergo a series of screenings, and whether or not a jury accurately reflects the region as a whole depends on this selection process. Normally, a trial is conducted in the same place the incident occurred. In California, however, the trial can be moved to another location when it is difficult to find impartial jurors because a case has received too much attention. Because the Rodney King beating was such a case, having received widespread coverage and made such an enormous impact nationwide, the court declared on July 23 that the trial would be moved. In addition, while an African American judge named Bernard J. Kamins had initially been appointed to try the case, he was replaced by the white Judge Stanley Weisberg due to "improper private communications between the judge and prosecutors" (Fukurai, Krooth, and Butler 1994, 81).

The prosecution requested the trial be moved to Alameda County near San Francisco, which had a racial makeup similar to that of the area where the incident had occurred. Judge Weisberg opted on November 23 to move the trial to Ventura County, however, due to questions of cost and convenience for LA residents. The racial makeup of Ventura County differed grossly from that of LA County, which was 40.8% white and 10.5% African American; Ventura County, by contrast, was 65.9% white and only 2.2% Black. The city of Simi Valley, where the Ventura County courthouse was located, was predominantly white, middle class, and "politically conservative and pro-police" (Fukurai, Krooth, and Butler 1994, 83).

Jury selection began in February 1992, with 2,000 initial candidates ultimately winnowed down to 12. These 12 jurors included 10 whites (6 women and 4 men), 1 Latinx woman, and 1 Asian woman. There was not a single African American person on the jury. Around 3 of the 12 jurors had relatives who served in police departments, and the majority had "positive opinions of police in general and the role of police officers."

The trial began on March 4. During deliberations, eight of the twelve jurors were inclined from the start to find the four officers not guilty, while the remainder wanted a guilty verdict only for Powell, the officer who had beaten King most severely. Despite the existence of positive evidence in the form of the Holliday tape, the jury's deliberations unfolded advantageously for the defense as the jurors who insisted on a not-guilty verdict felt that by resisting arrest, King had brought the beating on himself. The jury's decision was presented on April 29. While they deadlocked in Powell's case, they found the other three officers not guilty (Independent Commission on the Los Angeles Police Department [Christopher Commission] 1991, 55; Fukurai, Krooth, and Butler 1994, 86–87). Protests broke out in the wake of the verdict, as worsening unemployment and poverty, persistent and rampant police brutality, and the jury system's failure to check such repeated violence converged in the "multiracial city" of Los Angeles. Gross economic inequality, increased surveillance and police violence, and the exclusion of minoritized people from the jury system are deeply embroiled elements in the history of the 1992 uprising.

9.5 Multilayered Memories in Anna Deavere Smith's *Twilight: Los Angeles, 1992*

9.5.1 Between Drama and Oral History

The description of the LA uprising as the first "multiracial riot" largely evokes Black "animosity" toward Korean shopkeepers and the image of "minority youth" on a "rampage," delighting in looting and destruction of property. This subsumes African Americans, Korean shopkeepers, and Latinx residents under the heading of the "minorities" who make up the "multiracial city" of Los Angeles, but such focus on "racial antagonism" backgrounds white racism. It draws attention to the differences between these events and earlier "riots" caused by police violence against Black youth and distracts from the systemic issues that caused the uprising—and it lays the blame for the "riot" squarely on the shoulders of the African American, Korean, and Latinx communities (a form of the "inclusive exclusion" described by Katsuya Hirano in Chapter 2).

So how can we talk about the LA uprising without recreating the discourse of a "multiracial riot"? By lending an ear to the voices of the various "participants," what new image of history can we produce? In this section, I will examine *Twilight: Los Angeles, 1992*, actress and playwright Anna Deavere Smith's ground-breaking attempt to recuperate the multiplicity of voices drowned out by the discourse of the "multiracial riot." On April 29, the day the not-guilty verdict was rendered in the Rodney King trial, Smith was in New York preparing for rehearsals for her play *Fires in the Mirror* (Smith 1993). The theater was closed on the first day of rehearsals because of the uprising in LA, however, Smith joined a demonstration in Times Square to protest the verdict. The following month, director and producer Gordon Davidson approached her about creating a work on the subject of the LA uprising. After the play's run in New York ended, Smith flew to LA and began interviewing a total of 280 "participants" (Figure 9.3).

Based on this massive body of interviews, Smith worked with four dramaturges (cultural anthropologist Dorinne Kondo, LA Times reporter Hector Tobar, poet and scholar of English literature Elizabeth Alexander, and Oskar

FIGURE 9.3 Photo of Anna Deavere Smith (September 4, 1992)

Source: Randy Leffingwell/*Los Angeles Times* via Getty Images

Eustis, director of the Mark Taper Forum) to select 25 stories to bring to the stage (Smith 2000a, xxii–xxiii). Smith did not want to simply trace the process of the uprising but to draw out "a sea of associated causes" from the testimonies of the 25 people they had selected (Smith 1994, xviii). Below, I will examine the tale Smith wove from these oral histories.

Performances of *Twilight: Los Angeles, 1992* in Los Angeles and at the New York Shakespeare Festival were supplemented with interviews, and both book and film versions followed. The latter was created at the request of the late Supreme Court Justice Ruth Bader Ginsburg and her colleague Stephen G. Breyer, who were deeply affected by Smith's work and who had asked her to produce it for use as a teaching tool "in every high school in America." It was first screened at the 2000 Sundance Film Festival and was shown on television on April 29 of the following year (the ninth anniversary of the uprising) as part of the PBS series "Stage on Screen" (Afary 2009, 165).

Smith saw the words of the people she was performing on stage as "a means to evoking the character of the person who spoke them" (Smith 1994, xxiv). Because of this, she placed a great deal of importance on the actor's accuracy of language. This "accuracy" did not merely extend to using the same words, however, but meant getting as close as possible to the people themselves by imitating the flow and connections in their speech, right down to their hesitations and silences (Smith 2003, 4). This was because words could be "the doorway into the soul of a culture" (Smith 2000a, 12). Smith also writes: "In the theater we can't simply 'cover the material'; we 'become the material.' In fact our job is to *un*cover the material" (Smith 2000a, 96). Smith was endeavoring to uncover the "multifaceted identities" these individuals concealed within themselves and the "more complex language"—not something rigid, but rather a fluctuating, contradictory narration (Smith 1994, xxv).

When Smith was asked to produce a work about the LA uprising, she was expected to find a "unifying voice" to represent the entire "multiracial society" of the US (Smith 2000a, xxiv). In creating a work on the subject of the largest uprising in twentieth-century US history, which had rocked American society to its core, there were some who saw Smith as a savior and hoped she would offer immediate answers. Smith responds to these expectations as follows:

> It [Acting] is not a result, it is not an answer. It is not a solution. I am first looking for the humanness inside the problems, or the crises. The spoken word is evidence of the humanness. Perhaps the solutions come somewhere further down the road.
>
> *(Smith 1994, xxv)*

On the subject of costumes, sets, and props, Smith says, they can be "as minimal or as ornate as one imagines." She is merely endeavoring to be "as specific and individual as possible to avoid stereotypes." The tension between people of different races begins "with an inability to see the specific details of any person in front of you" (Smith 2003, 5).

9.5.2 Twilight: Los Angeles, 1992

Below I introduce eight of the people Smith portrays.

9.5.2.1 "A Weird Common Thread in Our Lives": Reginald O. Denny, Victim of Severe Beating

One notable character who appears in Smith's work is the white truck driver Reginald Denny, who accidentally drove into South Central on the first day of the uprising and was beaten by four African American men (Song 2005, 104; Afary 2009, 104–105). Denny relates:

> [I]t was just like a scene out of a movie. Total confusion and chaos. I was just in awe ... I didn't have a clue of what one [riot] looked like and I didn't know that the verdict had come down. I didn't pay any attention to that, because that was somebody else's problem I guess I thought at the

time … But when I knew something was wrong was when they bashed in the right window of my truck. That's the end of what I remember as far as anything until five or six days later.

(Smith 1994, 103–105)

Denny talks not about the people who beat him within an inch of his life but about his gratitude toward the four African American residents who saw it happening on live television and rushed to the scene, putting their lives on the line to save him and drive him to a nearby hospital.

> Someday when I, uh, get a house, I'm gonna have one of the rooms and it's just gonna be of all the riot stuff and it won't be a blood-and-guts memorial, it's not gonna be a sad, it's gonna be a happy room. It's gonna be … Of all the crazy things that I've got, all the, the love and compassion and the funny notes and the letters from faraway places, just framed, placed, and framed things, where a person will walk in and just have a good old time in there.
>
> *(Smith 1994, 110–111)*

Even as he voices his gratitude toward the people who saved him, Denny rages against the white people who look down on people of color: "you fool, you selfish little shit." Denny's simple honesty and optimism are compelling, particularly in comparison to the media's portrayal of Denny as "another victim" and of the intersection where he was attacked as a symbol of racial hatred.

9.5.2.2 "No Justice, No Peace": Paul Parker, Chairperson of the Free the LA Four Plus Defense Committee

Smith also portrays someone who directly repudiates Denny, however: Paul Parker, who stood up to defend the four men who beat Denny.

> Because Denny is white, that's the bottom line. If Denny was Latino, Indian, or black, they wouldn't give a damn, they would not give a damn … So the bottom line is it, it, it's a white victim, you know, beaten down by some blacks. 'Innocent.' … That white man, some feel that white boy just better be glad he's alive, 'cause a lot of us didn't make it.
>
> *(Smith 1994, 172–174)*

> No Justice No Peace. That's just more or less, I guess you could say, motto. When I finally get my house I'm gonna have just one room set aside. It's gonna be my No Justice No Peace room. Gonna have up on the wall No Justice, over here No Peace, and have all my articles and clippings and, um, everything else. I guess so my son can see, my children can grow up with it … It basically just means if there's no justice here then we not gonna give

them any peace. You know, we don't have any peace. They not gonna have no peace, a peace of mind, you know, a physical peace, you know, body.

(Smith 1994, 177–178)

9.5.2.3 "The Voice of the Unheard": Maxine Waters, Congressperson

Parker shows that while being white garners sympathy, African American citizens are treated as less than human by the police and their supporters, and their deaths are laid at their own door. According to Maxine Waters, a member of the House of Representatives for the district including South Central, the uprising constituted nothing more nor less than the "voice" of those who had been continually ignored.

> There was an insurrection in this city before and if I remember correctly it was sparked by police brutality. We had a Kerner Commission report. It talked about what was wrong with our society. It talked about institutionalized racism. It talked about a lack of services, lack of government responsiveness to the people. Today, as we stand here in 1992, if you go back and read the report it seems as though we are talking about what that report cited some twenty years ago still exists today ... Mr. President, our children's lives are at stake. We want to deal with the young men who have been dropped off of America's agenda ... Oh yes. We're angry, and yes, this Rodney King incident. The verdict. Oh, it was more than a slap in the face. It kind of reached in and grabbed you right here in the heart and it pulled at you and it hurts so bad ... I am angry. It is all right to be angry ... The fact of the matter is, whether we like it or not, riot is the voice of the unheard.
>
> *(Smith 1994, 159–162)*

9.5.2.4 "Why He Has to Get Shot?": June Park, Partner of Walter Park, a Shopkeeper Who Was Shot

What does "justice" for African American residents exposed to police brutality and the violence of poverty mean in the face of the voices of Korean immigrants, who suffered tremendously in the uprising? Below are the words of June Park, whose husband was shot during the uprising, and Young-Soon Han, owner of a liquor store that was looted.

> He [Walter Park] came to United States twenty-eight years ago. He was very high-educated and also very nice person to the people. And he has business about seven, what ten years, twenty years, so he work very hard and he so hard and he also donated a lot of money to the Compton area. And he knows the City Council, the policemen, they knows him. Then why, why he had to get shot? You know, I don't know why. So really angry, you know.
>
> *(Smith 1994, 147)*

9.5.2.5 "Where Is Justice?": Young-Soon Han, Former Liquor Store Owner

Until last year I believed America is the best … but as the year ends in '92 and we were still in turmoil and having all the financial problems and mental problems. Then a couple months ago I really realized that Korean immigrants were left out from this society and we were nothing. What is our right? Is it because we are Korean? Is it because we have no politicians? Is it because we don't speak good English? Why? Why do were have to be left out?

(Smith 1994, 245)

Han has this to say about the "victorious" verdict in the federal grand jury trial of the officers who beat Rodney King:

Where do I finda [sic] justice? Okay, Black people probably believe they won by the trial? … They were having party and then they celebrated, all of South-Central, all the churches. They finally found that justice exists in this society. Then where is the victims' rights? They got their rights. By destroying innocent Korean merchants …

(Smith 1994, 246–247)

They have fought for their rights [One hit simultaneous with the word "rights"] over two centuries [One hit simultaneous with "centuries"] and I have a lot of sympathy and understanding for them. Because of their effort and sacrificing, other minorities, like Hispanic or Asians, maybe we have suffer more by mainstream. You know, that's why I understand, and then I like to be part of their "joyment."

Smith 1994, 248

In Smith's performance, Park and Han raise the question of why they were victimized, despite the fact that they, too, had been marginalized in American society. Why must their lives be negated in the name of the "justice" Parker and Waters talk about? Why can't they share the future when they, too, are people of color? These questions resonate with the words of the Korean artist Jean Shin, whom Yasuko Takezawa introduces in Chapter 10: "You know so that … that again race should unite us, not divide us."

9.5.2.6 Persistent Police Brutality: Rudy Salas, Sculptor and Painter Wounded in the 1943 Zoot Suit Riots

Smith also introduces the voice of a Mexican American resident who was a victim of police brutality. Rudy Salas, who was beaten by police during the 1943 Zoot Suit Riots, has this to say:

[T]he insanity that I carried with me started when I took the beating from the police. Okay, that's where the insanity came in … I used to read the paper – it's awful, it's awful – if I would read about a cop shot down in the street, killed, dead, a human being! A fellow human being? I say, "So, you know, you know, so what, maybe he's one of those mother fuckers that, y'know ..." ... I'm hooked on the news at six and the newspapers and every morning I read injustices ...

(Smith 1994, 2–4)

Salas locates the Rodney King beating within the historical continuity of persistent police brutality. At the same time, he foregrounds the process by which not just African American residents but also their fellow Latinx neighbors become victims.

9.5.2.7 Who Are the "Victims"?: Elvira Evers, Pregnant General Worker and Cashier Hit by a Stray Bullet

Another memorable character is Elvira Evers, a pregnant Panamanian woman who was hit by a stray bullet during the uprising. Wearing an apron and periodically shushing her children, Elvira sits in her living room and speaks calmly about the events, her story made all the more shocking by contrast with her demeanor. Evers was out walking with a friend when she experienced a "tingling sensation"—like "itchin'." She only realized she'd be shot when her friend screamed. Despite the life-or-death situation she and her unborn child were in, Evers thought first of her friend and eldest son.

So I told my oldest son, I say, 'Amant, take care your brothers. I be right back' Well, by this time he was standing up there, he was crying, all of them was crying. What I did for them not to see the blood – I took the gown and I cover it and I didn't cry. That way they didn't get nervous.

(Smith 1994, 119–120)

Evers tried to drive herself to the hospital, but her friend put her in the passenger seat and drove her instead. As soon as they arrived, she was hooked up to a monitor; Evers says that "as long as I heard the baby heartbeat I calmed down."

[H]e [Evers' doctor] say, 'Um, she born, she had the bullet in her elbow, but when we remove ... when we clean her up we find out that the bullet was still between two joints, so we did operate on her and your daughter is fine and you are fine.' ... And her doctor, he told ... he explain to me that the bullet destroyed the placenta and went through me and she caught it in her arms. [Here you can hear the baby making noises, and a bell rings] If she didn't caught it in her arm, me and her would be dead.

(Smith 1994, 123)

In Smith's performance, Evers doesn't blame anyone, instead wryly telling the audience how lucky she was.

9.5.2.8 Fortress Beverly Hills Hotel: Elaine Young, Beverly Hills Real Estate Agent

While representations of the uprising as a "multiracial riot" include depictions of the confrontation between Koreans and African Americans on the one hand, and between the Black and Latinx communities and the police on the other hand, there is virtually no talk of white LA residents as "participants." And yet, the luxurious mansions of Beverly Hills, symbols of American affluence, sit a mere 35 kilometers from South Central, where the uprising took place. What were the residents of Beverly Hills thinking in the wake of the verdict and subsequent clashes between police and protesters, as the town was engulfed in flames and a curfew placed on the entire city?

One of the people Smith depicts is Elaine Young, a real estate agent who took shelter in the Beverly Hills Hotel. On the second day of the uprising, Young, overcome with anxiety, wanted to rendezvous with her boyfriend but discovered that stores and restaurants throughout the city were closed for business. Thinking that the restaurant in the Beverly Hills Hotel would be operating for the sake of its guests, she headed to the hotel only to find "the whole town, picture-business people." She spent the next three nights in the lounge, staying up until dawn with the others who had gathered there. Young says,

> It was like people hanging out together, like safety in numbers. No one can hurt us at the Beverly Hills Hotel cause it was like a fortress.
>
> *(Smith 1994, 155)*

While the discourse of the "multiracial riot" represents only African American, Latinx, and Korean residents as "participants," Smith also includes the affluent white people who barricaded themselves in the Beverly Hills Hotel while the smoke of the riots blanketed the city below them under that rubric.

9.6 Conclusion

The California African American Museum in South Central Los Angeles held an exhibit from March 8 to August 27, 2017, commemorating the 25th anniversary of the uprising, entitled "No Justice, No Peace: LA 1992." Curator Tyree Boyd Pates thought for a long time about how to depict "the history that led to the uprising" from the diverse viewpoints of the residents of Los Angeles, and *Twilight* was a point of reference for him. The exhibition, which also benefited from the cooperation of the families of both Harlins and King, was planned largely with the area's African American population in mind. However, Pates relates that much as Smith located the LA uprising within the intersecting narratives of its various "participants," he endeavored as much as possible to incorporate the voices of Mexican, Korean, and Anglo residents as constituents of the LA "community."[8]

The discourse surrounding "America's first multiracial riot" conceals the disparity and poverty, persistent police brutality, and problems with the jury system inherent in the urban space of Los Angeles by failing to properly register the people who share that space. These include those who experienced fierce rage and disappointment at the violence of the not-guilty verdict and the overt violence of Rodney King's beating; the Korean business owners and their families whose livelihoods were taken from them as protests in the name of "justice" transformed into an uprising; the Latinx residents who lost their homes and jobs; and the residents of Beverly Hills who holed up in a hotel for fear that the uprising would spread to their area. The LA uprising demands that we lend an ear to the voices of the various "participants" and face the multiplicity of competing memories. But what do we talk about, and from whose perspective? Smith attempted to reconstruct a multidimensional historical image by bringing together the words of the "participants" without glossing over the fissures between them.

In *Twilight*, various races/ethnicities, classes, genders, nationalities, ages, and ways of understanding the uprising converge in the person of Smith. Because of this, the speakers who appear in the play are both "others" and "ourselves." Through their interior experiences—of rage, fear, pain, contradiction—and their depictions of the past, present, and future of Los Angeles, the play brings to the fore the self-evident truth that, in fact, "we are all human." This mechanism is probably the reason why, in addition to winning Drama Desk and Theater World Awards and garnering attention in the realms of the performing arts and cultural studies, *Twilight* is used to this day in high school and college classrooms as a means of thinking about "multiculturalism."

The play is more than simple humanism or a paean to "multiculturalism," however. *Twilight* leaves it to the listeners/readers to use their imaginations to reconstruct the history of the LA uprising by observing the disparity and poverty, persistent police brutality, and systemic problems with the jury system buried in the stories of its diverse characters.

Twilight is rife with implications for the historian, whose job is to confront the "past." While the work is studded with "historical facts" recovered from its voluminous oral history, the audience or the reader cannot help but be conscious of Smith's constant presence—of the fact that these are nothing more than performed narratives (Smith 2011, 156). These narratives exist somewhere between "historical fact" and "embellished drama." Smith's exaggerated performance, which nonetheless homes in on the voices of the "participants," has the power to shake the very dichotomy between "fact" and "fiction." This confuses and perplexes the audience and, for that very reason, draws attention to the tales Smith weaves together—and to the way in which the LA uprising is represented, creating a critical viewpoint and encouraging dialogue regarding the events of 1992.

Acknowledgments

An earlier version of this chapter was translated by Daniel Joseph. I am grateful to him for his helpful comments.

Notes

1 "Acquittals," n.d., File 10, Box 1741, Mayor Tom Bradley Administrative Papers, 1920–1993, Special Collections, University of California, Los Angeles [hereafter Bradley Papers].
2 "Damage Reports," File 18, Box 4252, Bradley Papers.
3 RAND, "For Immediate Release: Rand Analysis Charts L.A. Riot Arrest and Crime Patterns Arrestees Show Distinctive Demographic Profile; Latinos Predominate," 1992, File "RAND Report: L.A. Riots Arrest & Crime Pattern—Demo. Pattern 1992," Box 4, The Los Angeles Webster Commission Records, Special Collections, University of Southern California, Los Angeles [hereafter Webster Commission Records].
4 "Open Letter from Concerned Korean-American Citizens," May 7, 1992, File 11, Box 4251, Bradley Papers.
5 "Statement by the National KAGRO, Korean American Grocers Association on the Recent Civil Unrest in Los Angeles, California," n.d., File 24, Box 4245, Bradley Papers.
6 "Latino Reconstruction Coalition Applicant List Update: June 1, 1992," File 3, Box 4360, Bradley Papers.
7 Paul Ong and Evelyn Blumenberg, "Racial and Ethnic Inequality in Los Angeles: Two Decades of Neglect 1970–1990," Graduate School of Architecture and Urban Planning, University of California, Los Angeles, June 27, 1992, File 8, Box 5, Webster Commission Records.
8 Tyree Boyd Pates, interview by author, August 14, 2017, California African American Museum, Los Angeles.

References

Abelmann, Nancy, and John Lie. 1995. *Blue Dreams: Korean Americans and the Los Angeles Riots*. Cambridge, MA: Harvard University Press.

Acuña, Rodolfo F. 1984. *A Community under Siege: A Chronicle of Chicanos East of the Los Angeles River, 1945–1975*. Los Angeles: Chicano Studies Research Center, University of California at Los Angeles.

Afary, Kamran. 2009. *Performance and Activism: Grassroots Discourse after the Los Angeles Rebellion of 1992*. Lanham: Lexington Books.

American Civil Liberties Union Foundation of Southern California [ACLU-SC]. 1992. *Civil Liberties in Crisis: Los Angeles during the Emergency*. Los Angeles: American Civil Liberties Union Foundation of Southern California.

Amnesty International. 1992. *Torture, Ill-Treatment and Excessive Force by Police in Los Angeles, California*. London: Amnesty International.

Anderson, Susan. 1996. "A City Called Heaven: Black Enchantment and Despair in Los Angeles." In *The City: Los Angeles at the End of the Twentieth Century*, edited by Allen J. Scott and Edward W. Soja, 336–364. Berkeley, CA: University of California Press.

Arregui, Edur Velasco, and Richard Roman. 2005. "Perilous Passage: Central American Migration through Mexico." In *Latino Los Angeles: Transformations, Communities, and Activism*, edited by Enrique C. Ochoa and Gilda L. Ochoa, 38–62. Tucson: University of Arizona Press.

Baldassare, Mark, ed. 1994. *The Los Angeles Riots: Lessons for the Urban Future*. Boulder, CO: Westview Press.

Bernstein, Shana. 2011. *Bridges of Reform: Interracial Civil Rights Activism in Twentieth-Century Los Angeles*. Oxford: Oxford University Press.

Budiman, Abby, Christine Tamir, Lauren Mora, and Luis Noe-Bustamante. August 20, 2020. "Facts on U.S. Immigrants, 2018: Statistical Portrait of the Foreign-born Population in the United States." Pew Research Center.

Bunch, Lonnie G. 1990. "A Past Not Necessarily Prologue: The African American in Los Angeles." In *20th Century Los Angeles: Power, Promotion, and Social Conflict*, edited by Norman M. Klein and Martin J. Schiesl. Claremont, CA: Regina Books.

California State Senate Office of Research. June 17, 1992. *The South-Central Los Angeles and Koreatown Riots: A Study of Civil Unrest.* Sacramento: Senate Office of Research.

Center for Pacific Rim Studies. 1993. *Losses in the Los Angeles Civil Unrest, April 29–May 1, 1992.* Los Angeles: Center for Pacific Studies, University of California, Los Angeles.

Chang, Edward T., and Russell C. Leong, eds. 1993. *Los Angeles—Struggles toward Multiethnic Community: Asian American, African American, and Latino Perspectives.* Seattle: University of Washington Press.

Davis, Mike. 1990. *City of Quartz: Excavating the Future in Los Angeles.* London: Verso.

Davis, Mike, and Jon Wiener. 2020. *Set the Night on Fire: L.A. in the Sixties.* London: Verso.

Dear, Michael J. 2002. *From Chicago to L.A.: Re-Visioning Urban Theory.* Thousand Oaks, CA: Sage Publications.

Felker-Kantor, Max. 2018. *Policing Los Angeles: Race, Resistance, and the Rise of the LAPD.* Chapel Hill, NC: The University of North Carolina Press.

Flamming, Douglas. 2005. *Bound for Freedom: Black Los Angeles in Jim Crow America.* Berkeley, CA: University of California Press.

Freer, Regina. 1994. "Black-Korean Conflict." In *The Los Angeles Riots: Lessons for the Urban Future*, edited by Mark Baldassare, 175–203. Boulder, CO: Westview Press.

Fukurai, Hiroshi, Richard Krooth, and Edgar W. Butler. 1994. "The Rodney King Beating Verdicts." In *The Los Angeles Riots: Lessons for the Urban Future*, edited by Mark Baldassare, 73–102. Boulder, CO: Westview Press.

Gonzalez, Juan. 2011. *Harvest of Empire: A History of Latinos in America.* Revised Ed. New York: Penguin Books.

Gooding-Williams, Robert. 1993. *Reading Rodney King, Reading Urban Uprising.* New York: Routledge.

Grant, David M., Melvin L. Oliver, and Angela D. James. 1996. "African Americans: Social and Economic Bifurcation." In *Ethnic Los Angeles*, edited by Roger Waldinger and Mehdi Bozorgmehar, 379–411. New York: Russell Sage Foundation.

Hernández, Kelly Lytle. 2017. *City of Inmates: Conquest, Rebellion, and the Rise of Human Caging in Los Angeles, 1771–1965.* Chapel Hill, NC: University of North Carolina Press.

Hinton, Elizabeth. 2016. *From the War on Poverty to the War on Crime: The Making of Mass Incarceration in America.* Cambridge, MA: Harvard University Press.

Hunt, Darnell M. 1997. *Screening the Los Angeles "riots": Race, Seeing, and Resistance.* Cambridge: Cambridge University Press.

Independent Commission on the Los Angeles Police Department [Christopher Commission]. 1991. *Report of the Independent Commission on the Los Angeles Police Department.* Los Angeles: Independent Commission on the Los Angeles Police Department.

Itagaki, Lynn Mie. 2016. *Civil Racism: The 1992 Los Angeles Rebellion and the Crisis of Racial Burnout.* Minneapolis, MN: University of Minnesota Press.

Jenkins, Destin, and Justin Leroy, eds. 2021. *Histories of Racial Capitalism.* New York: Columbia University Press.

Kun, Josh, and Laura Pulido, eds. 2014. *Black and Brown in Los Angeles: Beyond Conflict and Coalition.* Berkeley, CA: University of California Press.

Kurashige, Scott. 2008. *The Shifting Grounds of Race: Black and Japanese Americans in the Making of Multiethnic Los Angeles.* Princeton, NJ: Princeton University Press.

Lee, Erika. 2015. *The Making of Asian America: A History.* New York: Simon & Schuster Paperbacks.

Lewthwaite, Stephanie. 2009. *Race, Place, and Reform in Mexican Los Angeles: A Transnational Perspective, 1890–1940*. Tucson: University of Arizona Press.

Lionnet, Françoise, and Shu-mei Shih, eds. 2005. *Minor Transnationalism*. Durham: Duke University Press.

Lipsitz, George. 2010. *Midnight at the Barrelhouse: The Johnny Otis Story*. Minneapolis: University of Minnesota Press.

Lopez, David E., Eric Popkin, and Edward Telles. 1996. "Central Americans: At the Bottom, Struggling to Get Ahead." In *Ethnic Los Angeles*, edited by Roger Waldinger and Mehdi Bozorgmehar, 279–304. New York: Russell Sage Foundation.

Los Angeles County Commission on Human Relations. 1963. *Population and Housing in Los Angeles County: A Study in the Growth of Residential Segregation*. Los Angeles: Los Angeles County Commission on Human Relations.

Los Angeles County Commission on Human Relations. 1974. *Patterns of Social Change: Los Angeles County, 1960–73: A Statistical Review*. Los Angeles: Los Angeles County Commission on Human Relations.

Los Angeles Times. 1992. *Understanding the Riots: Los Angeles before and after the Rodney King Case*. Los Angeles: Los Angeles Times.

Madhubuti, Haki R., ed. 1993. *Why L.A. Happened: Implications of the '92 Los Angeles Rebellion*. Chicago: Third World Press.

Min, Pyong Gap. 1996. *Caught in the Middle: Korean Communities in New York and Los Angeles*. Berkeley, CA: University of California Press.

Molina, Natalia. 2014. *How Race Is Made in America: Immigration, Citizenship, and the Historical Power of Racial Scripts*. Berkeley, CA: University of California Press.

Morial, Earnet N., Marion Barry, Jr., and Edward M. Meyers (U.S. Conference of Mayors). 1986. *Rebuilding America's Cities: A Policy Analysis of the U.S. Conference of Mayors*. Cambridge, MA: Ballinger Publishing Company.

Morrison, Peter A., and Ira S. Lowry. 1994. "A Riot of Color: The Demographic Setting." In *The Los Angeles Riots: Lessons for the Urban Future*, edited by Mark Baldassare, 19–46. Boulder, CO: Westview Press.

Office of the Special Advisor to the Board of Police Commissioners, City of Los Angeles [Webster Commission]. October 21, 1992. *The City in Crisis: A Report by the Special Advisor to the Board of Police Commissioners on the Civil Disorder in Los Angeles*. Los Angeles: Office of the Special Advisor to the Board of Police Commissioners, City of Los Angeles.

Ong, Paul, Kye Young Park, and Yasmin Tong. 1994. "The Korean-Black Conflict and the State." In *The New Asian Immigration in Los Angeles and Global Restructuring*, edited by Paul Ong, Edna Bonacich, and Lucie Cheng, 264–294. Philadelphia, PA: Temple University Press.

O'Sullivan, Arthur, Terri A. Sexton, and Steven M. Sheffrin. 1995. *Property Taxes and Tax Revolts: The Legacy of Proposition 13*. Cambridge: Cambridge University Press.

Pagán, Eduardo Obregón. 2003. *Murder at the Sleepy Lagoon: Zoot Suits, Race, and Riot in Wartime L.A.* Chapel Hill, NC: University of North Carolina Press.

Payne, J. Gregory, and Scott C. Ratzan. 1986. *Tom Bradley: The Impossible Dream*. Santa Monica: Roundtable Publishing Inc.

Petersilia, Joan, and Allan Abrahamse. 1994. "A Profile of Those Arrested." In *The Los Angeles Riots: Lessons for the Urban Future*, edited by Mark Baldassare, 135–47. 1994. Boulder, CO: Westview Press.

Pulido, Laura. 2006. *Black, Brown, Yellow, and Left: Radical Activism in Los Angeles*. Berkeley, CA: University of California Press.

Romo, Ricardo. 1983. *East Los Angeles: History of A Barrio.* Austin, TX: University of Texas Press.

Rosas, Abigail. 2019. *South Central Is Home: Race and the Power of Community Investment in Los Angeles.* Stanford, CA: Stanford University Press.

Sánchez, George J. 1993. *Becoming Mexican American: Ethnicity, Culture, and Identity in Chicano Los Angeles, 1900–1945.* New York: Oxford University Press.

Scott, Allen J., and Edward W. Soja, eds. 1996. *The City: Los Angeles at the End of the Twentieth Century.* Berkeley, CA: University of California Press.

Sides, Josh. 2003. *L.A. City Limits: African American Los Angeles from the Great Depression to the Present.* Berkeley, CA: University of California Press.

Smith, Anna Deavere. 1993. *Fires in the Mirror: Crown Heights, Brooklyn and Other Identities.* New York: Anchor Books.

Smith, Anna Deavere. 1994. *Twilight: Los Angeles, 1992.* New York: Anchor Books.

Smith, Anna Deavere. 2000a. *Talk to Me: Listening between the Lines.* New York: Random House.

Smith, Anna Deavere. 2000b. "Twilight: Los Angeles." Translated by Anna Deavere Smith. In *Stage on Screen*, edited by Marc Levin. New York: PBS Home Video.

Smith, Anna Deavere. 2003. *Twilight: Los Angeles, 1992.* New York, Dramatists Play Service Inc.

Smith, Cherise. 2011. *Enacting Others: Politics of Identity in Eleanor Antin, Nikki S. Lee, Adrian Piper, and Anna Deavere Smith.* Durham: Duke University Press.

Soja, Edward, Rebecca Morales, and Goetz Wolff. April, 1983. "Urban Restructuring: An Analysis of Social and Spatial Change in Los Angeles." *Economic Geography* 59 (2): 195–230.

Soja, Edward W. 1987. "Economic Restructuring and the Internationalization of the Los Angeles Region." In *The Capitalist City: Global Restructuring and Community Politics*, edited by Michael Peter Smith and Joe R. Feagin, 178–198. Oxford: B. Blackwell.

Soja, Edward W. 2014. *My Los Angeles: From Urban Restructuring to Regional Urbanization.* Berkeley, CA: University of California Press.

Sonenshein, Raphael J. 1993. *Politics in Black and White: Race and Power in Los Angeles.* Princeton, NJ: Princeton University Press.

Song, Min Hyoung. 2005. *Strange Future: Pessimism and the 1992 Los Angeles Riots.* Durham: Duke University Press.

Stevenson, Brenda. 2015. *The Contested Murder of Latasha Harlins: Justice, Gender, and the Origins of the LA Riots.* Oxford, UK: Oxford University Press.

Taylor, Keeanga-Yamahtta. 2016. *From #BlackLivesMatter to Black Liberation.* Chicago: Haymarket Books.

The Governor's Commission on the Los Angeles Riots [McCone Commission]. 1969 [1965]. "Violence in the City: An End or a Beginning?." In *The Los Angeles Riots: Mass Violence in America*, compiled by Robert M. Fogelson, xi–110. New York: Arno Press and the New York Times.

Torres, Martin Valadez. 2005. "Indispensable Migrants: Mexican Workers and the Making of Twentieth-Century Los Angeles." In *Latino Los Angeles: Transformations, Communities, and Activism*, edited by Enrique C. Ochoa and Gilda L. Ochoa, 23–37. Tucson: University of Arizona Press.

Totten, George O., and H. Eric Schockman, eds. 1994. *Community in Crisis: The Korean American Community After the Los Angeles Civil Unrest of April 1992.* Los Angeles: Center for Multiethnic and Transnational Studies, University of Southern California.

Tsuchiya, Kazuyo. 2014. *Reinventing Citizenship: Black Los Angeles, Korean Kawasaki, and Community Participation.* Minneapolis, MN: University of Minnesota Press.

Tsuchiya, Kazuyo. 2017. "'Haihin' kara no sōzō: S. Rodia no Wattsu Tawā to Burakku Losu Angelusu [Creating from 'Junk': S. Rodia's Watts Towers and Black Los Angeles]." In *Hakai no ato no toshi kūkan: Posto katasutorophī no kioku* [Urban Spaces in the Aftermath of Destruction: Post-Catastrophe Memories], edited by Kensuke Kumagai, 287–317. Tokyo: Seikyusha.

US Congress. Congressional Budget Office. 1978. *Proposition 13, Its Impact on the Nation's Economy, Federal Revenues, and Federal Expenditures*. Washington, DC: G. P. O.

US Department of Housing and Urban Development (HUD). 1982. *The President's National Urban Policy Report, 1982*. Washington, DC: HUD.

Waldinger, Roger, and Mehdi Bozorgmehar, eds. 1996. *Ethnic Los Angeles*. New York: Russell Sage Foundation.

10

UNRAVELING AND CONNECTING IN THE TRANSPACIFIC

The Narratives and Work of Yoko Inoue and Jean Shin

Yasuko Takezawa

This chapter examines the flow of people, goods, and money in the transpacific—from East Asia to the US—through an analysis of the narratives and work of two immigrant artists, Yoko Inoue from Japan and Jean Shin from the Republic of Korea, by employing the concepts of both major- and minor-transnationalism.

The concept of *minor transnationalism*, as addressed in the introduction, highlights the horizontal relationship between transmigrants and/or between minoritized peoples (Lionnet and Shih 2005, see the introduction for more detail). In the previous two chapters, Crystal Uchino and Kazuyo Tsuchiya respectively shed light on the empathy, collaboration, and renewed relationships between Japanese Americans and other Asian Americans over the *hibakusha* (A-bomb survivors) and between Korean immigrants and African Americans in Los Angeles after the 1992 civil disturbances (Uchino, Ch. 8, Tsuchiya, Ch. 9).

Minor transnationalism contrasts with *major transnationalism* in the transpacific, a term which Hoskins and Nguyen use to reference the economic, political, and military contact zones between nation-states, incorporating the power dynamics between them (Nguyen and Hoskins 2014). As Naoki Sakai and Hyon Joo Yoo discuss (2012, 12, see the introduction for more detail), the US as a masculine presence dominated a feminized Asia while the stronger Asian powers exploited weaker Asian and Pacific countries. US intervention in the Korean and First Indochina Wars stimulated the development of capitalism in the nation-states of East and Southeast Asia, which allied themselves with the Western Bloc, and military cooperation from Japan, South Korea, Thailand, and the Philippines, in turn, helped support the Vietnam War (Nguyen and Hoskins 2014, 2–15). The role that the Korean War-era special procurements played in Japan's post-war economic recovery (detailed later in this chapter) provides another example of major transnationalism as well.

DOI: 10.4324/9781003266396-13

Affect and feelings, discussed in Tanabe's Chapter 6, will also play an important role in this chapter. However, in contrast to the ways in which affect and feelings are mobilized in India—where racialization and governmentality are strengthened against threat groups with the new technology of the biometric ID system—artwork generates affect and feelings to build collaborations, alliances, and new inclusive communities, as well as to counteract racism and sexism.

This chapter also draws on a number of sociological and anthropological studies of art. In *Distinction*, Pierre Bourdieu examined how the habitus born of the intersection between economic capital and cultural capital determines aesthetic choices and tastes (Bourdieu 1984). However, his argument ignores the explicit hierarchy that race has created in the art world. By contrast, the sociologist Howard Becker, who explicated the necessity of understanding art as the collective act of artists and the assistants and collaborators who support them (Becker 1982), and the cultural anthropologist Alfred Gell, who viewed art as "a system of action intended to change the world" and shed a light on the agency of art itself (Gell 1998), have emphasized the social relationality of art. Further, Tim Ingold asserts that a productive collaboration between cultural anthropology and art requires a methodology for retroactively explicating the process by which art is created (Ingold 2013). In analyzing the work of the two artists discussed below, we likewise recognize the collective nature of performance and the creative process, as well as art's agency in questioning society and promoting change. In this chapter, I will engage with the questions posed by the artwork of these women, with a close eye to race, gender, class, and the social status of the immigrant.

In this spirit, this chapter explores horizontal encounters, network-building, and alliances, and fosters conversations between minoritized and marginalized peoples in the transpacific by featuring the narratives and works of Yoko Inoue and Jean Shin. This study is based on my extensive interviews and exchanges with the two artists and a few curators of their shows in 2006 and from 2017 to 2021, as well as supplementary research on related topics; in particular, interviews and archival study carried out in 2018 on the ceramics industry in Nagoya, Japan.

10.1 Yoko Inoue

Yoko Inoue, who moved from Japan to New York first for work and again later for graduate school, has engaged in sculpture, installation, collaborative socially engaged art projects, and public intervention performance art. At the time of 9/11, Inoue was in the middle of preparing for a new performance art project as an artist-in-residence with Art in General, a non-profit organization in New York City.[1] In post-9/11 New York, with patriotism substantially elevated, Inoue personally experienced the precarity and weakness of being simultaneously a "non-American" and a "woman of color." On Canal Street, nearly all the immigrants covered their shops with American flags and had begun selling huge quantities of American flag merchandise while masking the identities of their homelands. It was their way of protecting themselves from the anti-immigrant bashing they feared in the wake of then President George W. Bush's pronouncement that "Either you are with us, or you are with the terrorists" (CNN 2001).

Through her daily observation of the crowds thronging Canal Street, she noticed that these vendors, exhibiting their humorous and talented performances despite the tragedy, attracted the most attention from people passing by. Inspired by these vendors, Inoue developed a performance art piece in which she took a mold of a *maneki-neko* (a common Japanese figurine in the shape of a cat believed to bring good luck to its owner) and used it to produce copies out of clay, which she then sold. She watched as the "pro-American" merchandise products sold by the other vendors, including sweaters modelled on Ralph Lauren's American Flag sweater collection, began to fly off the shelves, even though the majority of these sweaters were brought to the US by undocumented immigrants who made their livelihoods as intermediaries in the circulation of goods between Peru, Ecuador, and the US.

These vendors constantly kept an eye on one another, and sometimes when crowds of people on curator-led tours surrounded her *maneki-neko* stall, they would come out to spy on what was happening. At the same time, however, there were instances of cooperation and mutual protection, particularly when it came to the police. As Inoue explains:

> The presence of a mutual enemy [in the form of the police] brought everyone together. People would call out to each other or signal each other with their cell phones, and everyone would cover for each other. It brought a sense of unity. Things changed enormously in that regard; it is really interesting. Once people have seen you around, they come over to help, say "good morning," stuff like that.

Almost all these vendors were transmigrants of color, many of whom came from Latin America, with certain segments from other regions, such as Africa and Asia. According to Inoue, "9/11 has made things really tough," but it also generated a sense of mutual empathy among transmigrants including herself.

> Once we kind of got to know each other, we would stand around and chat over our cups of coffee. I met this Ecuadorian guy who made sweaters— for instance …. "Where are you from?" "Japan." "I am from Ecuador." "The Ecuadorian soccer team's doing well," I replied. Japan was hosting the World Cup that year …. We became friendly and ended up exchanging all kinds of information. Eventually he told me he was in charge of all the Latin American migrants selling the sweaters. He would bring them all there in his van. He told me, "There are around twenty villages up in the Andes in Ecuador … and I know all these communities."

Building on her friendship with many of the Peruvian and Ecuadorian transmigrants she met on Canal Street, Inoue began a long-term project entitled

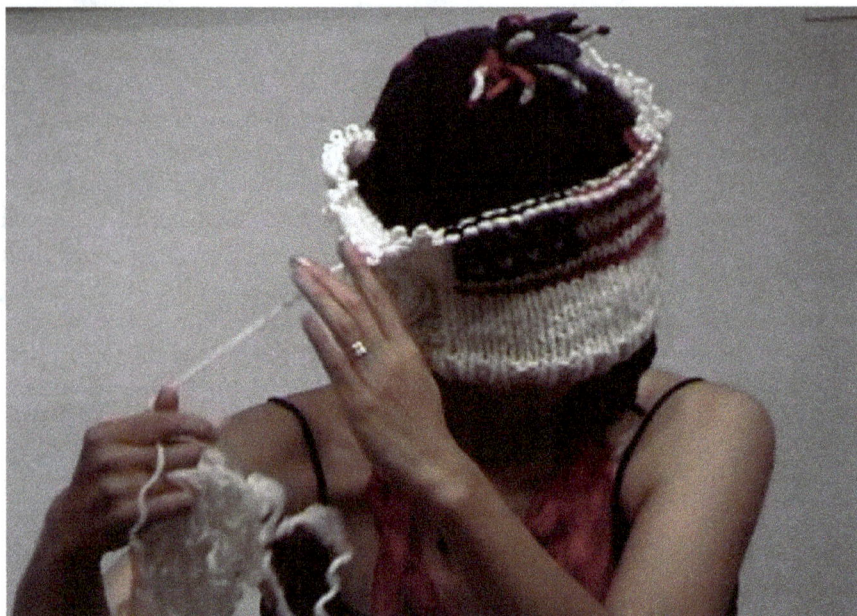

FIGURE 10.1 Yoko Inoue, *Transmigration of the Sold*, Site-Specific Installation, Canal Street, New York, NY, 2001

Source: Image Provided by the Artist

Transmigration of the Sold (2005–ongoing, New York/Otavalo, Ecuador/Amantani Island, Peru) with people in the Andes mountains and the "intermediary" transmigrants to New York. Inoue showcased her performance, *Community Alert*, in 2001 at the Rotunda Gallery of the Brooklyn Council of the Arts. It featured a knitted cap with an American flag design she had imported from the Andes.

The performance involved the unraveling of the cap she wore to reveal a Black headscarf underneath (Figure 10.1). At the time, metaphors conflating the 9/11 terrorists with the Zapatista Army of National Liberation[2] in Mexico and the Kamikaze special attack units of the Japanese Imperial Army were widespread. Non-white immigrants kept their identities hidden under cover of the stars and stripes in order to protect themselves from the gathering storm of xenophobia. The project demonstrated Inoue's way of challenging the tendency of mainstream American society to doubt the loyalty of anyone who was not a white American citizen that seemed particularly acute after 9/11. Her performance compelled audiences to consider the different ways in which dominant American society and non-white immigrants interpret what is revealed when the American flag is unraveled.

While in the Andes, Inoue learned that the three-color flag held during dances by the Quechua-speaking Indigenous people of Amantani Island (on the Peruvian side of Lake Titicaca in the Altiplano region) symbolizes the red, white,

FIGURE 10.2 Sweater Makers, Otavalo Ecuador 2008

Source: Image Provided by the Artist

and blue flowers of the potato plant, which they hold to be the source of life (Figure 10.2). The Indigenous people of the Andes deem potatoes and goats to be more precious than money as sources of sustenance.

The processes of globalization have led to Andean peoples knitting American-flag sweaters that are utterly disconnected from their own lives. The repetitious cross-border flow of people and goods led Inoue to begin considering the racial and geographical economic disparities between the global North and South. For her Canal Street performance, Inoue thus also repurposed the yarn unraveled from the American flag hats to make and sell tri-color bouquets symbolizing the flowers of the potato plant.

In 2017, Inoue presented a provocative performance at SFAI140 as part of an event at the Santa Fe Art Institute in New Mexico, which included the involvement of a Navajo pastry chef.[3] The event consisted of twenty 140-second presentations given by each of the invited artists. Inoue's performance was inspired by an old monotonous film justifying the use of the atomic bomb called *Hiroshima Nagasaki* (date unknown). The film is still being shown, according to Inoue; she had seen it some years before at the Bradbury Science Museum in nearby Los Alamos, where the then Los Alamos Scientific Laboratory (now Los Alamos National Laboratory) housed one of the sites of the Manhattan Project that researched and developed the atomic bomb during World War II. Inoue also recalled that she was deeply shocked to see a model of an enormous cake in the shape of a mushroom cloud on display at the Los Alamos History Museum.

> There was this model of a cake that was served at the ceremony [on November 5, 1946] celebrating the successful hydrogen bomb tests on Bikini Atoll. It was totally shocking. They were having a celebration! It was like a wedding cake or something. I was so surprised, I asked, "What on earth is this?"

She was also stunned to see archival photos of upper-class women on their way to a cocktail party wearing large mushroom cloud hats. When she saw the last scene of the film on Hiroshima and Nagasaki and its American-oriented narration ("We ended the war with only two bombs"—as if this was an adequate justification for the use of nuclear weapons), she thought, "Really? In 2017? It made me crazy. And I figured I needed to show it to the audience."

Inoue consulted a local wedding cake shop about commissioning a big cake resembling a mushroom cloud from nuclear bomb testings to use in her performance. When she showed the chef her drawing of how she imagined the cake, the chef responded, "Oh wow! I am a Navajo. I am happy to do this!" (Figure 10.3). The Navajo people had suffered for over a half-century from the contamination of

FIGURE 10.3 Yoko Inoue, Photograph of a Navajo Chef Making a Mushroom Cloud Cake for the Performance at SFAI140, Santa Fe Art Institute, Santa Fe, NM, 2017, 140-Second Performance

Source: Image Provided by the Artist

their land and the subsequent serious health damage caused by a series of nuclear tests and the large-scale uranium mining in the region. The secret Manhattan Project, which started on October 9, 1941, upon President Roosevelt's call for the development of an atomic bomb, had acquired an estimated 44,000 pounds of uranium on and near the Navajo reservation between 1943 and 1945 (Voyles 2015, 1–2).[4] The serious effects of uranium mining have continued to threaten the lives and resources of the Navajo Nation. Inoue decorated the cake stand with napkins that she had hand embroidered with each name of the Native American nations, whose tribal names had been appropriated to name the weapons used in the thermonuclear testings conducted at Bikini and Enewetak atolls in 1956. These napkins were intended to signal the message that the nuclear issue is not unique to Japan and the Japanese but also involves the US domestic encroachment on Native American nations.

Inoue's 140-second-long performance consisted of audience members more or less force-feeding cake into her mouth, while the aforementioned film *Hiroshima Nagasaki* played in the background (Figure 10.4). Inoue chose to use a real cake so that the participants would never forget the way it smelled as they fed it to her. Scientists and workers from Los Alamos mingled in the audience with the many white self-identified liberals from the art world, and Inoue was acutely aware of the crowd's emotional response to her performance (Inoue 2016).

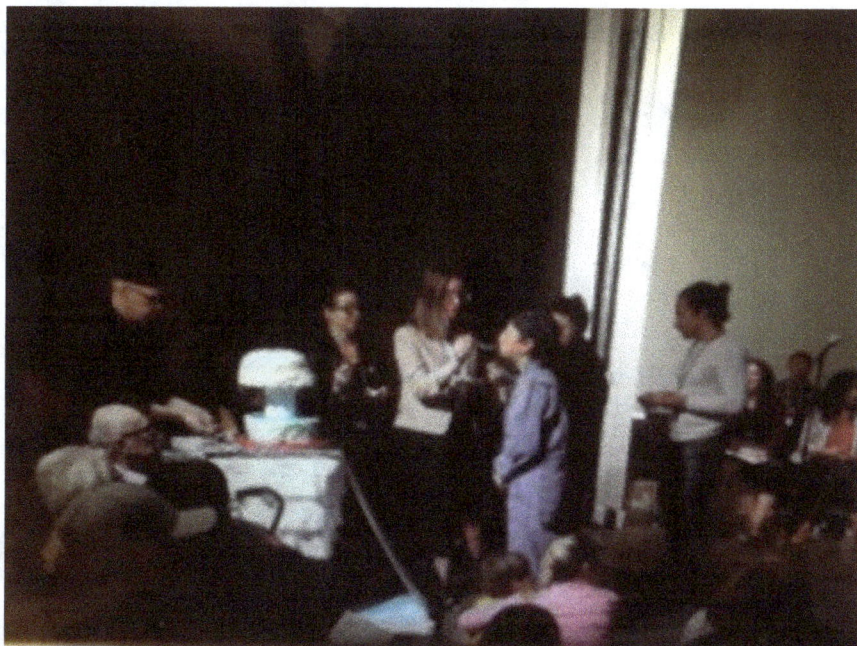

FIGURE 10.4 Yoko Inoue, Video Still of the Performers Being Fed Cake by the Audience at SFAI140, Santa Fe Art Institute, Santa Fe, NM, 2017, 140-Second Performance

Source: Image Provided by the Artist

In dealing with the memory of the atomic bomb, Inoue's work did not address Korean atomic bomb survivors and other victims of Japanese colonialism in Hiroshima and Nagasaki (see Uchino, Chapter 9, in this volume). Given that the audience at SFAI140 was composed almost entirely of Americans, Inoue prioritized a reconsideration of nuclear weapons in the US. When I asked her about Japanese colonialism in Asia before and during World War II and the debate in the US regarding the issue of comfort women, she gave her own view and expressed interest in someday attempting to produce a work addressing these issues.

In 2017, Inoue presented the installation *Tea Taste Democracy and Upside-Down Objects* at the SPACES Gallery in Cleveland, Ohio. On the wall were Western-style ceramic figurines affixed upside-down so that the viewer was confronted with the words "Made in Occupied Japan" inscribed on their bases (Figure 10.5). In a recessed display space, set up like a *tokonoma* decorative alcove in a Japanese-style room, the soundtrack from the *Hiroshima Nagasaki* film accompanies images of giant mushroom clouds and a photograph of a white housewife proudly displaying a mushroom cloud-shaped cake. Inoue's ceramic replicas of tea bowls, vases, and other everyday items are lined up on tables beside charred bento boxes she made, copying the well-known artifact displayed in the Hiroshima Peace Memorial Museum.

Inoue's work juxtaposes the contrasting "upside-down" memories of Hiroshima and Nagasaki between the US and Japan: the American celebratory

FIGURE 10.5 *Made in Occupied Japan* Nobilities Displayed at *Tea Taste Democracy and Upside-Down Objects*, Spaces Gallery, Cleveland, Ohio, 2017

Source: Image Provided by the Artist. IPhoto: SPACES GALLERY

narrative of the dropping of the atomic bomb in the film and the charred bento boxes; the proud smile of a woman showing off her cake, and anguished cries and groans represented through anime and manga. Noelle Giuffrida, then a professor of Asian art at Case Western Reserve University, praised Inoue's installation as "a jarring and thought-provoking group of polarizing images of the romanticizing of the atomic bombs on the American side, and then the devastation that they wrought in Japan" (Giuffrida 2017).

Inoue first encountered the phrase "Made in Occupied Japan (MIOJ)/(OJ)" when one of her students brought her an item discovered in a second-hand shop.[5] General Headquarters (GHQ), part of the Supreme Commander for the Allied Powers (SCAP), which administered occupied Japan from 1945 to 1952, had mandated this inscription be put on all products meant for overseas exportation produced in the five-year period between the resumption of private import/export trade in 1947 and the Peace Treaty of San Francisco in 1952 (Takashima 2014).[6]

During an art residency in early 2017 at the Cleveland Museum of Art (CMA), which boasts one of the finest collections of Asian art in the US on par with the collections in the Museum of Fine Arts in Boston and the Seattle Art Museum, she turned her attention to materials in the CMA archive related to the former museum director Sherman E. Lee (Cohen 1992, 134, 142; Satō 2003, 88).[7] Lee (1918–2008) was one of the "Monuments Men," people who went to Japan under US General Douglas MacArthur to survey the "effect of the ravages of war" (Satō 2003, 88) on art and artifacts.

Inoue's show *Tea Taste Democracy* (Lee 1963, 195–196) represents the bittersweet emotions brought up by the juxtaposition of the US justification for the dropping of the atomic bomb with the benefits Japan received from the US after the war. *Tea taste* refers to the bittersweet taste of green tea; Inoue is referencing the title of an essay by Sherman E. Lee, *Tea Taste in Japanese Art*, which is also the title of an exhibition Lee curated in 1963.

Through her research, Inoue discovered two types of objects brought across the Pacific to the US during the same period: traditional Japanese art considered "high art," and mass-market products seen as "low art." The post-war recovery is usually credited to Japanese "blood and sweat," but she came to realize it was also in large part due to the support of the US economy.

In addition to issues of economic inequality, Inoue's installation addresses gender inequality and the gendered division of labor. Gender and class inequality are critiqued in juxtaposing fancy tea utensils for the upper class, which are considered "high art" and usually made by men, with recreations of lunch boxes filled with food by women whose domestic labor often goes uncompensated and unrecognized.

Through this group of works, Inoue continues to ask what "justice" means in the US—the "justice" which is in peril now—while tensions between the US and its allies versus Russia, China, and North Korea leave the global community anxious about the possibility of World War III and the deployment of nuclear weapons. Inoue thinks of her work as "a first step"; the questions she posits offer the viewer the opportunity to think, even if only at an unconscious level.

Inoue's *Tea Taste Democracy and Upside-Down Objects* poses some key questions: What transpacific Japan–US dynamics are suggested by the existence of both the classic Japanese art objects Inoue encountered at the CMA and the consumer ceramic goods that were "Made in Occupied Japan"? What about the disparities in collective memories and narratives between Japan and the US, and between "high art" and "low art," all of which illustrate the Pacific as an interactive contact zone? Inspired by these questions Inoue raised, I set out to conduct my own interviews and archival research.

After the legal recognition of "Important Art Objects" in 1933, the 1950 Law for the Protection of Cultural Properties designated "Important Cultural Properties" and "National Treasures" as subcategories within "Important Art Objects." It is thought that amid the chaos in the aftermath of World War II, however, a large amount of national treasure-level artwork was lumped in with other "Important Art Objects" and, while not illegally, was also transported overseas from Japan in great numbers. The period of occupation from 1945 to 1952 was the only time since the promulgation of Japan's National Treasures Preservation Act in 1929 that foreigners were able to remove national treasure-level designated artwork from Japan (Cohen 1992).

While Sherman E. Lee, mentioned above, stayed in Japan as a Monuments Man, he and his former supervisor Howard Hollis inspected items housed in art museums and temples, private collections, and art dealer's shops, and reported on the location, condition, and storage circumstances of artworks and other tangible cultural property. Lee boasted about his role in the "democratization" of Japan's art museums (Lee 1997, 101). Hollis later became an art dealer working with Japanese clients in America, and Lee succeeded in bringing an extraordinary number of national-treasure level traditional Japanese art objects into the US.

Some in Japan, however, express skepticism about the methods Lee employed in acquiring a great many of the finest works of traditional Japanese art and sending them to the US. For example, critic Shimura writes:

> During his time in Japan, Sherman Lee exploited the authority of the occupation army to survey the entire country and compile a list of those artworks which were and were not legally certified, making off with the finest of the uncertified works.
>
> *Shimura 2014, 18*

Matsushita and others surmised in the discussion that: "They went after works that were valuable but had not been certified [as national treasures or important cultural properties]" (Matsushita et al. 1952, 12). As Satō adds, "The artworks flowing out of Japan during the occupation were in some sense spoils of war for the Americans" (Satō 2003, 88).[8]

Certain other circumstances render it impossible to declare that Japan was solely a victim. At the height of the San Francisco peace talks, the de Young

Museum in San Francisco held the exhibition *Art Treasures from Japan—A Special Loan Exhibition in Commemoration of the Signing of the Peace Treaty in San Francisco, September 1951*, prompting an overwhelmingly enthusiastic response from visitors.

Two facts deserve special attention in respect to major transnationalism: the exhibition was a collaboration between the de Young and the Cultural Properties Protection Commission of Japan, which had been established as a foreign bureau of the Ministry of Education; and the exhibition's subtitle included the words "in commemoration of the signing of the peace treaty." In the face of GHQ's absolute control and the chaos that reigned in the aftermath of World War II, the relevant Japanese authorities had no choice but to stand by and watch as a huge number of works that should have been classified as national treasures or important cultural properties flowed overseas. However, from the subtitle of this exhibition, we can infer that those in government sought to use this artwork—that had ended up in the collections of major American museums via Lee and his cohort—for political purposes.

It should come as no surprise that this artwork, as it crossed the Pacific and fascinated countless Americans in major art museums across the US, played an important role in recuperating the image of Japan from the country that "bombed Pearl Harbor" to a nation with a rich culture and traditions. Cohen writes:

> … if America had become the hegemon of East Asia and extracted art treasures as part of the tribute to which it was entitled, its client states were quick to recognize the value of art as an instrument of diplomacy. First the Japanese, then the Chinese, Koreans, and other Asian peoples sent their art on exhibition to win the respect and support of the American people.
>
> *Cohen 1992, 150–151*

Then how did the ceramics "Made in Occupied Japan" make their way to America? To find the answer, I set out for Nagoya, the center of Japan's ceramics industry, where both the Japan Association for the Promotion of Pottery Industry and the Nagoya Ceramics Hall are located. According to their archival materials,[9] while exports under the occupation counted as low as ¥960,000 in 1946, they grew exponentially to ¥470 million the following year, and by 1950 had reached ¥8.27 billion. In 1950, tableware accounted for ¥5.6 billion in exports, over seven times the 2010 tableware exports of ¥6.4 billion when adjusted for inflation (*Nagoya Tōjiki-kaikan* 1987: 574). In 1953, the first year for which data is available, the US was the largest importer of Japanese fine china and porcelain tableware, accounting for almost 40 percent of the total gross sales (*Nihon Yushutsu Tōjikishi Hensan Iinkai* 1967, 140–141).[10] For the import of dolls, animals, and other porcelain novelties like the ones Inoue uses in her work, the US accounted for nearly 75 percent of gross sales. According to Susumu Kondō, former managing director of the Japan Ceramics Export Association, during the time when the American middle- and working classes dreamed of adorning their cupboards with fine china dinner sets from companies like Wedgwood, they bought Japanese ceramics in great quantities because they were available at extremely inexpensive prices. As Kondo explains:

> GHQ cared about the quality of dinnerware .... When the American soldiers arrived after the war, they were delighted to discover that they too could afford to buy bone china. .... Japanese ceramics spread as they became [not just a product for the upper classes but] an object of aspiration for the American middle and lower classes as well.[11]

The following passage in *Nihon Yushutsu Tōjikishi* (The History of Japanese Ceramics Exports) underscores the historical reality that behind the post-war success of the Japanese ceramics industry lay the economic boom spurred by the Korean War.

> The special procurement boom that accompanied the beginning of the upheaval in Korea in 1951 led to a generally healthy economy. ... [T]otal gross from exports to countries such as Indonesia, Africa, and especially the United States ... increased by over 73% compared to the previous year.
> *Nihon Yushutsu Tōjikishi Hensan Iinkai 1967, 99*

Takafusa Nakamura, a renowned historian of the post-war Japanese economy, argues that special procurements resulting from the Korean War, in addition to financial aid from the US and loan agreements with the World Bank and elsewhere, played a major role in the revival of the Japanese economy (Nakamura 1976, 151). America's role in the post-war revival of the Japanese economy was not limited to the ceramics industry. Through the US, Japan also enjoyed some share of the economic effects of the struggle between the US and the Soviet Union over the sovereignty of the Korean peninsula.

Inoue's juxtaposition of refined art objects and cheap ceramics makes clear that American and Japanese interests at the time were two sides of the same coin. Ceramics is just one example which demonstrates the fact that the post-World War II Japanese export industry was tied to the US hegemonic intervention in Asia.

10.2 Jean Shin

Jean Shin moved to the US from the Republic of Korea when she was six, her family settling in the suburbs of Washington, DC.[12] In 1990, when Shin was a senior in high school, she was selected for the arts component of the prestigious Presidential Scholars program, winning a full scholarship to the Pratt Institute (Hallmark 2007, 194). Her sculptures and installations have been exhibited at America's premier institutions, including the Smithsonian American Art Museum and the Museum of Modern Art in New York. Despite this success, however, Shin has long harbored a fierce opposition to the disproportionate emphasis placed on traditional Western art in the academic context.

She was also irritated by "a Western gaze," seeing her as an Asian woman and reading an "Eastern gaze" in her work.

> You know, people would critique or whenever people would come into my studio, they would say "oh yes, and you're influence of calligraphy" and I sat there, going "what influence of calligraphy." You know because I took painting. Professors are Western .... so, it was very shocking to me that I kept getting this reference to calligraphy.

Shin eventually rejected traditional sculptural subjects and became interested in finding a novel artistic approach. The greatest influence on her during this time was David Hammons, a Harlem-based African American artist who would reuse materials intimately connected to Black people's everyday lives—fallen hair from the barbershop floor, hair beads, chicken bones, basketball hoops—to create works expressing Black daily experiences and identity expression.

Shin was inspired by Hammons' approach and began using discarded materials such as keys, sunglasses, slides, trophies, and pill bottles in her own work. She would gather these objects, often provided by friends and acquaintances, and transform their individual stories into enormous, unified pieces that reflected society as a whole. These pieces require meticulous handiwork and a great deal of time to complete, which is another important facet of her work (more on this to follow).

At first, the human body was the central theme of Shin's art, but ever since she began creating large-scale site-specific pieces, her work has become more about community participation and human interaction. This focus on ideas of participation and everyday life has become a massive trend in contemporary art in general since the turn of the twenty-first century.

Shin modeled her *Chance City* on an urban high-rise apartment complex, individually placing \$32,404 worth of scratch-off lottery tickets atop one another, relying solely on gravity and friction to hold them together without the use of any adhesive (Figure 10.6). These losing lottery tickets, now simply worthless scraps of paper, are filled with the aspirations of people who took a "chance" in the hopes of striking it rich so they could afford to buy a home, the enduring symbol of the "American Dream." Jean Shin gives form to these unrealized dreams in *Chance City*. The 9/11 attacks occurred while she was working on the piece, the twin towers of the World Trade Center so easily reduced to dust and rubble along with the lives of over 3,000 victims. Shin's work sounds the alarm about today's volatile global capitalist economy in which such massive amounts of capital circulate daily. When *Chance City* was constructed more quickly and on a smaller scale, the work was fragile and easily destroyed, but the larger it became and the longer it took to construct, the sturdier and more resilient it became.[13] At the same time, this work is imbued with the hope that even amid grief and chaos, solidarity and cooperation will someday enable the restoration of a city where everyone has a "chance."

In 2004 at MOMA, Shin had a solo show, *Cut Outs and Suspended Seam*, which utilized the used clothes of the museum's employees (Figure 10.7). Using the

FIGURE 10.6 Jean Shin, *Chance City,* 2002, 2004, and 2009

Source: Image Provided by the Artist

FIGURE 10.7 Jean Shin *Cut Outs and Suspended Seam* MOMA, 2004

Source: Image Provided by the Artist

cut-up cloth from their clothing, Shin covered the white walls with a sort of mosaic composed of the silhouettes of people of all shapes and sizes: short people like herself, big people, skinny people, and so on. The piece effaces the workplace hierarchy by arranging the clothing of all employees, from the museum director to the janitor, equally and without regard for their status. In doing so, it foregrounds the museum employees themselves, who ordinarily remain behind the scenes, and creates a space where they proudly point out the silhouettes of their used clothes and start talking to Shin to share their views about the museum. Through the process of creating this piece, the employees—centered around the curator—met, collaborated, and became aware of their identity as a collective entity.

Shin's *Unraveling* is a work that renders human "connections" even more overtly visible (Figure 10.8). When the Asia Society of New York invited her to participate in their exhibition *One Way or Another: Asian American Art Now* (2006), Shin solicited old sweaters from the people of the "Asian American community,"

FIGURE 10.8 Jean Shin, *Unraveling*

Source: Image Provided by the Artist

as she envisioned it. She began by patiently "unraveling" some of each sweater, then lined up what remained of the sweaters on three walls to form a gradient, after which she mapped the real-life human relationships that existed in the space between the sweaters by connecting them with the unraveled yarn. Finally, she decorated the entrance to the hall with a rainbow-colored sash composed of yarn from all of the assembled sweaters. My sweater was connected to Shin's; the sweaters donated by me, my husband, and my daughter were all connected to one another. *Unraveling* also included sweaters from the "white people" of the Asia Society who had been involved in the exhibition, as well as from non-Asian curators and staff members. For Shin, who has one son with her white husband, the "Asian American community" is not defined by essentialist attributes like bloodlines, ancestry, or nationality but is instead a loose network of people who share a common consciousness and common goals. She has found that unraveling is a way to build connections and new communities with the people she met or became even closer with throughout the duration of her project.[14]

Light green silhouettes of enormous vases decorate the wall of the Broadway Long Island Railroad station in the suburbs of New York City; entitled *Celadon Remnants* (2008), this work was commissioned by the MTA Arts for Transit in 2007 (Figure 10.9). Shin wanted to use materials that would remind the people who use the station, largely residents of the surrounding Korean American community, of their connection to their homeland. To this end, she visited Icheon, a city famous for its celadon porcelain. There she learned that in their traditional pursuit of a completely flawless product, the potters destroy the majority of the

FIGURE 10.9 Celadon Remnants, 2008, at the Broadway Long Island Railroad Station

Source: Photo by the Author

celadon objects they produce. Negotiations with the mayor led to the city of Icheon donating three tons of celadon fragments to New York, where Shin ultimately gave them new life in the form of this piece of public art in the Korean immigrant neighborhood of Flushing.

Shin has exhibited similar pieces made from shards of celadon, albeit on a smaller scale, alongside other works by Korean and Korean American artists at the US Embassy in Seoul and the Korean Embassy in Washington, DC. Shin views the celadon fragments "as a metaphor of the Korean diaspora, vibrant artifacts of the Korean people, their history and culture that are scattered all over the world to form new identities elsewhere."[15] For Shin, these silhouettes correspond to the form of the community that people from the Korean peninsula have reconstituted in the US, after leaving their homeland because of political or financial difficulties.

Shin sees both differences and commonalities between herself and the Korean immigrants who live in the Flushing community. Because her parents were both so busy when they lived in the suburbs of Washington, DC, Shin grew up spending a lot of time at the homes of her white American friends. She regards herself as both linguistically and culturally Americanized and feels "accepted" in American society. She has no need of a "mini-Seoul" where Koreans cluster to maintain their language, food, and culture. In that sense, she is an "outsider." At the same time, as a member of the Korean diaspora, she feels attached to that traditional culture. Another reason she chose to work with celadon was that she thought it would be easy for Koreans to recognize their own culture in this material which graces the halls of so many art museums. Conscious of the immigrants who, pressed by the exigencies of daily life, cannot visit the Metropolitan Museum of Art and view the celadon porcelain on display there, Shin approached the piece as a way to create a kind of public art museum.

In America, Shin constantly endures the gaze of those who see her as "an Oriental," but at the same time, she is open about her ambivalence toward the people of her homeland.

> So, for Koreanness, well, there is only one Korea. But, what happens to the diaspora? Some of us make communities like the Flushing community— they want to come together; they want to make another Seoul … it is interesting how Koreans [in Korea] can't accept flaws. If you are not 100 percent something, then there is a problem … they won't leave the country to do that. They think that my experience of being in America has just been a lonely walk.

She is critical of what she characterizes as the deeply rooted prejudice and discriminatory feelings Korean society harbors regarding the Korean diaspora.

Shin has been busy with child rearing in recent years and has largely turned her hand to community participation projects. Her installation *MAiZE* (2017), for instance, grew out of a commission from the city of Davenport, Iowa. *Maize* refers to fields of corn, which commonly symbolize the vastness and fertility of

FIGURE 10.10   MAiZE, 2017

Source: Image Provided by the Artist

the earth. In her installation, Shin represented corn fields with hundreds of green plastic corn syrup bottles that 800 volunteers had collected along the banks of the Mississippi River while cleaning up litter (Figure 10.10). This project not only created a bond among the people of the area in the form of a space of collaborative production, but it also created a space for the participants to think about and discuss environmental issues and their daily eating habits.

In 2018, *Unraveling* was exhibited for the first time in nine years as part of Shin's solo show at the Philadelphia Museum of Art. The curator, Hyunsoo Woo, told me about her view of Shin's art.

> A lot of people feel that *oh, contemporary is really difficult to understand.* But, the way that she [Shin] presents her exhibition, her works, is that she always uses this very familiar material. So, I think people already naturally engage more with her work … the way that she transforms them into an amazing visual arrangement is really, I think, a great talent that she has. And a lot of people, the visitors to this presentation would say, *Oh my god I had no idea that this was made out of you know shoe upper leather,* and *Oh my god, sweaters can be installed this way!* So, she really gives that unexpected transformation of the objects, you know …. So, she has a strong concept base, always about the identity of a person and then the network of those people and community. But at the same time, she has an amazing hand skill to make those into something else. And then the final product is always visually pleasing. So, I think she has a very well-balanced way of approaching her work.[16]

As *Unraveling* toured the US, Shin added sweaters reflecting the "Asian American" networks of the curators in each place the work was exhibited. Shin would divide the lineup on each wall by city, then further subdivide each by color to form a gradient. An examination of the names of those who donated sweaters seems to show that the racial, ethnic, and gender makeup of the group differs from place to place depending on the ethnic backgrounds and experiences of the curators themselves.[17] As the ethnic makeup of donors within the Asian community changes from city to city, so too do the colors of the sweaters, making this very much a site-specific artwork. For example, New York favored darker colors, whereas the sweaters from Hawai'i featured brighter ones.[18]

Shin's choice of old and worn-out materials, and her use of collage to express a single unified whole, are largely connected to her family history. This is something I did not learn from articles or critiques written about her but through conversation with Shin herself. Her parents had both been college professors in Korea, but after they came to the US, they encountered harsh racial discrimination and were unable to find employment in their fields, so they ended up running a convenience store in a poor Black neighborhood in the suburbs of Washington, DC.

> I can clearly see from my Asian American immigrant experience but really particular to my Korean American family coming, you know, in the late 70s with my parents working very hard trying to be the first-generation immigrants with really tough jobs that deal with lots of time and low wages and that kind of business owner mentality that all you did was just work all the time.
>
> So that notion of process. You know, like what are you doing, and how long does something take. And having to in some way validate that as being important and not necessarily the results ... the hard work is ... of value, you know.

Shin's work, which requires long hours of labor to create, is also laced with a critique of gender inequality.

> Unfortunately, because of inequities, women's labor and work is often undervalued, unacknowledged or invisible. In contrast to big quick actions often attributed to men, my work is purposefully labor-intensive and celebrates processes that are meticulous, repetitive and slow.

Shin places great emphasis on the artistic process described by Tim Ingold, as mentioned in the beginning of this chapter. At some point, she realized that her experience as an Asian immigrant, and in particular a Korean immigrant, had had a huge impact on her artistic style. She believes that growing up watching her parents eke out a living working long, anxious hours in their convenience store played a part in fixing the notion of process at the heart of her own work. She uses great quantities of similar objects in her art, which she says she "can clearly see" from her Asian American immigrant experience: her memories of helping her father stock the shelves of their convenience store always involve dozens of identical products, and she has no recollection of ever seeing single items on their own.

Shin shared her memories of her grandmother who she lived with:

> She [her grandmother] just saved everything. She just saved every tin, bottle, plastic in America with us. She would be so resourceful, she could make everything out of nothing, and she lived just like a hermit, you know, very self-contained …. A lot of people say *you are just like grandma* …. She was always in a mode of scarcity and resourcefulness …. And so that was also translated to me.

Shin learned the everyday wisdom of repurposing things rather than throwing them away from her grandmother, who had likely lived through the Japanese colonial period and the Korean War, then endured poverty and difficulty after coming to the US.

Shin also shared humorous memories from childhood of damaged goods that went unsold:

> When they had a supermarket, it was always the left-over fruit you know … What they always brought home was the stuff that was spoiled or just about to go bad, you know. So that was what we were kind of used to in our lives and you still make something delicious out of it, you still make something good out of something that maybe wasn't the most ideal for someone in the marketplace, you know. So, I think of all those relationships that link me toward my own history as being Asian American.

I asked Shin what drives her creativity. Among the Asian Americans I have interviewed, many answered "anger towards racial discrimination," but Shin's response was just the opposite: she had spent years watching people butting heads and shouting at each other, venting their hatred, and at the end of that road what she wanted was "to bring all these different voices that are fragmented … and revive them into an entity that only exists when I make it."

> I feel like what I've witnessed was a lot of that, people responding and acting out of anger and shouting and you know accusations and all this … like the fight.
>
> And I feel like because I saw it and am surrounded by it, where all I want to do is stop! Make it stop. That on a personal history level I think that if anything I've learned, you know, I just want to pick up the pieces and put them back together for someone. You know, could everyone stop fighting and stop being angry and just be quiet so we can just put … go to work you know in bringing things together.

The severe antagonism between Korean immigrants and African Americans in the part of the Washington suburbs where Shin and her family lived was similar to the social circumstances behind the 1992 LA uprising, which Kazuyo Tsuchiya has detailed in the previous chapter (Tsuchiya, Ch. 9). The Koreans were concerned about Black shoplifters, while the Black community felt the Koreans were bleeding poor Black people dry without giving anything back. Shin herself witnessed first-hand dozens of explosive or violent situations. Even as a child, she witnessed angry shouting and exchanges of verbal abuse, with accusations of theft traded for slurs like "Chinaman." She still recalls numerous occasions on which it seemed like her father and his customers would come to blows; her father, who had done compulsory military service in Korea, never backed down. Shin says the discrimination and hatred between the communities were shockingly fierce. While she was still in college, before her parents installed bulletproof glass in the store, Shin was terrified by the fact that they were defenseless, with no way of knowing who might come into their store or for what reason.

> I think probably in race history the tension between African Americans and Korean business owners were the worst in the 80s and early 90s. Literally every day … I imagined my parents being shot. And a lot of their friends died. They were just shot down. And so … knowing the many funerals that my parents attended or … so many business people that like they would drive by and say like, *Oh that person got shot on their way from home to the store.* On the day when I would help them work they would say, *Oh that person got shot, that person's in the hospital,* … You know, growing up thinking that your parents are going to be shot by a certain community just because they were Koreans and where they were living.

This is why she devoted herself to art, laying her prayers one atop the other within her creations. She says that in that sense, "perhaps those entities do come out of sadness and anger, and some of them come out of happiness and joy too."

As we can see from the fact that she avoids specifying "Black people" in the above quotation and uses instead the expression "a certain community," African Americans are not the target of her animosity; rather, she is empathetic to them as people marginalized by systemic racism and social inequality just as she and her family had been. For her, racial identity should be a tool for connection rather than antagonism.

> I really think that my philosophy about all the identity things is, I know that you are x y and z and have a certain history and therefore you're such and such, you know? However, you're still a human being and you're still here and on earth and as far as you know you live, and you die. And so, I really try to see our identity in a more universal way, and I think it's almost despite race though … race is important, I really would like to see it in a more universal connection.

> So again race should unite us, not divide us … the fact that you and I are
> Asian American but different … the part that says Asia, then that unites us
> as opposed to, say, no you're Japanese, I'm Korean.

Shin calls herself an "optimist": she believes that all the people who are endowed
with life in this world and who will eventually die should live together on this
planet in harmony. She takes as the twin aspects of her philosophy the universality
of human life and the commonalities that the loose connections of race can offer.

Shin's art is born of her formative experiences of witnessing first-hand the
deadly stakes of racial antagonism. Her work is oriented toward a new age when
conflict and despair are sublimated into connection and hope.

10.3 Minor Transnationalism as a Resistance to Nation-States' Hegemony

My analysis of the narratives and key cultural productions of the two artists in
this project revealed that major transnationalism and minor transnationalism are
two types of transpacific arenas of relationality and contiguity. In light of the
argument given at the beginning of the chapter, which understands the transpacific as an economic, political, and military contact zone between the US and
parts of Asia, Inoue's juxtaposition of fine artworks with cheap ceramic goods
in her *Tea Taste Democracy and Upside-Down Objects* demonstrates that US–Japan
national interests at the time were, in fact, inseparable and concordant.

During the occupation, the US exploited its total hegemony over Japan to
remove national treasure-level objects and other fine artwork as though they
were American property. Japan had little choice but to quietly acquiesce while
at the same time using these seizures to burnish Japan's image in the US as a
civilized and culturally advanced nation. Meanwhile, American individuals and
importers bought high-quality Japanese porcelain at bargain prices and looked
to Japan to supply increasing demand resulting from the Korean War, which
helped Japan's post-war economic recovery. Through its involvement in exports
to other Asian countries and in the Korean War, Japan was therefore complicit in
the US' hegemony in Asia. These high-art and low-art objects were crossing the
Pacific at roughly the same time during the post-war period.

However, their juxtaposition exposes a further contrastive narrative: Inoue
weaves into these objects the upside-down memory of the atomic bombings of
Hiroshima and Nagasaki, showing the contrast between the narrative that "the
bombs were dropped to end the war"—which remains the dominant discourse
in the US despite the fact that contemporary historical research has shown it to
be false—and the narrative of the horrors of the bomb which continues to be
told through Japanese popular culture, even as the Japanese government fails to
challenge the American suppression of public records concerning the bombings
(see Uchino, Chapter 8 as well).

For the audience who managed to experience the tactile element of Inoue's
work by interacting with the sweaters from the Andes and the potato flowers that

were subsequently woven from them, Inoue's *Transmigration of the Sold* provides a glance of the transmigrants who support the very economic foundations of the US. Viewers can connect the dots to see how economic and racial inequality is globalized, especially across the Pacific, and how they can even be (unintentionally) complicit in this inequality.

It is necessary to resituate the violence Shin witnessed between the Korean and Black communities within the context of its larger social framework, as discussed in Kazuyo Tsuchiya (Chapter 9). Lisa Lowe has pointed to the US' colonial/ neo-colonial role in the nations of Asia against the backdrop of the influx of "transpacific migrants" from Asia to the US. The advance of globalization and the expansion of American influence in Korea in the 1980s brought an influx of Korean capital into Korean American communities. At almost the same time, deindustrialization, the movement of factories overseas due to globalization, and the elimination of social welfare dealt a series of severe blows to the Black underclass who had come from the South and settled in urban areas (Lowe 2012, 64–65).

America is a space of encounter and negotiation among people with a long history of transatlantic migration on the one hand and people with a much shorter history of transpacific migration, including Koreans, on the other. It is undeniable that one source of friction between these groups is the relative lengths of time they have spent facing American racial discrimination and prejudice. Thus, the complex interaction between America's colonial role in Asia, the influx and outflux of global capital, and the inner-city encounters between newly arrived immigrants and established minorities who have been left behind by globalization gave rise to the particular composition of American "racial antagonism."

Furthermore, their artwork is significant not only for bringing embedded inequality in the vertical relationships between majority-minority or nation-states to our attention but for highlighting the agencies of transmigrants and other minoritized people in their resistance to nation-states' (or sometimes supra-nation states') hegemonic power and unevenness within this spatial realm. In the heightened atmosphere of xenophobia and racism after 9/11 and the partisan political climate which followed, transmigrant workers, whether legally documented or otherwise, were subject to widespread bigotry and hostility from the majority population despite the fact that the US continues to rely heavily on the labor force of these transmigrants. In an artistic reaction to address this, Inoue and her transmigrant friends came together to unite, comfort, and protect each other, and deepen their intercultural communication and understanding, thus establishing a cross-regional trans-local cultural pathway connecting the Andes with New York's Canal Street.

The empathy shown by the Navajo chef who baked a mushroom cloud cake for Inoue, and the empathy shown by Inoue in embroidering the names of Native American tribes onto napkins, were born of the encounter between these two minoritized people. Inoue was born in the one country that has suffered nuclear attack, and the Native American chef's people suffered greatly at the hands of America's hydrogen bomb tests as well as from nuclear programs involving uranium mining, which have continued to threaten the lives and resources of American Indians today.

For local audiences at SFAI 140, looking at the tribal names spelled out in red embroidery on the white napkins inevitably reminded them that the nuclear issue was not just about Japan, but their own country, and indeed the world in general, both past and present. In contrast to the vertical relationship of US hegemony suggested by having Inoue force-fed cake, the performance, enabled by the horizontal ties between the Japanese artist and the Navajo chef, drew audiences into this collective act of thought.

Shin's artwork is created through the cooperative relationship between artist and collaborator that Howard Becker highlights as the social organization of art (Becker 1982). The moment they leave their owners' hands, the items Shin uses as her materials lose their individual meaning and importance, but when she links them together, they take on a new significance through their participation in the message the collective entity sends.

Shin's art dismantles various social boundaries: essentialist boundaries based on race and ethnicity, workplace hierarchies, and the gendered division of labor. She does not, however, totally negate the social categories on which people found their identities through the extreme act of replacing them either with the smallest available unit—"the individual"—or the largest—"the human race." All of her works emphasize the community consciousness-turned-agency of the participants, thereby carrying out a "collective act" of art. And that community is staunchly liberating and inclusive, its horizontal connections ever growing.

When she offers "Asia" as an example of race, it is as a loose vessel for connecting people by discovering their commonalities. The structure of her pieces also expresses her strong stance against race as a force for division. And her pursuit of human universality stems from neither universalism nor absolutism but from a sense of the importance of respecting diversity, including the experiences and values of marginalized people.

In addition to the issue of economic disparity, another shared feature of Shin and Inoue's work lies in their engagement with issues of gender inequality and the gendered division of labor. Celadon porcelain is traditionally made by men, and it is the middle and upper classes who are able to visit the art museums where it is exhibited. On the other hand, the celadon collage that Shin, a female artist, created in Flushing has transcended gender and class, becoming an intimately familiar public art to everyone who uses the station it adorns. Shin's artwork requires meticulous handiwork that overlaps with the long working hours demanded of immigrants, and in her art, we can discern respect and affection for the Asian immigrant women who shoulder a significant portion of the work in the American garment industry.

Their works become a contact zone in which their audiences or participants of a project are invited to engage in a reconsideration of the complexity of trans-pacific dynamics. By blending elements of "high art" such as Japanese tea bowls and the Celadon, and "low art" such as anime and "Made in Occupied Japan" objects or used lottery tickets in their art works, they not only disrupt the divisions between that which is considered "high art" and "low art," but also reveal memories that have been suppressed by major-transnationalism. They also bring light to the everyday lives of peoples whose labor is often exploited and unrecognized in major transnationalism. The work of these two artists enables a practice of "minor transnationalism" in which transmigrants and other minoritized people are the subjects and actors in the creation of solidarity, cooperation, and friendly relations in opposition to the hegemony of US-led globalization as they intervene and ultimately reimagine the value of art in defiance of national boundaries and those of "high art" and "low art".

Inoue's art bears recognizing the importance of constantly questioning and thinking of the meanings of "democratization" and "justice" that are both often exploited for political and social purposes. Inoue's artwork encourages people to step back to consider again why it is imperative to continually recognize, reframe, and reconsider the fluid and alternative meanings associated with "democratization" and "justice," particularly as they engender a looped and warped contiguous understanding that may be taken advantage of by various parties within the transpacific power framework to advance their own political or socio-cultural ideologies and endowments.

For Shin, who pours her energy not into conflict or destruction but into creation, race is something that connects people, not something that divides them. She is shining a light on the people abandoned and marginalized by society, helping to create a community that will connect those people to mainstream society. She maintains an optimism that transforms despair into hope as she continues the steady, delicate task of unraveling in order to connect.

In these times of widespread overt racism and increasing intolerance, their message and the questions their art raises have greater relevance than ever. The everyday practices of "unraveling" and connecting have generated new forms of networks, communities, and cooperation among transmigrants and other minoritized people, out of mutual empathy and emotions, beyond reason or logic. They may represent a new attempt to open an alternative form of resistance against racism and xenophobia that shadows the world today.

After I completed the draft of this chapter, Shin and I enjoyed catching up when we met again at a café in New York. Shin recollected our interviews back then, particularly the conversation about her childhood when her parents ran a store in a predominantly Black neighborhood. Shin told me that for a long time she had suppressed the memories of those days because of her trauma she had carried over the years. It was too painful to even think about it. Our interview was the first time that she had talked about it to that extent. She suggested that she had finally reached a stage in her life when she could reflect on her childhood and tell someone about it. Because of that experience, she wanted to work with her hands, create something, connect people and create a new community, not hate each other.[19]

This made me realize just how deep Shin's childhood scars are. At the same time, I was deeply moved by the fact that the "optimism" she talks about is no empty ideal—it is a state of mind she has reached after long years of enduring the bitter, difficult realities of racism and the social system that surround it.

Acknowledgments

I would like to thank Yoko Inoue and Jean Shin for spending an enormous amount of time on this project. Special thanks go to Lyle De Souza, Crystal Uchino, and Laura Kina for their insightful comments. I thank Daniel Joseph for translating the earlier version of the article. Part I on Yoko Inoue and its related discussion are based on "Major and Minor Transnationalism in Yoko Inoue's Art," which appeared in *Asian Diasporic Visual Cultures and the Americas* 6 (2020): 27–47.

Notes

1 I first interviewed Yoko Inoue on March 9, 2006, but the interviews used in this article took place on the following dates at the following places: September 22, 2017, at Inoue's studio in Brooklyn, New York; May 8, 2018, at the Tokyo Office of Kyoto University; July 6, 2018, via Skype; in addition, we had numerous email exchanges over the following few years. All references to the artist, her biography and practice, as well as statements, are from these communications unless otherwise indicated.

2 The Zapatista is a guerrilla resistance organization based in Chiapas, Mexico, that fights against neoliberalism and discrimination against Indigenous peoples.

3 The chef's anonymity was agreed to by both parties.

4 See also United States Congress Senate Committee on Indian Affairs, "America's Nuclear Past: Examining the Effects of Radiation in Indian Country: Field Hearing before the Committee on Indian Affairs, United States Senate," One Hundred Sixteenth Congress, first session, October 7, 2019.

5 Present-day Japanese brands such as Tachikichi also had a hand in the production of MIOJ/OJ.

6 Japanese collectors living in America even held an exhibition of "OJ" in Roppongi, Tokyo in 2013.

7 The majority of the masterpieces held in the Asian art collection of the Seattle Museum of Art were acquired by Lee, the museum's future director, during the period between 1948 and 1952 after he left his post at GHQ.

8 See also (*Shūkanshinchō Henshūbu* 1970).

9 Mr. Susumu Kondō was kind enough to provide me with an Excel file of his calculations from trade statistics listed on the US Customs homepage.

10 Conversely, according to the US Department of Commerce's import data, among the countries from which the US imported ceramic tableware, Japan was first in gross imports at 65 percent (the UK was second at 17 percent) and also first in total number of items at 85 percent (second was West Germany at 6 percent); both cases accounted for an overwhelming market share. See endnote 9.

11 Interview with Susumu Kondō, November 22, 2018, at the Japan Association for the Promotion of Pottery Industry in Nagoya.

12 The interviews with Jean Shin used for the main text of this chapter took place on March 8, 2006 and September 9, 2017 at Shin's studio in Brooklyn, New York. In addition, there were numerous email exchanges over the years. All references to the artist, her biography and practice, as well as statements, are from these communications unless otherwise indicated.

13 *Chance City* was exhibited in 2002, 2004, and 2009, the scale increasing with every exhibition. For the 2009 exhibition at the Smithsonian American Art Museum, almost twice as many lottery tickets were used as in 2002, and the piece stood longer than in either previous instance.

14 An email response from Shin on January 29, 2019.

15 https://jeanshin.com/celadon-landscape accessed June 30, 2021.

16 From an interview with Hyunsoo Woo on August 14, 2018, at the Philadelphia Museum of Art.

17 This is reflected in the large representation of sweater donors of Korean descent at the Philadelphia Museum of Art, where Hyunsoo Woo served as the curator of her show. The breakdown of 22 donated sweaters at the Museum was: Korean descent 11, Japanese descent 4, Chinese descent 6, and Caucasian 1. (Information gathered from an interview with Hyunsoo Woo on August 14, 2018, at the Philadelphia Museum of Art.)

18 From an interview with Hyunsoo Woo on August 14, 2018, at the Philadelphia Museum of Art, where Shin's 2018 show was held.

19 From an interview on August 13, 2019, at a café in New York.

References

Becker, Howard S. 1982. *Art Worlds*. Berkeley, CA: University of California Press.

Bourdieu, Pierre. 1984. *Distinction: A Social Critique of the Judgment of Taste*, translated by Richard Nice. Cambridge, MA: Harvard University Press.

Cheng, Enoch. 2010. "Interview with Jean Shin," *Asian American Art (AAA) Newsletter*, June 17, 2010.

Cohen, Warren I. 1992. *East Asian Art and American Culture: A Study in International Relations*. New York: Columbia University Press.

CNN. 2001, "Transcript of President Bush's Address," CNN, September 21, 2001, viewed June 25, 2021, https://edition.cnn.com/2001/US/09/20/gen.bush.transcript/.

Cunningham, Michael R. 1998. "Kurīburando bijutsukan no toyō bijtsu (East Asian Art of the Cleveland Art Museum)." Translated by Ruriko Tsuchida, in *Kurīburando bijutsukan no toyō bijtsu*, edited by Nara National Museum. Nara: Nara National Museum.

Gell, Alfred. 1998. *Art and Agency: An Anthropological Theory*. New York: Clarendon Press.

Giuffrida, Noel. 2017. *SWAP #59: Yoko Inoue*, Spaces Gallery, YouTube, July 27, 2017, viewed June 25, 2021, https://www.youtube.com/watch?v=P6qXh6EOJB0.

Hallmark, Kara Kelly. 2007. "Jean Shin." In *Encyclopedia of Asian American Artist*, 194–197. Westport, Connecticut: Greenwood Press.

Hoskins, Janet A., and Nguyen Viet Thanh, eds. 2014. *Transpacific Studies: Framing an Emerging Field*. Honolulu: University of Hawai'i Press.

Ingold, Tim. 2013. *Making: Anthropology, Archaeology, Art and Architecture*. London: Routledge.

Inoue, Yoko. 2016. *SFAI 140—March 2016—Yoko Inoue*, Santa Fe Art Institute, March 2016, viewed June 25, 2021, https://vimeo.com/162389055.

Kondō, Susumu. 2011. "Tōgyōshi Kobore-banashi: "Made in Occupied Japan" (MIOJ) to Sono Jidai (Asides from the History of the Ceramics Industry 14: The Life and Times of 'Made in Occupied Japan)' (MIOJ)." *Japan Association for the Promotion of Pottery Industry Newsletter (June 2011)*: 4.

Lee, Sherman E., 1963. *Tea Taste in Japanese Art*. New York: Asia Society.

Lee, Sherman E. 1964. *History of Far Eastern Art*. London: Thames and Hudson.

Lee, Sherman E. 1997. "My Work in Japan: Arts and Monuments, 1946–1948." In *The Confusion Era: Art and Culture of Japan During the Allied Occupation, 1945–1952*, edited by Mark Sandler, Washington, DC: Arthur M. Sackler Gallery, Smithsonian Institution.

Lionnet, Françoise, and Shu-mei Shih, eds. 2005. "Introduction: Thinking through the Minor, Transnationally." In *Minor Transnationalism*. Durham: NC: Duke University Press.

Lowe, Lisa. 2012. "The Trans-Pacific Migrant and Area Studies." In *The Trans-Pacific Imagination: Rethinking Boundary, Culture and Society*, edited by Sakai Naoki and Hyon Joo Yoo, 61–74. New Jersey: World Scientific.

Matsushita, Takaaki, Ichitaro Kondō, Michiaki Kawakita, and Jirō Aoyama. 1952. "Zadankai: Kobijutsu no Kaigai Ryūshutsu to Sono Taisaku" [A Roundtable Discussion: The Overseas Flow of Art Treasures/Historical Art Objects and What to Do About It]. *Bijutsu hihyō* 8: 10–19.

Nagoya Tōjiki-kaikan (Nagoya Ceramics Hall), ed. 1987. *Nagoya Tōgyō no Hyakunen: Kaikan no Kabe wa Kiita Hyakugojūnin no Kaisō* [One Hundred Years of the Nagoya Ceramics Industry: Reflections of 150 People as Heard by the Walls of Nagoya Ceramics Hall]. Nagoya: Nagoya Tōjiki-kaikan.

Nakamura, Takahide. 1976. *Keizaigaku zenshū 25: Sengo nihonkeizai: Seichō to junkan* [Economics Collection 25: Post-War Japanese Economics—Growth and Cycles]. Tokyo: Chikumashobō.

Nihon Yushutsu Tōjikishi Hensan Iinkai (Editorial Committee on the History of Japanese Ceramics Exports), eds. 1967. *Nihon Yushutsu Tōjikishi* [The History of Japanese Ceramics Exports]. Nagoya: Nagoya Tōjiki-kaikan.

Nguyen, Viet Thanh, and Janet Hoskins. 2014. "Introduction: Transpacific Studies: Critical Perspectives on an Emerging Field." In *Transpacific Studies: Framing an Emerging Field*, edited by Hoskins, Janet, and Viet Thanh Nguyen, 1–38, Honolulu: University of Hawai'i Press.

Sakai, Naoki, and Hyon Joo Yoo, eds. 2012. "Introduction: The Trans-Pacific Imagination—Rethinking Boundary, Culture and Society." In *The Trans-Pacific Imagination: Rethinking Boundary, Culture and Society*, edited by Sakai, Naoki and Hyon Joo Yoo, 1–44. Hackensack, NJ: World Scientific.

Satō, K. 2003. "GHQ no bijutsu gyōsei: cie bijutsu kinenbutsuka niyoru 'bijutsu no min-shūka' to Yashiro Yukio [GHQ's Arts Administration: Yashiro Yukio and the cie Art Souvenir Division's 'Democratization of Art']." *Kindaigasetsu* 12: 80-95.

Shimura, S. 2014. "Shāman Rī to nihon bijutsu [Sherman Lee and Japanese Art]." *Akita University of Art Bulletin* 1: 15–24.

Shin, Jean. 2014. "Jean Shin." In *The Artist as Culture Producer: Living and Sustaining a Creative Life*, edited by Sharon Louden, 187–197. Bristol: Intellect Ltd.

Shūkanshinchō Henshūbu (Weekly Shinchō Editorial Department). 1970. *Makkāsā no nihon* [MacArthur's Japan]. Tokyo: Shinchōsha.

Takashima, S. 2014. "*2014 nen 3gatsu kenkyūkai hōkoku: MIOJ (Made in Occupied Japan) no hanashi*." March 2014 Conference Report: The Story of MIOJ (Made in Occupied Japan), Tokyo: All Japan Classic Camera Club, viewed June 25, 2021, http://www.ajcc.gr.jp/takashima_houkoku_2014_04.pdf.

Takezawa, Yasuko. 2011. "New Arts, New Resistance: Asian American Artists in the 'Post-race' Era." In *Racial Representations in Asia*, edited by Yasuko Takezawa. 93–123. Kyoto: Kyoto University Press.

Takezawa, Yasuko. 2016. "Negotiating Categories and Transforming (Mixed-) Race Identities: The Art and Narratives of Roger Shimomura, Laura Kina, and Shizu Saldamando." In *Trans-Pacific Japanese American Studies: Conversations on Race and Racializations*, edited by Yasuko Takezawa and Gary Y. Okihiro, 60–90. Honolulu: University of Hawai'i Press.

Velthuis, Olav. 2005. *Talking Prices: Symbolic Meanings of Prices on the Market for Contemporary Art*. Princeton, NJ: Princeton University Press.

Voyles, T.B. 2015. *Wastelanding: Legacies of Uranium Mining in Navajo Country*. Minneapolis, MN: University of Minnesota Press.

INDEX

For Product Safety Concerns and Information please contact our EU
representative GPSR@taylorandfrancis.com
Taylor & Francis Verlag GmbH, Kaufingerstraße 24, 80331 München, Germany